ASIAN SECURITY HANDBOOK

TERRORISM AND THE NEW SECURITY ENVIRONMENT

Foreword by Ambassador James R. Lilley

WILLIAM M. CARPENTER AND DAVID G. WIENCEK
EDITORS

AN EAST GATE BOOK

M.E.Sharpe
Armonk, New York
London, England

An East Gate Book

Copyright © 2005 by M.E. Sharpe, Inc.

All rights reserved. No part of this book may be reproduced in any form
without written permission from the publisher, M.E. Sharpe, Inc.,
80 Business Park Drive, Armonk, New York 10504.

Library of Congress Cataloging-in-Publication Data

Asian security handbook: terrorism and the new security environment / edited by William
M. Carpenter and David G. Wiencek.—3rd ed.
    p. cm.
"An East Gate book."
Includes bibliographical references and index.
ISBN 0-7656-1552-5 (cloth: alk. paper) ISBN 0-7656-1553-3 (pbk.: alk. paper)
  1. National security—Asia. 2. National security—Australia. 3. National security—New
Zealand. 4. Political stability—Asia. 5. Political stability—Australia. 6. Political
stability—New Zealand. I. Carpenter, William M. II. Wiencek, David G., 1958–

UA830.A842 2004
355′.03305—dc22   2004015637

Printed in the United States of America

The paper used in this publication meets the minimum requirements of
American National Standard for Information Sciences
Permanence of Paper for Printed Library Materials,
ANSI Z 39.48-1984.

∞

| BM (c) | 10 | 9 | 8 | 7 | 6 | 5 | 4 | 3 | 2 | 1 |
| BM (p) | 10 | 9 | 8 | 7 | 6 | 5 | 4 | 3 | 2 | 1 |

Contents

Foreword

The advent of global terrorism with its increasing threat to our vital interests, and those of our friends and allies, has obliged the United States to alter its priorities, methods, and commitments. The current Russian threat is inconsequential, the Chinese challenge is largely economic, and local ethnic clashes pale before the dangers of suicidal fanatics armed with high explosives and seeking weapons of mass destruction (WMD).

The arguments over whether China is a strategic partner or strategic competitor seem less important—we have no choice but to cooperate with China on Islamic fundamentalist terrorism and on rogue states such as North Korea, which has the capability and probably the will to make WMD available to other unstable and dangerous forces.

Taiwan has become a more vocal issue in U.S.-China relations, but the reality is that China, Taiwan, and the United States are part of the global supply chain in which each player is dependent on the other for resources, technology, and marketing in a competitive world. China has grown almost miraculously in the past two decades but it is now facing the huge problem of an advanced economy—tax reform, nonperforming loans, financial accountability, and corporate governance. Japan has fallen on hard times because it did not anticipate these problems and tried to sidestep from them in protectionism and crony capitalism. China's growing military is of concern as a key part of its comprehensive national power, but its military seems at least temporarily to be in check.

North Korea as an ugly and dangerous failed state has presented the region, not just the United States, with a continuing problem of instability, aggression, and a bizarre behavior pattern that has vexed and frustrated all regional parties. It has benefited enormously from its carefully calculated extortionism and its ability to split and torment surrounding states. The good news is that the surrounding states are beginning to view North Korea as a common problem, but to get effective cooperation from them is like herding cats—each country having its own agenda and parochial interests.

The emergence of India as a potential economic powerhouse, Taiwan's resilience and its experiment with political change, and continuing uncertainties in Southeast Asia all inject variables into the shifting balances in Asia. The divergence of U.S. interest to the Middle East has shaken Asia, but U.S. power remains crucial for Asian prosperity.

The authors are all well qualified to address the problems and prospects of the particular countries in Asia. Their comments and analyses are essential in tackling the big picture.

Ambassador James R. Lilley
September 2004

James R. Lilley is a resident fellow in Asian studies at the American Enterprise Institute (AEI), Washington, DC. Mr. Lilley was the U.S. ambassador to the People's Republic of China from 1989 to 1991, to the Republic of Korea from 1986 to 1989, and was the U.S. chief representative in Taiwan from 1982 to 1984. He served as assistant secretary of defense for international security affairs from 1991 to 1993. Mr. Lilley wrote forewords for the AEI books *Chinese Military Modernization, Over the Line: North Korea's Negotiating Strategy,* and *China's Military Faces the Future.* He is the coeditor of *Beyond MFN: Trade with China, American Interests and Crisis in the Taiwan Strait,* and the author of *China Hands: Nine Decades of Adventure, Espionage and Diplomacy in Asia.*

Editors' Note

This is the third edition of *Asian Security Handbook*. Our previous volumes were published in 1996 and 2000.[1] Because of the terrorist attacks of September 11, 2001, it is appropriate that we focus in this edition on the War on Terrorism and the still-unfolding impact it is having in Asia. The introductory chapter outlines the new security environment brought about by the events of September 11 and provides a context for the country profile chapters that follow.

Our country-specific chapters provide wide-ranging coverage of the political-security situation in twenty-three individual nations and update our previous assessments.[2] For this edition, new chapters on Bangladesh, Brunei, and Nepal have been added.

Our analysis is designed to offer regional breadth with the intention of providing a handbook or primer that is relevant and accessible to a general audience, including students and training classes, the business and investment community, as well as specialists in Asian studies and international security affairs. Given such comprehensive coverage, we believe this book will be a one-stop resource for those interested in geopolitical trends, terrorism and political risk, and defense and security issues in the Asia-Pacific region.

The chapters presented here bring together the insights and expertise of our contributors, a diverse group of international security analysts and Asian affairs experts from government, academia, and the private sector. They bring significant experience, as well as a variety of perspectives, to the book. They have written sharply focused chapters that are designed to be analytical and interpretive. A short bibliographic list for further reading and reference appears at the end of each chapter. The views expressed in each chapter are those of the individual author or authors.

As with the previous editions, this book is a collaborative effort between the editors and the contributors. We thank all our contributors for generously donating their time and expertise to this project. We are extremely grateful for the efforts they put into preparing the individual chapters. Finally, we note with sadness the passing of our colleague, Professor Henry S. Albinski, who contributed to the first two editions of *Asian Security Handbook* with chapters on security in the South Pacific region. Professor Albinski was an authority on Australia and New Zealand, and on Pacific Basin political-security affairs. He was a valued member of our team, and he is missed.

Notes

1. William M. Carpenter and David G. Wiencek, eds., *Asian Security Handbook: An Assessment of Political-Security Issues in the Asia-Pacific Region* (Armonk, NY: M.E. Sharpe, 1996), and William M. Carpenter and David G. Wiencek, eds., *Asian Security Handbook 2000* (Armonk, NY: M.E. Sharpe, 2000).

2. Although we have attempted to be as inclusive as possible, our coverage is admittedly selective and does not examine every Asia-Pacific nation. For example, Russia's role in the region is discussed at several points in the text, but there is no chapter on Russia.

Burma is officially named Myanmar, but in this book we use the former and more familiar name.

List of Illustrative Materials

Tables

Maps

Photographs

Figure

ASIAN
SECURITY
HANDBOOK

Introduction

Terrorism and
the New Security Environment

William M. Carpenter and David G. Wiencek

The terrorist attacks of September 11, 2001, have reshaped international politics and fundamentally restructured the international security environment. Important geopolitical shifts have taken place. Among these is a global strategic reorientation as a result of the strong response of the United States to the staggering events of 9/11. This response has highlighted the United States' political-military predominance in relation to other nations and its role as the world's sole remaining superpower.

This jolt to the world power situation has not come without political and diplomatic strains, particularly at the United Nations and between the United States and other major players, such as France, Germany, and Russia. As one senior U.S. official commented: "Like the end of the Cold War, and the end of World War II, September 11 was one of the relatively rare earthquakes in international politics. Long-established alliances and venerable institutions are being tested."[1] Sharp policy differences over how to respond to strategic threats in the aftermath of 9/11 split traditional allies France and Germany from the United States.[2] This fracturing of certain traditional alliance relationships, coupled with the emergence of new partnerships between the United States and a number of frontline states needed to help combat terrorism, is another key geopolitical shift that has resulted from 9/11.

Without 9/11 it is plausible that there would have been a continuation of previous strategic trends, with the United States as the leading power within what could generally be described as a loose multipower framework, consisting of the United States, Europe, and a rising China. But 9/11 prompted a stark realignment. It pushed the global correlation of forces dramatically to the side of the United States and its friends and allies, and has given rise to a clear unipolar world power structure.[3] In the new structure, the United States,

The Asia-Pacific Region

the world's sole superpower, is at the apex of an effort to thwart terrorism, Islamic extremism, and rogue states that threaten international stability. Such key traditional allies as the United Kingdom, Australia, and Spain, and new allies such as Poland have supported the United States in this effort. But shifts continue: the March 2004 election in Spain, for example, which followed by days a major terrorist attack in Madrid, brought about a reversal of key aspects of Spanish support for U.S. policies. Like Pearl Harbor more than sixty years earlier, the 9/11 attacks on the U.S. homeland wakened a sleeping giant. The attacks unified the country behind a newfound political will to bring the full measure of its power to bear against terrorists and rogue governments. This response, a sharp departure from U.S. policy in the 1990s, was one that the terrorists surely did not expect. America's strong resolve to act decisively since 9/11 has helped reshape the international security environment, and its impact will be felt for many years to come.

These developments also have had a pronounced impact on the security situation in Asia, which is the focus of this book. The following introductory analysis provides a context for the country-specific chapters that follow by highlighting the contours of the current and future regional security environment. Such an assessment must take as its point of departure the "new realities" brought into being by the terrorist attacks of 9/11. This survey is rounded out by a review of those security issues and trends that were at work prior to

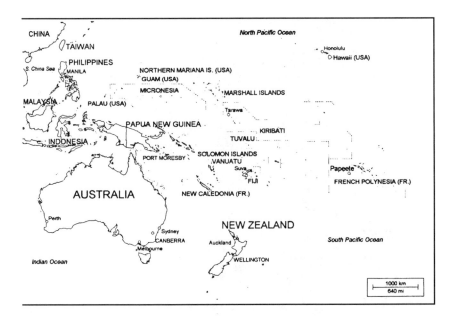

9/11. These "old realities" likewise continue to shape and strongly influence regional security dynamics.

September 11 and the War on Terrorism

On September 11, 2001, nineteen members of Osama bin Laden's al Qaeda terrorist network carried out a set of catastrophic attacks—the most lethal such attacks in history—against the United States. The attacks killed 3,016 people and caused billions of U.S. dollars in damages and economic losses. The terrorists hijacked four separate commercial jet airliners in a coordinated attack and crashed two into the World Trade Center towers in New York City, killing 2,792 people. The towers were among the tallest buildings in the world and a symbol of American economic might. In all, seven buildings were destroyed and many other surrounding structures were damaged. A third aircraft was crashed into the Pentagon building, home to the U.S. Department of Defense, just outside of Washington, DC, killing 125 people in the building and 59 aboard the aircraft. A fourth aircraft crashed in an open field near the small town of Shanksville, Pennsylvania, after a struggle between the terrorist hijackers and passengers determined to foil the plot. The crash killed all 33 passengers and 7 crew members.[4] That aircraft was en route to another presumed landmark target in Washington, DC, most likely the United States Capitol building or the White House.

September 11, 2001: Terrorist-controlled aircraft crashes into one of the World Trade Center towers in New York. The 9/11 attacks set in motion a fundamental restructuring of the international security environment. (AP/Wide World Photos)

These attacks sparked the adoption of unprecedented security measures in the United States and propelled the country into a long-term global assault against terrorist groups and their sponsors, hosts, and financial patrons—the War on Terrorism. In the days immediately after the attack, U.S. president, George W. Bush, outlined a new strategy that highlighted an intensified political will and national determination to confront those responsible for 9/11. President Bush stated:

Our war on terror begins with al Qaeda, but it does not end there. It will not end until every terrorist group of global reach has been found, stopped and defeated. . . . We will direct every resource at our command—every means of diplomacy, every tool of intelligence, every financial influence, and every necessary weapon of war—to the destruction of the global terrorist network.[5]

A strong U.S. military response followed and took its first form in Operation Enduring Freedom (OEF) launched on October 7, 2001, a scant twenty-six days after the 9/11 attacks. The primary aim of this (ongoing) operation is to destroy Osama bin Laden's Afghanistan-based al Qaeda terrorist network. The operation also sought to rid Afghanistan of the radical Taliban religious group, which for years had harbored bin Laden and wreaked havoc on the country with its harsh policies based on an extreme interpretation of Islam. OEF succeeded in bringing about the rapid fall of the Taliban, and Kabul was liberated on November 13, 2001. In December 2001, a new democratically oriented interim government was established and commenced rebuilding efforts. Despite these important successes, bin Laden remains at large and relatively small numbers of Taliban and al Qaeda remnants continue efforts inside Afghanistan to destabilize the emerging democratic government.

The United States then shifted its focus to Iraq. On March 19–20, 2003, another major military campaign, Operation Iraqi Freedom (OIF), was launched. OIF encompassed a U.S.-led international coalition to remove Iraqi dictator Saddam Hussein from power, eliminate his suspected weapons of mass destruction (WMD) capability, and forestall the possibility that such weapons—though none were actually found—could fall into the hands of terrorists. Overwhelming military force applied by the U.S. and its coalition partners, coupled with little Iraqi resistance, led to the fall of Baghdad on April 9, 2003, and the ousting of the Saddam regime. Saddam Hussein himself fled into hiding and then directed guerrilla and terrorist attacks against coalition forces over subsequent months until he was finally captured on December 13, 2003. Sovereignty was later restored to Iraq on June 28, 2004, when an interim government officially took power.

The liberation of Iraq succeeded in dislodging a major source of international instability and terror and put the country on a new, hopeful path toward representative self-government. Terrorist attacks, religious strife, and continued challenges to U.S. forces and the new governing authority, however, have plagued the postwar environment in Iraq.

The New U.S. Strategy

These two significant military operations, OEF and OIF, typify America's strong response to security threats in the post–9/11 world. Shocked by the viciousness of the events of September 11, Washington's new strategy is grounded in both the capability and the will to act decisively and, if necessary, preemptively. The underpinnings of this strategy were outlined by President Bush in June 2002 as follows:

> We must take the battle to the enemy, disrupt his plans, and confront the worst threats before they emerge. In the world we have entered, the only path to safety is the path of action. And this nation will act.[6]

The new strategy, also known as the Bush Doctrine, embraces the concept of preemptive military action in the face of severe potential threats to the American homeland, as well as U.S. interests around the world. The new emphasis on preemption is a departure from past U.S. policies built around deterrence and the containment of adversaries. This approach has been a source of controversy particularly among those who do not wish to see the United States assert its power so forcefully to shape world events. Previous policies created a strategic balance primarily through the prospect of massive (nuclear) retaliation that deterred attack against the U.S. homeland. But such calculations are more effective against state actors than they are in the new security environment against transnational terrorist groups with apocalyptic ideologies operating from diverse locations. Similarly, threats posed by terrorists or rogue entities in league with them, potentially armed with WMD, require proactive measures to prevent mass casualties on American soil or in the homelands of allies.

Under the new U.S. strategy, military force will necessarily be applied selectively:

> The United States will not use force in all cases to preempt emerging threats, nor should nations use preemption as a pretext for aggression. Yet in an age where the enemies of civilization openly and actively seek the world's most destructive technologies, the United States cannot remain idle while dangers gather.[7]

President Bush crystallized further the new post–9/11 threat environment when he said: "Any outlaw regime that has ties to terrorist groups, and seeks or possesses weapons of mass destruction, is a grave danger to the civilized world, and will be confronted."[8] This assessment built on the earlier identification of three primary rogue governments—Iraq, Iran, and North Korea—as comprising an Axis of Evil. The threat posed by Iraq has now fallen to U.S. power. It is likely that a range of strategies will be employed in due course to mitigate further threats from both Iran and North Korea, which continue to stand out as states seeking to disrupt international peace and stability.

The reelection of President Bush in November 2004 means that important elements of continuity are likely to govern U.S. policy going forward with continuing emphasis placed on dealing with the realities of the post–9/11 threat environment. These realities will define the international security environment for at least the next five to ten years. This new security environment thus couples the War on Terrorism with the parallel imperative to safeguard American and Western interests against WMD threats from terrorists and rogue governments.

The response since 9/11 is—and must be—built around "hard" power, that is, military power, and, we suggest, must continue as such to demonstrate convincingly and in unwavering terms that the United States is determined that its adversaries will be defeated. It further recognizes that long-festering security problems can no longer go unconfronted.

This approach is closely supported by what are sometimes called "soft" power solutions, that is, winning hearts and minds through economic and developmental assistance, cultural initiatives, and public diplomacy within the broader context of fostering democracy and free markets. In the Islamic world in particular, soft power is important in turning the tide away from jihad and radical interpretations of Islam, and is best addressed at the grassroots level and in the religious schools, or *madrasas,* through modern secular curricula.

U.S. Homeland Security

In the days following 9/11, the United States froze all commercial aviation for the first time in its history. Since then, there has been an intense effort to improve airport passenger screening and airline security. Air marshals are also being deployed in greater numbers on certain domestic and international flights.

Also following closely the attacks of 9/11, the security situation within the United States was further challenged by four anthrax-tainted letters delivered through the mail system. Five people were killed and thirteen others were infected in the states of Florida, New York, and Connecticut, and in Washington, DC. These attacks invoked more panic. They also simultaneously brought the WMD threat into sharper focus and created daunting new challenges for homeland defense. As of this writing, no perpetrator or group has been identified as masterminding the anthrax attacks. And it is not yet clear if they are linked to 9/11.

To handle such threats more effectively and coordinate all national activities in this area, President Bush created a new Department of Homeland Security (DHS). DHS brought together some twenty-two separate offices and agencies with over 170,000 employees into a single department in the largest governmental restructuring since World War II. In 2002 the U.S. military also created the U.S. Northern Command to take control of homeland defense and civil support missions. In short, the events of 9/11 led to a major reorientation of the U.S. security apparatus. Washington is pouring new resources into homeland defense. Military and intelligence budgets are expanding. A range of tools to cope with the new security challenges posed by 9/11 and continuing threats is being pursued, including in the areas of law enforcement, tracking of financial assets, and tighter border controls and immigration laws.

The Asian Security Environment: New Realities, Old Realities

It is against this fundamentally altered strategic backdrop that we turn our focus to Asia.

At the same time that 9/11 has brought into being new strategic realities in Asia, there remain a number of other issues and longer-term trends that were formed prior to 9/11 and which continue to shape Asia's security environment. Taken together, conflict potential in the region remains high and spans a full spectrum of low- to high-intensity threats. New security complexities raised by the events of 9/11 add further to preexisting regional instabilities.

Some of the new, interwoven regional security realities that have developed in the aftermath of 9/11 include:

- Growing Islamic fundamentalism in Southeast Asia. In many locations, this has been coupled with grassroots hostility to U.S. military action in Afghanistan and Iraq.
- Heightened political instability, most notably in Pakistan and Indonesia. In Pakistan, there have been assassination attempts against President Pervez Musharraf by hard-line Islamic elements, and the country remains a political tinderbox. In economically fragile Indonesia, former President Megawati Soekarnoputri navigated a narrow path between Islamist elements opposed to the United States, and those showing support for Washington's cause. In a hopeful sign for the future, newly elected president Soesilo Bambang Yudhoyono has called for stronger measures against terrorism in the world's most populous Muslim country.
- Increased security threats to Western interests, businesses, and travelers. These threats emerged early on and took the form mainly of protests at U.S. embassies in South and Southeast Asia and threats to boycott U.S. goods and products. There also were calls to "sweep" or forcibly expel American citizens from Indonesia; British, German, and Canadian citizens also were the targets of such actions. But these threats greatly expanded over time with revelations of major terrorist plots against the diplomatic establishments of the United States, the United

Kingdom, Australia, and other Western nations throughout Southeast Asia. The devastating 2002 bombing in Bali coupled with the suicide attacks in Jakarta on the J.W. Marriott Hotel in 2003 and the Australian embassy in 2004 clearly spotlight the continuing threat to Western interests, businesses, and travelers in the region.

Another noteworthy 9/11-related development is the forming of new relationships between the United States and frontline states in close proximity to Afghanistan, particularly Pakistan, Uzbekistan, Kyrgyzstan, and Tajikistan. Washington's newfound close ties with Islamabad, for example, mark a sharp reversal, as previous years had seen expanding ties between the United States and India, and relations with Pakistan were downgraded. This has changed with the War on Terrorism. Islamabad is now receiving major support from Washington, including debt relief and the lifting of sanctions put in place for nuclear proliferation violations. At the same time, India also has greatly expanded its political and defense ties with Washington. Broadly speaking, access arrangements with frontline states enhance U.S. military reach in the region and enable a more effective prosecution of the War on Terrorism.

The post–9/11 environment also has seen important changes in Japan. For the first time since World War II, Japanese forces became involved in military operations outside the home islands and surrounding areas. This action was made possible by a new antiterrorism law enacted in October 2001. The law permits Maritime Self-Defense Force (MSDF) ships to go into the Indian Ocean and provide rear-area support for the United States in Operation Enduring Freedom, involving supply, repair, communications, surveillance, and medical functions. In 2004, the overseas deployment trend was extended when Japanese ground support troops were sent to Iraq to assist coalition forces in noncombatant roles. As pointed out in Chapter 9, the Iraq deployment is the farthest distance Japanese military forces have ventured into a theater of war since 1915. The upshot of these developments is that Japan is beginning to play a more active role in international security affairs. Movement in this direction had been building inside Japan over recent years and took on greater urgency with the 1998 testing by North Korea of the Taepo Dong missile, which had a range sufficient to target Japan and beyond. The current manifestation marks another significant step in moving Japan away from its historic post–World War II pacifist posture and low-key profile in international crises. In short, Japan recognizes the new threats to its national security and is responding.

The issue of America's relationship with China is also evolving in the aftermath of the 9/11 attacks. Initially China came out in support of U.S. efforts and offered cooperation, albeit on a limited basis. But there is little evidence that China is actively assisting Washington in the War on Terrorism. Instead, under the pretext of fighting terrorism at home, Beijing has cracked down on its own separatists in Xinjiang and Tibet.

From its perspective, China sees its (limited) cooperation with the United States in the War on Terrorism as an opportunity to downplay the so-called "China threat theory"—that China is a long-term strategic competitor and potential adversary. But at the same time, Beijing is now worried that a new "encirclement" of China may be in the works with an expanding U.S. military presence in the frontline states of Central Asia, adding to the existing U.S. security network in East and Southeast Asia.

Al Qaeda and the Southeast Asian Terror Network

Of major significance, the events of 9/11 also led to the discovery of a previously unknown terrorist network in Southeast Asia. The first true signs of this clandestine network were uncovered in Singapore in late 2001. Subsequent investigations throughout the region revealed additional and complex linkages. This network derives support from and is closely linked ideologically with Osama bin Laden and al Qaeda.

By way of background, al Qaeda (translated as "the Base") is an international network of Islamic extremists formed in the late 1980s. The network grew out of the mujahideen (holy warriors) who fought against the forces of the former Soviet Union in Afghanistan. Al Qaeda's ideology is based on a militant vision that is rooted in the strict Wahhabi school of Islam. The group seeks to reestablish a caliphate that would unite Muslims worldwide under Islamic (sharia) law. To accomplish this, it wages jihad (holy war) to overthrow regimes in the Middle East and Asia that it believes are insufficiently Islamic and have "betrayed" the religion. The group also would expel Westerners from Muslim lands and banish Western cultural and political influences. Al Qaeda has designated the United States as a principal enemy based on a number of interrelated factors. These include: support for what al Qaeda sees as corrupt Islamic regimes; U.S. military presence in the Arabian peninsula (Saudi Arabia), which is home to the holy sites of Mecca and Medina; America's ties with Israel; and the United States' position as political, economic, and cultural leader of the West. As such, al Qaeda is locked in a life-or-death struggle with the United States and the West.[9]

As a formidable transnational organization, al Qaeda is believed to be active in over ninety countries and draws on members from some forty nationalities.[10] The network and its affiliates are responsible for a string of major terrorist incidents through the 1990s and up to and following 9/11, including:

- The 1993 bombing of the World Trade Center in New York
- The 1998 near-simultaneous bombings of U.S. embassies in Kenya and Tanzania
- The 2000 suicide maritime attack on the destroyer *USS Cole* in Aden harbor, Yemen
- The 2002 suicide bombing of an Israeli-owned hotel in Kenya, and the coordinated, but unsuccessful, shoulder-fired missile attack on an Israeli Boeing 757 passenger aircraft
- The 2003 suicide truck bombings of two synagogues in Istanbul, Turkey, and the subsequent attack on the British Consulate and a major London-based bank in Istanbul
- The 2004 coordinated bombing of commuter trains in Madrid, Spain, on the eve of the Spanish general elections, killing 191 and injuring some 1,600

So far, the War on Terrorism has achieved success in putting the organization on the defensive. For example, U.S. authorities report that nearly two-thirds of the top al Qaeda leadership identified before 9/11 has been killed or captured. But al Qaeda is adapting and the fight goes on. As the U.S. director of Central Intelligence explained in early 2004:

> Successive blows to al Qaeda's central leadership have transformed the organization into a loose collection of regional networks that operate more autonomously . . . Even as al Qaeda has been weakened, other extremist groups within the movement it influenced have become the next wave of the terrorist threat.[11]

The prospect remains of a long-term struggle with this diffuse organization, its like-minded affiliates drawing on hard-line interpretations of Islam, and its dispersed followers and foot soldiers.

Al Qaeda has a history of dealings in Southeast Asia that stretch back to at least the early 1990s, primarily in connection with the formative activities of the radical Abu Sayyaf Group (ASG) in the southern Philippines. But the newly uncovered Southeast Asian linchpin of al Qaeda's network is a jihadist group called Jemaah Islamiyah (JI) (Islamic group or Islamic community).[12] Operating principally from Indonesia, JI is an outgrowth of the earlier Darul Islam (House of Islam) movement that was active after independence and up to 1962. Darul Islam fought to establish an Islamic state in Indonesia. JI shares al Qaeda's jihadist ideology and major objectives. For its part, JI seeks to establish an Islamic superstate, headed by a caliph (supreme ruler), across Southeast Asia to include Indonesia, Malaysia,

Singapore, southern Thailand, the southern Philippines, Brunei, and northern Australia.

Working closely with al Qaeda, and Southeast Asian veterans of the Afghan war, JI forged links with the Moro Islamic Liberation Front (MILF), an established terrorist group in the Philippines. JI also created its own cells in Singapore, Malaysia, southern Thailand, Java, Mindanao, Sabah, Sulawsei, and Australia. JI operatives have been active in Cambodia as well. JI is further linked with another newly emerged terrorist group in Malaysia called Kumpulan Militan Malaysia (Malaysian Mujahideen Group or KMM). JI attempted to solidify its regional relationships through an alliance known as the Rabitatul Mujahideen (Mujahideen League or RM), comprised of the MILF, a southern Thailand-based jihadist group, and others.[13] Figure 1 provides a broad portrait in diagram form of this Southeast Asian terror network.

Top JI personalities include Abu Bakar Bashir, a JI founder and its emir ("spiritual leader"), and Riduan Isamuddin (also known as Hambali), a senior operational leader and, until his arrest in Thailand in August 2003, considered "the most wanted man in Asia." Bashir, a sixty-six-year-old hard-line Indonesian cleric of Yemeni background, was arrested after the October 2002 Bali bombing. In 2003, he was convicted in Indonesia of treason and sentenced to four years in prison, which many observers perceived as an unduly light sentence in view of his central role in the Southeast Asian terror network. Attempting to navigate a narrow path that would not further agitate Islamist elements, an Indonesian appeals court later dropped the treason charge and reduced his prison sentence to three years based on related charges. Bashir's term was subsequently cut in half without explanation. He was set free in April 2004, but immediately rearrested on new evidence linking him to terrorism. At that time, an unrepentant Bashir issued a new threat, telling an Australian interviewer: "I am convinced that sooner or later America, and the countries that assist it, will be destroyed in the name of Allah."

The thirty-nine-year-old Hambali, meanwhile, was a pivotal figure in the international jihad network with ties to Osama bin Laden, al Qaeda plotting throughout the 1990s, and the 9/11 attack itself. As an Indonesian, he was the only non-Arab member of the al Qaeda inner circle and reportedly was the organization's fourth highest-ranking leader.[14] Hambali masterminded the Bali attack and, upon his arrest in 2003, was believed to be involved in fresh targeting of Western diplomatic establishments in Thailand.

The activities of the Southeast Asian terror network are ongoing and raise serious continuing concerns. Regional authorities have been successful in making arrests and dismantling parts of the network. As a result, we may see changes over time in specific strategies and objectives and in the formation

Figure 1   **Southeast Asian Terror Network**

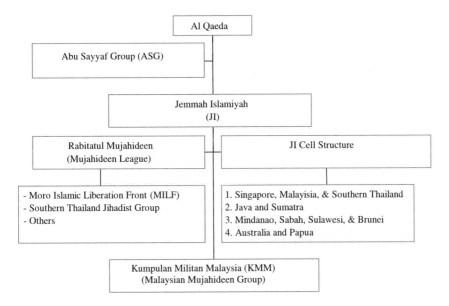

of splinter groups. Yet the underlying intentions of fostering an extreme vision of Islam remain in place, and the network is capable of making up for personnel losses with new members.[15] Thus, pursuing anti-U.S. and anti-Western activities will remain the network's broad mission, and this will result in persistent serious threats.

Plans for large-scale attacks on infrastructure targets, diplomatic establishments, military assets, and U.S. businesses have been disrupted. In Singapore, such attack planning was assessed to be operational and only a few days to a week away from implementation in late 2001.[16] The various plots that were uncovered but not carried out included:

- A USS *Cole* -like attack targeting a transiting U.S. warship off Singapore
- An attack on a U.S. warship off Surabaya, Indonesia, in May 2002
- An attack on a U.S. military bus in Singapore and against U.S. personnel in Malaysia
- Plans to crash a passenger plane into Changi Airport and to target other important infrastructure assets in Singapore
- Related plans to foment ethnic strife leading to interstate rivalry between Malaysia and Singapore intended to pave the way for JI political ascendancy
- Attacks on Western diplomatic establishments in Singapore, Malaysia, Indonesia, the Philippines, and Thailand

- Attacks on tourist resorts in Thailand
- The targeting of American businesses and the kidnapping of Western businessmen and diplomats

Al Qaeda's initial 9/11 attack planning also had a significant Asian component and called for the hijacking of U.S. aircraft flying Pacific routes. These aircraft were to be destroyed in midair. An alternate scenario apparently called for the hijacked planes to be crashed into U.S. targets in Japan, Singapore, or South Korea. This Asian dimension was to be carried out simultaneously with the attacks on America but was later set aside as being too complicated, and attack planning focused instead on targeting the United States.[17]

While these plots were thankfully averted, had any succeeded they would have increased regional instabilities, created substantial political-economic turmoil, and roiled regional and global investment markets.

JI did strike with devastating effect on October 12, 2002, in the nightclub district in Bali, Indonesia—one of the most lethal post–9/11 attacks (in terms of fatalities) by Islamic terrorists to date. The Bali attack killed 202 people, including 88 Australians, and left more than 300 injured. The U.S. secretary of state, Colin Powell, called the attack "Australia's 9/11," while the Australian prime minister, John Howard, confirmed that it was "the biggest loss of Australian life outside of war in a single incident." The incident cut sharply into Indonesia's tourism revenues and the direct economic impact was estimated to have reduced the country's gross domestic product (GDP) by 0.6 to 1 percentage point in 2003.

The Bali attack involved sophisticated tactics with multiple, near-simultaneous, remote-controlled detonations and also the use of a suicide bomber. Bali underlined the terrorists' formidable capabilities, and served as a further warning that Westerners visiting regional entertainment spots and other soft targets are vulnerable to attack. Bali was followed ten months later by another JI suicide attack on August 5, 2003, at the J.W. Marriott hotel in Jakarta. The attack occurred days before a verdict was handed down in the trial of one of the Bali bombers. The Marriott attack killed 12 people, including the Dutch expatriate manager of a Dutch-based bank in Jakarta, and left 150 injured.

On September 9, 2004, another suicide attack occurred in Jakarta and targeted the Australian embassy. This incident killed 9 and wounded 182, mostly Indonesians. The timing of the attack appeared designed to destabilize Indonesia days before the critical presidential election vote on September 20, 2004. Other likely objectives of the attack were to intimidate Australia, a key partner in the War on Terrorism, and demonstrate that JI retains its capacity to conduct major terrorist operations in Indonesia.

The charred ruins of the October 12, 2002, terrorist bomb blast in Bali, Indonesia. One of the most lethal post–9/11 attacks by Islamic radicals to date; 202 people were killed and more than 300 were injured. (AP/Wide World Photos)

Security Issues and Trends Independent of the Events of September 11

Alongside the factors that have developed so prominently since September 11, there is a full list of preexisting security issues and longer-term trends that continue to shape the Asian security environment. We have examined many of these issues in the two previous editions of *Asian Security Handbook*. The list includes:

- The potential for high-intensity, interstate conflict on the Korea Peninsula, across the Taiwan Strait, and between India and Pakistan stemming from long-running rivalries
- Religious and ethnic conflict and civil unrest in South and Southeast Asia
- Ongoing territorial disputes in the South China Sea
- Drug trafficking in the Golden Triangle area of Burma, Thailand, and Laos, as well as related narcotics threats emanating from neighboring Cambodia
- Maritime piracy in Asian waters
- Official corruption and linkages to organized crime

As noted below, two important deeper trends also stand out: (1) the nature of the Sino-American relationship, and (2) continued proliferation of WMD, primarily nuclear and missile capabilities and the related nexus with terrorism, rogue regimes, and regional power rivalries. Both are of crucial importance to future regional and global stability.

Prior to commenting on these two trends, we would offer a further word on maritime piracy, an issue that we examined closely in the previous editions of this book. Piracy had been played down in the past and for many years was of interest only to specialists and those in the business community directly affected, including the shipping and insurance industries. But this situation has changed with a steep increase in the number of piracy incidents reported in 2000 and a sustained high incident rate in subsequent years up to the present (see Table 1). Importantly, nearly two-thirds of all international piracy incidents over the last decade have occurred in Asian waters.

The surge in incidents, coupled with new post–9/11 concern about terrorist maritime threat potential, has greatly heightened interest in piracy, as well as shipping container and cargo security, port security, and in maritime security generally. Terrorists could hijack a vessel or use one in an attack scenario, to include attacks designed to have high political-economic impact. The February 2004 bombing of *Superferry 14* in Manila Bay is an example of this new threat. Claimed by ASG, that attack killed over 100 people.

Long-Term Trend 1: U.S.-China Strategic Competition

When it first assumed office, the Bush administration identified the People's Republic of China (PRC) as a strategic competitor with significant differences on issues ranging from Taiwan to missile defense, weapons proliferation, and human rights. The validity of this outlook was reaffirmed by the April 2001 incident involving a collision over the South China Sea between a Chinese F-8/J-8-II fighter employing aggressive tactics and a U.S. EP-3E reconnaissance plane. That same month President Bush stated that Washington would do "whatever it [takes] to help Taiwan defend herself." This statement came on the heels of the most comprehensive U.S. military package for Taiwan in a decade, which includes for the first time eight advanced diesel submarines, plus four Kidd-class destroyers, and 12 P-3 Orion antisubmarine aircraft.

These capabilities are intended to redress the military balance across the Taiwan Strait, which has been tilting to Beijing's advantage in recent years. China developed this edge through a wide-ranging conventional force and missile buildup, including a shopping spree in Russia involving advanced air and naval systems.[18] Hardware acquisition has been accompanied by the

Table 1

A Decade of Piracy in Asia, 1994–2003

Year	Total worldwide number of incidents	Number of incidents in Southeast Asia, South Asia, and Far East	Asian incidents as percentage of worldwide total
1994	90	73	81.1
1995	188	134	71.3
1996	228	165	72.4
1997	247	148	59.9
1998	202	121	59.9
1999	300	212	70.7
2000	469	355	75.9
2001	335	223	66.6
2002	370	222	60.0
2003	445	276	62.0

Sources: International Maritime Bureau (IMB), Regional Piracy Center (RPC), Kuala Lumpur, "Piracy and Armed Robbery Against Ships: Annual Report: 1st January–31st December 1998," January 1999, p. 3; RPC, "Piracy and Armed Robbery Against Ships: Report for the Period: 1st January–30th June 1999," 15 July 1999, p. 3; and IMB, "Piracy and Armed Robbery Against Ships: Annual Report:1 January–31 December 2003," January 2004.

Note: "Asia" as defined here does not include the Iran/Persian Gulf region.

exploitation of new technologies and the development of new asymmetrically designed war-fighting strategies, including information operations/information warfare.

Taiwan is a critical regional hot spot and a matter of the greatest strategic importance to East Asia and the entire international community. Heightened Chinese concerns over Taiwanese independence could lead to new pressures, threats, military maneuvers, or the outbreak of conflict on short notice, catapulting this issue to the forefront of international attention.

Despite the temporary lull brought on under the semblance of cooperation in the War on Terrorism, the interests of Beijing and Washington have the clear potential to clash in the years and decades ahead, if the relationship is not managed effectively. Military planners in the United States recognize this. As outlined in the September 2001 Quadrennial Defense Review (QDR) document, U.S. policy makers are shifting U.S. strategic priorities and force requirements to address future contingencies in East Asia in order to meet the long-term challenges posed by China. There are a number of broad indicators that, indeed, point to China as a long-term strategic competitor. First, the core interests of the United States and China diverge significantly on such key questions as democracy, human rights, Taiwan, and proliferation. Again, with respect to Taiwan, PRC authorities clearly have not ruled out the use of force to achieve future reunification. Any conflict over Taiwan would have enormous political, military, and economic consequences for the United States due to Washington's long-standing security commitments to Taipei. Similarly, China's record on proliferation is not good, and it appears that Beijing is all too content to see some weapons technology leakage to sensitive global conflict zones as a means of supporting China's allies while at the same time keeping the United States off balance.

Such realpolitik calculations extend also to the South China Sea—another regional flash point that is lying dormant for the moment. China has not backed off its expansive territorial claims in the South China Sea, and any future conflict there over disputed territory or natural resources most assuredly would impact the interests of the United States and its friends and allies in East and Southeast Asia. Worldwide shipping and commerce would also suffer from any crisis in the South China Sea.

A second major indicator of future competition stems from the People's Liberation Army's (PLA) continuing modernization program. This extensive modernization is buoyed by the availability of new economic resources and unfettered by any restraints except the capacity to absorb and deploy new weapon systems. Along the same lines, Chinese strategists and military planners also continue to identify the United States as a principal future adversary. Although the Chinese political leadership talks down notions of a strategic competition with the United States, there is a clear pattern of behavior with respect to military hardware acquisition, force modernization, and doctrinal development that points to acquiring the tools and strategies for power projection in Asia and beyond.

Yet, at the same time that significant tensions exist in the bilateral relationship, there are powerful economic and trade forces pushing the two sides together. Some observers in fact see the economic dimension as a defining determinant of future relations. This is based in many respects on the view that the "China market" will drive future global growth given a continuing forecasted expansion of the Chinese economy. China's voracious appetite for commodities, energy resources, and other economic inputs will deepen the country's free market orientation and could become the basis for the creation of a huge middle class. Under this view, a policy of bilateral strategic cooperation or partnership is therefore a necessary foundation for economic interaction, and such cooperation cannot be achieved with the two countries in a distinctly competitive mode. Taken further, this view holds out the possibility that economic development could be a springboard for future democracy.

But the China market thesis also presents a dilemma in that greater economic integration built around significant industrial manufacturing and technology transfer to China will end up only strengthening the country's military and security apparatus, and runs the risk of creating a strategic competitor. Newfound economic power could make the existing communist dictatorship stronger and more resistant to change. The country would be better positioned to pursue its interests in Asia and beyond and to pose a significant challenge to the United States.

In late 2003 the Bush administration began reversing its earlier emphasis on the strategic competition aspects of the bilateral relationship and indeed the phrase "strategic competitor" was essentially banned from official usage. A policy of tactical accommodation emerged under which the United States sought to play down its significant differences with China, particularly over the issue of Taiwan, and to instead focus on the commonality of interests between the two countries. This policy shift apparently came about in recognition of overriding U.S. priorities in the War on Terrorism. But gazing into the future, as the War on Terrorism winds down, the competition between these two powers is likely to heat up as their interests continue to clash.

Managing what will be basically a long-term competitive relationship will be a critical challenge for policy makers in both Washington and Beijing. As the ultimate guarantor of peace and stability in the region, the United States must of necessity maintain a strategic equilibrium that balances the rising power aspirations of China by means of deterrence and strong defense capabilities. Prudent U.S. and allied strategists must also seek to integrate China into the world system in a cooperative manner.

Long-Term Trend 2: WMD and the Nexus of Terrorism, Rogue Regimes, and Regional Rivalries

As examined in depth in the two previous editions of this book, WMD proliferation has been a burgeoning problem for quite some time, mainly in the context of regional power rivalries in East and South Asia. But it is now an issue that has taken on much greater urgency in recognition of the fact that these weapons would pose grave threats in the hands of a terrorist organization such as al Qaeda. It is also an issue that has burst into daily news headlines as a result of continuing post–9/11 concerns, as well as the controversy that developed after Operation Iraqi Freedom surrounding the full extent of Saddam Hussein's WMD programs.

Given its continuing desire to inflict mass casualties on its enemies, al Qaeda has shown a strong interest in obtaining and employing biological or chemical weapons, radiological dispersal devices ("dirty bombs"), or potentially nuclear weapons.[19] Aided by a rogue state or through covert transactions on the inter national black market, the prospect of terrorists gaining access to WMD poses daunting challenges for Western defense and security planners.

This prospect is all the more worrying in light of revelations of illegal technology transfers from elements within Pakistan's nuclear establishment to Iran, Libya, North Korea, and possibly others. The key figure in this still unfolding matter is Abdul Qadeer (A.Q.) Khan, father of Pakistan's nuclear bomb, who utilized an extensive international black market network and middlemen to spread nuclear weapons components and technologies. Khan and his associates, for example, used a factory in Malaysia to manufacture key parts for centrifuges built to enrich uranium. Other parts and components were purchased through operatives based in Europe, the Middle East, and Africa.

Similarly, North Korea itself has boasted that it may be prepared to commit a brazen act of proliferation and transfer nuclear know-how or capabilities to a terrorist group or other rogue elements. As noted earlier, the United States has made the defeating of this nexus of terrorism, rogue regimes, and WMD proliferation a defining feature of its post–9/11 security strategies.

An added element in this challenging situation is the continued pursuit of WMD capabilities throughout Asia and the consequential reactions this is producing. Table 2 illustrates selected WMD-related developments in Asia in recent years. In particular, nuclear and missile capabilities continue to spread in East and South Asia, creating dangerous new instabilities and tensions in the conflict zones between North and South Korea, China and Taiwan, and India and Pakistan.

A key consequential impact is that an opponent must be seen to match his adversary's capabilities for prestige purposes, in order to maintain deterrence, and to have a response-in-kind defense should deterrence fail. In short, this situation has led to a new nuclear arms and missile race in Asia. This is certainly the case in the dynamics we see between India and Pakistan. For its part, China's across-the-board buildup of ballistic and cruise missiles is in effect forcing Taiwan to develop similar counterforce capabilities. China has positioned nearly five hundred ballistic missiles opposite Taiwan, and this number continues to grow. As a result, Taiwan is moving toward missile systems that can hold at risk Shanghai, Hong Kong, or other valuable political-military targets in southeastern China, and possibly extending to the targeting of the Three Gorges dam.

There also has been talk in Japan of playing the nuclear card in response to North Korea's missile threat. But so far Japan has chosen a lower-key response as a first option—a new missile defense system being developed in cooperation with the United States. Japan itself does not deploy offensive ballistic missiles, but its extensive space launch vehicle (SLV) program provides an inherent capability for developing ballistic missiles. Japan's SLV program puts it in a position to create a missile force quickly if it chooses to do so. In addition,

Table 2

Weapons of Mass Destruction in Asia: Selected Developments, 2002–2004

2002

January   **India**: flight test of Agni 1, a new rail or road deployable medium-range ballistic missile (MRBM) with a range of 700–900 km/435–559 miles.

April   **Japan**: Ichiro Ozawa, leader, Liberal Party (former-Liberal Democratic Party) states: "We have plenty of plutonium in our nuclear power plants, so it's possible for us to produce 3,000 to 4,000 nuclear warheads. If we get serious, we will never be beaten in terms of military power."

May   **Pakistan**: multiple flight tests of Ghauri MRBM and Hatf 2 & 3 short-range ballistic missiles (SRBMs).

July   **China**: tests DF-21 Mod 2 MRBM with 6–7 penetration aids.

August   **Yemen**: confirms receipt in the late 1990s of North Korean Scud SRBMs.
    Pakistan: purchases 4–6 No-Dong/Ghauri MRBMs from North Korea. Ships them to Islamabad via C-130 aircraft.

September   **South Korea**: Defense Ministry says North Korea has a stockpile of 2,500–5,000 metric tons of chemical weapons and is capable of producing 1 ton of biological weapons per year.

October   **North Korea**: admits to uranium-based nuclear weapons program.

December   **Yemen**: receives 15 Scud SRBMs (believed to be Scud Cs) and 15 conventional high-explosive warheads shipped via the *So San*, a North Korea merchant vessel.
    North Korea: restarts work at Yongbyon nuclear facilities.

2003

January   **India**: flight test of Agni 1.
    North Korea: withdraws from the Nuclear Non-Proliferation Treaty (NPT).

February   **India**: tests nuclear-capable Brahmos antiship cruise missile (ASCM) (under a joint program with Russia).

March   **India**: tests Prithvi SRBM.
    Pakistan: tests Abdali SRBM.

April   **North Korea**: admits to possessing nuclear weapons—is now the world's 9th nuclear power?

May   **United States**: announces the Proliferation Security Initiative (PSI).

July   **Japan**: government official reports that North Korea has deployed about 200 No-Dong MRBMs capable of targeting Japan.
    United States: imposes sanctions on one North Korean and five Chinese entities for providing WMD materials to Iran.

(continued)

Table 2 *(continued)*

August	**Taiwan**: reports development of the Hsiung-Feng IIE, a land-attack cruise missile (LACM) prototype with a potential range of 1,000 km/ 622 miles.
October	**Pakistan**: tests Hatf 3 and Hatf 4 (Shaheen 1) SRBMs.
	India: confirms that it has established nuclear command and control centers.
	Iraq: paid US$10 million to North Korea for No-Dong MRBMs and missile production technology in late 2002, according to post-Iraq war investigations, but North Korea never completed delivery.
	Taiwan: may have recently tested a new ballistic missile with a range of 600–900 km/373–559 miles capable of targeting Shanghai, Hong Kong, and major coastal centers in southeastern China.
November	**Burma**: sent a contingent of military officers to North Korea to study nuclear technology and may purchase missiles from Pyongyang.
	Taiwan: President Chen Shui-bian reveals China targets Taiwan with 496 ballistic missiles.
December	**Pakistan**: initiates investigation of nuclear scientists engaged in illegal technology transfers.

2004

January	**Pakistan**: dismisses prominent nuclear scientist Abdul Qadeer (A.Q.) Khan on revelations of illegal technology transfers.
	Nigeria: reportedly in talks about acquiring missile technology from North Korea.
February	**Pakistan**: A.Q. Khan admits to illegal WMD dealings but is pardoned by President Musharraf. International Atomic Energy Agency (IAEA) chief says Khan's revelations are the "tip of an iceberg" of the international WMD black market.
	Libya/Pakistan/China: nuclear warhead designs obtained by Libya from A.Q. Khan originated in China.
	Malaysia: local company affiliated with A.Q. Khan identified as source of centrifuge components for Libyan nuclear program.
April	**North Korea**: U.S. intelligence reportedly raise estimate of number of North Korean nuclear weapons from "possibly two" to at least eight.
July	**North Korea**: reportedly deploying two new intermediate-range ballistic missiles (IRBMs) with ranges of 2,500–4,000 km/1,550–2,480 miles that are based on a Soviet-era submarine-launched ballistic missile (SLBM).
August	**India**: flight test of Agni 2, an IRBM with a range of 2,500 km/1,550 miles.
September	**South Korea**: publicly acknowledges carrying out secret nuclear fuel experiment in early 2000, enriching uranium to near-bomb grade level.

Source: Prepared by David G. Wiencek based on multiple sources.

the country's vast supply of plutonium could be adapted for a nuclear weapons program if existing threat trends become even more pronounced.

North Korea's WMD threats truly stand out and pose an imminent threat to regional and global security. Pyongyang has amassed a force of some 800 ballistic missiles and is the world's largest exporter of ballistic missiles and associated technology. It deploys the No-Dong medium-range ballistic missile, which can target Japan, and, by mid-2004, had reportedly developed two new intermediate-range ballistic missiles (IRBMs) based on a Soviet–era submarine-launched ballistic missile. One of these new IRBMs, with a range of 2,500–4,000 km/1,550–2,480 miles, is being deployed in a land-based version, while the operational status of the other missile, a ship or submarine-based variant with a range of 2,500 km/1,550 miles, is not yet known.

North Korea is also working on the longer-range Taepo Dong system. In 1998 North Korea conducted a flight test of the Taepo Dong 1. As the U.S. Central Intelligence Agency later noted, if the Taepo Dong 1 "were flown successfully on an ICBM [intercontinental ballistic missile] trajectory, it would have been able to deliver a small biological or chemical weapon to American soil." A two-stage Taepo Dong 2, a more capable system under development, "could reach parts of the United States with a nuclear-sized payload, while [a] three-stage version could reach anywhere in Europe or the United States."[20]

In 2002–2003, the stakes were raised further when North Korea reopened its Yongbyon facilities and reportedly completed the reprocessing of spent fuel rods into weapons-grade plutonium. Subsequently a senior official acknowledged that the country in fact possessed nuclear weapons and was prepared to conduct a "demonstration" (a nuclear test) or "transfer them," which was interpreted as a not-so veiled threat to export nuclear capabilities to others, including terrorists. These developments prompted a new round of diplomacy, the so-called six party talks, aimed at containing Pyongyang's threatening posture. Reflecting on the seriousness of North Korea's nuclear breakout, one senior U.S. official has commented:

> Pyongyang's open pursuit of additional nuclear weapons is the most serious challenge to U.S. regional interests in a generation. . . . The outcome of the current crisis will shape relations in Northeast Asia for years to come.[21]

The Proliferation Security Initiative

One new response to deal with North Korean and other rogue WMD challenges is the Proliferation Security Initiative (PSI) launched by President Bush in May 2003. The PSI seeks to interdict the transfer of and trade in

WMD components and materials. So far, eleven nations have agreed to participate in this effort: Australia, France, Germany, Italy, Japan, the Netherlands, Poland, Portugal, Spain, the United Kingdom, and the United States. The PSI goes beyond previous diplomatic efforts and actively seeks to prevent clandestine WMD transactions from taking place. The participating nations agree to share information and to use force to stop, board, and search suspect vessels, aircraft, or ground-based transports and seize prohibited cargo.

A key impetus for the PSI came from a high profile incident in December 2002 when a North Korean vessel, the *So San,* was intercepted by a task force of Spanish and U.S. vessels in the Arabian Sea. The *So San* was a North Korean merchant ship that had departed the port of Nampo in mid-November 2002. It sailed unflagged, but claimed Cambodian registry, and the original name of the ship had been painted over to conceal its North Korean identity. The *So San* was purportedly carrying two thousand tons of cement.

But when it was stopped and forcibly boarded, Spanish and U.S. forces found hidden beneath bags of cement fifteen Scud missiles (believed to be Scud Cs with a range of approximately 500 km/310 miles), warheads, fuel, and drums of unidentified chemicals. After a standoff the *So San* was allowed to proceed to Yemen, its designated port of call and the true buyer of the Scud missiles. In an unfortunate proliferation policy lapse, Washington calculated that Yemen's assistance in the War on Terrorism was vital and, to avoid a diplomatic row, decided to allow the shipment to proceed. Yet the incident in which North Korea was caught red-handed shipping missile systems increased the focus on the need for better counter-proliferation interdiction policies.

The *So San* episode was followed by an incident in April 2003 in the waters off Sydney, Australia. Another North Korean merchant vessel, the *Pong Su,* evaded authorities during a four-day chase until Australian special forces forcibly boarded it. While not carrying WMD components, the *Pong Su* carried 125 kilograms (276 pounds) of pure heroin worth approximately US$120 million. The incident highlighted North Korea's trade in illicit activities and showed that, in addition to WMD proliferation, it was involved in state-sponsored narco-trafficking. Proliferation and drug trafficking, along with currency counterfeiting and other related illegal activities, are designed to earn hard currency to keep the Kim Jong-il dictatorship in power at all costs. These other concerns are being dealt with under a separate program, the DPRK Illicit Activities Initiative, operated in parallel with the PSI.[22]

Although the details have yet to be made public, similar efforts reportedly played a pivotal role in achieving a subsequent counter-proliferation policy victory: the surprise announcement in late 2003 that Libya would renounce its long-running clandestine WMD programs. Under this gesture, Libya agreed to dismantle unilaterally its nuclear weapons program, destroy its chemical

A sailor is lowered from a Spanish helicopter onto the *So San,* a North Korean merchant vessel carrying Scud missiles to Yemen. The boarding took place on December 9, 2002, in the Arabian Sea and highlighted North Korea's trade in weapons of mass destruction systems. (AP/Wide World Photos)

weapons stockpile, and voluntarily subject itself to international inspections. The interdiction of WMD components bound for Libya was an important factor in leader Moammar Gaddafi's decision to come clean, give up his WMD capabilities, and reach out to the United States, United Kingdom, and the West for normal relations.

The timing of the Libyan overture, which initially took place around the start of Operation Iraqi Freedom, also suggests that the demonstration effect of the robust new U.S. strategy should not be underestimated. America's strong resolve to act decisively is likely affecting the calculations of such rogue states as Libya, who now must take very seriously Washington's commitment to stop terrorism and prevent WMD technology from spreading, particularly to terrorist groups. Libya's reaction in this regard is therefore significant.

Missile Defense

Missile defense is an important and vital response to ever growing ballistic and cruise missile threats in Asia. In the United States, missile defense has taken on a new significance in light of the post–9/11 requirement to secure the homeland from rogue or terrorist attack.

Missile defenses are stabilizing and help deter attack. They also help prevent nuclear blackmail and intimidation. If deterrence fails, missile defenses provide a means to blunt an attack and help protect population centers and critical military assets.

U.S. missile defense systems proved their effectiveness during Operation Iraqi Freedom, successfully intercepting nine of nine Iraqi short-range ballistic missiles (five other Iraqi ballistic missiles fell harmlessly in the desert or in the waters of the Persian Gulf). One engagement was particularly crucial: an Iraqi missile was intercepted "two miles before it would have struck the allied command center" in Kuwait. As the *New York Times* reported, "Later analysis indicated the missile was dead on target when it was intercepted," and the intercept averted an "Iraqi attempt to decapitate the allied military leadership."[23]

In the face of rapidly expanding missile threats from China and North Korea, Japan has decided to deploy over the coming years a layered missile defense system. One tier of the system will consist of the U.S.-developed, sea-based Standard missile (SM)-3 deployed aboard Japanese Aegis destroyers for intercepting a missile in the upper reaches of its flight path, while the ground-based Patriot Advanced Capability (PAC)-3 is intended for lower-tier interception. Taiwan, meanwhile, also has expressed an interest in the PAC-3 as a means of countering Beijing's massive missile buildup. In South Korea, U.S. forces have acquired the PAC-3 while South Korean forces are also examining the possibility of obtaining the PAC-3 for themselves and establishing links with U.S. antimissile capabilities. In 2003 Australia announced that it too would participate in U.S. missile defense efforts. The United States itself began deployment in 2004 of an initial capability to defend against long-range missile attack known as the Ground-based Midcourse Defense (GMD). When completed by late 2005, this initial capability will consist of up to twenty interceptors based at Fort Greely, Alaska, and Vandenberg Air Force Base in California. These capabilities will be expanded over time as missile defense technologies mature further.

Conclusions and Outlook

The events of September 11 have ushered in many changes for the United States and the world. The international security environment has been transformed and the global power balance has shifted as a direct result of 9/11. The power and influence of the United States has grown in relation to others. The unipolar power structure creates new dangers in that the United States is now the principal target of many hostile elements, and those nations that have seen their power diminished will potentially look for new ways to challenge U.S. supremacy and keep the United States off balance.

All indications point to the War on Terrorism lasting many years and being conducted in many locales, including throughout Central, South, and Southeast Asia. The U.S. homeland will also remain vulnerable to follow-on terrorist attacks.

In Asia the new security complexities raised by the events of September 11 add further to preexisting instabilities, and conflict potential in the region remains high, spanning a full spectrum of low- to high-intensity threats. This situation, coupled with ongoing political developments, high stakes elections, and such pressing region-wide health problems as severe acute respiratory syndrome (SARS) and avian flu, place a premium on timely analysis and assessment of the risk factors that will influence future political, economic, and military trends in Asia.

Structure of the Book

The chapters that follow analyze such factors and political-security conditions throughout the region on a country-by-country basis. Given our terrorism focus, each chapter contains a "Terrorism Threat and Response" section describing the extent to which 9/11 has had an impact on that country's interests and to what extent that country is engaged with the United States and others in the region in the War on Terrorism. North Korea clearly stands out as a nation outside this antiterror framework and such considerations do not apply in its case.

Our comprehensive treatment of country-specific concerns now extends to twenty-three individual nations, with Bangladesh, Brunei, and Nepal new to this edition. The profiles describe the country's framework for assessing political-security issues and contain a risk assessment that highlights the key internal and external security problems facing the country. The profiles also review the role of the armed forces, military force structure, and defense policy issues. Suggestions for further reading are included at the end of each chapter, which point to useful reference resources. Finally, additional reference material is contained in two appendices. Appendix 1 shows in table form comparative data on the countries surveyed in this book. Appendix 2 contains a list of official United States government-designated Foreign Terrorist Organizations (FTOs) in Asia mentioned throughout the text.

Notes

1. Comment of Condoleezza Rice, U.S. National Security Adviser, "Our Coalition," *The Wall Street Journal,* March 26, 2003.
2. Spain's foreign minister, Ana Palacio, went further in describing the fissures between the United States and some of its traditional allies prior to the war in Iraq in

March 2003. She wrote: "At the root of some countries positions'—particularly France and Germany—appears to be the desire to play the role of 'counterweight' to the U.S. on the world stage. This desire to set up a rival pole and offer the world an alternative to U.S. power sometimes takes priority over any other link with the U.S. and even leads to confrontation on the international stage." See Ana Palacio, "Allies, Not 'Counterweights,'" *The Wall Street Journal,* March 25, 2003. The British prime minister, Tony Blair, shared this assessment and has said that "some want a so-called multipolar world where you have different centres of power, and I believe that will very quickly develop into rival centres of power." Quoted in "Full transcript of the interview with Tony Blair," *Financial Times,* April 28, 2003, at www.ft.com.

3. The unipolar world power structure is best described by commentator Charles Krauthammer in his seminal article "The Unipolar Moment," *Foreign Affairs: America and the World* (1990/01), vol. 70, no. 1, and his updated analysis, "The Unipolar Moment Revisited," *The National Interest,* Winter 2002/03, no. 70, pp. 5–17. Also along these lines, Mr. Blair comments that "we need one polar power . . . which encompasses a strategic partnership between Europe and America and other countries too—Russia, China—where we are trying to ensure that we develop . . . a common global agenda. Because I think the danger of rival poles of power is that you end up reawakening some of the problems that we had in the old cold war with countries playing different centres of power off against each other, with countries who really should be together falling out over issues, and that destabilises the world." See "Full transcript of the interview with Tony Blair," *Financial Times.* For related analysis, see Lionel Barber, "The Power Paradox: The US Moves towards Selective Alliances and Away from 'Mindless Multilateralism,'" *Financial Times,* December 19, 2003, p. 11.

4. September 11 casualty figures as posted on memorial panels at the World Trade Center site in New York by the Port Authority of New York and New Jersey and reproduced at "September 11 Panels" (Downtown Restoration Program section), at www.panynj.gov. Regarding the economic impact of the attacks, see U.S. General Accounting Office (GAO), *Review of Studies of the Economic Impact of the September 11, 2001, Terrorist Attacks on the World Trade Center,* GAO-02–700R, May 29, 2002, at www.gao.gov. Also see Peter Grant and Motoko Rich, "How Damaged Is Downtown?" *The Wall Street Journal,* September 11, 2002, pp. B1 and B6.

5. Transcript of President Bush's Address to a Joint Session of Congress, *Washington Post,* September 21, 2001, p. A24.

6. President George W. Bush, "Remarks by the President at 2002 Graduation Exercise of the United States Military Academy, West Point, New York," June 1, 2002, at www.whitehouse.gov. The conceptual framework for the new U.S. strategy is further discussed in *The National Security Strategy of the United States of America,* September 2002, particularly in the introduction and chap. 5, at www.whitehouse.gov/nsc/nss.html.

7. *The National Security Strategy of the United States of America,* chap. 5, at www.whitehouse.gov/nsc/nss.html.

8. President George W. Bush, remarks from the deck of the aircraft carrier USS *Abraham Lincoln,* in "'The Battle of Iraq Is One Victory in a War on Terror,' president says," *Washington Times,* May 2, 2003, p. A15.

9. For background on al Qaeda, see Peter L. Bergen, *Holy War, Inc.: Inside the Secret World of Osama Bin Laden* (New York: Touchstone, 2001), and Rohan Gunaratna, *Inside Al Qaeda: Global Network of Terror* (New York: Columbia Uni-

versity Press, 2002). For another valuable resource that places al Qaeda's views within the broader context of Islamic history and current trends within Islam, see: Bernard Lewis, *The Crisis of Islam: Holy War and Unholy Terror* (New York: The Modern Library, 2003). For an authoritative official account of al Qaeda plotting and the events leading to 9/11, see National Commission on Terrorist Attacks Upon the United States, *The 9/11 Commission Report* (New York: W.W. Norton, 2004), chaps. 2, 4, and 6.

10. Dr. Rohan Gunaratna, "Al-Qaeda is Replicating, Rejuvenating and Reorganising to Strike in the Region," *Straits Times*, September 13, 2002.

11. George J. Tenet, "The Worldwide Threat 2004: Challenges in a Changing Global Context," Testimony of the director of Central Intelligence before the Senate Armed Services Committee, March 9, 2004 (as prepared for delivery), at www.cia.gov. Also see Keith Johnson and David Crawford, "New Breed of Islamic Warrior is Emerging," *The Wall Street Journal*, March 29, 2004, p. A16 and Dan Eggen and John Lancaster, "Al Qaeda Shows New Signs of Life," *Washington Post*, August 14, 2004, pp. A1 and A13.

12. For background on the Southeast Asian terrorist network, see Ministry of Home Affairs, Republic of Singapore, *White Paper: The Jemaah Islamiyah Arrests and the Threat of Terrorism*, January 7, 2003, at www2.mha.gov.sg; Gunaratna, *Inside Al Qaeda*, particularly chap. 4; Zachary Abuza, *Militant Islam in Southeast Asia: Crucible of Terror* (Boulder: Lynne Rienner Publishers, 2003); and Maria A. Ressa, *Seeds of Terror: An Eyewitness Account of Al-Qaeda's Newest Center of Operations in Southeast Asia* (New York: Free Press, 2003).

13. See "Singapore Government Press Statement on Further Arrests under the Internal Security Act," September 19, 2002, at www2.mha.gov.sg, and Ministry of Home Affairs, Republic of Singapore, *White Paper: The Jemaah Islamiyah Arrests and the Threat of Terrorism*, p. 7. Zachary Abuza writes that the Rabitatul Mujahideen (RM) consisted of leaders from JI and the Mujahideen Council of Indonesia (MMI), an overt umbrella group linking various Indonesian militant organizations, and "representatives from Aceh, Thailand, Myanmar, and Bangladesh," Abuza, *Militant Islam in Southeast Asia*, p. 171. Abuza also reports that the RM met only three times, the last time was November 2000, and that all meetings took place in Malaysia. Other sources indicate that a JI-linked paramilitary group, Laskar Jundallah, also was part of the RM. Singapore also includes an unnamed self-exiled Rohingyas group based in Bangladesh as part of the RM.

14. Don Greenlees, "Still a Force to be Feared," *Far Eastern Economic Review*, January 22, 2004, p. 14. Also see *The 9/11 Commission Report*, pp. 150–152.

15. Ellen Nakashima, "Indonesian Militants 'Keep Regenerating,'" *Washington Post*, March 25, 2004, p. A17; Leslie Lopez, "Islamic Militants Shift Strategy in Southeast Asia," *The Wall Street Journal*, March 9, 2004, pp. A14–A15; and James Hookway, "A Dangerous New Alliance," *Far Eastern Economic Review*, May 6, 2004, pp. 12–14. Also see comments of Sidney Jones, Indonesia Project Director, International Crisis Group before the United States-Indonesia Society (USINDO), Washington, DC, February 23, 2004, in USINDO "Brief: Major Security Concerns in Indonesia, Sidney Jones 2/23/04."

16. This is the judgment of the U.S. ambassador to Singapore, Frank Lavin, as quoted in Elizabeth Sullivan, "Ambassador Says U.S. Ship, Transport Targeted in al-Qaida's Singapore Plot," *The (Cleveland) Plain Dealer*, June 19, 2002, online edition.

17. As recounted in *The 9/11 Commission Report*, p. 156.

18. See, for example, Richard D. Fisher Jr., "The Impact of Foreign Weapons and Technology on the Modernization of China's People's Liberation Army." A Report for the U.S.-China Economic and Security Review Commission, January 2004, at www.uscc.gov/researchreports/2004/04fisher_report/04_01_01fisherreport.htm.

19. For background, see U.S. Central Intelligence Agency, "Terrorist CBRN [Chemical-Biological-Radiological-Nuclear]: Materials and Effects," June 2003, at www.cia.gov, and Bill Gertz, "CIA Says al Qaeda Ready to Use Nukes," *Washington Times,* June 3, 2003, pp. A1 and A8.

20. See remarks of the deputy director of Central Intelligence John E. McLaughlin at the Fourth Annual Space and Missile Defense Conference, Huntsville, Alabama, August 21, 2001, and "Foreign Missile Developments and the Ballistic Missile Threat Through 2015," National Intelligence Estimate, December 2001, at www.cia.gov.

21. Vice Admiral Lowell E. Jacoby, USN, director, Defense Intelligence Agency, "Statement for the Record," before the U.S. Senate Armed Services Committee, February 12, 2003.

22. As reported by Steven R. Weisman, "U.S. to Send Signal to North Koreans in Naval Exercise," *New York Times,* August 18, 2003, at www.nytimes.com.

23. Michael R. Gordon, "Dispatches: A Poor Man's Air Force," *New York Times,* June 19, 2003, at www.nytimes.com. Also see Col. Charles A. Anderson, "Air and Missile Defense: Operation Iraqi Freedom," *Army Magazine,* January 2004, at www.ausa.org. Note: there were two unfortunate fratricide incidents involving Patriot missile defense systems and a British GR-4 Tornado and a U.S. Navy FA-18. Also, five Iraqi-modified, Chinese-designed CSS-3 cruise missiles were launched at Kuwait. These missiles were not intercepted and produced no casualties.

Country Profiles

1

Australia

America's Closest Ally

Bruce Vaughn

Introduction

The terrorist attacks on the United States of September 11, 2001, have, when combined with America's newfound sense of insecurity, produced fundamental changes in the way the United States interacts with the world. This has had a profound effect on the way other nations perceive the United States, and it has, in many cases, damaged America's relations with friends, allies, and neutral states. Some observers have gone so far as to speculate that present realities threaten to render the existing system of American alliances "superfluous."[1] While this may increasingly be the case in Europe, Australia stands in Asia as a state that has drawn closer to the United States since 9/11. Australia has traditionally sought to involve the United States in its corner of the world and has welcomed America's Asia-Pacific presence. Australia has also increasingly played an active role in promoting stability in its region. Since 9/11 this has in part been justified by the need to prevent failing states from becoming failed states from which terrorists could potentially draw arms and support or use for money laundering. It is also drawing Australia to cooperate with moderate Islam and to nurture closer relations with Indonesia and other Southeast Asian states as it attempts to mitigate extremist Islamic threats that could arise in the region.[2]

Australia's actions since 9/11 have provided further evidence to support the assertion that Australia is indeed America's closest ally. Australia and the United States have been treaty allies since the signing of the trilateral 1951 ANZUS treaty, between Australia, New Zealand, and the United States. At that time, Australia was seeking to keep America engaged in the western Pacific to hedge against a resurgent Japan. Australia had viewed the Korean War in 1951 as an opportunity to demonstrate to its would-be ally, America,

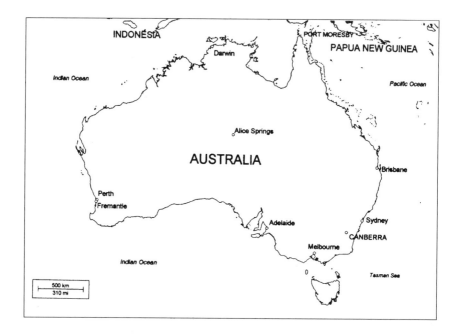

that it would continue to carry its weight in Asia-Pacific configurations in the post–World War II period. Nonetheless, Australian and American forces did not begin their shared experience in war at this time. During World War I the United States and Australian forces began in earnest what is now a longstanding experience as brothers in arms. United States and Australian forces have also fought shoulder to shoulder in Vietnam, the first Gulf War, Afghanistan, and, most recently, Iraq. This shared history is a testament to the enduring bonds of mutual values and culture. A key turning point in Australia's shift from reliance on Great Britain to the United States as its closest ally was World War II. The fall of the British bastion at Singapore and the military assistance that the United States gave in the Pacific, most notably at the Battle of the Coral Sea and Guadalcanal, convinced Australians that the United States was best positioned to help Australia should it again be threatened.

Political Framework

Australia is approximately the size of the continental United States, with a population of 20 million. It is also a parliamentary democracy dominated by two key political parties. On the left is the Labor Party, and on the right is the Liberal Party, with its National Party ally. The political spectrum in Australia does not extend as far to the right as it does in the United States. Voting is compulsory, there is a preferential ballot, and the upper house of parliament, the Senate, is elected on a proportional basis. While there is a degree of involvement by the parliament in defense and foreign affairs, it is not on the same level as that exerted by the United States Congress—due to the structural dynamics of a parliamentary, as opposed to a congressional checks-and-balances style, democracy. There is a large degree of bipartisanship in defense and foreign policy, though some differences are discernable. The Labor Hawke and Keating governments were enthusiastic promoters of defining Australia's destiny in and with Asia. They were also supporters of the American alliance. The Liberal Howard government, however, has drawn back from a Keating-style Asian engagement and steered Australia more firmly into line with its more traditional ally, the United States. This is particularly evident in defense and trade policy. The Howard government has also emphasized the importance of Asia as demonstrated by its growing relationship with China, and is increasingly drawn into regional affairs as a result of the widening war against terror.

Prime Minister John Howard came to office in 1996 seeking to reinvigorate what was already a very close defense and intelligence relationship between the United States and Australia. Howard remained steadfast on this policy, marking a shift away from the previous government of Paul Keating. Keating's policy had been described as Asian "engagement" or "enmeshment." It proved to be too far out in front of average Australians who did not see themselves as "Asian." A large majority of Australians trace their ethnic roots to the United Kingdom, Ireland, or elsewhere in Europe. Howard's commitment to the American alliance has been reified by combined joint exercises, intelligence sharing, the commitment of Australian forces to United States military operations, and a strong push for a free-trade agreement with the United States.

Internal Security Environment

Australia is unlike most Asian states in that it is a largely cohesive state that has not experienced significant regional autonomous or secessionist movements. Its population is largely of the same ethnic origin (aborigines account for approximately 1 percent of the population, while Asians account for about 7 percent), and there are no troubling regional differences that might lead to conflict—other than on the rugby field. While aboriginal grievances have been expressed, they are largely being worked out in a societal context that is increasingly understanding of past hardships that the original settlers imposed on the aborigines. More recent waves of immigration sometimes encounter social conflict with the dominant Anglo-Celtic culture, but these differences are also declining over time, as the society has become largely tolerant of difference.

Discussion of internal security concerns in Australia has grown as a result of the war against terror, though it is still relatively slight. It has now come to light that the Jemaah Islamiyah (JI) (Islamic group or Islamic community) terrorist network, which has ties to al Qaeda, has plans to establish a caliphate in Southeast Asia that would include Indonesia, Malaysia, Brunei, the southern Philippines, and northern Australia. JI's leader, Abu Bakar Bashir, has traveled to Australia numerous times to establish a terrorist network there. This was known as Mantiqi Four. Little is yet known of the inner working of the cell, although it is thought that the group sought to attack the 2000 Olympics held in Sydney. That effort was reportedly disrupted when Australian Federal Police raided what was thought to be a small arms training site near Canberra.[3]

External Security Environment

Australia's external security perceptions are shaped by its past, as well as by conceptions of its future. World War II came to occupy a central place in Australia's threat perception in a way that it did not for America, despite the Japanese attack on Pearl Harbor. The Japanese had bombed Darwin and other northern Australian cities. Japanese submarines had been in Sydney Harbor and fears arose that if Papua New Guinea were to fall, Australia would be next. That, when combined with traditional ethnic fears of "the Asian hordes," has often led Australia to often seek security *from* Asia. Juxtaposed with this vision of the external security environment is a more progressive overview that sees a future for Australia working *with* Asia. This took root as Australia found northeast Asia to be a consumer of its exports in the post–World War II period. It reached a high point under Prime Minister Paul Keating and Foreign Minister Gareth Evans.

A key aspect of this policy was the signing of a security pact by Prime Minister Keating and President Soeharto of Indonesia that demonstrated that Australia was seeking security in cooperation with its Asian neighbor, rather than from it. The pact has since lapsed as a result of Indonesian displeasure with Australia over its involvement in the independence of East Timor, a former province of Indonesia since 1975. East Timor had previously been a Portuguese colony. In 1999, the people of East Timor voted for independence from Indonesia and in 2002 it was internationally recognized as an independent nation.

Indonesia remains a key strategic focus for Australia. It is Australia's closest neighbor. With its 235 million people it also dwarfs the 20 million population of Australia. Given the geography of Southeast Asia and Australia, any military threat to Australia would likely have to come from, or go through, the Indonesian archipelago. That said, the War on Terrorism is changing the role of geography as distant globalized networks can be the source of new threats.

While Australia has from time to time looked to India and the Indian Ocean, it is the Asia-Pacific that occupies most of its strategic concern. Southeast Asia and the Southwest Pacific constitute Australia's region of greatest direct strategic interest. This has been demonstrated by the Australian involvement in United Nations operations in Cambodia, as well as in East Timor. Recently Australia has, together with New Zealand and other regional states, become more actively involved in the South Pacific. Examples of this are its activities in Bougainville in Papua New Guinea as well as most recently in the Solomon Islands. Australia has also taken a more active role in the Pacific Islands Forum by promoting such ideas as establishing a regional police force enabled to act more effectively across the region. Further, Australia has supported island nations through its patrol boat program that helps island states patrol their fisheries resources.

Terrorism Threat and Response

The strong bonds between Australia and the United States were reaffirmed when Prime Minister Howard evoked the ANZUS treaty and called on Australia to come to the assistance of the United States in the aftermath of the 9/11 attacks. Coincidentally, Prime Minister Howard was in Washington on 9/11. Australia's commitment to the war against terror was redoubled when 88 Australians were killed in the bombing of a popular Australian tourist destination in Bali, Indonesia, in October 2002. The small but significant Australian forces have demonstrated their value in Afghanistan and in Iraq while fighting alongside American forces. Australian Federal Police have worked closely with their Indonesian counterparts to uncover information related to the Bali bombing. The investigation has led to the arrest of 35 suspects in Indonesia in connection with the bombing, which killed a total of 202 people. Three of these have received death sentences. Despite this, JI is not an illegal organization in Indonesia.

Australia's commitment to regional cooperation in the war against terror was illustrated by its cohosting with Indonesia of a twenty-six-nation conference in February 2004 in Bali. The conference proposed the establishment of a Transnational Crime Center in Jakarta, which would improve antiterror cooperation and training. Foreign Minister Alexander Downer of Australia stated that the establishment of the center could lead to the posting of additional Australian Federal Police officers in Indonesia to provide intelligence and advice for regional states. It is thought that the center could also offer training in forensics, bomb disposal, antiterror techniques and act as a center for information sharing. While some two hundred JI operatives have been apprehended across the region, key operatives remain at large. "JI remains highly resilient and committed to its cause," Minister Downer stated. Australia hopes that its unprecedented cooperation with Indonesia over the Bali bombing will serve as a template for further regional cooperation. The U.S. attorney general, John Ashcroft, also attended the conference.[4] Despite these positive signs, the bilateral Australia-Indonesia relationship continues to have an element of distrust. In January 2004 Indonesia criticized Australia for announcing plans to join the United States in missile defense, stating that it perceived such a move as "offensive," and adding that the decision could push China in a direction that would undermine regional security. The ongoing nature of the threat was demonstrated in February 2004 by information indicating that a group of hard-liners, known as the Mujahideen Kompak, had broken away from JI to form a new militant Islamic militia in Sulawesi,[5] east of Borneo.

Military Structure and Defense Policy

Australia's defense force is robust for a small-to-midsize nation with a per capita gross national product (GNP) of approximately US$20,585. Australia's defense budget has increased from A$14.3 billion in 2001, to A$14.6 in 2002 and A$15.8 in 2003. The Australian Defence Force (ADF) has been deployed more in the recent past than at any time since the Vietnam War. Some 2,000 army, navy, and air force servicemen and -women were committed in support of Operation Falconer in Iraq in 2003. Australia also provided 1,700 military and police, out of a total force of 2,250, in Operation Helpem Fren as part of the Regional Assistance Mission to the Solomon Islands (RAMSI) in July 2003. Partially as a result of this increased coalition experience, Australia has moved to augment its capabilities for coalition warfare. Australia has 53,650 active forces and 20,300 reserves. Key weapons systems include: 71 Leopard tanks; 255 light armored vehicles; 364 armored personnel carriers; 105-mm and 155-mm artillery; mortars; surface-to-air missiles; 6 Collins class submarines; 11 frigates (including 5 ANZAC class); various patrol boats, mine sweepers, and amphibious ships; 35 F-111 aircraft; 71 F/A-18 aircraft, as well as various airlift and helicopters. Australia also has *Harpoon*, *Sidewinder* and *Sparrow* missiles.[6]

There are two pivotal themes in Australian defense policy. The first is expeditionary warfare—the strategy that views the defense of Australia as being best served by configuring Australia's military forces to fight in coalition with its key alliance partner. The second theme is continental defense, or the defense of Australia (DoA). This policy places priority on defending the territory of Australia from attack by denying the sea-air gap that separates Australia from Southeast Asia and the southwest Pacific. The Dibb review of 1986 was instrumental in establishing the centrality of the DoA concept.[7] A related theme is that of self-reliance within an alliance framework, which tacitly recognizes that the viable defense of Australia against an attack similar in scale to what the Japanese might have mounted in World War II would require the support of a great and powerful friend. Self-reliance is also dependent on strong logistical support from the United States.

Australia needs to devise a new policy to avoid being caught between these two approaches. To focus on the DoA to the exclusion of key alliance issues with the United States could lessen American enthusiasm for the alliance and jeopardize potential rewards. The benefits of enhanced Australia-U.S. bilateral defense cooperation have been described as securing "a credible U.S. extended deterrence commitment . . . indispensable and cost effective access to American technology, and the prospect of economic and diplomatic payoff that were previously beyond Australia's reach."[8] Conversely, too enthusiastic an approach to the United States could come with costs in terms of Australia's relationship with Southeast Asia. Australia's increasingly close trade relationship with China may present difficulties in the future over such issues as supporting the United States in a potential conflict over Taiwan.

It is important to understand these themes to fathom the mind-set that the strategic community in Australia has as it seeks to grapple with the new challenges of asymmetrical warfare in the age of terrorism. The old debate between continental defense and forward defense has been overtaken by events since 9/11. What is needed now, and recent policy documents indicate that this is beginning to be realized, is a fundamental reconceptualization of the nature of war and a comprehension that its changed nature requires Australia to be able to wage war across the full spectrum of conflict. It also requires Australia to reconceptualize its sense of geography.

The Australian Defence Force will have to adjust and reconfigure itself to deal with asymmetrical and transnational threats as they expand. This will also require an increasingly integrated approach to security from a wide array of governmental agencies. The Howard government's Defense White Paper *Defence 2000: Our Future Defence Force* was most recently updated by the document *Australia's National Security: A Defence Update, 2003.* The update describes Australia's strategic environment as being shaped by "the twin global threats of terrorism and weapons of mass destruction and continued instability in Australia's immediate region." Some analysts in Australia have taken the position that the construct of the global War on Terrorism has been overplayed and obscures for Australia its more enduring strategic interests, "Our security environment is shaped by the interaction of these global trends [terrorism, weapons of mass destruction, state failure, malaise with the United Nations] with some much older, more durable regional issues."[9] Australia seeks to promote its security interests in the region through a web of bilateral and multilateral ties. Australia has sought to emphasize "the close alignment of our strategic interests with those of our Southeast Asian neighbors, to enhance regional cooperation among the Southeast Asian states, and to help where we can in the development of appropriate regional military capabilities."[10]

Expanding the update's vision somewhat, we can see four interrelated key drivers behind Australia's defense posture in the years ahead.

1. The alliance relationship with the United States:
   - The war against terror has brought Australia and the United States closer together and will likely continue to do so.
   - Networks with the United States in the areas of intelligence, arms procurement, and so forth reinforce the relationship.
2. The War on Terrorism, weapons of mass destruction, and growing asymmetrical and transnational nature of conflict:
   - Combating regional and global terrorist groups that threaten Australian interests.
   - The need for counterterror cooperation is drawing Australia back into the Southeast Asian region.
3. Globalization:
   - Forces of globalization are drawing Australia closer to the United States, such as with the free trade agreement.
4. Regional instability:
   - There is an arc of crisis to the north of Australia: Aceh, East Timor, Papua New Guinea, Bougainville, Solomon Islands, and so forth.
   - The Taiwan-China conflict and South China Sea disputes may increase.
   - The disputes on the Korea Peninsula may grow worse.
   - A lack of momentum in ASEAN, the ARF, or APEC may lead to a breakdown of these groups.

Australia is moving to address these four challenges. The *Defence Update* makes several observations and recommendations, including the following. Terror and weapons of mass destruction present real threats to Australia, while conventional attack is more remote. Australia's immediate region is vulnerable to transnational threats, and ADF involvement in coalition operations is likely to continue. ADF coalition contributions will likely be best made through niche contributions, such as special forces, and there may be increased call on the ADF in the immediate region. These dynamics will require some reconfiguration of the force. It should be noted that while these recommendations point to the way ahead, there will undoubtedly be a degree of resistance from Australians who remain tied to older conceptions of Australia's security environment that focus to a larger extent on geography and the DoA.

Australia's ongoing desire to draw closer to the United States in a strategic sense was demonstrated by the decision announced in December 2003 to join United States' missile defense efforts. The announcement formalized what had been an informal process of cooperation and sharing in programs related to missile defense. Australia has long been a partner of the United States in missile warning through such systems as the Defense Support Program, which has been supported by joint facilities in Australia. The United States and Australia have cooperated in subsequent early warning experiments such as the DUNDEE (down under early-warning experiment) trials, which tested the Jindalee over-the-horizon radar's capability to detect missile launches. A sea-based missile defense system is the most likely option for Australia as the Royal Australian Navy is set to acquire three *Aegis*-class destroyers from the United States.[11]

Conclusions and Outlook

Australia is in the process of reconfiguring its force and doctrine to more effectively deal with the security environment it faces in the age of the war against terror. That said, it recognizes that more traditional and other ongoing security concerns and issues remain salient. Indeed, the revolution in military affairs had already triggered an examination of the force prior to 9/11 with an eye to ascertaining if its capabilities were the best suited for most likely missions. As with all armed forces, the strategic vision and desired force structure to fulfill likely missions will have to be balanced against available resources. In recent years Australia has demonstrated its desire to increase the available resources to meet the new challenges it faces. Australia's current strategic path will likely continue to lead to increased cooperation with the United States, as well as a continuing active role in its region of strategic concern.

Notes

The views expressed in this chapter are the author's own and do not necessarily reflect the views of the Congressional Research Service.

1. Rajan Menon, "The End of Alliances," *World Policy Journal,* Summer 2003.

2. Rod Lyon, "Australia's Security and the Threat of Islamic Extremism in Southeast Asia," *Cambridge Review of International Affairs,* October 2003.

3. For additional information, see Mark Manyin, Richard Cronin, Larry Niksch, and Bruce Vaughn, "Terrorism in Southeast Asia," Congressional Research Service Report, RL31672, updated periodically.

4. "More Regional Attacks are Inevitable, Antiterror Conference is Told," *Channelnewsasia,* February 4, 2004.

5. "Morning Intelligence Brief: Indonesia," *STRAFOR,* January 16, 2004; and Raymond Bonner, "Terror Expert Reports on New Militant Group in Indonesia," *New York Times,* February 4, 2004.

6. The above paragraph is drawn extensively from information in The International Institute of Strategic Studies, *The Military Balance 2003–4* (London: Oxford University Press, 2003).

7. Paul Dibb, *Review of Australia's Defence Capabilities* (Canberra: Report to the Minister for Defence, 1986).

8. William Tow and Rod Lyon, *The Future of the Australian-U.S. Security Relationship* (Carlisle: U.S. Army War College, 2003).

9. Hugh White, "Beyond the War on Terror: Australian Defence Policy in an Age of Uncertainty." Address to the National Press Club, Canberra, October 2003.

10. Defence 2000: *Our Future Defence Force,* (Commonwealth of Australia: Defence Publishing Service, DPS Oct010/2000), p. 39.

11. Gregor Furgeson, "Australia Will Join U.S. Missile Defense Program Efforts," *Defense News,* December 15, 2003.

Suggested Readings

Advancing the National Interest: Australia's Foreign and Trade Policy White Paper, at www.dfat.gov.au/ani/index.html.

Australian Journal of International Affairs, Australian Institute of International Affairs, Carfax Publishing, ISSN 1035–7718.

Dalrymple, Rawdon. *Continental Drift: Australia's Search for a Regional Identity*. Aldershot: Ashgate Publishers, 2003.

Edwards, Peter, and David Goldsworthy. *Facing North: A Century of Australian Engagement with Asia*, vols. I & II. Melbourne: Melbourne University Press, 2003.

Hill, The Honorable Robert. *Australia's National Security: A Defence Update*. Minister for Defence's Office, February 2003.

Tow, William, and Rod Lyon. *The Future of the Australian-U.S. Security Relationship*. Carlisle: U.S. Army War College, 2003.

Vaughn, Bruce, ed. *The Unraveling of Island Asia? Governmental, Communal, and Regional Instability.* Westport, CT: Praeger Publishers, 2002.

2

Bangladesh

Growing Islamic Identity and Continued Political Gridlock

M.A. Thomas

Introduction

The People's Republic of Bangladesh, the fourth largest Muslim nation, with a population of 139 million, is commonly known for being victimized by frequently recurring natural disasters such as cyclones and floods. Enveloped by India, Burma, and the Bay of Bengal, the South Asian nation suffers from weak democratic institutions, pervasive corruption, and rampant poverty. In recent years, moreover, Bangladesh's moderate image has been called into question. Islamist elements and anti-American views have worked their way to the forefront of the country's consciousness following the September 11, 2001, attacks and the subsequent U.S.-led global War on Terrorism. Interventions in Afghanistan and Iraq by the United States and public diplomacy in the Middle East have further provided Islamists in Bangladesh with fodder to espouse their anti-American sentiments. Rumors and reports indicate that al Qaeda and Taliban elements may have taken refuge in the country after their routing from Afghanistan by the United States.

Ethnicity and Language

Unlike most other South Asian nations, Bangladesh is ethnically homogeneous with 98 percent of the population comprised of Bengalis. Bengalis speak Bangla, the official language of the country. Bangla, which belongs to the Indo-European family of languages, has a rich cultural heritage in literature, music, and poetry. In addition to Bangla, English is considered an important language for business and international communication in Bangladesh.

Biharis, on the other hand, constitute less than 1 percent of the population. They are Urdu-speaking non-Bengalis who derived from the Indian state of

Bihar. Tribal groups, found mainly in the rural areas of the Chittagong Hill Tracts (CHT) and surrounding regions, together represent just over 1 percent of the population. Characterized by Mongoloid features, they are of Sino-Tibetan descent and speak Tibeto-Burman languages.

The four largest tribes are the Chakmas, Marmas, Tipperas, and Mros. The Chakmas, the largest of the tribes, and the Marmas both display formal tribal organization. Unlike the others, these two tribes inhabit the highland valleys. The tribes in general tend to intermingle, however, distinguishing one another by differences in their dialect, dress, and customs. The Marmas, who are of Burmese ancestry, consider Burma as the font of their cultural life. The Tipperas migrated southward from the northern Chittagong Hills. Northern Tipperas had been influenced by Bengali culture. The Mros, thought to be the original inhabitants of the CHT, have no written language of their own, but some have adopted the Bangla and Burmese scripts.

The Role of Islam in Society

About 83 percent of the country's population is Muslim, making Islam by far the dominant religion in Bangladesh's society. The vast majority of Bangladeshi Muslims practice the Sunni form of Islam. Small Shia communities can be found primarily in the urban areas of Dhaka (or Dacca) and Chittagong.

Sufism, widely regarded as a tolerant and compassionate form of Islam, also has an underlying influence on Muslims in Bangladesh. Sufi missionaries have been responsible for a considerable number of conversions among Hindus who find a natural appeal and some common ground with this form of Islam. The largest Sufi orders in the country include the Qadiri, Naqshbandhis, and Chishtis.

The influence of Hinduism, and to a lesser extent Buddhism, has caused Islam in Bangladesh to develop its own unique characteristics that differ from other Islamic trends found in South Asia. The practice of Islamic rituals and the observance of Islam's tenets vary according to social position, locale, and personal considerations. In some rural regions, for example, Muslims have incorporated their local beliefs and practices into Islamic ceremonies that differ from and often conflict with orthodox Islam.

The government-run Islamic Foundation sponsors training for imams (Islamic leaders), issue publications, sets holy days, and supports research on Islamic culture. The foundation also provides free medical care to the poor through its twenty-eight missions around the country. Unlike many other Islamic countries, the judiciary in Bangladesh has traditionally operated without any official sharia (Islamic law) courts. Muslim judges, however, are often requested to preside over Muslim marriages and to advise on such matters of personal law, as inheritance, divorce, and the administration of religious endowments.

The following examples further demonstrate how Bangladeshi society differs from more orthodox Muslim societies: Bangladeshi women are seldom completely veiled and often are seen in public without any head covering or male escort; women form a large percentage of the workforce, especially in the export-oriented garment industry; and alcohol, while illegal for Muslims, is consumed socially by the urban elite.

For the most part, Bangladeshi Muslims are accommodating toward followers of other religions, especially Hindus, who constitute 16 percent of the population. It is not uncommon for Hindus and Muslims in Bangladesh to share traditions and festivals. In some cases, villagers would fail to distinguish between Hindu and Muslims shrines.

Political Framework

Bangladesh is a constitutional republic with a parliamentary democratic form of government. Though the president is the head of state, the position is largely ceremonial, except at times when the parliament is dissolved and a caretaker government is installed pending national elections. The president is elected by the national parliament (Jatiya Sangsad) for a five-year term. The prime minister, who wields the executive power in Bangladesh, is the leader of the political party that wins the greatest number of seats in the unicameral parliament during a national election. National elections must be held every five years.

Bengali nationalism is an emotive rallying point for Bangladeshis. Before Bangladesh (formerly East Pakistan) wrested its independence from West Pakistan in 1971, it had endured amid an atmosphere of discontent and discrimination, dominated by West Pakistan. The following factors contributed to a sense of alienation among East Pakistanis: Bengali underrepresentation in the government, civil service, and the military; the second-class status accorded the Bangla language; economic inequities that favored West Pakistan despite East Pakistan's larger generation of revenue; and West Pakistani perceptions of Bengalis as being ethnically inferior. A strong nationalist pride in Bengali heritage and culture united East Pakistanis to revolt successfully against West Pakistan and, with the help of the Indian armed forces, to form the independent nation of Bangladesh.

Bangladesh, inheriting Pakistan's praetorian society, succumbed to military intervention within only a few years of its independence (see Military Structure and Defense Policy below for a list of military coups). Indeed, only in February 1991 was continuous civilian rule established in Bangladesh, when Begum Khaleda Zia, leader of the Bangladesh Nationalist Party (BNP), was sworn in as prime minister. The constitution was changed shortly thereafter, transforming the government from presidential rule to a Westminster-parliamentary form of government. In June 1996 Sheikh Hasina Wajed, leader of the Awami League, assumed power after winning national elections. In October 2001 Begum Khaleda Zia was once again installed as prime minister after successfully contesting elections in a four-party alliance.

The bitter and often violent rivalry between the governing BNP and the opposition Awami League has led to an atmosphere of sustained political gridlock in Bangladesh. The female leaders of both parties abhor each other and have a profound mistrust of the other's intentions. Prime Minister Khaleda Zia is the widow of the late General Ziaur Rahman (commonly referred to as General Zia), a benign and popular dictator who ruled Bangladesh from 1975–1981 until he was assassinated by a rival general. The leader of the opposition, Sheikh Hasina Wajed, is the daughter of Sheikh Mujibur Rahman (popularly known as Sheikh Mujib), considered by many as the founder of Bangladesh. Sheikh Mujib ruled Bangladesh for three years after independence until he and his family were assassinated during a military coup. Sheikh Hasina was the only family member who happened to be abroad at that time.

Of the two largest political parties, the BNP tends to incorporate more Islamic symbols and themes in its political rhetoric than does the Awami League. As a result, those who support increased Islamization in politics tend to support the BNP over the Awami League. The Awami League enjoys closer relations with neighboring India than does the BNP, which is distrustful of India's intentions in the region. Both parties have abandoned democratic avenues for political expression of their opposition by boycotting parliament, calling for general strikes, and inciting street agitation against the government.

With the deterioration of democratic institutions for political expression, student activism has become a focal instrument in the country's politics. In general, students among Bangladeshi public universities are highly politicized, owing allegiance and demonstrating loyalty to a particular political party. Politicians rely on students supporting their party to provide the muscle for general strikes, street agitations, and conflicts with opposing parties that often turn violent. It is not unusual for universities in Bangladesh to shut down for long periods of time and for students to take up to a decade to complete a three-year degree.

The Role of Islam in Politics

Bangladesh initially adopted a secular nationalist ideology. Its secular identity was subsequently replaced with an Islamic one, however, following a string of constitutional amendments and government proclamations. Though the constitution establishes Islam as the state religion, it nonetheless stipulates that individuals have the right to practice the religion of their choice.

Traditionally, moderate Muslims in Bangladesh have looked down upon the minority of Islamic extremists, viewing them as traitors during the Liberation War against Pakistan in 1971. This minority of ardent Islamists in Bangladesh collaborated with West Pakistan, believing that rebelling against Pakistan, the "land of the pure," was anti-Islamic.

Indications are that Islamic extremism has made some inroads into Bangladesh, especially in the post–9/11 era. Attacks against minority Hindus by Muslim radicals have been documented. What is more, the government has banned publications of the Ahmadiyya community, a moderate group of Muslims that has been declared as un-Islamic by religious hard-liners. Finally, the two Islamic political parties, the Jama'at-e Islami (Islamic Society or JI) and the Islami Oikya Jote (Islamic United Front, or IOJ) in Prime Minister Khaleda Zia's four-party alliance have a support base of Islamic radicals.

The JI, the most popular Islamic political party in Bangladesh, is known for its grassroots organization and its discipline. It is the more moderate of the two Islamic parties that belong to the governing BNP-led alliance. JI leaders state that their ultimate aim is to transform Bangladesh into a humanitarian Islamic state run according to sharia law. Party workers regularly engage in educational efforts and developmental relief projects. Its student wing, the Islami Chatra Shibir, is influential on several university campuses. The JI has traditionally received financial support from abroad, particularly from Saudi Arabia. The Islami Oikya Jote is the smaller and less moderate of the two Islamic parties that belong to the four-party alliance. In 2001 the IOJ coordinated anti-American rallies in Bangladesh to protest the bombing campaign in Afghanistan.

The Islami Constitution Movement (ICM) is a breakaway faction of the IOJ. ICM leader Mawlana Fazlul Karim parted ways with the IOJ in 1999 after its leadership decided to join the BNP-led four-party alliance. Karim subsequently formed a partnership with the Jatiya Party, a non-Islamic political party that is led by former president Hussain Mohammed Ershad. Both parties agreed to launch an alliance termed Islami Jatiya Oikya (IJO). The IJO declared that the ICM and the Jatiya Party would work together toward the dissemination of Islam, among other goals. Disagreements on the role of women in politics, however, prevented the relationship from flourishing. The ICM felt that women should be barred from politics altogether, whereas the Jatiya Party's second in command is the wife of Ershad.

Bangladesh is an important center for the Jama'at al-Tabligh (Preaching Group). Small groups of individuals organized by various chapters of the organization go house-to-house inviting people to join the Tabligh and to visit local mosques. Each January the Jama'at al-Tabligh organizes and conducts the Biswa Ijtema (World Congregation) in Bangladesh, considered the second-largest gathering of Muslims in the world after the hajj (pilgrimage to Mecca). The government and private organizations assist the Tabligh by providing medical care, transportation, water, and sanitation facilities at the congregation. After the annual event, many devotees embark on a *chilla*, a forty-day preaching mission inside and outside of Bangladesh.

Internal Security Environment

The potential flare-up of insurgent activity in the CHT, a stretch of territory along Bangladesh's southeast border with Burma, remains a key security concern for the government. The insurgency began when Sheikh Mujib began to relocate Bengali settlers into the tribal-dominated CHT during the mid-1970s. The conflict intensified during the mid-1980s when thousands of tribal refugees poured into neighboring India as result of violence between the Bengali settlers and the Chakmas, the dominant tribal group in the region. The government and the Shanti Bahini (Peace Force), tribal insurgents vying for independence, were engaged in a protracted conflict until a ceasefire was declared in 1992.

Sporadic violence continued even after the Awami League government signed a controversial peace accord in 1997 with the Parbatya Chattagram Jana Sanghati Samiti (PCJSS), the political wing of the Shanti Bahini. The peace accord promised that most Bengali settlers, constituting almost half of the CHT population, would return to the plains, and the military would return to the barracks. In return, the PCJSS downgraded their demand for independence to one of increased autonomy. Little has been accomplished, though, to fulfill the terms of the peace accord since the current BNP-led administration, which campaigned to revise the accord, assumed power in October 2001. The PCJSS has cautioned the government of a return to hostilities if the conditions of the peace accord are not honored. Tensions continue to smolder between the tribal groups and the Bengali settlers.

External Security Environment

Bangladesh's relationship with India is a politically charged issue in Bangladeshi politics. Relations with India constitute Bangladesh's principal foreign policy concern. Initially, expectations of positive bilateral relations between the two countries were high, especially after the Indian government aided Sheikh Mujib and the Awami League in securing Bangladesh's independence from Pakistan in 1971. However, the lingering presence of Indian troops in Dhaka heightened suspicions about India's intentions in the region among a growing opposition to Sheikh Mujib. Opponents of the Awami League's close relationship with India feared that Bangladeshi leaders would simply serve as puppets of the Indian government—a sentiment that continues to be expressed by Awami League detractors. After Sheikh Mujib's assassination, relations between the two neighbors soured immediately as Bangladesh entered a period largely dominated by military rule. The governing BNP routinely exploits the Awami League's India-friendly posture as a partisan political issue. India has accused Bangladesh of harboring a number of insurgent groups operating in India's northeast.

Despite Bangladesh's violent struggle for independence from Pakistan, poor relations between the two Islamic nations were short-lived. The Islamic factor and interpersonal relationships between both militaries contributed to the establishment of favorable relations. China, originally opposed to the formation of Bangladesh, came around and forged positive ties with Bangladesh to offset strained Sino-Indian relations. Bangladesh has procured the bulk of its military hardware from China. It views its relations with China as a deterrent against Indian aggression. China, along with the United Kingdom and the United States, regulaıly provides military training to the Bangladeshi armed forces. The status of Rohingya refugees has been a contentious issue between Bangladesh and Burma. Bangladesh incurred an economic burden when a quarter of a million Rohingya Muslims fled across the border from Burma in 1991 to escape a crackdown from Burmese military authorities. Most Rohingyas from that group have since been repatriated; however, the remaining 22,000 refugees are of concern to Bangladesh's government.

Terrorism Threat and Response

The Harakat ul-Jihad-I-Islami/Bangladesh (HUJI-B) (Movement of Islamic Holy War) is a terrorist group that operates in Bangladesh. The goal of the HUJI-B, led by Shauqat Osman, is to establish Islamic rule in Bangladesh. The group has connections to the Pakistani militant groups Harakat ul-Jihad-i-Islami (HUJI) and Harakat ul-Mujahidin (HUM) (Movement of Holy Warriors), who advocate similar objectives in Pakistan and Kashmir. The HUJI-B was accused of stabbing a senior Bangladeshi journalist in November 2000 for making a documentary on the plight of Hindus in Bangladesh. In addition, the group was suspected in the July 2000 assassination attempt of Prime Minister Sheikh Hasina of Bangladesh. Its strength is estimated to number more than several thousand members. Funding of the HUJI-B comes primarily from the increasing number of madrasas (Islamic schools) in Bangladesh and from militants in Pakistan.[1]

The HUJI-B is thought to be close to al Qaeda and other affiliated organizations in Pakistan. As previously mentioned, uncorroborated reports have suggested that al Qaeda and Taliban elements may have taken refuge in the country after their forced expulsion from Afghanistan by the United States. A *Time* magazine source alleged that two hundred members of al Qaeda and the Taliban had been transported to Bangladesh from Afghanistan and Pakistan by a ship named MV *Mecca* during two separate voyages.[2]

Prime Minister Khaleda Zia has rhetorically pledged her administration's support against terrorism. Nevertheless, the BNP administration has repeatedly downplayed the presence of al Qaeda and Taliban fighters on Bangladeshi soil. In addition, it has turned a blind eye to activities of Islamic radicals in the country. First, the BNP is reluctant to provoke the extremist support base of the two Islamic political parties in the ruling alliance. Second, it views the extremist elements as providing a counterbalance to the opposition Awami League internally and to India externally.

Military Structure and Defense Policy

Bangladesh's military consists of the army, navy, air force, and coast guard. Paramilitary units include the Bangladesh Rifles, Bangladesh Ansars, Village

Defense Parties, Armed Police Battalions, and the National Cadet Corps. The 110,000-strong army is the most prominent of the armed forces, and constitutes a critical institution in the country. Traditionally, the army has been divided between "freedom fighters" and "repatriates." Freedom fighters fought in the war for independence against West Pakistan. They tend to have political links to the Awami League and exhibit loyalty to Sheikh Hasina Wajed. Repatriates were confined in West Pakistan during the war for independence. They identify closely with the BNP and Prime Minister Khaleda Zia. Both the BNP and the Awami League, when in power, have frequently purged military officials linked to the opposition. Generally speaking, the army supports the BNP over the Awami League. This is mainly due to the charismatic influence of the late General Zia as well as its skepticism toward India.

Since independence, the army has frequently usurped the civil administration of the country through military coups. Also, it has significantly influenced civilian governments and has often exercised a de facto veto power over major policy decisions. Following is a list of military coups staged in Bangladesh.

August 15, 1975: In the so-called majors' plot, thirty middle-ranking officers assassinated Sheikh Mujib and members of his family. These officers, many of whom were repatriates, asked General Zia to become the army chief of staff. Khondakar Mushtaque Ahmed became the figurehead president.

November 3, 1975: Freedom fighter elements countered the original coup and seized the government under the leadership of Brigadier Khaled Musharraf. General Zia was placed under arrest, and the ringleaders of the majors' plot were exiled to Libya.

November 7, 1975: Loyalists to General Zia secured his release and staged a third coup in which Brigadier Musharraf was killed. General Zia established firm control over the army and was made chief martial law administrator. General Zia ruled Bangladesh until May 30, 1981.

May 30, 1981: General Muhammad Manzur Ahmed, scheduled to be transferred to an undesirable noncommand position, assassinated General Zia. Army chief of staff General Hussain Muhammad Ershad put down the rebellion, killing General Manzur. A civilian government then assumed power.

March 24, 1982: After almost a year of weak, ineffectual civilian rule, General Ershad dismissed the government and assumed full powers under martial law. General Ershad ruled until December 1990, when he was deposed following antigovernment protests. He was subsequently tried, convicted of a number of offenses, and jailed.

It is noteworthy, however, that the army has refrained from seizing control of the government since the fall of Ershad. Nevertheless, it remains a powerful and influential institution in Bangladesh.

Conclusions and Outlook

Political gridlock will prevail in Bangladesh's predominantly two-party system as long as the BNP and the Awami League continue to engage one another in belligerent partisan politics. There have been glimmerings of a "third force" emerging on the country's political scene, but it has yet to find a foothold. The inclusion of two Islamic parties in the government is unprecedented in Bangladesh's history. Islamic groups and individuals have always exercised considerable influence in shaping public opinion, but traditionally have had limited electoral appeal to Bangladeshi voters. With respect to the CHT, the government will have to temper its policies with the tribal groups to prevent a resurgence of hostilities in the region.

Corruption in the country is on the rise and is endemic among all sectors of government and society. Bangladesh has been stigmatized as remaining at the top of Transparency International's corruption perception index for the third straight year. Though it was referred to as a basket case by the Clinton administration, Bangladesh's economy seems to have improved with a favorable growth rate of above 5 percent, strong overseas remittances, a rising foreign reserve level, and a manageable fiscal deficit.

The United States and Bangladesh have traditionally enjoyed cordial relations. Though its government has voted with the United States on all terrorism-related United Nations Security Council resolutions, Bangladesh is being challenged with a rise in Islamic extremism and a possible infiltration of foreign terrorists. Extremist tendencies tend to surface in the country whenever perceptions arise that Islam is under attack by the United States and the West. A small number of individuals among members of parliament belonging to the two Islamic parties in the government openly supported Saddam Hussein and the Taliban. Nonetheless, the United States considers Bangladesh a friendly and moderate Islamic nation. The U.S.-government promotes human rights in Bangladesh through a variety of programs to improve the professionalism of the military and police. The United States, along with Japan and a number of Middle Eastern and European countries, remains a major aid donor to Bangladesh.

Notes

The views presented in this chapter are those of the author and do not necessarily represent the views of the Department of Defense or any of its components.

Portions of this chapter have been drawn from unclassified writings by the author in studies written for the U.S. Army Special Operations 4th Psychological Operations Group (Airborne).

1. U.S. Department of State, *Patterns of Global Terrorism* (Washington, DC: U.S. Government Printing Office, 2003), pp. 133–34.

2. *Time* magazine, *Deadly Cargo,* October 15, 2002.

Suggested Readings

Ahmed, A.F. Salahuddin. *Bengali Nationalism and the Emergence of Bangladesh: An Introductory Outline.* Dhaka: International Centre for Bengal Studies University Press, 1994.

Baxter, Craig. *Bangladesh: From a Nation to a State.* Boulder, CO: Westview Press, 1998.

Sisson, Richard, and Leo E. Rose. *War and Secession: Pakistan, India, and the Creation of Bangladesh.* Berkeley and Los Angeles: University of California Press, 1991.

Stern, Robert W. *Democracy and Dictatorship in South Asia: Dominant Classes and Political Outcomes in India, Pakistan, and Bangladesh.* Westport, CT: Praeger Publishers, 2001.

Zafarullah, Habib. *The Zia Episode in Bangladesh Politics.* Dhaka: University Press, 1996.

3

Brunei

Multifaceted Survival Strategies of a Small State

Cheng-Chwee Kuik and Bridget Welsh

Introduction

With a population of 360,000 people and a territory about the size of the U.S. state of Delaware, Negara Brunei Darussalam is an emblematic example of a vulnerable "small state" in the international system that protects itself by curbing domestic security threats to the regime, by developing good relationships with its neighbors, and by forging ties with international organizations, especially the Association of Southeast Asian Nations (ASEAN). Unlike other small states, Brunei fortunately has a rich resource base derived from oil and gas, which gives it funds to foster domestic legitimacy and forge strategic regional ties. This minuscule state's vulnerability stems from its geography. Located on the northern coast of Borneo, Brunei's territory is divided into two disconnected sections by the Malaysian district of Limbang and lies adjacent to Indonesia and the Philippines. In the post–Cold War era, especially after the September 11 attacks, security concerns have expanded, moving from traditional security apprehension regarding territory to nontraditional issues of terrorism and other transnational threats. Brunei is one of three majority Muslim countries in Southeast Asia that has used religion to consolidate domestic support; however, since it borders states that have radical groups, Brunei has become linked with radical Islamic extremism in the region, thus increasing attention to the sultanate.

While the new security concerns are legitimate, Brunei has enjoyed a high level of internal security and external stability since it gained its independence from Britain in 1984. This trend is likely to continue, as Brunei carefully mobilizes resources to address security issues. Most small states have sought to offset their inherent weaknesses by developing governing capacity through forging interstate cooperation and strengthening legitimacy at home.

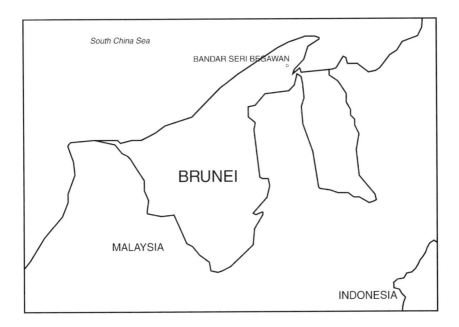

Brunei is no exception. The sultanate has successfully adopted a dynamic security strategy, which has skillfully capitalized its institutional linkages with various regional and international arrangements, and has mobilized its economic and defense resources in addressing security challenges. The regime has relied primarily on economic legitimacy at home, on limiting political openness, and on strategic relations with neighbors, especially Singapore and Indonesia.

Political Framework

Brunei is Southeast Asia's only absolute ruling monarchy. The present ruler, Sultan Hassanal Bolkiah, is both the chief of state and the head of government, who appoints and presides over an eleven-member cabinet. In addition to his being prime minister, the sultan also holds the positions of minister of defense and minister of finance. Prince Mohamad Bolkiah, the eldest of the sultan's three younger brothers, serves as the minister of foreign affairs. The sultan is advised by his cabinet and assisted by the Privy Council, the Council of Succession, and the Religious Council.

There is no representative form of government in Brunei. The country's last election was held in September 1962 during the reign of Sultan Hassanal's father, Sultan Omar Ali Saifuddin, when the country was still a British colony.

The elections gave the majority of elected seats to the Parti Ra'yat Brunei (the People's Party of Brunei, or PRB), led by A.M. Azahari. When Sultan Omar refused to convene the Legislative Council, the military wing of the PRB launched a revolt in December 1962. The rebellion was subsequently put down within days by British military intervention, but a state of emergency remains to this day. The PRB leadership fled to Malaysia and remains in exile. Popular support for the PRB has waned considerably during Sultan Hassanal's rule.

At present, Brunei has registered only two political parties, the Parti Perpaduan Kebangsaan Brunei (PPKB or Brunei National Solidarity Party) and the Parti Kesedaran Rakyat Brunei (PAKAR or Brunei Peoples' Awareness Party). Neither party engages actively in politics. Rather, they serve primarily as personal vehicles for party leaders who occasionally comment on political events. Nor has either managed to attract many followers. The PPKB, for example, has fewer than two hundred registered party members. Without elections, Brunei's political parties have been marginalized and are seen as ineffective.[1]

Brunei's ineffective political parties are a by-product of the depoliticization of society; civil servants and security personnel, who comprise the over 60 percent of the workforce, are banned from engaging in political activity. Nongovernmental organization activism is restricted to such specific areas as consumer concerns, and is actively regulated. Citizenship is automatically granted to Malays or indigenous groups. The Chinese, who comprise 12 percent of the population, have to pass a difficult test to obtain citizenship, and immigrants, who comprise over 60,000 of the country's residents, cannot obtain citizenship. Essentially, over a quarter of Brunei's population lacks equal political and economic rights.

The media remains on the periphery. There are only two newspapers—the English-language *Borneo Bulletin* and the Malay-language daily *Media Permata* (launched in 1998). Both have close links to the royal family and are strictly monitored. A second English newspaper, the *News Express,* was launched in July 1999 but stopped printing in 2002 when its owner was declared bankrupt and its journalists were sanctioned for publishing a column on grievances. In October 2001 the government enacted a far-reaching law—the Local Newspapers (Amendment) Order 2001, giving the home affairs minister power to suspend local newspapers and withdraw permits for imported publications. The revised law imposes stiff fines and jail sentences on journalists who publish false news, requires local presses to obtain a yearly permit to operate, and restricts all directors of newspapers to be Brunei citizens or Brunei permanent residents. The government controls the electronic media through Radio Television Brunei. These measures have limited political discourse. Most Brunei residents rely on the Internet or satellite television for news, with minimal open discussion of domestic issues.

With an authoritarian political system, the sultanate has had to turn to other forms of legitimacy to maintain power. One indispensable feature of Brunei's political system is the national ideology of *Melayu Islam Beraja* (MIB or Malay Islamic Monarchy), which has been used to consolidate power since 1991. The sultan has strategically linked conservative Islamic values with traditional Malay culture to unify support for the monarchy and fend off appeals of Muslim fundamentalism.[2] The MIB concept is used in school curricula as well as ministerial statements. Brunei's leaders, like those in Indonesia and Malaysia, have co-opted Islam for political purposes, using religion for legitimacy. This has increased the Islamization of the country, and cloaked the sultan with moral authority.

Although the MIB ideological base underlies the regime, the main source of legitimacy has been economic development and an effective distribution of resources. Sultan Hassanal inherited his kingdom with the promise of improving economic conditions. His tenure has seen a rapid and impressive growth of the economy, investment in infrastructure and improvements in living standards. Citizens are given free social services, including health care and education. Telecommunications, housing, and electricity are subsidized. Salaries are high, with a comparatively low cost of living. Unlike other countries in Southeast Asia, Brunei did not suffer during the 1997 Asian financial crisis. At well over US$14,000 annually, Brunei citizens have the second highest per capita income in the region. Brunei's middle class (which comprises the majority of the population), like that in Malaysia and Singapore, is largely dependent on the state for its livelihood and high living standard, and rarely challenges the regime.

Internal Security Environment

The closed nature of Brunei's political system assures that the country's main internal security problem is defined by the protection of the established political order. Any acts that are perceived to undermine this order are considered "matters of national security."

Foremost, the regime is concerned with any challenges to the royal family's power. In 1985 the now-defunct Partai Kebangsaan Demokratik Brunei (PKDB or Brunei National Democratic Party) was formed with the objective of creating a system of parliamentary democracy under a constitutional monarchy. In the following year PKDB leaders crossed the red line by calling for elections and for the sultan to give up his position as prime minister so that his royal position would not be sullied by involvement in politics.[3] The monarch responded by arresting these leaders and deregistering PKDB in 1988. Although the political atmosphere in Brunei is more open today than it was in the 1980s, there is no indication that the monarchy's sensitivity over the issue of regime authority has been relaxed. In fact, actions taken by the Internal Security Department (ISD) in July 1998 against a few individuals for possession of poison-pen letters against corruption by public officials and members of the royal family show that unchallenged royal authority remains a central concern. The Prime Minister's Office accused these letter writers of jeopardizing "the security of the nation."[4] While criticism of the 1998 Amedeo scandal involving the misappropriation of US$14.8 billion by the sultan's brother Prince Jeffri Bolkiah was allowed, open dissent of the sultan is not tolerated.

Protest has increasingly taken the form of religious activism, since religion has remained one of the few areas of political interaction that was relatively unregulated. The blurred line between politics and daily life within Islam has allowed for open discussion of domestic politics, increasing attention to such issues as corruption and good governance. At the same time, it has deepened the links between Bruneins and others in the *umma,* the Muslim community, including Muslims in the Middle East. This has broadened international ties with Muslim charities and has exposed Bruneins to a range of discourse in Islam. Islamization has also inadvertently increased the threat of religious extremism.

This security concern was an issue in Brunei before 9/11. "Deviationist" religious elements have quietly taken root in this tiny sultanate. In July 2000 the ISD questioned and detained a number of local and immigrant workers under the Internal Security Act (ISA), for their suspected involvement with the Malaysian deviationist movement Al-Ma'unah. Investigations by ISD revealed that Al-Ma'unah had set up a branch in Brunei in December 1999 without registering itself with Brunei's Registrar of Societies. The branch was comprised of twenty-seven members, twenty of whom were Bruneins and one who was a military officer.[5] It was also discovered that the Malaysian founder of the group, Mohamad Amin Razali, had made four trips to Brunei since November 1999. The Ministry of Religious Affairs disclosed that books published by Al-Ma'unah were found to contain teachings deviating from Islamic tenets.[6] Government imams (preachers) in mosques stood up to support the draconian response and cautioned Muslim followers against "attempts by certain undesirable elements."[7]

The Al-Ma'unah is not the only "deviant" Muslim group that worries the Brunei government. The Al-Arqam, a Malaysian religious cult that has been banned by Brunei since 1991, is also on the government's watch list. In September 2003 the ISD detained six local followers of Al-Arqam under the

ISA, for their involvement in reviving the movement. Although later investigation by the ISD indicated that the Al-Arqam group in Brunei has no connection with any regional terrorist group, the fact that two deviationist movements have gained a foothold in the sultanate, presents a grave concern to the government. This is especially so following growing global attention to terrorism in Southeast Asia.

The control of religion has extended to Christian groups. The government forbids the proselytizing of Christianity among Muslims in the sultanate. Brunei law prohibits the conversion of Muslims to any other religion. In March 2001 the Ministry of Religious Affairs revealed that over two dozen people were questioned for their alleged involvement in spreading Christianity among Muslim followers. Three persons were later detained under the ISA. The ISD claimed that the activities of these individuals could "jeopardize religious harmony and stability in Brunei because they were directed towards certain Muslim establishments."[8] The dependence on the regime for Islamic legitimacy limits the scope of religious freedom in the state and implicitly characterizes religion as an internal security issue.

External Security Environment

Brunei has enjoyed a benign and relatively peaceful external security environment since it got its independence in 1984. The security of this small kingdom has not been threatened by any external power. This is remarkable progress if one contrasts the present climate with the sultanate's acute sense of insecurity and vulnerability in the 1960s and 1970s. Brunei's unpleasant earlier interaction with its immediate neighbors—for instance, Indonesia's involvement in the 1962 revolt and Malaysia's sanctuary for PRB leaders— made the tiny state fearful that its larger neighbors might continue to undermine its security. Mainly due to such fear, the sultan was reluctant to assume full independence from Britain. Developments in the late 1970s, however, served to encourage Brunei to accept full independence. The signing of the treaty of friendship with Britain in 1979 and the evident cohesion of ASEAN, to which Indonesia and Malaysia were strongly committed, both served to reassure Brunei that the threats of neighbors had waned.[9] Singapore's experience in the regional organization, in particular, was persuasive, as Brunei began to think that ASEAN—with its pledges to uphold the sanctity of national sovereignty and nonintervention among its members—could be a source and a form of future security.

It was not a coincidence, therefore, that Brunei joined ASEAN on January 7, 1984, just one week after it assumed its full independence. Brunei's membership in ASEAN not only allowed it to strengthen its relations with former foes, but also boosted this small sultanate's international legitimacy, thus significantly improving its immediate security environment. Considering ASEAN's enormous value to the country, it is thus not surprising that Brunei views ASEAN as the cornerstone of its foreign policy. This is clearly reflected by the country's active participation in ASEAN activities throughout the past two decades. The kingdom assumed the chairmanship of ASEAN in 1995–1996 and again in 2001–2002, hosting the important events of the ASEAN Summit, the ASEAN Ministerial Meeting (AMM), the ASEAN Regional Forum (ARF), the Post-Ministerial Conference (PMC), and the ASEAN Plus Three (APT) Meeting.

While it is necessary to emphasize the significance of ASEAN to Brunei, it would be misleading to attribute Brunei's enduring security to this single factor alone. Since its independence, Brunei has relied on a three-pronged strategy in ameliorating its external security vulnerability and strengthening its international position.

The first element refers to Brunei's involvement in multilateral institutions, both regional and international. These include ASEAN, the United Nations (UN), the British Commonwealth, and the Organization of Islamic Conference (OIC) that Brunei joined in 1984 upon attainment of its full independence, as well as the Asia-Pacific Economic Cooperation (APEC) organization, the Non-Aligned Movement (NAM) and the Asia-Europe Meeting (ASEM) that Brunei joined in 1989, 1992, and 1996 respectively. Brunei hosted the APEC Leaders' Summit in December 2000 and was appointed by the OIC in August 2001 as a member of the Committee of Eight to monitor the implementation of peace and development in Mindanao in the southern Philippines. Such international links have given Brunei a remarkable status and disproportionate influence in world affairs.

Brunei also uses economic cooperation to pave the way for closer political relations. Making use of the country's financial strength, this strategy takes a few forms: (1) promoting regional economic cooperation (especially but not exclusively, the Brunei-Indonesia-Malaysia-Philippines East ASEAN Growth Area, BIMP-EAGA); (2) investing in ASEAN countries' infrastructure projects; (3) pledging funds to support neighboring countries' currencies during financial crisis (US$500 million to the International Monetary Fund package to Thailand, a B$1 billion cash investment to help Malaysia's ailing financial sector, and B$1.88 billion as a standby credit to assist Indonesia); as well as (4) promoting bilateral trade and investment cooperation through joint commissions for bilateral cooperation with individual countries (for instance, the Brunei-Malaysia Joint Commission was set up in 1994, whereas the first sessions of the Brunei-Thai and Brunei-Indonesia Joint Commissions were held in April 2003 and July 2003 respectively).

Brunei's efforts also extend to forging military relations with major powers and neighboring countries. Brunei conducts a wide range of bilateral military exercises with countries in Southeast Asia, especially Singapore and Malaysia, and with the United States. These military exercises strengthen Brunei's bilateral ties by fostering good working relationships between the Royal Brunei Armed Forces (RBAF) and external forces. In the process they also enhance the RBAF's inter-operability and improve the skills of military personnel.

This multifaceted strategy has significantly improved Brunei's overall security position in general, and its capacity to address the problems of territorial disputes in particular, notably the overlapping territorial and maritime claims between Brunei and Malaysia, and the Spratly Islands dispute that is contested by Brunei, China, Taiwan, Vietnam, Malaysia, and the Philippines. Although a full settlement is unlikely in either case, progress has been made in reducing the potential of conflict among the claimant countries.

In the former, Brunei and Malaysia have overlapping land claims over the Limbang area as well as the maritime claims concerning offshore waters and associated hydrocarbon rights. After a naval standoff between the two countries in early 2003 at the Kikeh area, the leaders of both countries have held rounds of discussions and have made arrangement for further talks.[10]

In the case of the Spratly dispute, Brunei and other ASEAN countries have managed to make progress on their talks with China since 1995, principally through the ASEAN-China Senior Official Consultations. In 2000 the two sides agreed to create a working group to discuss the establishment of a code of conduct in the South China Sea. After three years of discussion, China and ASEAN eventually signed a "Declaration on the Conduct of Parties in the South China Sea" in November 2002. Although the declaration is merely a political document and not the binding code of conduct that some parties had originally hoped for, it has nonetheless reduced the risks of armed conflict in the disputed area, thus preserving a peaceful security environment for all countries, including Brunei.

Military Structure and Defense Policy

Brunei's defense force, the RBAF, plays a critical role in maintaining this security. Founded on May 31, 1961, the RBAF was originally known as *Askar Melayu Brunei* or the Brunei Malay Regiment. Upon the attainment of independence on January 1, 1984, it was renamed *Angkatan Bersenjata Diraja Brunei* or Royal Brunei Armed Forces. As a result of a restructuring in 1991, the RBAF now consists of five major units, namely, the Royal Brunei Land Forces, the Royal Brunei Air Force, the Royal Brunei Navy, the Royal Brunei Services Forces and the Royal Brunei Armed Forces Training Centre.

There are two main divisions under Brunei's Ministry of Defense (MOD).[11] The Military Staff Division is headed by the commander of the Royal Brunei Armed Forces, whereas the Civilian Staff Division is headed by the Permanent Secretary, MOD. Under these divisions there are six military directorates (Operations and Plans, Intelligence and Security, Training and Staff Duties/Doctrine, Personnel and Administration, Logistics, and Strategic Planning) and four civilian directorates (Administration and Manpower, Politics and Organization, Development and Work Services, Finance and Procurement).

Brunei's defense posture has three main characteristics, first, a small active manpower, second, close military relations with Western powers, specifically the United Kingdom and the United States, and third, the above-mentioned web of bilateral military exercise with countries in the Asia Pacific region.

Brunei's military has only 5,000 personnel—the smallest armed forces in the region. Unlike the Singapore Armed Forces that is supported by a large citizen reserve, Brunei does not maintain reserve forces. In fact, Brunei's military personnel are all-volunteer forces. The strength of RBAF is augmented by a battalion of British Gurkha Rifles, which had been stationed in the oil town of Seria. This battalion has since been garrisoned on rotation from its brigade headquarters after the unsuccessful revolt in 1962. Brunei's military structure reflects that the main security concern is not external, but internally focused on preventing revolt from within and safeguarding its hydrocarbon assets in the offshore areas. In 2000 the Second Battalion of the Royal Gurkha Rifles was replaced by the 1,000-strong First Battalion Royal Gurkha Rifles from the UK.[12] In early January 2003 the sultan signed a renewal agreement with Britain under which the Gurkhas would continue to be stationed in Brunei for another five years, through 2008.

The stationing of the Gurkha infantry battalion is part of the deep defense links between Brunei and Britain. The British army has a Bell 212 Helicopter Flight of the Army Air Corps permanently stationed in the sultanate. The UK is also the main source for Brunei armed forces' arms acquisitions. BAE Systems Marine has built three Offshore Patrol Vessels (OPVs) for the Royal Brunei Navy. The first two ships, named KDB (Kapal Diraja Brunei) *Nakhoda Ragam* and KDB *Bendahara Sakam* respectively, had already been launched and delivered to the sultanate. The third ship, the US$95-million KDB *Jerambak,* was delivered in 2003. Based at the sultanate's main naval base in Muara, these corvettes are designed for offshore patrols and surveillance in Brunei's territorial waters and its Exclusive Economic Zone.[13]

The Brunei-British defense tie was further enhanced by the creation of the Joint Commission on Defense Cooperation (JDC) on December 31, 2002.

The first and second JDC meetings were held in January 2003 and June 2003 respectively. The meetings, which were attended by senior military officers from both countries, were aimed at discussing military cooperation and general political and security issues, as well as promoting better ties and understanding between the two countries.

The sultanate has also maintained a strong military relationship with the United States. The two governments signed an agreement on cooperation pertaining to defense affairs and equipment on November 29, 1994. A joint defense working committee was established subsequently to strengthen military cooperation between the two countries. The fifth joint defense working committee meeting was held in October 2003, attended by senior officials from Brunei's Ministry of Defense and from the U.S. Pacific Command. Since the late 1980s the Royal Brunei Navy has engaged with the U.S. Navy in an annual bilateral exercise code-named Kingfisher/Carat. Besides this, the Royal Brunei Land Force and the U.S. Marine Corps also hold a battalion exercise called Green Canopy.

Brunei also holds a bilateral series of military exercises with other countries in the region, especially Singapore and Malaysia. Since 1978 Brunei and Singapore have had joint naval exercises, code-named Pelican, and military exercises code-named Latihan Rintis Bersama and Maju Bersama. Brunei and Malaysia have had joint military and naval exercises since 1985, known as Brumal Setia and Hornbill respectively. Brunei has joint naval exercises, code-named Seagull and Helang Laut, with the Philippines and Indonesia, respectively, and joint land forces exercises known as Mallee Bull with Australia.

Terrorism Threat and Response

Despite the robust military activity, Brunei presently is not faced with any immediate traditional external security threat. The sultanate's more pressing concerns are associated with nontraditional security issues, particularly potential threats posed by international terrorism. In the aftermath of the terrorist attacks on the United States on September 11, 2001, Brunei joined other countries all over the world in expressing sympathy to the United States and condemning terrorism. In a statement addressed before the UN General Assembly on October 4, 2001, Brunei's permanent representative to the UN remarked:

> The September 11th incident showed that no country, big or small, is safe from terrorist attacks. It has significant effects on the stability of nations and adverse consequences on social and economic developments. Such indiscriminate acts disrespect human life and dignity and deny peace and harmony as professed by all religions.[14]

Although Brunei has been free from any terrorist attacks to date, the country obviously does not see itself as immune from the transnational threat. Brunei has been consistently vigilant about religious extremism. The government regards any such organization as an internal security problem that, if left uncontrolled, would threaten the sultan's rule. The existence of Al-Ma'unah and Al-Arqam within Brunei, despite their insignificant number of followers, has alerted the authorities that religious deviationist groups that originated in a neighboring country could take root and gradually gain strength on its own territory.

It is in this regard that the arrest of several members of the Jemaah Islamiyah (JI) (Islamic group or Islamic community) in Singapore and Malaysia—and the subsequent exposure of the JI network in the region—appears to be particularly alarming to the sultanate. The JI movement seeks to establish a pan-Islamic state in the region that encompasses Indonesia, Singapore, Malaysia, Brunei, and the southern Philippines. Furthermore, unlike Al-Ma'unah, which attracts only a small number of followers in Malaysia and Brunei, JI has developed a much more extensive and sophisticated network in the region, as demonstrated in its ability in plotting the 2002 Bali bombing, the bombings of the J.W. Marriott Hotel and Australian Embassy in 2003 and 2004 respectively in Jakarta, as well as other unsuccessful schemes against U.S. and Western targets in the region.

Moreover, the fact that some JI members are found to be native Singaporeans reflects that it is a mistake to assume that "only Southeast Asia's poorer and more weakly governed societies posed an extremist threat."[15] One lesson to be learned is that citizens in all sorts of societies—rich or poor, strong or weak—are all prospective recruiting targets for religious extremist groups. Brunei knows it is no exception. The close proximity to the conflict in the southern Philippines and a steady flow of immigrant labor compounds these concerns. Not surprisingly, therefore, Brunei has been quietly but firmly supportive of the War on Terrorism. It aims to prevent al Qaeda and its associated groups from using the sultanate as a gateway or a launching pad and limits religious extremist groups from gaining a foothold in its own society.

Thus far, Brunei has responded to the terrorism threat by collaborating with the United States and other countries in the region. In November 2001 Sultan Hassanal, together with his ASEAN counterparts, signed a Declaration on Joint Action to Counter Terrorism at the seventh ASEAN Summit. Later, in August 2002, the leaders of ASEAN and the United States gathered in Brunei to sign the U.S.-ASEAN Joint Declaration on Combating Terrorism, which called for expanded intelligence sharing and more effective counterterrorism policies. Brunei and the United State issued a joint statement in December 2002, in which the two countries agreed on the need "to strengthen cooperation to identify and destroy terrorist networks; exchange information and intelligence about terrorists and terrorist organizations; disrupt the movement of terrorists and the tools of terror across international borders; and cut off sources of funding for terrorist acts, especially in Southeast Asia."[16] On the international level, Brunei acceded to the International Convention for the Suppression of the Financing of Terrorism in the same year.

Brunei has also engaged in closer cooperation and coordination with APEC members. A Counter Terrorism Task Force was set up within the APEC framework to tackle terrorism. At the task force meeting held in August 2003, Brunei submitted a Counter Terrorism Action Plan, in which the kingdom committed to taking concrete actions aimed at protecting cargo, ships, international aviation, people in transit; halting terrorist financing; as well as promoting cyber security.

The above collaborations are made in tandem with other regional and bilateral cooperation, which is, in fact, the main thrust of Brunei's counterterrorism efforts. Such an approach is understandable, given that Brunei is most concerned about the possible threats of the regional-based extremist movements, and that policy coordination among immediate neighbors is seen to be more effective in combating terrorism. In July 2002 Brunei, Indonesia, Malaysia, and the Philippines agreed to adopt common policies on customs, immigration, quarantine, and security (CIQS) to fight human and goods smuggling, as well as threats to regional and national security. On October 5, 2003, Brunei joined the ranks of five other ASEAN members in accession to the agreement on Information Exchange and Establishment of Communication Procedures, which was initially signed by Indonesia, Malaysia, and the Philippines in May 2002, and joined by Thailand and Cambodia later. With the accession, Brunei agreed to facilitate coordination and collaboration during security or border incidents, transnational crimes, and other illegal activities with these countries. Under the agreement, the six countries are obliged to cooperate with each other in the issues of terrorism, money laundering, goods smuggling, piracy, hijacking, illegal entry, drug trafficking, illicit trafficking in arms, as well as other transnational problems. The commitment was solidified with the signing of the ASEAN Bali Concord in 1993.

Terrorism is seen as a menace that threatens not only the security of individual countries, but also the viability of ASEAN as a regional organization, the durability of peace and stability, and the economic prospect of the region as a whole. The sultan's keynote address at the opening of the 35th ASEAN Ministerial Meeting on July 29, 2002, expressed this clearly:

> At its deepest level terrorism directly threatens all international order. It is therefore an attack on the very structure of our association [ASEAN]. . . . Without peace and stability, all ASEAN's work will ultimately founder.[17]

Brunei's antiterrorism commitment has been implemented quietly, without the fanfare of an open alliance with the United States. Like many Muslim countries, Brunei has concerns about the tenor of the United States-led War on Terrorism, especially the invasion of Iraq. Too close an alliance with the United States could undermine support for the sultan at home. It is in this vein that internal efforts to address religious extremism have been ratchetted up, including closer regulation of religious schools in 2002 and monitoring of visas.

Conclusions and Outlook

Brunei illustrates that a small state may not necessarily be vulnerable to internal challenges and external perils. Brunei's enduring security for the past two decades shows that a multifaceted strategy that dexterously mobilizes its diplomatic skills and economic resources, is capable of mitigating its inherent vulnerabilities.

Since the 1962 revolt, Brunei's internal security problems, which overlap with growing transnational security concerns, have remained its most pressing concerns. This is likely to continue. Although Brunei's territorial disputes are still far from resolution, it is unlikely that those controversies will lead to extensive interstate conflicts. The regional terrorist threat reinforces this observation, as more attention is domestically focused to curb extremism and regional collaborative efforts deepen.

Brunei's security problems, as those of most small states, are closely linked to developments in its neighboring countries. This is true for problems like environmental degradation, drug trafficking, transnational crimes, and, as discussed above, religious extremism. Despite a well-trained security force, Brunei cannot resolve the problems alone. It is thus imperative for Brunei to continue forging regional cooperation. It also cannot rely exclusively on domestic coercion and needs to create such domestic conditions as more political space, in order to dampen potential extremism.

Since attaining independence, Brunei's membership in ASEAN has enabled the sultanate to ameliorate its relationships with its former foes and to engage in regional affairs on equal footing with its much larger neighbors. Brunei's multifaceted security strategy has given the tiny state a notable international status and allowed its voice to be heard on the world stage. International cooperation will remain the cornerstone of Brunei's strategy in dealing with future security challenges.

Notes

1. Mohamad Yusop bin Awang Damit, "Negara Brunei Darussalam: Light at the End of the Tunnel," *Southeast Asian Affairs,* 2002, p. 89.

2. Michael Leifer, *Dictionary of the Modern Politics of South-East Asia* (London: Routledge, 1996), p. 172.

3. Clark D. Neher, *Southeast Asia in the New International Era,* 4th ed., (Boulder, CO: Westview Press, 2002), p. 180.

4. *Borneo Bulletin,* July 31, 1998.

5. Zachary Abuza, "The Last Frontier? Jemaah Islamiya, Al Qaeda and the Potential for Terrorist Infiltration in Brunei." Unpublished paper, October 2002.

6. *Borneo Bulletin,* July 13, 2000.

7. *Borneo Bulletin,* July 29, 2000.

8. "Brunei Detains 3 for Pushing Christianity," *The Australian,* March 26, 2001.

9. Leifer, *Dictionary of the Modern Politics of South-East Asia,* p. 4.

10. S. Jayasankaran and John McBeth. "Malaysia and Brunei: Oil and Water," *Far Eastern Economic Review,* July 3, 2003, p. 7.

11. Joint Statement between the United States and Negara Brunei Darussalam, December 16, 2002, at www.state.gov/p/sa/rls/pr/16038.htm.

12. *Borneo Bulletin,* July 30, 2002.

13. Brunei's Ministry of Defense's home page, at www.mindef.gov.bn

14. Statement by His Excellency Ambassador Serbini Ali, Permanent Representative of Brunei Darussalam to the United Nations on Agenda Item 166: "Measures To Eliminate International Terrorism" at the 56th Session of the United Nations General Assembly, New York, October 4, 2001.

15. Catharin Dalpino and David Steinberg, eds., *Georgetown Southeast Asia Survey 2002–2003* (Washington, DC: Georgetown University, 2003), p. 2.

16. A.V.M. Horton, "Negara Brunei Darussalam: Economic Gloom and the APEC Summit," *Southeast Asian Affairs,* 2001.

17. *Borneo Bulletin,* July 8, 2002.

Suggested Readings

Case, William. "Brunei Darussalam in 1996." *Asian Survey,* vol. 37, no. 2, February 1997, pp. 194–98.

Damit, Mohamad Yusop. "Negara Brunei Darussalam: Weathering the Storm." *Southeast Asian Affairs,* 2000, pp. 87–96.

Gunn, Geoffrey. *New World Hegemony in the Malay World.* Lawrenceville, NJ: Red Sea Press, 2000.

Sulaiman, Hamzah. "Negara Brunei Darussalam: Socio-Economic Concerns Amid Stability and Plenty." *Southeast Asian Affairs,* 2003, pp. 71–79.

4

Burma

Plus ça Change

Maureen Aung-Thwin

Introduction

Burma, also known as Myanmar, is a resource-rich, Buddhist nation whose fiercely patriotic citizens have endured harsh military rule for over forty years. Even the regime's opponents are impressed by the military's durable ability to stay unified and maintain power. The Burmese armed forces, or Tatmadaw, are a bigger and better-equipped force today than ever before in its history; the Tatmadaw has the second largest army in Southeast Asia and the sixteenth largest armed force in the world.[1]

Much of the world became aware of Burma in 1988, when a popular uprising against the dictatorship was brutally crushed. The generals insist they are an interim power until a multiparty democracy—Burmese style and according to the military's timetable—can be established. Under the current junta, called the State Peace and Development Council (SPDC), Burma has evolved from a xenophobic, pseudosocialist, strictly nonaligned dictatorship into a slightly outward-looking, pseudocapitalist dictatorship beholden to China.

Every so often Burma moves into the global spotlight, reminding the international community of the continuing political impasse between the military regime and Burma's democratic opposition. The junta came under global opprobrium for viciously attacking a convoy of democracy leader and Nobel Peace laureate Daw Aung San Suu Kyi and her colleagues from the National League for Democracy (NLD) on May 30, 2003. The attack by agents and supporters of the junta underscore a serious lack of consensus among top regime officers on how to deal with their biggest obstacle to remaining in power. Soon after the attack, the regime floated a supposedly new road map to democracy, an offer that appeased many external regime critics suffering

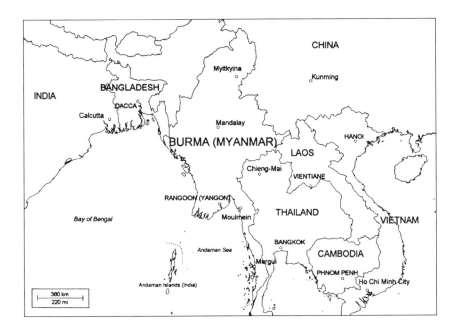

from "Burma fatigue" and raised hopes for a genuine breakthrough leading to peaceful reconciliation in Burma.

The glass is half full or half empty, depending on who is describing Burma. The regime proudly boasts of having built roads, bridges, hotels, and other visible infrastructure; it also points to ending almost all ethnic insurgencies that have plagued Burma since its independence from British colonial rule in 1948. Regime detractors underscore the junta's use of rape, forced labor, and other abuses against the civilian population; they also criticize the state's monopolistic exploitation of natural resources to pay for expansion of the Tatmadaw at the cost of education and social services.

Burma has raised eyebrows within Asia and in Washington, DC, for trying to purchase a nuclear reactor from Russia in 2002, for reported reliance on North Korea for nuclear technology, and for possible links between some of its disenchanted Muslim minority and global Islamic terrorist groups.

The opaque nature of military rule in Burma makes impossible cogent analysis of the country based on reliable statistics or checkable facts. Open for interpretation is everything from the exact nature of the relationship between the Burmese military regime and China, its chief patron, to fissures among the Burmese army leadership. In the last decade, perhaps because of the challenge to decipher one of the last world's remaining exotic countries, interest in Burma has grown tremendously among academics, travelers, and policy makers. Since the regime does not allow public discussion of its policies by its citizens and refuses to issue visas to outside critics, any study of Burma has to take into account not only myriad rumors and increasingly sophisticated propaganda but the contrast between the official rhetoric and the actual practice of an unpredictable military regime.

The United States and the European Union are constantly under pressure to reassess their hard-line policies toward Burma whenever its generals sing a conciliatory note. In 2006 it is Burma's turn to host the annual meetings of the Association of Southeast Asian Nations (ASEAN), which accepted Burma as a member in a whirl of controversy in 1997. ASEAN stands to lose colossal face at its most prestigious annual event were it to be ruined by its most recalcitrant member.

Around the region there is palpable pressure on the Burmese generals to enter into a genuine and sustained dialogue with the democratic forces of the country—including Burma's ethnic leaders—in an effort to end Burma's long nightmare.

Political Framework

Since 1962, when General Ne Win took over power in a relatively bloodless military coup, military men have dominated politics in Burma. The Tatmadaw is convinced that without its oversight the country would break up like the former Yugoslavia. Burmese leaders, civilian and military, have been keen observers of global affairs and were not always isolated from—or shunned by—the world. During the brief episode of parliamentary democracy in the 1950s, between the end of British colonial rule and Ne Win's coup, politically-neutral Burmese diplomats were well regarded in international circles. Burma's academics studied everything and everywhere; its civil servants were well informed. The Burmese considered as friends Israel's Ben Gurion and Yugoslavia's Marshall Tito, as well as the U.S. presidents Dwight D. Eisenhower and Richard M. Nixon. Burma was one of the first nations to recognize the People's Republic of China in 1949. In 1979 true to its beliefs, Burma quit the Non-Aligned Movement (NAM), which it helped found, because it perceived many NAM member nations were tilted towards the then Soviet bloc.

After more than forty years in power, the generals are still struggling with how to run an ethnically diverse, resource rich, failing state. In the 1970s General Ne Win tried to reinvigorate what he termed the Burmese Way to Socialism. By 1987 the Old Man, as General Ne Win was also known, faced a major economic crisis. After years of economic mismanagement, he authorized a series of sudden demonetizations of banknotes without compensating holders of the old currency. He resigned, then audaciously—and presciently—suggested that Burma try a multiparty democracy.

The summer of 1988, Burmese from all walks of life took to the streets to demand just that. The popular uprising demanding an end to military rule was crushed by General Ne Win's slightly younger successors. They declared his disastrous Burmese Way to Socialism officially dead and cautiously introduced some free market ideas. In 1990 the military was soundly defeated in free elections, but simply ignored the results.

As Ne Win did in the 1970s, the current junta is looking now for ways to civilianize its rule and maintain power through legitimate means. After the 2003 attack on the NLD, SPDC General Khin Nyunt, apparently the most moderate of the top junta hierarchy, became prime minister. He introduced a seven-point road map to reconvene a stalled national convention on the constitution, which he hoped would lead to elections and the establishment of a government dominated by the military.

By fall 2004, a power struggle was clearly underway; the hardliners in the junta forced the fifteenth cabinet shakeup in seven years. By mid October an internal coup and subsequent witch hunt purged General Khin Nyunt and the entire military intelligence sector.

An essential piece of the political jigsaw of Burma is the ethnic element. Much of the natural wealth of Burma—timber, gems, oil—lies in areas populated by ethnic groups, some of whom in precolonial days ruled the equivalent of their own kingdoms. Colonial rule favored some of these tribes over Burmans who were slightly in the majority. Under the British, the ethnic nationalities made up the bulk of Burma's armed forces. However, the army that later routed first the colonial British and then the fascist Japanese occupation forces during World War II was composed of Burman nationalists led by General Aung San, the father of Daw Aung Suu Kyi. A political rival assassinated General Aung San before he could assume the position of independent Burma's first head of state. Some regard his daughter's mission as Burma's second struggle for independence.

Senior General Than Shwe, the Burmese Tatmadaw's top—and most xenophobic—official makes it quite clear that he disagrees. In a veiled reference to Daw Aung San Suu Kyi's purported closeness to the West, where she spent much of her life, the general recently reiterated in a speech:

> Sovereignty is the lifeblood of a nation. The three powers—legislative, executive and judicial—must be understood as sovereignty. These three powers must be in the hands of our citizens and our national races. We cannot put them in the hands of any alien directly or indirectly. Once the sovereignty of our country is influenced in any way by others, it is tantamount to

indirect enslavement under neo-colonialism. Hence, the Tatmadaw must ensure perpetuation of sovereignty at the risk of lives.[2]

Internal Security Environment

"Non-Disintegration of the Union" has been the military's mantra since 1962. This is the organizing principle around which the regime rationalizes its existence—and its main excuse for maintaining a huge army. Throughout history Burma has been cautiously correct in relating to such immediate neighbors as Thailand and Bangladesh and regional powers like India and China. Since the end of World War II, Burma has experienced only a few border disputes, one with China in the early 1960s and a few with Thailand in the context of Burmese ethnic wars abutting the country's eastern border. While arming its forces as if the country faced an urgent external threat, Burma's gravest problems come from within. The most serious threat to internal security is the Burmese military's continued repressive, illegitimate rule. Other elements of instability inside Burma include:

- Ethnic expectations: Burma under any regime, even a democratic one, will not know permanent peace within its own borders unless ethnic nationalities are given a voice and a genuine partnership in a federal union. The regime's current cease-fires are a quick fix based on the junta's need to reallocate soldiers and expenses to contain the more threatening urban opposition against its rule.
- Drugs: Burma's poppy cultivation is slightly down, but it is still the world's second largest supplier of opium. The regime has been unable or unwilling to combat criminal drug groups, largely ethnic Chinese and Wa who produce and market narcotics, particularly *yaa baa* or methamphetamine, to the region and beyond. *Yaa baa* has been facetiously described as "the most effective crop substitution program in the Golden Triangle."[3]
- HIV-AIDS: The regime finally appears to have acknowledged that it has a problem and has begun to allow some programs on prevention. Burma's infection rate is the second highest in Southeast Asia, after Cambodia, but with comprehensive testing, Burma could well be the highest.
- Terrorism: For all the talk about the junta's tight control of the country, Burma is vulnerable to domestic—and perhaps global—terrorism. Over the years the junta has been woefully unable to gauge the level of hostility toward its rule or control what foreign terrorists might do on its soil.
- Economic factors: All the elements that threaten domestic stability are related in some way to the mismanagement of the economy. Burma faces

a widening gap between rich and poor. It risks renewed social unrest due to the inability of the SPDC to run a modern economy and provide more than a minimal level of education, health, and social services.

The Burmese regime is not the first dictatorship to grapple with how to hold on to power by force, without creating domestic instability. A modicum of the rule of law, the junta realizes, is necessary for sustained foreign investment and economic growth. Indonesia under President Soeharto has served as a model for the Burmese junta. After Soeharto's sudden ouster followed by the near-secession of the oil-rich province of Aceh, interest in this model understandably waned. Today, however, the Burmese are no doubt watching Indonesia with renewed interest. A decade after its transition to democracy, Indonesia's economy is still dominated by special interests linked to the military. In 2004, a retired military general, Soesilo Bambang Yudhoyono, trounced civilian housewife Megawati Soekarnoputri in the nation's first direct presidential elections. The junta in Burma prides itself for ending the decades of civil war and ethnic insurgencies, but these cease-fires have come at a price. The military now has a permanent presence in almost every part of the country. In the areas where traditional non-Burman ethnic populations live, this presence is seen as an army of occupation rather than a stabilizing force. Amnesty International reports human rights abuses continue, especially forced labor and forced relocation.[4]

As long as there is no negotiated political settlement in Burma and the junta rules by force and fear rather than popular support, the internal security environment always will be unstable.

External Security Environment

The regional security environment in Southeast Asia has become more complex after the terrorist events of September 11. The Soviet Union and China once were the great powers that shaped regional and national policies. Today all eyes are on China and, to an extent, the United States.

The willingness of the United States to use military might against sovereign nations that it dislikes has alarmed the paranoid dictators of Burma. In 1988 many Burmese prodemocracy demonstrators (including some in the military) expected the U.S. Navy's Seventh Fleet to come in and oust the Burmese military regime.

Burma's defense policies are based on a heightened sense of vulnerability to external attack—as well as what the Burmese military thinks is now in their national interest. At the same time, the Burmese regime is exploiting the country's prominence as a crucial crossroads between South and Southeast

Asia and between the two regional superpowers—India and China. China is Burma's main supplier of arms and military aid; in return China may be allowed to use one of Burma's Coco Islands as an intelligence outpost. Soon after September 11, the Burmese regime reportedly let two Pakistani nuclear scientists seek refuge inside its territory (presumably to help with the running of the proposed nuclear reactor). India has begun a new Look East policy, which, under the guise of promoting regional economic integration, would also be looking out to counter China's influence in countries like Burma. Already India has entered into several agreements with Burma to build transnational highways and discussed mutual defense strategies against ethnic insurgents active in the shared border of India's northeast.

Eager to cultivate allies wherever it can, the regime in the last several years has made overtures to a motley range of nations. The junta's newfound friends have included such other pariah states as Belarus, Saddam Hussein's Iraq, and North Korea. Regardless of the regime's rhetoric, many Burmese, including some in the military, would prefer to be closer to the United States, with whom there were once warm relations.

Terrorism Threat and Response

The junta has long labeled opponents of the regime as "terrorists," while dissidents have called the junta a "terrorist regime." Burma's response to the international terrorism threat after September 11 is affected by its questionable intelligence-gathering capability, an uneasy relationship with the United States, and shabby treatment of Burma's Muslim minorities.

As the Burmese junta continues to upgrade the capacity of its fighting forces, it also expanded the reach of its intelligence arm. Since the inception of military rule in 1962, any type of security agency or individual dealing with gathering intelligence became known among the public (and even among foreigners) by the generic name "MI" (for military intelligence). In recent years MI capabilities expanded to include better intelligence gathering and monitoring equipment and increased potential for shared intelligence with neighboring China and India.

The Burmese military rules mostly by fear. Most Burmese assume that the MI is all-powerful and omniscient, but the spontaneous popular uprising in 1988 against military rule demonstrated to the generals that the MI needed major upgrading. Only a few years earlier, in 1983, North Korean agents carried out a bombing that killed several visiting South Korean cabinet members in Rangoon in a botched attempt to assassinate the South Korean president. Since 1988, the MI have also failed to anticipate sporadic terrorist activity in and around Burmese cities, including a parcel bomb mailed to a Burmese general's house that blew up his daughter. Now with the MI gone, the hardcore army must recreate an intelligence network.

Advances in information technology over the past decade have been both a blessing and a challenge to the Burmese military. Burmese urbanites have expensive and very limited access to the Internet and international phone lines, all of which are monitored. The challenge of gathering—and evaluating—intelligence on its own citizens, including the armed forces (many of whom voted in 1990 for the NLD), as well as potentially subversive foreign visitors, will only grow greater.

If global terrorism today implies acts of violence by Islamic extremists, Burma is probably not yet very vulnerable, although it could be in the future. Muslim minority groups have long suffered under majority Burman rule in a predominantly Buddhist country. For complex reasons rooted in the country's colonial history, foreigners are distrusted and often become a scapegoat for political and societal ills.

Southeast Asia has over 200 million Muslims (of an estimated 1.2 billion around the world).[5] After September 11, Burma's Muslims—a long-ignored community—received renewed scrutiny, as have all Muslim communities in the region. Estimates for the numbers of Muslims residing in Burma range from 4 percent (or 2 million of a population of upward of 50 million), to 16 percent or 8 million. Besides the unreliability of statistical information on Burma, the range in the estimate reflects the discrimination and disregard of Burma's Muslims by the central government.[6] The Buddhist military leaders of Burma actively discourage the practice of non-Buddhist religions, particularly Christianity and Islam.

Antiforeign attitudes by not only the military junta but by ordinary Burman Buddhists toward the Muslim minority in Burma, go back to colonial times when large numbers of Bengali Muslims were first brought from India by the British to work as laborers, clerks, and civil servants. Rohingyas, the largest of Burma's four main Muslim groups, have resided mainly in Arakan State in western Burma for centuries, but are still not considered true Burmese citizens.

Among the few Burmese Muslim groups that advocate armed struggle, only one faction of one group, the Rohingya Solidarity Organization, or RSO, may have links to hard-line international Islamic organizations. A few Burmese Rohingya mujahideen apparently were found fighting for the Taliban in 2001, but these included Pakistanis of Burmese descent who had never been to Burma.[7]

If the Burmese military junta continues to use the U.S.-initiated global War on Terrorism as an added excuse to clamp down on local Muslim minority groups calling for religious freedom and the right to genuine citizenship, the situation may change.

Military Structure and Defense Policy

In the Burmese Tatmadaw, the army is the most privileged sector of the three forces. The Burmese military has ruled for four decades largely through the intimidation of its military intelligence apparatus and the brute strength of its well-seasoned army. The command structure of the Tatmadaw has evolved over the years, honed by real and imagined internal and external threats. Burma's army grew from a respected, heroic force that ousted foreign occupiers to become an occupying army over its fellow countrymen. Consequently all of the military government's policies, including defense, are shaped by perceived threats to Burma's sovereignty and to sustaining the power of the Tatmadaw.

Serving military officers did not always run the Burmese government. In 1974, when General Ne Win introduced a new constitution and even a People's Assembly, or *hlutaw,* many retired military officers took over political duties, adding the civilian honorific "U" in front of their names to civilianize the process. Everything changed in 1988. Confronted by the biggest national uprising against their rule, active military officers retook political control as the State Law and Order Restoration Council (SLORC).[8] The Tatmadaw hierarchy was reorganized, and most senior officers were upgraded by two ranks.[9] Within ten years the SLORC's members, who also held cabinet posts, had swollen to thirty-eight. In 1997 the SLORC was renamed the State Peace and Development Council or SPDC, with the membership pared down to nineteen members.

For many years, the entire command structure of Burma's military has been dominated by the whims of the most dogmatic and powerful junta figure—the reclusive and narrow-minded Senior General Than Shwe. Until his ouster, high-level foreign visitors usually dealt with the more English-proficient General Khin Nyunt, the head of the military intelligence and prime minister.

Burmese military rulers have built up a vast military structure and weapons arsenal at the expense of the civilian population. Arms and military equipment account for more than one fifth of the country's total imports.[10] The forbearance of the Burmese populace to repressive rule may be explained by the intense faith in Buddhism and the belief in karma by Burmese. The military came into power in 1962, but it took the general population until 1988 to rebel. Another tranquilizing influence is a dual economy, including an unregulated, mostly barter system that helps over 75 percent of the Burmese to subsist. Though poor, people are shielded from effects of foreign currency fluctuations and economic sanctions.

The military or military-related interests control the most lucrative sectors of Burma's formal economy. All major foreign investment requires joint ventures with the Union of Myanmar Economic Holdings (UMEH), the country's largest holding company. Shares in the Myanmar Economic Corporation (MEC), are open only to active-duty military personnel. The petroleum sector is run by the Myanma Oil and Gas Enterprise (MOGE), while other related state companies have exclusive rights to develop and produce petroleum.

The Tatmadaw not only uses Burma's rich resources to pay for military imports, but also receives additional, hidden, subsidies in the form of free or below-cost, goods and services. Regular citizens and foreign residents pay enormous rates for electricity, much of which is free to the military. Staples such as rice, oil, and gasoline are available to military families at below market prices and then resold by officials for a profit.[11] On a per-capita basis, Burmese government expenditures on health and education are among the world's lowest, and even part of the miniscule health budget is diverted to special health and education services open only to military personnel and their families.

Even with such sources of revenue, the army central command has to stretch to meet the cost of paying and supplying its soldiers. Over the last several years regional commanders have been ordered to meet basic needs for their troops locally, resulting in abuses against rural farmers.

Since 1988 Burma's air force and navy have also modernized, though they still lag behind the Burmese army as a priority for the junta, all army men. Burma's air force since its inception just prior to independence in 1948 mostly has been a counterinsurgency force—and not a very effective one. Lack of funds for aircraft, spare parts, and training, due to ambivalence about foreign military aid, impeded the modernization of Burma's air force for decades. When the Tatmadaw was finally ready to modernize and expand—after the 1988 uprising—arms embargoes against the regime stifled the upgrading of equipment. In recent years the Tatmadaw has acquired military equipment from India, Pakistan, and China, and such western nations as the Ukraine, Serbia, and Montenegro, the remnant of Burma's former close ally Yugoslavia.

The Burmese navy is undergoing a vast modernization program with the aid of China and India, expanding its capabilities from guarding sovereign territory against external enemies to guarding Burma's marine resources, offshore extractive industries and it is suggested, keeping routes to the Middle East oil fields open for China.[12]

Conclusions and Outlook

The key to lasting peace in Burma is a truly representative federal union of a plural society. Therefore, a serious political settlement must be the result of genuine tripartite negotiations among the military, the ethnic nationalities, and the democratic opposition led by the National League for Democracy.

The SPDC regime could turn Burma toward lasting peace—if it acts courageously and correctly, soon. First, all political prisoners must be freed. And whenever the national convention is reconvened, it must include Daw Aung San Suu Kyi and the NLD plus leaders of the ethnic nationalities, including the Karen National Union (KNU), the largest and longest-running insurgency force, who have started tentative peace talks with the SPDC. However fragile the premise, the long road to reconciliation must begin with these first steps. ASEAN countries should send observers to the national convention. A successful convention would have a huge consequence on how the regime is regarded—and rewarded—by the international community, but more importantly, by the citizens of Burma.

Notes

1. U.S. Department of State, *World Military Expenditures and Arms Transfers, 1999–2000,* released February 6, 2003, at www.state.gov. William Ashton, in "The arms keep coming but who pays?" *Irrawaddy,* July 14, 2004 calls it the fifteenth largest in the world.

2. Senior General Than Shwe, excerpt from reprinted speech, "New Light of Myanmar," March 14, 2004.

3. Altsean Special Report, *Ready, Aim, Sanction,* Bangkok, November 2003, p. 126.

4. Amnesty International, "Myanmar: Lack of Security in Counter-Insurgency Areas," July 2002.

5. Robert W. Hefner, "Islam and Asian Security," in Richard J. Ellings and Aaron L. Friedberg, eds., *Strategic Asia 2002–03: Asian Aftershocks* (Seattle, WA: National Bureau of Asian Research, 2002), p. 351.

6. Andrew Selth, "Burma's Muslims: Terrorists or Terrorised?" *Canberra Papers on Strategy and Defence,* no. 150, Australia, August 2003.

7. Selth, "Burma's Muslims: Terrorists or Terrorised?" p. 18.

8. Andrew Selth, *Burma's Armed Forces: Power Without Glory* (Norwalk, CT: EastBridge, 2002), p. 71.

9. Tin Maung Maung Than in Selth, p. 55.

10. United Nations Development Program, UNDP Human Development Report 1994.

11. U.S. Embassy, Rangoon, "Foreign Economic Trends Report," 1996.

12. Selth, *Burma's Armed Forces: Power Without Glory,* p. 197.

Suggested Readings

Ashton, William. "The arms keep coming but who pays?" *Irrawaddy*, July 14, 2004, at www.irrawaddy.org.

Altsean. *Burma Briefing: Issues and Concerns.* Volume 1. November 2004, at www.altsean.org.

Altsean Special Report. *Ready, Aim, Sanction.* Bangkok: November 2003, at www.altsean.org.

Council on Foreign Relations. *Burma: Time for Change.* Independent Task Force Report, June 2003.

KWO Report: *Shattering Silences*, April 2004, at www.ibiblio.org/obl/docs/Shattering_Silences.htm.

Fink, Christina. *Living Silence: Burma under Military Rule.* London: Zed Books, 2001.

Human Rights Watch. "Out of Sight, Out of Mind: Thai Policy toward Burmese Refugees and Migrants." February 2004, at http://hrw.org/reports/2004/thailand0204/.

Khoo Thwe, Pascal. *From the Land of Green Ghosts: A Burmese Odyssey.* New York: HarperCollins, 2002.

Marshall, Andrew. *The Trouser People: A Story of Burma in the Shadow of the Empire.* New York: Counterpoint Press, 2003.

Smith, Martin J. *Burma: Insurgency and the Politics of Ethnicity,* 2nd ed. London: Zed Books, 1999.

Steinberg, David I. *Burma: The State of Myanmar.* Washington, DC: Georgetown University Press, 2001.

Takano, Hideyuki. *The Shore Beyond Good and Evil: A Report from Inside Burma's Opium Kingdom.* Boston: Charles E. Tuttle Co., 2002.

Tucker, Shelby. *Among Insurgents: Walking Through Burma.* New York: HarperCollins, 2002.

United Nations Development Program, *UNDP Human Development Report 2003,* at http://hdr.undp.org/reports/global/2003/.

United States Department of State. *Country Reports on Human Rights Practices* (Burma), 2003.

Suggested Web sites

General Information:

Online Burma Library:
www.burmalibrary.org
Burma Project, Open Society Institute
www.burmaproject.org
Human Rights Watch
www.hrw.org

News Sources:

www.burmanet.org
www.burmadaily.com

www.irrawaddy.org
www.shanland.org
www.yangonglobe.com

SPDC government links:

www.myanmar.com/
www.myanmar.com/myanmartimes/
www.myanmar.com/nlm/

Myanmar information sheets (by year)

www.myanmar-information.net
www.myanmar-information.net/political/english.pdf

Ministry of Defence. 9 volumes of "The Truth: An Analysis of the Announcements issued by the National League for Democracy." www.myanmar-information.net/truth/truth.html

5

Cambodia

A Gathering Danger

Paul C. Grove

Introduction

The absence of the rule of law as well as corruption in Cambodia provides Asian criminals and regional terrorists with safe havens and bases of operations in Southeast Asia. Transnational crimes emanating from Cambodia, particularly narcotics and human trafficking, pose significant and growing threats to regional neighbors.

Efforts to promote democracy in Cambodia have largely failed. While space exists for opposition political parties and a donor-dependent civil society, opportunities for meaningful political reform have repeatedly been undermined and subverted by the Vietnamese-installed Cambodian People's Party (CPP). Opposition activists and reporters are intimidated and often murdered.

Elections in Cambodia are mostly hollow events. Controlled by the CPP through the manipulation of the election bureaucracy, the electoral environment and broadcast media, flawed polls in Cambodia provide the CPP with a veneer of legitimacy.

For the past decade, international donors and financial institutions have time and again failed to hold the CPP accountable for its lawless and repressive actions. Perpetuation of the status quo serves only to encourage senior CPP officials to continue illicit activities that undermine the development of Cambodia—whether deforestation, drug trafficking, or the demobilization of "ghost soldiers."

Political Framework

In theory, Cambodia is a multiparty democracy and a constitutional monarchy with Norodom Sihamoni as king. In practice, the country is a dictatorship

under the thumb of the CPP and its repressive leader, Hun Sen, who has served as prime minister since 1985.

Parliamentary polls in Cambodia in 1993, 1998, and 2003 bore the trappings of electoral events, but failed to serve as catalysts for political change.

In 1993 the CPP placed second to the royalist United Front for an Independent, Neutral, and Peaceful Cambodia (FUNCINPEC) party in elections mandated by the 1991 Paris Agreements and sponsored by the United Nations. Post-election threats of violence by the CPP resulted in a lopsided power-sharing agreement that enabled continued CPP control of key ministries and the head of the government. Despite losing the election, Hun Sen emerged as Cambodia's "Second Prime Minister."

By July 1997 this power-sharing charade collapsed when Hun Sen launched a bloody coup d'état to oust his royalist rivals. Over one hundred FUNCINPEC government officials were murdered, and opposition political party structures were decimated. The coup was financed by a US$1 million contribution to the CPP by Cambodian drug kingpin Theng Boonma.[1]

Elections in 1998 and 2003 were also marred by violence, limited access to media by CPP challengers (FUNCINPEC and the Sam Rainsy Party or SRP), and the total control of the election bureaucracy by the CPP.[2] In both polls, the CPP failed to secure a two-thirds majority required to form a new government, and pressed its royalist rival into joining a coalition government.

Once burned and understandably wary, FUNCINPEC was reluctant to engage in a coalition and again become a powerless partner in a Hun Sen–dominated government. Under intense pressure from King Sihanouk and the international community in 1998, however, FUNCINPEC capitulated to the CPP's demands.

An eleven month stalemate followed the controversial 2003 polls, during which the royalist party initially joined forces with the SRP in an "Alliance of Democrats" against the CPP to demand that the new government be committed to political and legal reforms. Repeated attempts by King Sihanouk to broker a coalition failed, and the Alliance collapsed when FUNCINPEC agreed to join the CPP in a government consisting of 186 cabinet members—twice as many as the previous one. In addition to betraying the principles of the Alliance and creating among the world's most bloated bureaucracies, FUNCINPEC's sellout to the CPP served to cement Hun Sen's primacy in Cambodian politics and to undercut SRP's reform agenda.

Nonetheless, CPP leaders recognize the popularity of the SRP and violence against opposition activists is commonplace in Cambodia. Rather than dispiriting grassroots members and national leaders, political killings and intimidation appear to steel the determination of activists to crack the CPP's monopoly on power. Such was the case with the January 2004 assassination of SRP founding member and union leader Chea Vichea, which brought 15,000 mourners into the streets of Phnom Penh, many demanding Hun Sen's resignation.

Blatant attempts by the CPP to destroy its competition include a March 1997 grenade attack against opposition leader Sam Rainsy and his supporters in Phnom Penh, and the July 1997 coup d'état. An October 1999 report on the grenade attack by United States Senate Foreign Relations Committee staff states that "sufficient evidence exists in order to yield *a very obvious conclusion: Hun Sen and his Bodyguard Forces were behind this crime.*"[3]

The CPP directly controls and/or influences national and local governments, the judiciary, the police, and the military. A 123-member National Assembly is unprofessional and powerless and cannot provide a check to the CPP's monopoly on power. The Senate is similarly ineffective. Once a political force and the conscience of the Cambodian people, the influence of the monarchy has waned, and its future uncertain under new King Sihamoni, who replaced his father in late 2004.

It is clear that Hun Sen intends to remain in power regardless of political processes or public opinion. On December 6, 2003, he stated: "I will always stay because I have stayed since 1979 [the year of Vietnam's invasion of Cambodia]. No one can replace Hun Sen, including the CPP."[4]

Internal Security Environment

Lawlessness and Corruption: The absence of the rule of law and functioning democratic institutions poses serious challenges to domestic security and stability in Cambodia. Human rights abuses and crimes against the Cambodian people by government, police, and military officials occur with regularity and impunity. They include land confiscation, political killings, torture, and restrictions on such constitutional rights as freedom of speech and assembly.

The single greatest threat to Cambodia's internal security comes from the corruption perpetuated by the CPP, which is pandemic at all levels and branches of government. According to the Center for Social Development in Cambodia, corruption costs as much as US$400 million a year. Despite pledges to international donors by Prime Minister Hun Sen in 2002, Cambodia has yet to enact an anticorruption law creating an anticorruption board or to require public disclosure of assets and liabilities. Substantial challenges to increasing transparency and accountability will remain even if such a law were enacted—particularly to enforcement of the law and relevant regulations.

Corruption and the politicization of donor aid also undermine the development of the country. According to the U.N. World Food Programme, from January 2003 to April 2004 some 4,000 metric tons of rice provided to twelve Cambodian provinces through food-for-work projects was stolen and sold for cash. Government officials and CPP village chiefs, among others, were involved in the US$2 million rice scam.

Political Instability: Political repressiveness and instability limit economic opportunities for the majority of Cambodians. With the exceptions of the garment industry and tourism, Cambodia's unreliable infrastructure and weak legal system attract mostly high-risk investors. While nearly half the population continues to live below the poverty line, the quality of life for most Cambodians has improved since the genocidal days of the Khmer Rouge regime. Cambodia's political opposition points out that the benchmark for the country's development should not be the Khmer Rouge but international standards of development and justice.

Anti-Thai Riot: As the January 2003 anti-Thai riot in Phnom Penh illustrates, foreign interests in Phnom Penh are not immune to Cambodia's lawlessness—or CPP's control of security forces. Following an alleged slight against Cambodia by a popular Thai actress, Thailand's diplomatic mission and private businesses were attacked and destroyed by Cambodian mobs. Despite repeated official pleas made by the Thai ambassador, Chatchawed Chartsuwan (and a call from the Thai prime minister, Thaksin Shinawatra, to the Cambodian prime minister, Hun Sen), senior Cambodian military, police, and government officials failed to safeguard the diplomatic compound and personnel or to protect Thai private businesses. Over US$50 million damage was done to Thai interests in Phnom Penh.

A U.S. State Department report implicated CPP-backed thugs known as the "Pagoda Boys" in instigating the violence, and noted that senior police officials were unable to respond to the riots as no authorization by Hun Sen or his closest aides was given. The CPP blamed "extremists" for the riot, and initiated a crackdown on their political opponents and independent broadcasters. Sam Rainsy sought—and was given—refuge in the U.S. embassy.

While Thailand temporarily suspended diplomatic relations with Cambodia over the riots, neither Thailand nor Cambodia has credibly investigated or punished the perpetrators of the riots.

Deforestation: Cambodia's greatest natural resource—and source of illicit profits for the Cambodian military and the CPP—is its forests. With ready timber markets in neighboring Vietnam and Thailand, Cambodia's forests are rapidly dwindling. This comes at a high cost to Cambodian farmers and to the environment, which is impacted by severe flooding during the rainy season, caused by deforestation.

In 1998 environmental watchdog Global Witness warned that the country's forests could be commercially depleted within five years. The group exposed a logging deal with Vietnam worth US$130 million—money destined for the pockets of senior Cambodian military and government officials, including Prime Minister Hun Sen.[5] In contrast, Global Witness noted that a paltry US$12.7 million in official revenue went into government coffers in 1997.

One year later Global Witness was appointed the official forestry monitor for the Cambodian government, but was unceremoniously sacked in 2003. In an April 22, 2003, press release, Global Witness took aim at its critics: "These individuals at the heart of government and the public administration no doubt see the termination of Global Witness' official role as the surest way to maintain their illicit revenue streams and thereby their power."

Further injustice was delivered to the Cambodian people as international donors and the World Bank readily acquiesced to the removal of the only effective check against rampant deforestation in Cambodia.

Domestic Drug Abuse: According to Cambodian narcotics officials, drug abuse in Cambodia is on the rise. From 2002 to 2003 unofficial figures note a 100 percent increase in the number of drug addicts. The actual increase is probably significantly higher. The drug of choice appears to be amphetamine-type stimulants (known as "yama" in Khmer). Drugs are reportedly distributed to Cambodian youth by organized networks linked to foreign traffickers, with heaviest use in Battambang, Phnom Penh, and Banteay Meanchey provinces. In September 2004 police in Kratie province seized 559,600 yama tablets – the largest amphetamine drug bust in Cambodia's history.

Drug abuse further disadvantages Cambodian youth whose educational and economic opportunities are already severely limited. This point appears to be lost on senior Cambodian government, military, and police officials reportedly involved in the lucrative drug trade.

HIV/AIDS: Cambodia has among the highest HIV/AIDS infection rates in Southeast Asia. The disease is spread almost entirely by sexual transmission, and the prevalence rate among sex workers is estimated at nearly 30 percent. Given the extent of human trafficking through Cambodia, and between Vietnam and Cambodia, HIV/AIDS poses an internal security challenge, as well as a regional problem. By some estimates, as many as 55,000 Cambodian children have lost parents to HIV/AIDS.

HIV/AIDS health programs are not immune from corruption. The effectiveness of the "100% Condom Campaign" was undermined by bribes paid by sex workers to avoid attending sexually transmitted disease (STD) clinics and by the sale of condoms by brothel owners to prostitutes,[6] instead of distributing them free as required by the anti-AIDS campaign.

External Security Environment

Foreign Policy: Cambodia's foreign policy is most closely aligned with Vietnam and the People's Republic of China. Despite historically close ties with the CPP, Vietnam is becoming increasingly concerned with transnational crimes emanating from Cambodia, notably narcotics and human trafficking. Hanoi is aware that Cambodian officials are involved in the transit of heroin and other narcotics to Vietnam and in the flourishing sex industry in Cambodia. Vietnamese girls are regularly trafficked to neighboring Cambodia, where, by some estimates, they comprise 78 percent of all prostitutes.[7] Vietnamese officials are wary of the impact Asian criminal syndicates in Cambodia may have on the development of indigenous criminal networks. Vietnamese officials are also concerned about growing ties between their historic adversary, China, and Cambodia.

The relationship between China and the CPP continues to grow and is recognized by senior Cambodian officials as particularly important because China unconditionally provides foreign assistance. Chinese cooperation spans business investments, cultural preservation, friendship associations, educational activities, and foreign assistance. In November 2003 China provided the Cambodian government with a US$6.1 million grant for unspecified activities and a US$24.1 million interest-free loan for capital improvements. According to the Cambodian foreign minister, China extended six interest-free loans to Cambodia since 1994, and provided three grants worth US$6.1 million since 2002. Trade between China and Cambodia was expected to reach US$300 million in 2003, an increase of 15 percent over 2002.

Vietnamese and Chinese interests directly clash over the proposed Khmer Rouge tribunal, which the Cambodian government approved officially in November 2004. Former battlefield foes, Vietnam supports a tribunal as it believes it may legitimize its invasion of Cambodia in 1979. China is concerned that a tribunal will expose the depth of its relationship with Pol Pot and the Khmer Rouge.

Cambodia's relations with the United States were largely defined by the violent events of 1997. The U.S. Congress strongly condemned the March grenade attack and July coup d'état, and restricted assistance to the government of Cambodia. With few exceptions (including human trafficking and HIV/AIDS), U.S. assistance to the government is still prohibited. Given growing concerns with drugs and terrorism in Cambodia, however, Congress may ease restrictions on counternarcotics and military assistance to enhance border control capabilities.

Although over 50 percent of Cambodia's national budget is composed of foreign aid, international donors have been unwilling or unable to use this leverage to affect meaningful political, legal, and economic reforms in Cambodia.

Asian Criminal Syndicates: Beginning in the early 1990s, Asian criminal syndicates from Hong Kong, Taiwan, Macao, and mainland China migrated to Cambodia—attracted by a lawless and permissive environment.[8] With these gangsters came illicit activities, including narcotics trafficking and production, human trafficking, money laundering and prostitution. Today, the 14K and Bamboo Union triads are known to operate in Phnom Penh.

Asian criminals bought ready access to senior government officials. Following the 1997 coup d'état, Chen Chi-li of Taiwan's Bamboo Union triad acquired an honorary title from the Cambodian government (reportedly purchased by a contribution of US$100,000 or more) as well as an official position as an adviser to CPP Senate President Chea Sim.[9]

Such close relationships with the CPP ensure that Asian triads will be a fixture in Cambodia for the foreseeable future.

Narcotics: Cambodia is increasingly becoming a distribution point for heroin from the Golden Triangle destined for Asia, Australia, Europe, and the United States. It remains a significant producer and exporter of marijuana. The marijuana market operates under the control of foreign criminal syndicates. Cambodian drug officials indicate that small-scale drug laboratories were seized in 2003 in Phnom Penh, Koh Kong, Banteay Meanchey, and Battambang provinces. Precursor chemicals for these labs are thought to come from China via Vietnam.

According to Cambodian narcotics officials, heroin entering Cambodia today comes from the northern border, by way of the Mekong River, and passes through Stung Treng and Preah Vihear provinces on its way to southern Vietnam. The U.N. Office on Drugs and Crime (UNODC) estimates that 10 to 20 kilograms of heroin is trafficked from Laos each week, and that heroin is stockpiled in the country for future transshipment. As late as 2001, heroin routes entered through the country's western borders. This shift may be a result of the 2003 narcotics crackdown in Thailand.

Cambodian military, police, and government officials are reportedly involved in the drug trade. Punishment for officials implicated in trafficking is either nonexistent or insufficient (monetary fine) to dissuade complicity in the drug trade. Corrupt courts and protection by senior officials undermine drug interdiction efforts.

The National Authority for Combating Drugs (NACD) is responsible for coordinating antidrug efforts of the Cambodian government. Its four-pronged strategy is simplistic: cut demand, cut supply, increase law enforcement, and increase international cooperation on narcotics interdiction. The NADC's annual budget is roughly US$250,000, of which some US$100,000 is for administrative expenses.

Casinos owned by the CPP elite are suspected of laundering profits from the illegal narcotics trade in Cambodia and neighboring Vietnam.[10] These casinos are also thought to be linked to criminal organizations.

Terrorism Threat and Response

Beginning in the 1990s, Cambodia served as an arms market for such terrorist groups as the Tamil Tigers, which reportedly purchased assault rifles and SA-7 surface-to-air missiles in Phnom Penh.[11] In 1996 Japanese Red Army terrorist Yoshimi Tanaka was apprehended in Svay Rieng province (at the border with Vietnam) carrying a North Korean passport and counterfeit U.S. currency.

More recently, al Qaeda's top Southeast Asian operative and Jemaah Islamiyah (JI) chief Riduan Isamuddin (aka Hambali) found safe haven in Cambodia from September 2002 to March 2003.[12] Hambali reportedly was interested in using Cambodia to launch terrorist attacks in the region.[13]

Cambodia's ethnic Muslim Cham communities offer convenient cover for regional Islamic extremists. Saudi and Kuwaiti charities (including the Om Al Qura Charity Organization and the Revival of Islamic Heritage Society) surfaced in these communities in the early 1990s. These organizations provided assistance to communities that converted to the Wahhabi branch of Islam, building schools, orphanages, and mosques for faithful followers, and educating young Cham in Cambodia and abroad.[14]

The U.S. State Department estimates a population of 700,000 Chams in Cambodia, of which 6 percent adhere to Wahhabism. In other words, 42,000 Cambodian Wahhabis reside in Phnom Penh today, only one of whom needs to be recruited to conduct a terrorist attack against a domestic or international target.

The presence of Hambali in Cambodia forced the Cambodian government to take action against foreign Islamic charities, and in May 2003 they closed two Islamic schools funded by Om Al Qura and arrested two Thais and one Egyptian for alleged connections with JI. Other foreign nationals affiliated with the schools were deported. In June 2003 a Cambodian ethnic Cham also was arrested. Although the four were slated to stand trial in Cambodia's notoriously corrupt judicial system in February 2004 on charges of terrorism, they remain imprisoned despite a six-month pre-trail detention limit, and face new charges of attempted murder. Accusation by Thai officials of missile proliferation in Cambodia prompted the Cambodian government to undertake again counterterrorism measures. Initially denying that they even possessed such weaponry, the government disclosed that it possessed 233 surface-to-air missiles in its arsenals, which it intended to destroy.[15]

Endemic corruption may provide additional opportunities for international terrorists and criminals. In September 2004 Cambodian police broke up a sophisticated forgery ring in Phnom Penh that provided an estimated thirty foreigners with counterfeit Cambodian passports, fake Cambodian citizenship, and other documentation.[16]

Senior CPP officials admit that their interests in cracking down on terrorism are primarily economic in nature. They well understand that an international terrorist attack on Cambodian soil would devastate tourism to Cambodia—a major revenue source for the government.

Military Structure and Defense Policy

The Royal Cambodian Armed Forces (RCAF) poses no immediate military threat to Thailand, Laos, or Vietnam. The demise of the Khmer Rouge insurgency significantly reduces the need for a large Cambodian military.

According to the RCAF's "Strategic Review—2002," Cambodia's defense priorities include: (1) enhancing border control capabilities, including maritime patrols; (2) expediting military reforms, including demobilization, unit restructuring, and refocusing on training systems; (3) establishing mechanisms for force mobilization; (4) expanding military participation in national development, including engineering projects and humanitarian relief activities; and, (5) participating in regional and international military activities, including United Nations peacekeeping operations.

According to the Review, defense cooperation with the People's Republic of China has been "significantly enhanced" to include human resources training, military base and training facility construction, health care support, and engineering and other material assistance. India, France, Thailand, Malaysia, the Philippines, Indonesia, Singapore, Vietnam, and Australia cooperate militarily with RCAF.

The Cambodian government estimates a current force size of 130,000 soldiers, which it intends to reduce over a five-year period to between 70,000–80,000 soldiers. In contrast, the U.S. State Department's *World Military Expenditures and Arms Transfers* (WMEAT) report released in February 2003 estimates a force size of only 60,000.

Demobilization efforts supported by the World Bank and international donors have been compromised by corruption and scandal. A US$42 million program to demobilize 30,000 soldiers (each would receive US$240 in cash, and the choice of a sewing machine, water pump, or motorcycle) was suspended after the World Bank discovered "misprocurement" that included individuals' paying between US$23 to US$200 to secure their names on personnel rolls.[17] The World Bank was negligent in its fiduciary duties to its members, as the presence of "ghost soldiers" on military rosters was a well-known risk prior to the awarding of the US$18 million demobilization loan.

According to senior RCAF officials, 80 to 90 percent of Cambodian forces are aging soldiers. Some officials advocate compulsory service as a means to introduce younger soldiers into the military, but it is unclear how concurrent force reduction and conscription might occur. This conundrum is compounded by unreliable data on force structure and size.

Estimates of military expenditure as a percent of gross domestic product vary from 3 to 4 percent. The State Department's WMEAT report pegs expenditures at US$332 million, of which US$5 million is used for the importation of arms.

Except for soldiers tasked with protecting the prime minister, the military is plagued by unprofessional and undisciplined troops, and aging and broken military hardware. According to senior RCAF officials, few aircraft, vessels, or tanks are operational or adequately maintained.

RCAF officials are complicit in narcotics and human trafficking, illegal logging, land confiscation, and gross human rights abuses against the Cambodian people. These crimes are committed with impunity.

Conclusions and Outlook

The lack of responsive and responsible leadership in Cambodia has resulted in the establishment of an additional narco-state in Southeast Asia that poses immediate threats to its neighbors. Prime Minister Hun Sen's nearly twenty-year dictatorship has forced a continuous cycle of poverty and violence on the Cambodian people. By failing to hold the CPP accountable for its abuses, international donors and financial institutions have perpetuated an environment of lawlessness and injustice since the 1993 parliamentary elections.

Cambodia's myriad problems—from narcotics and human trafficking to terrorism and HIV/AIDS infection rates—have become too large to ignore. It is incumbent upon international donors to use foreign assistance as leverage to force the implementation of much needed reforms. Foreign capitals should make clear their support for democracy and human rights activism in Cambodia through words and deeds. Failure to do so will have significant repercussions not only for the Cambodian people and their regional neighbors, but also for U.S. interests in Cambodia and throughout the region.

Drugs and human trafficking ensure that Cambodia is no longer a "sideshow." It is imperative that it does not become a bull's-eye for terrorism.

Notes

The views expressed in this chapter are those of the author and do not reflect the official position of the U.S. Government.

1. Bertil Lintner, *Blood Brothers: Crime, Business and Politics in Asia* (Thailand: Silkworm Books, 2002), p. 217.

2. In contrast to the United Nations-sponsored polls in 1993 in which responsibility for the conduct and oversight of elections resided with seventy-two international personnel, primary authority for organizing and conducting the 1998 and 2003 polls rested with eleven and five, respectively, Cambodian officials handpicked by the CPP.

3. James Doran, *The March 30, 1997 Grenade Attack in Cambodia*, U.S. Senate Foreign Relations Committee (S. Prt. 106–32), October 1999, p. 1.

4. Yun Samean, "Parties Agree to Convene Assembly," *The Cambodia Daily*, December 8, 2003.

5. Global Witness Press Release, "ASEM Members Plunder Cambodia's Forest, 3–5 Years Left," March 20, 1998.

6. Patrick Falby, "Corruption Slows Condom Campaign," *Phnom Penh Post*, April 11–24, 2003.

7. United Nations Office on Drugs and Crime, "Country Profile on Vietnam—2003," p. 34.

8. Linter, *Blood Brothers: Crime, Business and Politics in Asia*, p. 219.

9. Phelim Kyne, "Taiwan's 'Dry Duck' Gets His Feathers Clipped," *Phnom Penh Post*, July 21–August 3, 2000.

10. United Nations Office on Drugs and Crime, "Country Profile on Vietnam—2003," p. 31.

11. Linter, *Blood Brothers: Crime, Business and Politics in Asia*, pp. 218–19.

12. Kevin Doyle and Phann Ana, "Hambali Left Gentle Impression on Phnom Penh," *The Cambodia Daily*, August 22, 2003.

13. Ibid.

14. Stephen O'Connell and Bou Saroeun, "Arabian Zealots Pour Dollars into 'Purifying' Cham," *Phnom Penh Post,* July 7–20, 2000.

15. Ker Munthit, "Hun Sen Orders Missiles Destroyed in Anti-Terrorism Move," *Associated Press,* December 16, 2003.

16. Phann Ana, "Five Charged in High-Tech Forgery Ring," *The Cambodia Daily,* September 9, 2004.

17. U.N. Wire, "World Bank Cuts Loan for Cambodia's Demobilization Program," July 9, 2003.

Suggested Readings

Becker, Elizabeth. *When the War Was Over.* New York: Simon and Schuster, 1986.

Brown, MacAlister, and Zasloff, Joseph. *Cambodia Confounds the Peacemakers: 1979–1999.* New York: Cornell University Press, 1998.

Chandler, David. *The Tragedy of Cambodian History.* New York: Vail-Ballou Press, 1991.

Doran, James. *The March 30, 1997, Grenade Attack in Cambodia.* U.S. Senate Foreign Relations Committee, October 1999.

Gottesman, Evan. *Cambodia After the Khmer Rouge: Inside the Politics of Nation Building.* New Haven, CT: Yale University Press, 2002.

Kamm, Henry. *Cambodia: Report From a Stricken Land.* New York: Arcade Publishing, 1998.

6

China

The Rising Power in Asia and Its Relations with Preemptive America—Emerging Strategic Partnership, Temporary Tactical Accommodation, or Both?

Joseph G. D. (Geoff) Babb

Introduction

International and regional relationships in Asia are undergoing significant changes in the aftermath of the events of September 11, 2001. There has been a noteworthy focus on the Abu Sayyaf Group in the southern Philippines, the terrorist bombing in Bali, Indonesia, the arrests of terror suspects in Malaysia and Singapore, and the changing relationship between India and Pakistan in light of the removal of the Taliban regime in Afghanistan. What should not be overlooked about changes in Asia after 9/11 are the continuing political, economic, military, and social developments in China (officially, the People's Republic of China or PRC) and, perhaps more importantly, ongoing and perhaps historic changes in Sino-American relations.

During the December 2003 visit to the United States of the Chinese premier, Wen Jiabao, both the United States and the PRC took the opportunity to reiterate issues that have previously discouraged movement toward greater strategic cooperation. Fundamental disagreements over human rights, religious freedom, discriminatory economic policies, the trade imbalance, and Taiwan continue to militate against anything more than temporary and turbulent periods of accommodation. Since September 11, 2001, and the Bush administration's subsequent declaration of a global War on Terrorism, however, an outline of a more mature and potentially more enduring strategic relationship has steadily emerged between the two countries. This fragile modus vivendi is being fostered by a rapidly changing

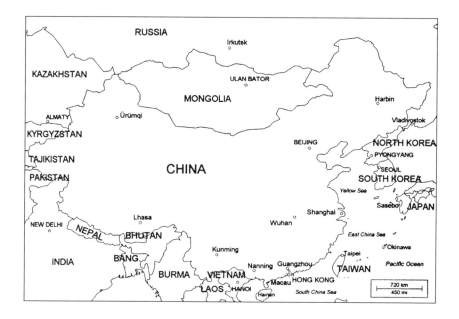

global environment, a clearer understanding of areas of shared concern for Asian regional stability, and a grudging recognition of a growing economic and diplomatic interdependence.

At a time of rising tensions between the PRC and the Chen Shui-bian government on Taiwan, the Bush administration appears to have returned, no doubt reluctantly, to a policy more reminiscent of the Nixon-Kissinger era of Sino-American relations. The restatement of adherence to a "one-China" policy and a return to the days of greater "strategic ambiguity" in terms of the use of U.S. military force to defend Taiwan if attacked by China, has at least temporarily assuaged the PRC. Taiwan has been duly warned—in these troubled times as America addresses a worldwide terrorist threat to its own homeland—that the maintenance of a U.S. strategic relationship with the PRC is more important than support for an independent, democratic Taiwan.

For its part, China has stepped into the breach to take a leading role in mediating the problem of a nuclear-armed North Korea with a history of the proliferation of key building blocks of weapons of mass destruction (WMD). This can be seen as clear-eyed recognition by the United States of China's growing power and influence in Asia. This move by Beijing, however, is not without risk. The success of the six-party talks is now a matter of "face" for the PRC, and the American position is clearly understood—nuclear weapons in North Korea are unacceptable, and the sale of materials related to WMD will not be tolerated.

China has also benefited from the controversial agreement by the United States to include Uighur independence movements in Xinjiang Province in western China on its list of terrorist organizations. There is a quid pro quo for this support as a new Great Game emerges in Central Asia. China has quietly acquiesced to the United States building stronger relationships in the region, upgrading military facilities, and conducting broad-based efforts to "democratize" Afghanistan from bases in Pakistan, Uzbekistan, and Tajikistan. At least for the time being China, as well as Russia, sees the pragmatic need for access to energy resources, regional stability, and predictability in international relations as trumping history, ideology, and chronic xenophobia.

> The United States seeks a constructive relationship with a changing China. We already cooperate well where our interests overlap, including the current war on terrorism and in promoting stability on the Korean peninsula. Likewise, we have coordinated on the future of Afghanistan and have initiated a comprehensive dialogue on counterterrorism and similar transnational concerns. Shared health and environmental threats such as the spread of HIV/AIDS, challenge us to promote jointly the welfare of our citizens.[1]

As the above excerpt from the U.S. *National Security Strategy* suggests, the United States and China appear to be developing a mutual recognition of shared interests and of the need to cooperate in dealing with critical regional issues. The military and economic problems of Northeast Asia—the ominous and growing radical Muslim terrorist threat in Southeast Asia, the potential for a catastrophic nuclear exchange between India and Pakistan, coupled with rising instability within an old mutual ally, Pakistan, in South Asia—is changing the face of Sino-American relations. The two major players in Asia share common "actionable" national interests for a stable region and for dealing with nonmilitary issues of international importance.

In the late 1970s and early 1980s there was strategic congruence in opposing Soviet military power. There are again signs that China and the United States have opened another window of improving relations based on a significant overlap of strategic interests. Unlike the earlier period that ended in the late 1980s with the fall of the Soviet Union and the crushing of the democracy protesters in Tiananmen Square, however, there is no single, clear, overriding strategic issue that the political leaderships of both countries can use to quell domestic political dissent or assuage nagging doubts over what many see as the inevitable clash of two great powers. Nevertheless, despite a rough period from the U.S. bombing of the Chinese embassy in Belgrade in 1999 at the end of the Clinton administration, through the April

2001 EP-3 incident and stern warnings to China over Taiwan early in the Bush administration, U.S.-PRC relations are on a markedly improving path—leading perhaps to a longer term, mutually beneficial strategic relationship.

Political Framework

The Chinese Communist Party (CCP) continues to run China through the state bureaucracy. While the National People's Congress is starting to play more of a role, it is still predominantly a rubber stamp for the CCP. Through the Central Military Commission (CMC) the Politburo oversees the security apparatus, which remains firmly in place and in control of a nation and a political system in transition. In 2001 China peacefully passed along its national and party leadership. Jiang Zemin turned over key elements of the reins of power to Hu Jintao. Jiang retained a key post in the leading military organization, the CMC, through September 2004, then stepped to the background, indicating that a clear transition to Hu's leadership had begun.

Hu assumed power in a period of continued economic growth and prosperity, but also at a time when the founding ideology of the party—Marxist-Leninist-Mao Zedong Thought—continues to erode in the face of the success of China's market economy and the rising wealth and independence of its private sector. Ironically, continued movement to the capitalist free market and economic growth are critical for the CCP to maintain power and legitimacy. An economic downturn is perhaps the most dangerous threat to China's internal security—that is not to say that the CCP does not have other concerns for domestic stability.

Internal Security Environment

The People's Armed Police (PAP) emerged in the 1990s as the key organization for the maintenance of domestic security after the international embarrassment of using the tanks of the People's Liberation Army (PLA) to brutally suppress the "democracy" movement in Tiananmen Square. While the PLA remains the ultimate guarantor of the political power of the CCP, the PAP, lightly armed and equipped and greatly increased in size over the last decade, conducts the day-to-day security tasks and maintenance of internal and border security. Outlined below are several of the key areas of concern with current or potential impacts on domestic stability.

Korean Refugees

Reports of food shortages and famine in North Korea (the Democratic People's Republic of Korea or DPRK) by international and nongovernmental humanitarian and aid agencies underscore North Korea's problems. While the focus remains on the DPRK's role in WMD proliferation and its development of nuclear weapons, thousands of North Koreans have fled into China, hiding among the Chinese Korean minorities in the region or moving through China hoping to reach the safety of South Korea (the Republic of Korea or ROK). China has refused to treat the escaping Koreans as political refugees and continues to conduct forced repatriation in contravention of international law. Not only has this been an international embarrassment for China, but it also has caused problems in its bilateral relations with South Korea, a relationship it has nurtured diplomatically and economically since the late 1980s. Recently China has reportedly moved additional security forces, including elements of the PLA, into the region to deal more forcefully with the problem.

The Tibetan Problem

An independent theocracy in Tibet, an area China sees as vital to its national security, is troubling for the Beijing government. Foremost are the historic problems with India and of control along the long common border between India and Tibet. India provides a home for the exiled Dalai Lama and thousands of his followers. China fears the looming security problems of this vast region should Tibet come under Indian suzerainty, as are Bhutan and Sikkim. China also fears religion as a unifying and guiding ideology. A free and independent Tibet could serve as a model for other minority groups occupying key strategic zones and autonomous regions along China's long land borders. China will continue to "modernize" Tibet with economic development and continue to use Han Chinese emigrants to change the social and ethnic structure of Tibet, but it will not under any circumstances let go of its strong grip of this region.

The Problem of Chinese Muslims

The issue of Muslim terrorists in Xinjiang will be addressed later in this chapter. It is important to note, however, that the Islamic faith has been a part of Chinese society since before the time of Marco Polo. The legacy of trade, both by sea to eastern ports and over the Silk Road along several routes through Central Asia, is a large dispersed Muslim population throughout the country, not only in western China. Since the founding of the PRC, the Beijing government has systematically, but not continuously, attempted to resettle Muslim areas with Han Chinese and has discouraged Muslims from practicing their faith. While these anti-Muslim policies have not been consistently enforced, it is clear that the practice of any religion in China has been and will remain a matter of grave concern for a CCP clearly worried about its borders and its domestic stability. The rise of radical, militant, fundamentalist Muslim organizations in Southeast Asia as well as changes in the internal political dynamics of a Muslim crescent bordering western China from Pakistan through Kazakhstan cannot be lost on Beijing.

Other Religious Groups

The Falun Gong, a religious sect based on indigenous religious foundations, has been brutally suppressed despite international pressure and extensive embarrassing media coverage. Christians in China, perhaps numbering into the tens of millions, continue to be persecuted and must practice their faith covertly or risk imprisonment. Given the communist policy of prohibiting the free practice of religion, the ruling party oligarchs in Beijing continue to fear religion as a dangerous organizing political device. China's consistent lack of concern with international outcries over its repressive policies is indicative of the remote possibility of any real change in terms of religious freedom in China.

Farmers, Rural Areas

China now feeds herself and even exports food. The agriculture sector led China's economic reforms in the late 1970s and 1980s. Farm prices have stagnated, however, and the government's desire to keep prices low have meant that the approximately 60 percent of the Chinese population living and working in the agricultural sector have not been able to keep pace in terms of wages and buying power with their countrymen in urban areas. In comparison with the more prosperous eastern coastal regions, China's interior provinces are seeing an increase in areas of rural poverty that have given rise to demonstrations and local antigovernment activity. The unevenness of economic growth regionally and in different sectors of the economy will only get worse without significant governmental intervention and increased investment in key areas of its interior.

Workers from State-Owned Industries

Another area of potential internal security problems is laid-off workers, while the process of closing down and transitioning state-owned industries continues. These old and often inefficient manufacturing plants and complexes are a drain on resources and, especially, on much needed investment capital. The closing of such facilities is putting hundreds of thousands of workers out of jobs at the same time as the "iron rice bowl" of socialist "cradle-to-grave" care is being dismantled. This significant alteration of both the job market and social benefit packages, including pensions, may be even more destabilizing than discontent in the rural sector.

Political Dissidents

Beijing continues to move quickly against antigovernment dissenters, although more popular involvement in local political activities appears to be encouraged at the grassroots level. As long as the economy keeps improving and the average Chinese sees his or her daily life getting better, most dissent will remain localized, nonviolent, and not focused on changing the CCP or national-level political control. Another Tiananmen is unlikely without significant deterioration in the economic situation—that is not to say that demonstrations and riots at the local level will not occur. It is unlikely, however, that such actions would spread regionally or nationally without a momentous economic decline.

Spies

The key role of intelligence and espionage in China is outlined in the concluding chapter of Sun Tzu's 2,500-year-old treatise on war. Recently several Taiwanese were arrested for spying. This should be seen in terms of continuing Beijing-Taipei sparring over China's perception of Taiwan's movement in the direction of independence. China is playing a complicated game of keeping Taiwan in line while not scaring off billions of Taiwanese investment dollars and the accompanying entrepreneurial talent that is important to China's continued economic growth. The global acquisition of technology, both military and civilian, through the use of a global network of intelligence operatives and overt collectors should not come as a surprise to any government or business working in China or with Chinese businessmen and students living and working abroad.

The Internet

Chinese attempts to control domestic use of the Internet and the detention of individuals perceived to misuse this powerful medium can be expected to continue, despite the difficulties. It remains to be seen how successful the government can be in terms of monitoring the types of information allowed on the net and how that information can be used. What probably cannot be stopped is access to outside sources of news. What can be curtailed is use of the Internet for overt antigovernment or antiparty activities. There should also be no doubt that the government fully understands the power of information-age media and the need to control it, if at all possible. In addition to a defensive effort to protect and use the Internet for domestic control, its use as an offensive tool diplomatically, economically, and militarily cannot be undervalued.

Corruption

Going in the "back door," seeking government favors through payoffs, and such illegal practices by politically connected businessmen as the seizure of property is perhaps the most serious threat to internal stability in China today. Corruption fundamentally undermines the ongoing growth of the economy. Periodic anticorruption campaigns have been part of the PRC from its founding. Corruption and attacks against the moneyed class by government officials and illegal activities practiced by those who have amassed great personal wealth over the last two decades of economic reform are having and will have an increasingly detrimental effect on the economy. If history is any guide, corruption in China cannot be stopped. It is likely that the government will make greater attempts to manage the problem, however, as the negative effects on the economy become more obvious. Nevertheless, show trials and draconian public punishment of the most egregious perpetrators or those unlucky enough to get caught is more likely than any systemic approach.

Arguably, over the short- to midterm, maintaining internal security and transitioning from the communism of Mao and Deng Xiaoping and its political accoutrements to some form of single-party, controlled, democratic, market-oriented China with socialist characteristics is the biggest task of the current leadership. The most appropriate characterization of the next decade might be the rise of neonationalist market socialist China. Central to this stabilizing maintenance effort will be the conscious building of a CCP-sponsored nationalism. A critical part of this will be a shared perception of the external threats confronting China.

External Security Environment

Modern China has historic threats and challenges along its borders and from over the seas dating back far beyond the arrival of Western traders and the Opium Wars of the mid-nineteenth century. Unsettled borders, real or imagined animosities, and China's rise as a regional power have both the potential to ignite crises and to provide opportunities to further its position as the emerging dominant regional power in Asia—secure internally and strong on its periphery. The United States is a major player in Asia, with key alliance relationships and a significant regional military presence, especially in terms of air and sea power. By virtue of its status as the world's lone remaining superpower, militarily and economically, the United States, the hegemon, has to be seen as a threat by China. The facts that the United States has been involved in three major conflicts in the Pacific area after establishing itself in the region with its victory over the Spanish and the Philippine rebels at the turn of the twentieth century and that it maintains significant forces in the area are objective proof for China's political and military leadership. Because the United States is a principal player in the region, it is a potential Chinese foe. Outlined below is a brief region-by-region synopsis of these threats and challenges to China, and the potential U.S. regional roles—complementary and conflicting.

Northeast Asia (Taiwan, Korean Peninsula, Japan, and Russia)

If Taiwan, officially the Republic of China (ROC), declares independence, the PRC will do whatever it needs to do to prevent that reality from coming to pass. The gravity of this situation is now clearly apparent in Washington, and the Bush administration moved both to clarify its position and reduce the tensions, despite domestic political opposition within President George W. Bush's own party. The PRC is committed to reunification with Taiwan, Taiwan appears to be committed to independence, and the United States is committed to a peaceful process of national reconciliation. Is any kind of middle ground possible? A military conflict in the Taiwan Strait would be disastrous for Asia and for the global economy.

The military balance across the strait appears to be moving increasingly in the PRC's favor, and although Taiwan has a competent, well-trained and well-equipped force, without U.S. assistance, a successful defense cannot be assured. The potential casualties on both sides would greatly exceed those of the two Gulf wars combined. Having benchmarked its support in 1996 with the quick dispatch of two carrier battle groups, the United States showed its commitment to Taiwan, but the global War on Terrorism, large military commitments to Iraq and Afghanistan, and continuing stationing of forces in Europe and Korea have currently stretched U.S. forces thin. It is also possible that the continued loss of American lives in Iraq could reduce the American public's support for Taiwan should it be attacked. This would be especially problematic if Taiwan were to declare independence, for all intents and purposes igniting the war. While Taiwan is China's most pressing security problem (which it considers to be an internal rather than an external problem), North Korea is Northeast Asia's most dangerous and complex flashpoint.

North Korea serves as a buffer between the United States and its ally, South Korea. Increasingly beset by economic problems, the leader of the DPRK, Kim Jong-il has used the proliferation of missile and nuclear technologies to gain international leverage to obtain food, energy, and security. The breakdown of the 1994 Agreed Framework designed to end the DPRK's nuclear program and the recent self-admission that North Korea was in possession of nuclear weapons has rekindled another crisis in the region. Currently China is working directly with North Korea to continue the six-party talks (United States, PRC, ROK, DPRK, Russia, and Japan) to help resolve the volatile issue. This leading role by China is critical to a peaceful solution.

A nuclear-armed North Korea with the appropriate delivery systems is a clear threat to the ROK, the United States, and Japan. While China is an ally of the DPRK and its forces fought alongside the North Koreans from 1950–1953, its current influence over the North is much debated and will be tested in the near term as the negotiation process moves forward. Arguably, a nuclear-armed North Korea destabilizes the region and is not in China's national interest. As part of the Bush administration's "Axis of Evil," the DPRK is a potential target of U.S. offensive action if the nuclear issue cannot be resolved. Perhaps more importantly for China, the DPRK threat could provoke a large-scale rearming of Japan, itself a serious national security threat for the PRC.

Japan has been a bitter rival of China and of Korea since the late nineteenth century. For nearly fifty years, Japan controlled significant portions of Chinese and Korean territory. Chinese and Korean memories of colonization, economic exploitation, and military occupation continue to influence regional relationships. Today there is both economic competition and cooperation in the region, but as Japan sends major military formations off to United Nations duty and to Iraq in support of the U.S. effort there, concerns over a more active and capable Japanese military are part of any future regional calculus in Northeast Asia—a prospect China would like to avoid.

One should not leave any discussion of this region without examining the role of Russia. The economic successes of the PRC, the ROK, and Japan have not been attained by Asian Russia. Nevertheless, the resources and transportation systems in the maritime provinces of Russia and Siberia and key links to European Russia have the potential to play a major role in the future. Whether this will be as a trading partner and economic collaborator or as an area of economic, and possibly military, competition is problematic. Japan and Russia have still not resolved the residual World War II territorial sovereignty issue of the Kurile Islands. The requirements and competition for access to oil and key resources by Japan, the Koreas, and China could turn this area into a future battleground. Chinese actions in the coming months and years will provide key insights into the future relations of the major powers there, whether the United States is a key player or a bystander in Northeast Asia.

Northwest and Central Asia (Mongolia, and the "—Stans")

Any future potential regional competition places Mongolia, a large country landwise, but with only slightly more than 2 million people, in the middle of the action. A former Soviet Republic that garrisoned several army divisions during the Cold War, Mongolia (Outer) has ethnic ties to Chinese Mongolia (Inner). Mongolia sits astride a major invasion corridor into China that has historically seen its most dangerous security threat coming from the north. Isolated and landlocked, Mongolia, having gained its independence in the early 1990s, now must develop without Russian economic or military assistance. Mongolia has tried to build a more representative government and to take advantage of its natural resources and its potential for tourism. Mongolia's future lies in maintaining cordial relations and economic ties with both Russia and China.

In 1996 China, Russia, Kazakhstan, Tajikistan, and Kyrgyzstan (Uzbekistan joined later) formed the Shanghai Cooperation Organization (SCO) ostensibly to further regional stability and increase peaceful resolution of a wide variety of issues, including economic cooperation and the development of energy resources. The movement of the United States into this part of the world to build and maintain military bases to support the global War on Terrorism and the operations in Afghanistan has complicated great-power relations in the region. China shares a short border with Afghanistan, but has a long history of dealing with tribal and ethnic threats in and from these regional states.

South Asia (Pakistan, India, Nepal, and Bangladesh)

Pakistan has been a solid ally of the PRC since 1950 and continues to maintain a close relationship with this pivotal nation in South Asia. Pakistan, China, and the United States worked together to provide weapons, training, and support to the mujahideen fighting the Soviets in Afghanistan from 1979 to 1989. In an effort to further stability in the region, China has been working to improve its relationship with India and could potentially play a key role in defusing the crises in the Kashmir (China claims part of this area, as well as India and Pakistan) and especially in regards to any future regional nuclear confrontation.

The Maoist insurgency in Nepal is also an area of concern in the region. Thousands have died when the rebels attacked local landowners and the traditional governmental system while calling for major changes in how the nation is ruled and administered. While Maoist in ideology, the insurgents do not appear to be supported by China; rather, this seems to be a classic indigenous insurgent movement with limited outside support. Muslim Bangladesh, formerly East Pakistan, also has had a long and close relationship with China. Poor, overpopulated, but geographically located to serve as a potential staging area in any future conflict between China and India, the PRC continues to maintain a friendly relationship and to make modest weapons systems available. Bangladesh also shares a border with Burma (Myanmar), a transition state to the economically dynamic and politically complex Southeast Asian region.

Southeast Asia (ASEAN Economics, the Burmese Basket Case, Muslim Terrorists, and the South China Sea)

The Association of Southeast Asian Nations (ASEAN) is currently composed of ten countries (Burma, Laos, Thailand, Cambodia, Vietnam, Singapore, Indonesia, Malaysia, Philippines, and Brunei). With a combined population of approximately a half a billion, it is extremely diverse politically, militarily, culturally, and economically. ASEAN members have significant potential as a regional economic grouping. Individually, several also have the potential, history, and geographic location to play influential roles in China's rise to regional power.

Burma (Myanmar) is run by one of the most egregious human-rights-abusing regimes in the world. The opium crop, environmental destruction, smuggling of drugs and natural resources, and trafficking in human beings are central to this regime's stability, economy, and longevity. Burma's key strategic location and resources have caused China and other neighbors to generally overlook its shortcomings and build mutually beneficial relationships. Chinese access to intelligence collection facilities and arms sales serve to advance Chinese long-term interests in access to the Indian Ocean and regional surveillance, and the landline of communication into Southeast Asia from Yunnan Province.

Burma, China, Vietnam, Cambodia, and Thailand all border the small, troubled communist nation of Laos. Its location as a landlocked internal line of communication in Southeast Asia gives it a regional importance that is often overlooked.

Thailand, a United States treaty ally, maintains cordial relations with China but not with Burma. China has the potential to play a role as interlocutor between Burma and Thailand should a crisis occur. A friendly relationship with China was to a certain extent forced on the government in Bangkok in the early 1970s when the United States withdrew from Vietnam and Southeast Asia, leaving Thailand alone and isolated.

In the late 1970s Vietnam, now fully estranged from China and with at least the acquiescence of its Russian allies, invaded and occupied Pol Pot's Kampuchea (Cambodia). This was in direct contravention to Chinese demands for Vietnam not to invade. With Vietnamese forces now on the Thai border and refugees occupying its territory, the Bangkok government turned to China for support and assistance. Through the 1980s China, Thailand, and eventually the United States shared a common enemy, Vietnam, and all three provided aid to their client factions in Cambodia. After Vietnam pulled out of Cambodia in the mid-1990s, China became heavily involved in providing economic assistance to the government in Phnom Penh, helping to nurture friendly relations and position itself for future influence in this centrally located impoverished nation.

Currently, the relationship between China and Vietnam, who fought a short but costly war in 1979, has greatly improved. Likewise, the United States' relationship with Vietnam is much improved and moving toward closer economic and diplomatic relations, possibly including enhanced military-to-military relations. China still casts a wary eye toward Vietnam and would likely look very unfavorably on any base access or long-term use by the U.S. military. American forces using bases in Vietnam would not be seen in the same light as similar activities in Thailand, Singapore, or the Philippines that do not have a recent history as a direct threat to China.

China's relations with the predominantly ethnic Chinese city-state of Singapore, located on perhaps the most strategic choke point on any oceanic line of communication in the world, has been excellent since the Deng Xiaoping era in China. In the predominantly Muslim states of Indonesia and Malaysia, however, that surround Singapore, China has had a more troubled history and continued strained relations despite increased economic trade. Both of these states have small ethnic Chinese minority populations with significant business clout that are often made the scapegoats of domestic political and financial shortcomings. Furthermore, these two states remain suspicious of the potential for Beijing to exercise influence in their internal affairs.

An upsurge in radical Muslim terrorist activity in an arc from Indonesia through the Philippines has the potential to adversely affect the region's economic growth and political stability. China, Japan, and the United States have significant interests and markets in this area. The Philippines is a treaty ally of the United States and is perhaps the most strategically located territory in the Asia-Pacific region. While U.S. military bases closed in the early 1990s, recent terrorist activities by the Abu Sayyaf Group on several of the southern islands prompted a request for the return of U.S. military units. The United States continues to provide forces to train and work with the armed forces of the Philippines as it tries to deal with the terrorist threats and maintain stability in the face of other domestic perils.

The "Chinas," the PRC and the ROC (Taiwan), have long-standing territorial disputes and overlapping claims with the Philippines, Vietnam, Brunei, and Malaysia in the South China Sea. While no major oil fields have yet been discovered in or near the Spratly (Nansha) or the Paracel (Xisha) islands, the South China Sea has prime fishing areas. The PRC claims sovereignty over virtually all of these island groups and has established and manned small outposts and facilities. Although there has been no repeat of the late 1980s sea battle where PRC forces attacked and destroyed Vietnamese naval vessels, China does not hesitate to use military power to protect its claims. Despite the potential for conflict, the PRC has soft-pedaled its disagreement with the regional players and has concentrated on improving economic relations and building positive relations with ASEAN and its member states.

At least for the near term, China sees its primary security task as maintaining domestic stability, which is best accomplished by continued economic growth and international trade. At this time, China really has no significant external threats or challenges to its sovereignty. Its military forces remain defensively arrayed while it slowly but steadily builds a more professional force that will be better manned, trained, and equipped for modern warfare.

Terrorism Threat and Response

In the aftermath of September 11 and President Bush's announcement of the global War on Terrorism, the PRC was provided an opportunity to gain international legitimacy in its long battle against the predominantly Muslim populations in Xinjiang (New Territories) in China's far west. Seen by some as "freedom fighters" or persecuted minorities, the non-Han Chinese populations of Turkic Uighurs and other Muslim ethnic groups of Central Asia are now part of the global terrorist infrastructure—and now fair game for harsher treatment at the hands of the PRC government and security apparatus. This has provided China an opportunity to play the role of the good global citizen while continuing its harsh treatment on these ethnic minorities.

There are more than fifty officially recognized minority groups that inhabit the key border regions of China from Korea to Afghanistan to Vietnam. A major portion of the People's Liberation Army and elements of the PAP are deployed to permanently garrison key minority areas or to be available as a quick-reaction force in the case of local or regional instability anywhere on the periphery of China.

Military Structure and Defense Policy

Since the beginning of the Deng era after the decade of internal turbulence of the Great Proletarian Cultural Revolution, the PLA and its subordinate elements (the PLA ground forces; the People's Liberation Army Air Force or PLAAF; the People's Liberation Army Navy or PLAN that now includes a small marine corps; and the 2nd Artillery, which constitutes its strategic missile force) have been streamlined and professionalized. In addition, the PRC maintains a huge militia force capable of returning to "People's War," should the security situation dictate. Since its inception in the early 1980s and spurred on by the embarrassment of the use of PLA tanks in Tiananmen Square, the PAP has steadily grown in size and capability while greatly increasing its role in domestic security missions. While military modernization was the last of the PRC's "four modernizations" announced in the 1970s, today the PLA has moved far beyond the doctrine, tactics, and manning of Mao-era People's War.

Defense White Paper

For several years now the PRC has published a national defense white paper outlining its view of the current security situation, its overall strategy, and the status of its national defense policy and organizations. In the 2002 edition of its white paper, China lists its interests as:

> Safeguarding state sovereignty, unity, territorial integrity, and security; upholding economic development as its central task and unremittingly enhancing the overall national strength; adhering to and improving the socialist system; maintaining and promoting social stability and harmony; and striving for an international environment of lasting peace and a favorable climate in China's periphery.[1]

The underlying foundations of this "defensive" doctrine are clear—internal stability, secure borders, and return of lost territories (Taiwan). What is also clear is that without a strong economy the means for providing a strong defense establishment suitable for China's emerging military strategy of "active defense," is not possible. To be capable of winning local wars under modern, especially high-tech conditions, China's military will have to continue a transformation that really began in the 1970s when Deng Xiaoping called for a streamlining of the PLA and movement from a People's Army that was more "red than expert" to a smaller, better equipped, more rapidly deployable force. This is not an inexpensive proposition for any developing country. China's post–Deng Xiaoping Communist Party leadership does not have revolutionary military credentials or close connections with the PLA leadership. Perhaps more problematic is the fact that the more money spent on improvements in the military detracts from investment in national infrastructure and loans to businesses. Exploiting emerging technologies to underpin the continued economic growth is critical to the party's legitimacy and national stability.

Defense Budget

Much is made of the double-digit increases in the PLA's funding over the last decade. The exact amount of defense spending is difficult to ascertain, but even doubling official figures of over US$20 billion, China's defense budget pales in comparison to that of the United States (10–15 percent of U.S. expenditures). What is also hard to ascertain are the resultant costs of the "soft" upgrades: increased education for the officer corps; improved training for all ranks; large-scale joint exercise programs; and a better lifestyle to retain this smaller, but more professional, better equipped, and ready force. China's fiscal outlays to accomplish even modest military transformation are enormous. While terrorism, guerrilla wars, and violent insurgent activities are ongoing in Iraq and Afghanistan, the rapidity of the collapse of national armies and conventional forces in the face of America's overwhelming military power cannot be lost on China. Luring a foreign invader in and reverting to a People's War is always an option for a nation nearly the size of the United States, populated with almost a fifth of mankind. If the PRC wants to project power regionally or successfully defend foreign incursions on its periphery, however, expensive weapons systems—not "made in China"—must be procured, trained on, maintained, and exercised to effectively transform the PLA into a force capable of successfully conducting modern war.

Weapons Sales and Purchases

To make a bad paraphrase, "One man's arms sales are another man's proliferation of WMD." When two of the PRC's long-term and close allies, North Korea and Pakistan, have nuclear weapons and missile technology, can there be much doubt that China has played a significant role? The PRC has and will sell its indigenously produced weapons to friends, allies, and potential security partners to further its own national interests and to make money. After 9/11 and with greater international calls for adhering to proliferation protocols, China is likely to be more circumspect in its sale of components of WMD and delivery means.

China will likely continue to sell conventional weapons to Pakistan, Bangladesh, Burma, and other friendly states in Asia and Africa who want and can afford, for the most part, outdated but generally reliable military equipment. China's most pressing problem, however, is not what it sells, but what to buy. China's senior military policy makers are making critical decisions on what to purchase, in what quantities, and where and how these systems should be deployed. The PLA must acquire advanced systems, especially for its air and naval arms, that can make a difference and are capable of competing with modern American and European arms and military technology found throughout the Asian-Pacific region.

Although there are reports that France, Germany, and Israel may be willing to begin selling arms to China in the future, any sale of U.S. weapons to China as happened in the 1980s is unlikely but not impossible. Russia remains China's only major provider of modern weapons systems. A brief discussion follows of some weapons acquisitions by the PLA.[2]

Air

Two modern Russian fighter aircraft, the Su-30 and the Su-27 with advanced air-to-air missiles and possibly air-to-ship missiles, have been acquired over the last several years for employment in the PLAAF and People's Liberation Army Navy Air Force (PLANAF). While currently the numbers are relatively small, with licensed production significant quantities may be added to the force. In addition, China is purchasing key enhancements for its air forces: the A-50 Mainstay, a Russian version of airborne warning-and-control aircraft system (AWACS); electronic warfare aircraft and unmanned aerial vehicles (UAV); and an air-to-air refueling capability. These systems procured in sufficient numbers and flown by competent and well-practiced crews would constitute a significant upgrading of the PLA's air capability.

Sea/Amphibious

Much has been made of China's impressive "Naval Leap Forward." In addition to adding improved indigenously produced frigates and destroyers, the acquisition of up to four Russian Sovremennyy guided missile destroyers with an advance ship-to-ship missile system and ten to twelve Kilo-class diesel submarines, as well as the domestic development and production of attack and ballistic missile submarines are significant upgrades to the PLAN. Rumors remain afloat about China's plans for an aircraft carrier, either purchased from a foreign source or domestically developed. While the prestige and status of adding a carrier battle group to the PLAN would be significant, a true carrier naval warfare capability would require more than one carrier and the necessary support ships. The cost of procuring, maintaining, and operating the carrier battle group ships and its air complement would seem to be prohibitive for at least a decade and probably longer.

China is expanding and improving its naval infantry, or marines. There are also indications of an increase in the indigenous production of modern amphibious shipping. A marine force with sufficient lift to attack Taiwan with multiple divisions does not yet exist. Any amphibious assault on Taiwan would demand a complex and practiced command and control system and the ability to coordinate a huge joint force of air, land, and, especially, sea elements. Having a naval force capable of giving the U.S. Navy pause in operations around Taiwan may be within China's grasp. Having modern equipment and having a competent naval force, especially given the PRC's lack of naval tradition, however, are two very different matters.

Land

The PLA is a force being reduced in size to more effectively utilize the improvements in its indigenously produced land warfare equipment. A modern, technologically advanced tank, the Type 96, is being built in significant numbers, while older systems are being up-gunned and fitted with more technologically advanced systems. With more than twenty corps-size units (the United States currently fields four corps) and over eighty division and brigade-size formations, the cost of upgrading the entire force with modern combined arms warfare-capable systems is immense. The PLA is probably still the largest land force in the world, but its modernization and transformation is uneven. More to the point, this is not a force that is currently capable of force projection and is generally garrisoned throughout the country to secure China's vast borders. While several quick-reaction units have been formed, China continues to equip and man a Cold War model land force.

Space and Missile Technology

China has put a man into space and shows every indication that it will continue to move forward in manned-space activities. In addition, China has developed missile technology to the point where it is able to orbit and maintain a space-based intelligence collection, surveillance, and global positioning and navigation capability for military use. China is building and improving its intercontinental ballistic missile capability that can range the entire U.S. mainland. China also continues to build and deploy hundreds of short-range systems that threaten Taiwan. The advantages of being a modern space power with capable and survivable short, medium, and long-range missiles have not been lost on China.

Special Operations

Very little has been published on the PLA's Special Operations capability. However, given the Soviet Spetnaz model, the extensive North Korean capability, its own guerilla warfare tradition, and the fact that Special Operations is not highly reliant on advanced technology, China certainly has the potential to build a large and competent Special Operations capability, including small commando units that would be very useful in a wide variety of missions along the border areas of China, not to mention in an attack on Taiwan.

Information Operations/Information Warfare (IO/IW)

In the 1990s the Chinese began to write and publish extensively on information warfare. This has created a major debate in the United States on just how extensive and advanced China's capability really is. Despite some obvious similarities with U.S. IO/IW doctrine and thought, it became clear that China is making a major effort in this emerging area of modern warfare. IO/IW is a key capability for conducting asymmetrical warfare. Western technical advances in precision strike capability and computer- and advanced communications-aided military decision making and intelligence data handling are highly dependent on information systems not only for targeting but also for guidance, command, and control. China cannot hope to compete with modern U.S. military technology without using asymmetrical measures to even the playing field.

Emerging Military Capability

The future path for China's military is slowly emerging. Over the next ten to fifteen years, given even modest economic growth, the PLA can certainly transform into a more modern and capable military establishment. This force will be smaller, professionally trained and educated, equipped with modern foreign-supplied and improved indigenous weapons systems. However, traditional weaknesses in logistics, in transportation, and in joint command and control are only slowly being turned around. Nevertheless, the PLA will provide the military strength to enhance the Beijing government's economic and diplomatic influence in regional affairs.

Conclusions and Outlook

The primary focus of the PLA and the PAP will likely remain as insuring domestic stability especially in the vulnerable regions on China's periphery (Yunnan, Tibet, Xinjiang, Inner Mongolia, and along the Korean border). Over the next five years the military balance on the Taiwan Strait will begin to tip to Beijing's advantage unless Taiwan gains access to Western military technology and the will to acquire key defensive military systems. The re-arming of Japan, a major withdrawal of U.S. forces, or a significant change on the Korea Peninsula (war or reunification) would likely cause China to relook at its commitments in terms of the pace and extent of its military transformation.

The outlook for the near term is for Sino-American relations to continue to improve. Today's strategic and tactical accommodations could rapidly evaporate, however, as China and the United States, two great powers with a presence in Asia, come to grips not only with the security dynamic unleashed by the September 11 attacks, but also with areas of fundamental and real disagreement. As the U.S. *National Security Strategy* cautions:

> There are, however, other areas in which we have profound disagreement. Our commitment to the self-defense of Taiwan under the Taiwan Relations Act is one. Human rights is another. We expect China to adhere to its non-proliferation commitments. We will work to narrow differences where they exist, but not allow them to preclude cooperation where we agree.[4]

Notes

This chapter reflects the opinions of the author and is not the official position of the U.S. Army or the U.S. government.

1. *The National Security Strategy of the United States of America,* September 2002, page 27.

2. See www.china.org.cn/e-white/20021209/index.htm.

3. A primary official source for information on what systems the Chinese have and will acquire is U.S. Department of Defense, *FY04 Report to Congress on PRC Military Power: Annual Report of the Military Power of the People's Republic of China,* May 28, 2004.

4. *The National Security Strategy of the United States of America,* September 2002, page 28.

Suggested Readings

Bernstein, Richard and Ross H. Munro. *The Coming Conflict with China.* New York: Alfred Knopf, 1997.

Garver, John W. *Face Off: China, the United States, and Taiwan's Democratization.* Seattle: University of Washington Press, 1997.

Griffith, Samuel B. *Mao Tse-tung On Guerilla War.* New York: Praeger Publishers, 1961.

———. *Sun Tzu Art of War.* New York: Oxford University Press, 1963.

Kristof, Nickolas D., and Sheryl WuDunn. *China Wakes.* New York: Random House, 1994.

Lieberthal, Kenneth. *Governing China: From Revolution Through Reform.* New York: W.W. Norton, 1995.

Overholt, William H. *The Rise of China: How Economic Reform is Creating a Superpower.* New York: W.W. Norton, 1993.

Shambaugh, David. *Modernizing China's Military: Progress, Problems, and Prospects.* Berkeley: University of California Press, 2002.

Spence, Jonathan. *Mao Zedong.* New York: Viking Penguin Group, 1999.

———. *The Search for Modern China.* New York: W.W. Norton, 1990.

7

India

Confidence amid Change

Satu P. Limaye

Introduction

India at the beginning of the twenty-first century continues the transitions under way at the end of the twentieth. India's efforts to reshape itself internally and redefine itself abroad are proceeding, taking into account India's internal conditions and external realities. The country's recent politics are characterized by the rise of the conservative, nationalist Bharatiya Janata Party (BJP), the weakening of the once dominant Congress Party (INC), and coalition governments. India's economy is edging toward faster rates of growth and fewer restrictions on trade and investment. India's identity struggle between secularism and Hinduism is today stronger than in earlier years when major domestic conflicts revolved around regional and caste identities. And its relations with the world exhibit a combination of diplomatic outreach and self-assertion. In all of these ways India's once vaunted Nehruvian Consensus [1] (named after the country's first and longest-serving prime minister, Jawaharlal Nehru) on socialism, secularism, and nonalignment has eroded but has not been eradicated.

India's commitment to a highly regulated, inward-looking economy began to weaken in the 1990s, following a debt crisis in 1991. The reforms that were launched have lifted India's economic growth rates to nearly double the level of the preceding forty years (from roughly 3.5 percent to 6 percent on average), but still below the rates of India's fast-growing neighbors in Southeast and East Asia—most noticeably China. On the other hand, partly because of India's marginal reliance on external capital, India has been less susceptible to the kinds of economic, social, and political dislocations produced by the 1997 Asian financial crisis. India's economic reforms continue to be the subject of political wrangling, obstruction by vested interests, and

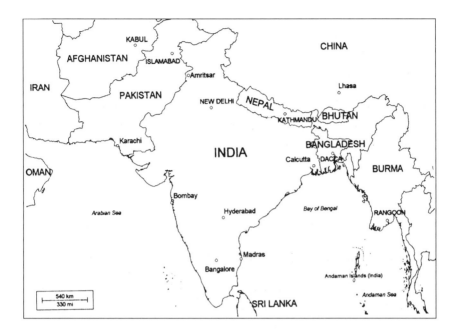

ideological debate—though there is virtually no prospect of the steps taken thus far being reversed. The key questions are whether India will build on its record of reforms and at what pace. A number of legal and regulatory changes have been pushed through to liberalize trade and investment both at home and from abroad. Three continuing problems of India's economy are high fiscal deficits, an inflexible labor market, and poor infrastructure.[2] Reforms and the resulting faster growth rates, when combined with a rate of population growth that is burdensome but manageable, could lead to reductions in the still high levels of poverty. As yet, India's economic impact on the world is marginal. While India has 17 percent of the world's population, it has only 2 percent of the world's gross domestic product (GDP) and 1 percent of world trade.[3] On the positive side, India is internationally acknowledged as a profitable destination for outsourcing of services and expertise in software and computers.

Contrary to some expectations, India's international posture and external security environment have not collapsed following the end of the Cold War. Though India did lose its main political, economic, and military partner in the former Soviet Union, India has managed to adjust to the new context with some notable successes, including constructive ties with the United States, renewed ties with China, and enhanced ties with Southeast Asia. India was not formally recognized as a nuclear weapons state, following its

1998 tests, and the diplomatic and political fallout of its nuclear tests has been largely overcome. India-Pakistan relations remain poor, despite highly publicized efforts over the past decade to initiate improvements—including, most recently, in 2004. Fundamentally, India remains wary of a unipolar international order in which its room for maneuver is constrained. It continues to seek strategic autonomy and a multipolar order, with India as one pole.

India's commitment to democracy has not faded, though it is a different democracy than in Prime Minister Nehru's tenure. India's democracy today is in some ways deeper and more inclusive than in the past. The power of the elite continues to ebb, however unevenly and fitfully, with the rise of lower caste involvement in politics at the national, state, and local levels, not only as voters, but also as officials at the highest levels. India's governance is being indigenized. A common complaint in India is that these changes produce more political turbulence and unpredictability in the form of short-lived governments, rougher politics, and the hurly-burly of coalition machinations. But India is also edging its way toward a more inclusive politics that is reflective of the country's underlying forces and its people. That these processes of social transformation, economic reform, and foreign policy adjustment are being undertaken within a democratic framework is a testament to India's innate strengths.

India's national security and defense attitudes and its policies are also showing signs of change. India's 1998 decision to conduct five nuclear tests and declare itself a nuclear weapons state (NWS) is the most cited and dramatic element of departure from the past. The Kargil conflict in 1999 (when Pakistan-backed fighters intruded into Indian-occupied Kashmir and were dislodged by Indian soldiers) spurred a number of major studies on India's defense structure and organizations. India's military forces are firmly under the control of the elected political leadership and civilian bureaucrats. At times there is chafing about what members of the military perceive as excessive civilian control and oversight, but there is little push for fundamental change, and civilian control of the military is extremely unlikely to diminish. The Indian defense budget hovers at around US$15 billion, with steady increases over the past several years. This amount is about 2.5 percent of India's GDP. Military requirements and capabilities, defense doctrines, and decision-making structures remain under ongoing review.

Political Framework

India's democracy persists, albeit with flaws. A boisterous political process is carried out openly at the local, state, and national levels. Indeed, to the chagrin of some, India seems always to be in the midst of an election. Civic, professional, and nongovernmental organizations are active and free of government control. A thriving English and vernacular-language media reports, reflects, shapes—and at times distorts—public debates. In spite of India's courts being infamous for their inefficiencies and delays, they are largely respected and increasingly activist in holding government to account for implementing its own laws. Key national organizations such as the National Human Rights Commission and the National Election Commission are seen as independent and impartial although human rights violations and electoral irregularities do sometimes occur. The creation of new states has gone hand in hand with the devolution of power to states and village councils, though the central government retains considerable powers. Regional and other "identity" political parties (e.g., lower castes) encompass a large segment of voters and require accommodation from the two national political parties—the BJP and the INC.

India is a parliamentary democracy comprising the House of the People (Lok Sabha) and the House of the States (Rajya Sabha). The prime minister is the head of government, though the president is the head of state and the Supreme Commander of the Indian armed forces. Apart from the formal structures of the government, a number of notable developments have occurred in India's politics. First, the BJP, with its conservative, nationalist agenda, has emerged as a national party, garnering support in the north and south and across social and economic groups. BJP-led coalitions have governed India since 1999. Second, there has been a substantial weakening of the previously dominant INC. By 2000, in fact, the INC had lost three consecutive national elections, and India had completed a decade without a Nehru or Gandhi family member (the founders and stalwarts of the INC) as prime minister. Mrs. Sonia Gandhi, the widow of assassinated former Prime Minister Rajiv Gandhi, took the helm of the party that year, and in the 2004 national elections Congress pulled off a stunning upset by defeating the BJP. However, Mrs. Sonia Gandhi declined the prime ministership and instead supported Dr. Manmohan Singh as prime minister. Third, India's politics are now coalition politics. Neither the BJP nor the INC is likely to take power without the support of regional and other parties—as proved to be the case with Congress' victory in the 2004 elections. The net effect of these three macro changes in Indian politics is that two major parties continue to battle for national preeminence but rely on coalition partners to form governments.

Internal Security Environment

India faces a plethora of internal security challenges ranging from insurgencies and secessionist movements to religious strife and social unrest. The most pronounced insurgencies are in Jammu and Kashmir and northeast

India (i.e., mainly in Assam and Nagaland). A violent insurgency in Punjab state in the 1980s has faded, and a full political process has been reestablished in the state. In addition to these insurgencies and secessionist movements, there continues to be religious strife between Hindus and Muslims. The 2002 communal carnage that led to the deaths of an estimated one thousand Muslims in the state of Gujarat is the most recent manifestation of religious violence that has been rising for over two decades. In the past several years there has also been a rise in violence against Christians, and intense controversy surrounds the conversion of tribal peoples to both Hinduism and Christianity. Caste conflict is also an endemic feature of Indian political and social life—particularly in rural areas where most of India's population lives.

India's internal problems are a drain on the country's coffers and security forces. One report noted that from 1975 to 1996, the ratio of government troops to the population rose 71 percent—mostly in the form of paramilitary forces. Aside from the increase in the number and use of security forces for internal security, the effects of doing so can be devastating. A case in point was the use of the army to storm the Sikh religion's holiest temple two decades ago. Operation Bluestar resulted in mutinies by Sikh soldiers, and India's then Prime Minister Mrs. Indira Gandhi was assassinated by her Sikh bodyguards. While a mix of carrots and sticks have been employed by the Indian government to manage internal conflicts, some of which are likely to be matters of ongoing governance rather than swift and complete solutions.

External Security Environment

Many analysts predicted that the end of the Cold War would be calamitous for India because its main military and economic patron and diplomatic shield, the former Soviet Union, collapsed. But all has not been bleak for India's external security environment. The most difficult challenge continues to be the ongoing insurgency in Jammu and Kashmir, supported by India's neighbor Pakistan. The Kashmir conflict has led India and Pakistan to war twice (three times if one counts the brief but bloody Kargil conflict in the summer of 1999). The Kargil conflict derailed a heady attempt at rapprochement between the Indian prime minister, Atal Bihari Vajpayee, and his then Pakistani counterpart Nawaz Sharif (deposed in a coup by the current president, General Pervez Musharraf in 2001). More recently, tensions over Kashmir once again brought India-Pakistan animosity to new heights when explosions rocked the Jammu and Kashmir legislative assembly in October 2001, and when militants opened fire in India's parliament compound in December. For roughly the next eighteen months, acute tensions and the cut off of transit services and the withdrawal of emissaries bedeviled bilateral relations.

By early 2004, however, India and Pakistan began "talks about talks" that are supposed to lead to a "composite dialogue," including ones about the Kashmir dispute. While the reopening of transit and diplomatic ties are encouraging, few expect any quick or final resolution of the Kashmir problem or of underlying India-Pakistan tensions.

Other developments relating to India's external security are much more hopeful. With the United States there has been a steady warming of relations since former President Bill Clinton visited India in the spring of 2000—the first sitting American president to visit the country since 1978. Under the George W. Bush administration, relations with India have improved further. Though India declined to send troops to Iraq to support reconstruction and peacekeeping following the end of major combat operations there, the United States and India have strengthened their cooperation through the renewal of military ties (suspended following India's nuclear tests in 1998), cooperation on missile defense, and a warmer, fuller political dialogue. Nevertheless, divergences on a number of international security and economic interests, nuclear issues, and low levels of trade and investment continue to inhibit a full blossoming of the bilateral relationship.

India has also made considerable progress in its Look East policy of improving ties with Southeast Asia and East Asia. India has not only improved bilateral relations with a number of individual states, but it has been accepted as a member of a number of regional organizations such as the Association of Southeast Asian Nations (ASEAN) Regional Forum (ARF) and now holds an annual "ASEAN Plus India" bilateral dialogue (separate from, but on par with, the dialogue between ASEAN and China, South Korea, and Japan).[4]

Even relations with China have improved somewhat in the last few years. While a contested border and China's support to India's arch rival Pakistan with military supplies and alleged weapons of mass destruction continue to rankle Indian strategists and officials, incremental progress has been made on the border problem, political dialogue has picked up, and Sino-Indian trade ties are booming. Though suspicions and doubts about China persist, and though Indian defense planners continue to make decisions about doctrines and acquisitions with at least an eye toward China, India-China relations today are much improved. Overall, India's international political profile is higher than during the past four decades, though its economic role remains far below potential.

Terrorism Threat and Response

From India's point of view, its main terrorist problem is in Kashmir, and Pakistan is the "epicenter" of terrorism directed at India both in Kashmir and elsewhere in the country. The fifteen-year-old Kashmir insurgency has been the focus of India's antiterrorism military and diplomatic initiatives.

The September 11, 2001, terrorist attacks on the United States had profound impacts on India, as did the subsequent attacks by militants on the Jammu and Kashmir legislative assembly in October and on India's national parliament in December 2001. First, India offered immediate and substantial military and other forms of assistance to the United States following the September 11 attacks. Indeed, there was considerable surprise within the United States about the nature and content of India's offer, given its earlier sensitivity and reticence about military cooperation with the United States. Second, India sought to link the attacks on the United States with its own antiterrorist efforts in Kashmir by having the Bush administration place certain militant groups on the U.S. State Department's Foreign Terrorist Organization (FTO) list, and press Pakistan to halt its support for cross-border infiltration. On both counts India achieved considerable success despite the fact that Pakistan became a frontline state in Operation Enduring Freedom (OEF) to capture and bring to justice al Qaeda and Taliban elements in neighboring Afghanistan. India employed coercive diplomacy to move the United States toward these twin objectives. This coercive diplomacy involved mobilizing troops along the India-Pakistan border and along the Line of Control (LOC) in Kashmir, and threatening war if Pakistan did not cease infiltration and eliminate the infrastructure of terrorism within its territory.

Support for the United States after September 11 and efforts to get its backing regarding India's complaints about Pakistan have not been without problems and divergences between Washington and New Delhi. India has complained that the United States is narrowly concerned with terrorism against its interests but less willing to recognize terrorism against the interests of other countries. Indians, including officials, have made charges that Washington has double standards about terrorism. At especially acute points of tension over the past two years, Indians have also pointed out that while the Bush administration counsels dialogue to address India's concerns about Pakistan, it pursues preemption and the use of military force to root out anti-American terrorists. India has made complaints about Washington's unwillingness to label Pakistan a terrorist state, about its highly selective approaches to naming FTOs, and its calls for restraint and dialogue. Nevertheless, the fact is that India's post–December 13, 2001, coercive diplomacy has brought numerous changes in tone and substance to U.S. positions regarding Kashmir that are favorable to U.S.-India relations. First, the United States has characterized the Kashmir issue as a terrorist problem, placing less emphasis on the human rights and other problems there. Second, the United States moved to put certain organizations that India has long deemed as terrorist outfits on its own FTO list. Third, the United States moved to squarely place a degree of responsibility on Pakistan and its leadership to halt infiltration across the LOC.

While India's engagement on the terrorism issue has focused on the United States, given its ability to influence Pakistan, New Delhi has also sought to use the terrorism issue as part of its diplomacy more generally. For example, India, in its diplomatic outreach to Southeast Asia, has signed a number of counterterrorism, information sharing, and extradition agreements with regional countries. India has perceived that shared concerns about militant Islamic terrorism are an additional factor of commonality between itself and several states in Southeast Asia. Meanwhile, India's wider diplomacy continues to beat on the terrorism drum to rally support for pressure on Pakistan.

Military Structure and Defense Policy

India maintains the second-largest army in the world, with total armed forces of 1.3 million active servicemen and servicewomen and first-line reserves of another 535,000. India's army traditionally has been the dominant service, receiving the largest share of the military budget. This reflects not only historical factors, but the reality that India's primary security threats are land-based, emanating from Pakistan and China. While the army's primus inter pares ("first among equals") role is unlikely to change, India has begun to allocate increased funds to the navy, which has had few capital improvements since the mid-1980s. The navy is also expected to incorporate some major purchases such as the aircraft carrier *Admiral Gorshkov* from Russia. The Indian defense budget hovers at around US$15 billion and has had steady increases over the past several years. Current defense spending is about 2.5 percent of India's GDP. No sharp changes in the defense budget are expected.

India's ongoing efforts to modernize its armed forces are constrained by budgetary, bureaucratic, personnel, and technology constraints. India's approach to equipping its armed forces has been twofold: develop indigenous systems and procure equipment from abroad. India has a vast defense production network, but the output generally has been delayed and less satisfactory than the military desires. Among the projects that have been delayed or faced technical difficulties are the Arjun Main Battle Tank (ABT), the Light Combat Aircraft (LCA), the Advanced Light Helicopter (ALH), and the Advanced Technology Vessel (ATV) nuclear-powered submarine. Better success has been achieved in missile development. There have been some efforts to bring in private sector investment into the state-controlled and over-staffed defense industry, but this has had only limited success due to resistance from vested interests. On the procurement front, the collapse of the Soviet Union,

India's main military supplier, was a heavy blow. Since the mid-1990s, however, Moscow and New Delhi have worked diligently to devise new modes of cooperation going beyond barter deals and outright purchases to deals that involve greater technology transfers, personnel exchanges, and joint development and production of major weapons systems. An example of the India-Russia military relationship is the agreement for joint production and development of the SU-30MKs fighter aircraft. India continues to seek other Western suppliers of defense equipment as well, including the United Kingdom and France. Israel has also emerged as an increasingly important military partner of India. With improving U.S.-India military ties, there is also greater scope for Indian military purchases from the United States.

Another feature of India's military and defense posture worth noting is the expansion of links with other countries. Apart from continued ties with Russia and enhanced connections with the United States and Israel, India has improved military logistics with Iran, Kazakhstan, Tajikistan, and Uzbekistan and is increasing military cooperation with such Southeast Asian states as Singapore, Indonesia, Thailand, and Vietnam.

The Kargil conflict in 1999 led to a series of recommendations about the structure of the armed forces and defense policy. Among the key suggestions were a new headquarters for the three military services, the creation of a Chief of Defense Staff (CDS), and the establishment of a Defense Intelligence Agency (DIA). Since then there have indeed been some modifications, including the establishment of an Integrated Defense Staff (IDS) to push "jointness" among the three military services. However, despite announced plans to do so, it is not certain that a CDS will be appointed because of interservice differences as well as concerns about civilian control of the military. Two other developments are the creation of a tri-service command at Port Blair in India's Andaman Islands and a Strategic Forces Command to coordinate control over India's nuclear delivery systems.[5]

India's military structure and defense policy remains firmly under the control of civilian bureaucrats and the elected political leadership of the country. The key national security decision-making authority is the Cabinet Committee on Security (CCS) chaired by the prime minister and comprising the home, defense, external affairs and finance ministers, the National Security Advisor, and the chiefs of the Intelligence Bureau (IB), Research and Analysis Wing (RAW), and the three military services.

Conclusions and Outlook

India is undergoing important transitions in the political, economic, foreign policy, and defense realms. As might be expected, in a country of over one billion people, with a dizzying diversity of ethnicities, languages, religions, and identities, change is both slow and at times difficult to discern. Amid change, a significant continuity in India is likely to be democracy, which continues to be regarded, especially by weaker elements of the society, as critical to having their voices heard and their demands met. India's identity appears to be slowly morphing toward a more conservative, nationalist, and Hindu outlook, though secularism is unlikely to be jettisoned officially. India's economic reforms will continue to be pursued but not at a "shock therapy" pace. India is exhibiting a more realistic and pragmatic approach to its external relations, but with a dose of self-assertion backed by its self-declared nuclear capabilities. On the whole, India appears more confident about its prospects in the post–Cold War and post–September 11 world.

Notes

The views expressed in this chapter are those of the author and do not reflect the official policy or position of the U.S. Department of Defense, the United States Pacific Command, or the Asia-Pacific Center for Security Studies.

1. The preamble of India's constitution commits the country to socialism, secularism, and democracy.

2. "India: Country Outlook," *EIU Views Wire*, Economist Intelligence Unit, January 8, 2004.

3. "India's Shining Hopes: A Survey of India," *The Economist*, February 21, 2004.

4. See Satu P. Limaye, "India's Relations with Southeast Asia Take a Wing," in Daljit Singh and Chin Kin Wah, eds., *Southeast Asian Affairs 2003* (Singapore: Institute of Southeast Asian Studies, 2003).

5. For an overview of India's armed forces, see, "Jane's Sentinel Security Assessment—South Asia," *Jane's International Defense Review*, posted February 25, 2004, at www4.janes.com/K2/.

Suggested Readings

Bajpai, K. Shankar. "Untangling India and Pakistan." *Foreign Affairs*, May/June 2003.

"India's Shining Hopes: A Survey of India." *The Economist*, February 21, 2004.

Kux, Dennis, and Ispahani, Mahnaz. *New Priorities in South Asia*. Council on Foreign Relations, October 2003.

Limaye, Satu. "Mediating Kashmir: A Bridge Too Far." *The Washington Quarterly*, vol. 26, no. 1, Winter 2002–2003, pp. 157–67.

Perkovich, George. "Is India a Major Power?" *The Washington Quarterly*, vol. 27, no. 1, Winter 2003–2004, pp. 129–44.

Saez, Lawrence. "India in 2002: The BJP's Faltering Mandate and the Morphology of Nuclear War." *Asian Survey*, vol. 43, no. 1, pp. 186–97.

Swamy, Arun R. "Deja Vu All Over Again? Why Dialogue Won't Solve the Kashmir Dispute." East-West Center: *Asia Pacific Issues*, no. 56, October 2001.

———. "Nationalist Ideologies and Misperceptions in India-U.S. Relations." Foreign Policy in Focus: Special Report no. 11, May 2000, at www.fpif.org/papers/india/index_body.html.

8

Indonesia

A Difficult Transition to Democracy

John B. Haseman

Introduction

Indonesia is one of the largest, most populous, and most diverse countries in the world. With a population of almost 230 million people, Indonesia is the world's fourth most populous country. It is the most populous Islamic country in the world with more than 180 million Muslims, most of whom practice a moderate form of Islam, in contrast to more strident strains common in the Middle East.[1] The country consists of more than 17,000 islands strung out along the equator. Superimposed on a map of the United States, Indonesia would stretch from San Francisco to Bermuda and from Canada to Mexico.

The country occupies one of the most strategically important locations in the world. The waterways between its thousands of islands link the Pacific and Indian oceans, and the country forms a series of stepping-stones between Asia and Australia. Indonesia's international straits are key strategic lines of communication vital to the movement of commercial and military shipping between the Pacific Basin and Europe, the Middle East, and South Asia. Millions of barrels of oil, huge amounts of cargo, and the commercial and military shipping of many nations pass through Indonesian waterways.

The Strait of Malacca is the heaviest-traveled waterway in the world. It is a matter of both international and regional concern, however, that its waters now experience the largest incidence of piracy anywhere in the world. The implications for security, given the rise of international terrorism, are obvious. Because of their huge size, the largest cargo ships and tankers and such major warships as aircraft carriers do not use the Strait of Malacca but rather travel a longer route through the wider, deeper, and less congested Makassar Strait (between Sulawesi and Kalimantan) and the Ombai Strait (west of the island of Timor).

In the sixth year of a difficult transition from autocracy to democracy, Indonesia in 2004 is a country with deep political and economic problems, social pressures, and internal security challenges. In addition to the difficulties inherent in any major political transition, the country must simultaneously cope with economic recovery, repair a badly torn social fabric, and manage separatist violence at opposite ends of the archipelago. Any one of these challenges is difficult enough, yet Indonesia must cope with all of them at the same time. Superimposed on these systemic problems is terrorism. The October 2002 bombing of nightclubs in Kuta, Bali, and the August 2003 bombing at the J.W. Marriott Hotel in Jakarta were carried out by both Indonesian and foreign terrorists.

Indonesia's political crisis began with the collapse in 1998 of longtime president Soeharto's authoritarian New Order government. Soeharto was forced from office in large part by the impact of the 1997–1998 Asian financial crisis, exacerbated in Indonesia by high levels of corruption among the political elite as well as Soeharto's inability to discern the rising tide of opinion against him. Since Soeharto's resignation in May 1998, Indonesia has stumbled through three presidents. Vice President B.J. Habibie succeeded Soeharto. He held office for only eighteen months and failed in his bid for reelection. Abdurrahman Wahid was elected president by parliament in October 1999 after skillful political maneuvering, even though his party had not won a plurality. Vice President Megawati Soekarnoputri succeeded to the presidency in July 2001, following Wahid's impeachment for incompetence.

The 1997–1998 Asian financial crisis hit Indonesia harder than any other country. Indonesia was forced to accept a US$5 billion emergency bailout package from the International Monetary Fund in November 1997. The nation's leadership fulfilled the terms of the loan agreement, which ended on December 31, 2003. Although considerable progress has been made toward restoring macroeconomic fundamentals, Indonesia has lagged behind the rest of Southeast Asia in its economic recovery, and it remains uncertain whether growth will ever return to the robust rates of the 1990s.

These economic travails are partly responsible for the outbreak of communal and religious violence throughout the country. The Soeharto era security apparatus kept a tight lid on domestic conflict, but in the years since then and with a less intrusive security apparatus, those tensions have erupted into the open. Economic difficulties and a more open society have also resulted in an increased support for radical Muslim organizations. The appeal of such groups as Laskar Jihad (LJ) and others, which have contributed to an expansion in recruitment of extremist terrorists, is a worrisome trend. Indonesia's first civilian defense minister in forty years, Yuwono Sudarsono, told an international audience that Indonesia remains one of the least prepared nations for developing the required social and economic institutional underpinnings that facilitate greater democracy.[2]

Indonesia's halting transition from autocracy to democracy has revealed one of Soeharto's greatest disservices to his country—his authoritarian rule prevented the development of alternative leadership capable of steering Indonesia into a more democratic era. The same tiny political elite that was a part of the New Order system and that benefited from decades of authoritarian government and corruption still largely controls Indonesia. While President Megawati herself could hardly be called a Soeharto associate, most of her government and the current members of parliament were holdovers from the Soeharto years. Newly elected President Soesilo Bambang Yudhoyono, although he served on active duty during the Soeharto era, was never a member of the inner circle of power and frequently clashed (quietly and behind the scenes) with the more hard line officers associated with Soeharto.

Political Framework

Indonesia is a country subject to multiple centrifugal forces, with fragmented geography, ethnic and religious diversity, and glaring imbalances in income distribution. Five years of muddled leadership and policy drift have adversely affected political and economic development within Indonesia and allowed security challenges to worsen. Many Indonesians believe that the country needs a strong central government to keep its volatile population at peace. While many of these people simply long for the relative stability of the Soeharto years, some are actively working behind the scenes to reinstall a new form of autocracy. Others are hoping instead that the transition to democracy, as well as decentralization of power to the provinces and regencies, will encourage alternative and competing power centers while maintaining national unity.

Indonesia must address its many challenges in the aftermath of a major electoral season which is fraught with political change and perhaps the start of a new era in Indonesian politics. Indonesia's parliamentary and presidential elections showed that the populace is more sophisticated than old-time political leaders gave it credit for. The new president will have less than a political majority in parliament and will have to govern with the cooperation of a legislature in which supporters of his opponent will be in formal opposition. This first-ever direct election of the president and vice president went smoothly and virtually without violence or marked voter fraud. This is in stark contrast to the past 35 years, during which Indonesia's constitution mandated the selection of the president by parliament, which was nothing more than a rubber stamp for Soeharto's rulings. Passage of constitutional amendments in 2002 providing for popular direct election of the president and vice president as a team is one of the most significant political measures enacted since the fall of Soeharto.

Parliamentary elections under the new legislation were held on April 5, 2004. In what became the largest one-day election in world history, more than 120 million Indonesians went to the polls to elect two houses of parliament. The election provided several interesting surprises. Most major parties lost voter share from the previous election in 1999. Two new parties combined to win almost 15 percent of the vote. This election, and the two rounds of the presidential election have provided the most interesting Indonesian political season in many years. The five major presidential candidates all selected vice presidential running mates from other political parties, continuing the de facto coalition politics that characterized the Indonesian presidency after Soeharto. No candidate won an outright majority in the July 2004 election. The winner, with about one third of the vote, was former chief security minister Soesilo Bambang Yudhoyono, a retired army general considered to be a political moderate and reformist. Mrs. Megawati won 26 percent of the vote, an improvement over her party's parliamentary showing of 18.5 percent. Mrs. Megawati's campaign performance improved, but she had to contend with a record of vacillating leadership, charges of cronyism and corruption, and the challenge posed by the potential alliance of Muslim political parties. [3]

Internal Security Environment

Indonesia's greatest internal security threat is that posed by separatist rebels in Aceh and Papua.[4] There are, however, important differences between secessionist guerrillas, whose goal is to secede from the country and gain independence, and the less doctrinaire members of popular movements whose grievances center around economic and social exploitation by the central government and who seek greater autonomy rather than formal independence.

The Acehnese have historically resisted rule from Jakarta, whether by the Dutch colonial government or that of an independent Indonesia. The most recent period of violence in the province began in the 1970s and escalated dramatically following the fall of Soeharto. After several unsuccessful cease-fire efforts, the government of Indonesia and the Free Aceh Movement (Gerakan Aceh Merdeka or GAM) signed an agreement to end hostilities in December 2002, facilitated by the Switzerland-based Henry Dunant Center.

The agreement unraveled in May 2003 due to irreconcilable differences over the basic issue of Aceh's future status as either a province of Indonesia or an independent state. The GAM never stopped pursuing a goal of independence in its propaganda and public statements, and used the five months of peace to step up recruiting and acquire new weapons. For its part, Jakarta would not change election laws to give the GAM status as a political party and will never agree to Aceh's separation from Indonesia.

When peace talks broke down, President Megawati declared martial law in Aceh in May 2003, and the military launched its largest operation since the 1975 invasion of East Timor.[5] Military leaders initially predicted a six-month operation to destroy the GAM once and for all, although the head of the armed forces, General Endriartono Sutarto, in July 2003 acknowledged that the fighting might last years.[6] President Megawati eventually extended martial law through mid-May 2004, when the improved government posture allowed a downgrade of the security situation to that of "civil emergency," and returned governing responsibility to the civilian administration in the province. Security forces continue their strong operational presence in Aceh, and have seriously degraded the size and capabilities of the GAM.

The military and the president have overwhelming public and political support for their tough stands on Aceh. President Megawati strengthened her leadership credentials by her unyielding position on the issue of territorial integrity and national unity. Most Indonesians and political leaders support the high level of military operations and strongly oppose the GAM's goal of separation from the country. Newly elected President Soesilo Bambang Yudhoyono was the primary advocate of the attempt to gain a political settlement in Aceh, and he is likely again to attempt to end the secessionist challenge by both political as well as military means.

At the opposite end of the country Papua also remains a security concern. Small and uncoordinated separatist groups have conducted antigovernment operations in the region for years. Those groups have begun to coordinate and communicate among one another since the late 1990s, and have increased political pressure as well. Grievances in Papua include the small return to the province of the fruits of its enormous natural resources, concern about a huge government-sponsored influx of non-Papuan transmigrants, and resentment of the government's and the military's attitude toward local tribal populations. Both Aceh and Papua benefit from special autonomy legislation that allows the two, among other benefits, to retain a far larger share of the income from petroleum and forestry production than in the past.

Given the vast natural resources in both Aceh and Papua and the importance of national unity and territorial integrity to Indonesia's political and military leaders, Jakarta will never allow either Aceh or Papua to secede. Resolving the security problems in both provinces will require a reduction in tensions between the government and the people, agreement on effective local autonomy, and, on the part of the security apparatus, moderation when carrying out legitimate police and defense operations. Without such efforts, the outlook is years of sporadic conflict and inflamed relations between Jakarta and these two far-flung provinces.

Quite aside from the threat of separatist insurgencies in Aceh and Papua, Indonesia also must face the internal threat posed by continual outbreaks of severe violence among ethnic and religious groups—known in Indonesia as SARA (SARA stands for "ethnicity, religion, race, and intergroup" conflict). The reputations of the Indonesian police and military have been damaged by revelations of human rights abuses throughout the country. The police and armed forces are further hampered in their domestic security responsibilities by a lack of training and equipment for nonlethal crowd control. Selected military and police units in some urban areas have received this kind of training and equipment, but when violent incidents occur frequently, in widely scattered areas of the country, trained units and equipment do not stretch nearly far enough, and quick-reaction transport is far from adequate.

A more disturbing phenomenon is a legacy of deliberately instigated violence in which the government or powerful individuals incite or inflame SARA incidents for political purposes. Soeharto was a master at using the security and intelligence agencies as agents provocateurs to control or eliminate potential rivals and to fragment political opposition In the years since his downfall, ambitious and powerful groups and individuals have also employed violence as a political tool. Whether the desired goal is to destabilize a presidency, protect business and financial interests, or to assert political power, violence remains an unfortunate element in Indonesia's political equation.

The most notorious recent example of this was the formation and deployment of the radical Muslim group LJ. This extremist organization was initially the tool of a shadowy cabal of hard-line military and civilian figures opposed to the reform efforts of former president Abdurrahman Wahid. LJ was designed as a zealous Islamic militia intended to confront Christian gangs in the Moluccas (also spelled Malukus), as well as to embarrass the president. The organization is widely believed to have been formed, financed, trained, and equipped with the assistance of army, police, and civilian government officials. Despite presidential orders to prevent LJ from becoming involved in the Moluccas violence, thousands of its fighters were transported across Java and moved by ship to the islands, where they were primarily responsible for expanding the sectarian conflict there. Once involved in the sectarian violence in the Moluccas and the Poso region of central Sulawesi, LJ expanded in size and power and was soon beyond the control of its sponsors.

LJ leaders announced in the aftermath of the Bali bombings that the organization had disbanded. Nevertheless, it is more likely that it has merely moved into the shadows and can be quickly reformed on call. There are disturbing reports that LJ cells have moved into several cities in Papua, where they could become involved in sectarian violence similar to that perpetrated in the Moluccas.[7]

External Security Environment

Indonesia is blessed with its regional neighborhood. No country poses a threat to Indonesia's security, though nonstate external threats include international terrorism, piracy, and transnational crime.[8] By far the most serious of these is the threat posed to Indonesia, as well as to the region and the national interests of a plethora of countries, including the United States, by international terrorists and terrorist organizations.

The continuing revelations of the inroads made by Jemaah Islamiyah (JI) (Islamic group or Islamic community), the Southeast Asia terrorist organization, indicate a serious peril to Indonesia. The goal of JI is to create a Muslim state comprising Indonesia, Singapore, Malaysia, Brunei, and the southern areas of Thailand and the Philippines. The organization, its role and plans, and composition of JI and other terrorist and extremist groups are beyond the scope of this chapter. (See Suggested Readings below for recommended works that examine the subject in more detail.) It goes without saying, however, that JI's ability to carry out three major bombing attacks against targets in Indonesia demonstrates that it will be a significant security threat for some time to come.

In addition to terrorism, external threats to Indonesia include piracy, fishery poaching, smuggling of goods and humans, and drug trafficking. These issues are primarily economic in nature and do not constitute a security threat that would endanger the state. But the great cost of these economic crimes drains away from Indonesia billions of U.S. dollars a year—a considerable amount.

Piracy in Indonesian waters is a significant threat both to Indonesia and to the world's shipping. In 2003 the International Maritime Bureau recorded 121 instances of piracy against merchant shipping in Indonesian waters— over one-fourth of the 445 incidents recorded worldwide.[9] While many of these were attacks against small ships for the purpose of crew robbery, there has been a disturbing rise in the number of cases in which ships were actually stolen for the purpose of the resale of their cargoes. The potential for terrorists to seize ships and use them as weapons against ports, warships, or other terrorist targets is a real danger.

Terrorism Threat and Response

Terrorism and counterterrorism have become high priorities in Indonesia, and terrorism constitutes the country's greatest externally based threat. For many months after the September 2001 terrorist attacks in the United States, however, Indonesian politicians, particularly those associated with Muslim political parties, denied that Islamic extremist groups were involved in terrorism and even refused to admit that terrorism had made inroads in Indonesia. Indonesia's population and political leadership retain an ambivalent attitude toward terrorism. Many believe, through ignorance, isolation, or zealotry, that the worldwide counterterrorism campaign is a deliberate attack on the Muslim religion and fail to see the difference between "terrorists who are Muslims" and "Muslim-sponsored terrorism."

The tragic October 2002 bombing incident in Kuta, Bali, that claimed more than two hundred lives and the August 2003 bombing at the J.W. Marriott Hotel in Jakarta that killed twelve brought home to the country the reality of international involvement in domestic terrorism. The Indonesian police gained credit for acting promptly, with international assistance, to investigate those incidents. More than three dozen men involved in the terrorist bombings have been convicted, and several were sentenced to death or life in prison. Investigation revealed ties between many of the suspects in these attacks to a spate of terrorist incidents in several Indonesian cities that took place between 2000 and 2002.

A third major bombing attack in September 2004 at the Australian Embassy in Jakarta killed 10 and injured more than 180 people—almost all of them Indonesians. In the aftermath of this bombing the leaders of several of Indonesia's largest Muslim organizations publicly condemned JI and terrorism, a marked contrast to earlier times when many Indonesians ignored or attempted to rationalize away the terrorist threat in their midst.

Evidence confirms that the Bali and the two Jakarta attacks were planned and carried out by the regional terrorist organization JI, which also is accused of numerous other terrorist plans and attacks across Southeast Asia. There still are lingering concerns, however, that Indonesian political leaders are reluctant, for domestic political reasons, to become more assertive in regional and international counterterrorism efforts because of misplaced perceptions that counterterrorism policies are inherently anti-Muslim. While Indonesian officials strike the proper notes in overseas meetings and speeches, few senior Indonesian government officials have delivered strong antiterrorism messages to the public at home.

Despite the dozens of arrests of those involved in terrorist attacks in Indonesia, several important terrorist leaders, both Indonesian and foreigners, remain at large. There is also a worrisome likelihood that there are many more Indonesians involved in domestic and regional terrorist planning. Radical Indonesian Muslims, initially tolerated because there was little publicity about their possible involvement in both domestic and international terrorism, continue to join JI and other local extremist groups from which terrorists recruit their cadre. For example, investigations have tied together individuals from LJ, the Sulawesi radical organization Laskar Jundullah, and the regional terrorist organization JI. Laskar Jundullah members have been convicted of terrorist bombings in Makassar, the provincial capital of South Sulawesi Province, and one of its key leaders, who is also connected to JI, was tried and convicted of a terrorist bombing in the Philippines.[10]

Investigations into the Bali and Jakarta bombings, and persistent research and analysis by several regional experts, uncovered a complex web of ties among extremist religious groups and criminals, as well as the deep involvement of regional and international terrorist organizations in Indonesia.[11] The worrisome reality is that, despite being a tiny minority within Indonesia's large, predominantly moderate Muslim population, violence-prone radicals can quickly gain a foothold by exploiting organizations created for other purposes. For example, Indonesian security forces have a history of controlling "rent a thug" groups for political power reasons. It seems apparent that there are many more trained terrorists and willing recruits in Indonesia than police and intelligence agencies have thus far identified. The implications for the international War on Terrorism are many, but certainly two of the most topical for Indonesia are the fertile ground for recruitment of terrorists and their support network, and the ability of terrorists to move, train, and, when necessary, escape from the country without attracting official attention.

Indonesia prosecuted those accused of involvement in the Bali bombing under the provisions of a hastily-enacted anti-terrorism law which was not passed by parliament until after the Bali bombing. In June 2004 the Indonesian Supreme Court ruled that the use of a retroactive law was unconstitutional. Adding to a confused and controversial situation, however, the court did not overturn the convictions of those involved in the Bali bombings. Indonesia will most likely have to re-try the suspects under pre-existing laws, such as those dealing with murder, assault, conspiracy, and treason. However the anti-terrorism law itself was not ruled unconstitutional, so prosecution of those arrested after enactment of that law remain legally valid, and the law has been cited in the case of the J.W. Marriott Hotel bombing and subsequent terrorist attacks in Indonesia.

Despite the political and psychological conditions affecting Indonesians' perceptions of terrorism and counterterrorism, elements of the government security apparatus have responded to efforts by the United States and regional neighbors to energize Indonesia in the counterterrorism campaign. The United States is helping to train, equip, and fund a new national police counterterrorism organization called Detachment 88. The first trainees have already entered active police duties and have distinguished themselves in the arrest of several accused Indonesian and foreign terrorists. When fully manned and trained, Detachment 88 will have a strength of four hundred and will become Indonesia's first-line counterterrorism unit. The army's Unit 81, an element of the Army Special Forces Command, is a highly skilled world-class counterterrorism organization. U.S. political constraints, however, currently prevent full military-to-military cooperation with Indonesia's armed forces because of ongoing human rights concerns. The attack on the Australian Embassy also gained new and broader powers for the chief of Indonesia's National Intelligence Agency (BIN), U.S.-trained retired general A.M. Hendropriyono. He had long called for stronger powers to direct intelligence operations of the military and other governmental departments and for the power to detain suspected terrorists without first gaining police assistance.

Military Structure and Defense Policy

The military is the single most powerful and influential force in Indonesian society. Beginning with its significant role in the struggle for independence from the Dutch, the military has always wielded enormous power in Indonesia. Indonesia's military force—approximately 350,000 in all services—is

Table 3

Indonesian Armed Forces Strength

Army	265,000
(Kostrad)	(30,000)
(Kopassus)	(5,000)
Navy	57,000
(Marine Corps)	(15,000)
Air Force	24,000
Total Strength	346,000

Source: Order of Battle data in this section is from John B. Haseman, *Indonesia,* in Jane's Information Group, *Jane's Sentinel Security Assessment: Indonesia* (London: Jane's Information Group, updated regularly).

small for the size of the country's population and huge geographical spread (see Table 3). The army is by far the dominant service, both in size and political power. The air force and navy are much smaller in size and influence.

From 1965 until 1998 the Indonesian military was known as Angkatan Bersenjata Republik Indonesia (ABRI)—Armed Forces of the Republic of Indonesia. In 1998, as a symbol of reform, the armed forces renamed itself the Tentara Nasional Indonesia (TNI or Indonesian National Armed Forces). The change reflected the devolvement of the Indonesian National Police (INP), which had previously been a fourth branch of the military, alongside the army, navy, and air force. The Department of Defense and Security was likewise renamed the Department of Defense to indicate the removal of internal security from the military's mission.

Since 1998, the TNI has implemented some important reforms that have reduced its dominant role in Indonesian politics. The military has withdrawn from day-to-day involvement in politics and does not support any political party. It remained neutral in parliamentary elections since 1998 as well as both rounds of the 2004 presidential election. It has accepted the elimination of its dedicated seats in parliament. In addition, military personnel must now retire from active service before they can occupy the thousands of civil government posts once traditionally filled by military appointees.

The country's largest and most important tactical command is the Komando Strategis Angkatan Darat-Kostrad (Army Strategic Reserve Command). Composed entirely of army personnel, but with navy and air force liaison officers assigned to its headquarters and major subordinate commands, Kostrad falls under the army chief of staff for training, personnel, and administration. However, it comes directly under the armed forces' commander in chief for operational command and deployment. In that respect, the command follows U.S. military doctrine.

Table 4

Indonesian Army Territorial Commands

Command designation, area of responsibility	Headquarters location
Kodam I/Bukit Barisan: Northern Sumatra	Medan, North Sumatra
Kodam II/Sriwijaya: Southern Sumatra	Palembang, South Sumatra
Kodam III/Siliwangi: Western Java	Bandung, West Java
Kodam IV/Diponegoro: Central Java	Semarang, Central Java
Kodam V/Brawijaya: Eastern Java	Surabaya, East Java
Kodam VI/Tanjungpura: all of Kalimantan	Balikpapan, East Kalimantan
Kodam VII/Wiribuana: all of Sulawesi	Makassar, South Sulawesi
Kodam VIII/Trikora: Papua	Jayapura, Papua
Kodam IX/Udayana: Eastern Indonesian islands	Denpasar, Bali
Kodam Jaya: Jakarta	Jakarta
Kodam Iskandar Muda: Aceh	Banda Aceh, Aceh
Kodam Pattimura: the Maluku islands	Ambon, Maluku

Source: Data in this section is from John B. Haseman, *Indonesia*, in Jane's Information Group, *Jane's Sentinel Security Assessment: Indonesia* (London: Jane's Information Group, updated regularly).

The basic structure of Kostrad consists of two combat divisions, each composed of both airborne and standard infantry brigades and battalions; a separate infantry brigade; and the expected combat support and combat service support units. In the event of impending hostilities, it would be deployed to meet the primary external threat. In the domestic security structure, its battalions can be deployed anywhere in the country where police or territorial army battalions cannot cope with disorder. Kostrad keeps a standby battalion on alert for immediate deployment.

The army's other major tactical command is the Komando Pasukan Khusus—Kopassus (Army Special Forces Command). Kopassus has played a crucial part in counterinsurgency operations in East Timor, Aceh, and Papua as well as in domestic intelligence operations. For many years Kopassus has had close links with the Australian and British Special Air Service regiments and the U.S. Army Special Forces. Many of those relationships, however, have been suspended because of allegations that its personnel were involved in directing violence in East Timor and for systemic human rights abuses elsewhere in Indonesia. Kopassus has a strength of about five thousand, organized in three operational groups, plus a training center and a counterterrorist unit.

The military's base of political power emerges from the army's territorial organization. Consisting of twelve Komando Daerah Militer—Kodam (Military Regional Commands) commanded by major generals, more than half of the army's personnel is assigned in this geographically-oriented structure that parallels civil government from the national level down to the tens of thousands of villages at the base of the population pyramid (see Table 4).

The territorial system has its base in Indonesian military doctrine, which stresses guerrilla warfare and the involvement of the entire population in any struggle against outside invasion. Under Soeharto, the territorial system became a primary instrument of political power, and it has remained so to this day. By its presence at the province, regency, district, and village levels, the military strongly influences every element of society. The territorial system is a basic element of control that continues to guarantee to the military significant political and economic powers. Political leverage throughout the civilian governmental structure is assured through posts effectively reserved for recently retired military officers.

The air force and navy feature two major tactical commands (Air Operations Commands and Fleets, respectively) each, geographically divided into eastern and western areas of operations. Both services are armed with an international variety of weapons systems, including U.S. F-5 and F-15 fighters and C-130 transports, and capital ships from the United States, the Netherlands, South Korea, and East Germany. Because of arms embargoes imposed by traditional suppliers, however, Indonesia is increasingly turning to new suppliers. Among other new equipment and arms purchases, in May 2003 President Megawati announced the purchase of Russian jet fighters and helicopters financed largely through commodity countertrade. The Ukraine, South Korea, and the Netherlands have also won contracts for major weapons systems. Poland will provide helicopters. The United States has not sold a major weapons system to Indonesia for almost fifteen years.

Indonesia has a long history of underfunding its military and police requirements, which has given rise to a huge military business empire (the police have a similar system). The government's budget provides only about one-third of Indonesia's military and police funds. The remaining two-thirds of funds for administrative, operational, and capital expenditures must be raised through an extensive business empire of both legal and illicit enterprises. For example, all three military services and the INP use their transportation assets for profit, and the army in particular has extensive holdings in the timber industry as well as many other economic sectors. On a less salubrious level, military and police personnel are involved in protection and extortion rackets, gambling, and prostitution. The size of the business empire and the amount of income it generates are among the military's most closely guarded secrets. The system was refined during the Soeharto era as a tool to control the military leadership as well as a means to allow the government to give higher priority to other funding requirements. The territorial system is the keystone of the pervasive powers of the military business empire; the two cannot be effectively separated. Although widely criticized as a tool for the enrichment of senior officers, the military business empire is in fact an important source of administrative and operational funding. Without these revenues the military could not adequately pay, feed, and house its troops, maintain its equipment, buy spare parts, or train and exercise its personnel.

Conclusions and Outlook

Indonesia is important to U.S. strategic interests in Asia and the world. The country's strategic location, natural resources, investment and market potential, and a large moderate Muslim population make it an important consideration in many U.S. policy objectives. For many years, Indonesia has been a welcome, temperate voice in international forums. A longtime leader in ASEAN and the Asia-Pacific Economic Cooperation (APEC) forum, Indonesia has played an important role in regional and global political and economic affairs.

Prior to the mid-1990s the United States enjoyed a successful multifaceted relationship with Indonesia. After the shooting of dozens of civilians by the military in Dili, East Timor, in November 1991, however, human rights issues became a determining factor in U.S. policy toward Indonesia, particularly in security matters. The cutoff of overseas military education in Western countries since the early 1990s has adversely affected the TNI's software—its personnel and leadership. A dearth of overseas experience has resulted in an inward-looking military leadership that views the world without the breadth of international experience.

After the TNI was found complicit in the egregious violence that swept through East Timor in 1999 after its populace voted to separate from Indonesia, the United States and several other countries ceased military-to-military relations and arms sales. Rather than address international concerns over human rights abuses, TNI's leadership is increasingly turning to other sources of weaponry and equipment. It is frustrated by embargoes imposed by its traditional suppliers and so far has been unwilling to make the political sacrifices demanded for resumption of normal military-to-military relations.

Since the end of U.S. military training provided to Indonesian military personnel, a generation of Indonesian military officers has been denied the professional education and personal relationships that had resulted from exposure to the role of the U.S. military in American society.[12] There are virtually no senior Indonesian military officers personally familiar with the United States and its culture, society, and policy objectives. The one-to-one friendships that make international relations and policy discussions move more smoothly are no longer present. Indonesia needs the training and both countries will benefit when Indonesia's senior officers have an appreciation of the role of the military in a democratic society.

There remains, however, a strong counterpoint. Many observers in the United States believe that brutality is ingrained in the Indonesian security forces as part of a decades-long culture of violence as a political tool and of immunity from prosecution. Those who oppose restoring the military-to-military relationship think that it would be naive to believe that either the TNI, which routinely uses soldiers as enforcers for its own businesses (illicit and legal), or those civilians willing to pay for the services they offered, would punish soldiers whose violence becomes the focus of international attention. The chain of command is ineffective in controlling the behavior of troops in the field, where most abuses occur, through its lack of supervision and failure to discipline miscreants.

The election of a former military officer as president, a man with extensive international education and experience, could lead to changes both in the untrammeled authority of the TNI, and in the relationship of the TNI and Indonesia with the U.S. and other western countries. Mr. Yudhoyono was the preferred presidential candidate in the 2004 election, which he won by the decisive vote of 60 percent to 40 percent. He was seen to be more receptive to reform within the military establishment and more politically attuned to the need for better relations with regional and world powers. His announced priorities—to fight corruption, improve Indonesia's abysmal judicial system, and move strongly against terrorism—anger well for improved economic and political security.

An economically and politically strong Indonesia would play an important role in addressing America's strategic concerns in the region and the world. Internal developments in Indonesia in the coming years will strongly influence the nation's direction for many years to come. Two possibilities seem most likely. One is that an increasingly nationalistic Indonesia becomes more and more isolated from Western influences and, beset by seemingly endless domestic problems, withdraws from its long years of beneficial international involvement. The other is that Indonesia addresses issues currently limiting some country-to-country relations, so that the dominant national interests of the United States and Indonesia determine policy across a bilateral relationship and once again the two countries can together examine the important strategic issues in the region.

In the first scenario, Indonesia could return to its situation of the 1950s and early 1960s—a nearly failed state led by nationalists who rally its population against an outside world that is blamed for the nation's problems and kept at bay by bellicose rhetoric and obstructionist policies.

A far better outcome would be an Indonesia reengaged with its neighbors and friends. A cooperating (not hectoring) military-to-military relationship will be an important aspect of the bilateral relationship because, regardless of the halting progress of Indonesia's move to democratization, the TNI will remain the most powerful element in Indonesian society. The greatest challenges to achieve this goal appear to be to communicate the issues effectively and to find a cooperative path to success. Given its size, location, and religious majority, a democratic Indonesia, fully engaged to meet common strategic objectives, would be a vital partner in addressing strategic challenges confronting the United States.

Notes

1. See Robert W. Hefner, *Civil Islam: Muslims and Democratization in Indonesia* (Princeton, NJ: Princeton University Press, 2000).

2. Address to the United States-Indonesia Society, Washington, DC, April 11, 2000. Mr. Sudarsono was appointed Minister of Defense in October 2004, the second time he has held that office.

3. Concise information on the 2004 elections can be found in International Crisis Group, *Indonesia Backgrounder: A Guide to the 2004 Elections* (ICG Asia Report No. 71) (Brussels: International Crisis Group, December 18, 2003). This, and all other ICG documents cited in this chapter, can be accessed online in PDF format at the ICG Web site at www.crisisweb.org.

4. Indonesia's view of its domestic and international security threats are described in its 2003 defense white paper: Indonesia Department of Defense, *Indonesia: Mempertahankan Tanah Air Memasuki Abad 21 (Indonesia: Defense of the State Entering the 21st Century)* (Jakarta, Indonesia: Department of Defense, March 31, 2003).

5. For excellent detailed coverage of Aceh developments, see, inter alia, the following reports: International Crisis Group: *Aceh: Why the Military Option Still Won't Work.* Indonesia Briefing, May 9, 2003; *Aceh: A Fragile Peace.* ICG Asia Report No. 47, February 2003; and Edward Aspinall and Harold Crouch, *The Aceh Peace Process: Why it Failed* (Washington, DC: East-West Center, 2003), at the East-West Center Web site at www.eastwestcenterwashington.org.

6. BBC World Service, "Aceh Offensive Could Take Years," July 7, 2003; Jane Perlez, "Indonesia Says Drive Against Separatists Will Not End Soon," *New York Times,* July 9, 2003.

7. See, inter alia, International Crisis Group, *Indonesia: Resources and Conflict in Papua.* Indonesia Report, September 13, 2002 (Brussels: International Crisis Group, 2002).

8. Indonesia Department of Defense, *Indonesia: Mempertahankan Tanah Air Memasuki Abad 21* (Indonesia: Defense of the State Entering the 21st Century).

9. "Piracy Rife in Indonesia Archipelago," Associated Press, July 24, 2003; John C.K. Daly, "The Terrorism Maritime Threat," United Press International, December 29, 2003; and International Maritime Bureau, "Piracy and Armed Robbery Against Ships: Annual Report: 1 January–31 December 2003," January 2004.

10. Jane's Terrorism and Insurgency Centre, at www.janes.co.uk, carries a lengthy series of short articles on terrorism and counterterrorism in Indonesia.

11. For a superb summary of these interlocking connections, see Sidney Jones, *Al Qaeda in Southeast Asia: The Case of The "Ngruki Network" in Indonesia,* International Crisis Group, August 9, 2002 (Brussels: International Crisis Group, 2002).

12. For background, see John B. Haseman, *The United States, IMET, and Indonesia,* USINDO Report, Issue No. 3, (January 1998) (Washington, DC: United States-Indonesia Society, 1998).

Suggested Readings

Haseman, John B. "Indonesia—Turbulent Times, From Autocracy to Democracy," in Richard J. Ellings, and Aaron L. Friedberg, eds., *Fragility and Crisis: Strategic Asia 2003–2004.* Seattle: The National Bureau of Asian Research, 2003.

International Crisis Group (various reports). *Indonesia: Overcoming Murder and Chaos in Maluku,* December 19, 2000; *Communal Violence in Indonesia: Lessons from Kalimantan,* June 27, 2001; and *Indonesia: The Search for Peace in Maluku,* February 8, 2002. These reports provide excellent detailed firsthand analysis on communal and religious violence in Indonesia are available at www.crisisweb.org.

Lowry, Robert. *The Armed Forces of Indonesia.* Sydney: Allen & Unwin, 1996. This is the most detailed study of the organization of the Indonesian armed forces.

Manning, Chris, and Peter Van Diermen. *Indonesia in Transition: Social Aspects of Reformasi and Crisis.* Singapore: Institute of Southeast Asian Studies, 2000. This publication provides varied views on the social, economic, and political history of Indonesia since Soeharto.

O'Rourke, Kevin. *Reformasi: The Struggle for Power in Post-Soeharto Indonesia.* Sydney: Allen & Unwin, 2002. This book is a fascinating and detailed account of the tumultuous weeks surrounding Soeharto's resignation and the economic, financial, political, and military machinations involved in the most important event in modern Indonesian political history.

Rabasa, Angel, and John B. Haseman. *The Military and Democracy in Indonesia: Challenges, Politics, and Power.* Santa Monica, CA: Rand Corporation, 2002. This report is an excellent analysis of current political and security trends in Indonesia.

Schwarz, Adam. *A Nation in Waiting: Indonesia's Search for Stability.* 2nd ed. Boulder, CO: Westview Press, 1999. This book is a thoughtful examination of Indonesia's political and economic history since the mid-1960s.

9

Japan

Untangling the Contradictions

Steven R. Saunders

Introduction

September 11, 2001, and actions in Iraq and North Korea have more profoundly affected Japan than any other U.S. ally. Combined with the challenges of the last decade—at the end of which nationalism had become respectably mainstream, "checkbook diplomacy" had been discredited, and constitutional reform was regarded as both desirable and inevitable—these events have produced historic and far-reaching changes in Japanese policy and attitudes. Japan is reemerging as an independent power in the Pacific, but many Western observers, missing the forest for the trees, persist in regarding Japan simply as a tangle of contradictions.

The Chinese character (Japanese: *kanji*) for the word "contradiction" combines the characters for "sword" and "shield," an allusion to a famous armor maker in ancient China who boasted that his spears could pierce any shield and his shields could withstand any spear. A visitor asked, but what if one of your spears is thrown at one of your shields?

Japan is attempting to address these contradictions: the world's second largest economy helplessly mired in sequential recession and deflation since the burst of the "bubble economy" in 1990; the world's fourth largest standing military establishment maintained by a nation with a "peace constitution" (Article 9) that, strictly construed, barely permits self-defense; a nation whose people are overwhelmingly pacifist suddenly feeling they are being bullied and provoked in a region that is not pacifist and that plays by different rules—and where bitter memories of World War II still prompt distrust of future Japanese military ambitions; a functioning multiparty democracy that has had almost uninterrupted one-party rule by the conservative Liberal Democratic Party (LDP) for over half a century; a nation producing a dazzling

143

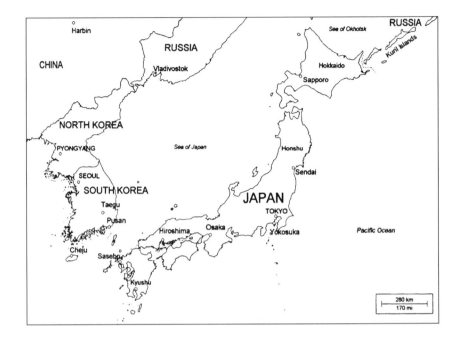

array of innovative technologies that lags behind China in its ability to put satellites into orbit; a stable society that has had forty-two prime ministers since the end of World War II, thirteen since 1981; a conservative but aging country, where the combination of low birthrates and resistance to immigration could produce a 50 percent drop in the population by the end of this century.

Since the simultaneous collapse of the external Soviet threat and the domestic bubble economy in 1990 these contradictions have prompted an intense national debate in Japan on fundamental questions about its place in the world, including the security alliance with the United States that has been the controversial core of Japanese defense and foreign policy since 1951. Even more important are issues of the floundering economy, chronic weakness in national leadership, and popular disgust with the ruling LDP and the influence of "money politics."

This debate has been conducted in an atmosphere of pessimism born of gloomy economic news, turmoil in traditional party politics, heightened regional military anxieties about North Korea and China, and domestic terrorism. But this process has produced what are, in Japanese terms, rapid and dramatic changes in public attitudes toward government, weakening bureaucratic control of the private sector, and favoring the emergence of such stronger national leaders as Prime Minister Junichiro Koizumi in 2001. It also jump-started an emerging national consensus—still reluctant and fragile—that international conditions and its own perceived self-interest impel Japan to change the way it participates in collective defense arrangements. Such changes go beyond the limited deployment of peacekeeping troops in Iraq and will require constitutional revision of Article 9, an inevitability now accepted by major Japanese political parties.

During the 1990s Japan was viewed by the United States and the European Union (EU) in the broader context of global security and political issues instead of the narrow tunnel-vision focus on trade and economic friction of 1960–1995. There have been no high profile trade disputes between Japan and the United States since 1995.

Political Framework

Japan is a parliamentary democracy with a powerless constitutional monarch. The bicameral National Diet (parliament) consists of a lower chamber, the House of Representatives, the source of real power, similar to the British House of Commons, and an upper chamber, the House of Councilors, with limited powers over the national budget. The first elections to the Diet were held in 1890 under a restricted voter franchise. Women did not gain the vote until universal suffrage was introduced in 1946.

Executive power is vested in the prime minister and the cabinet, who are responsible to the National Diet but effectively are accountable primarily to the lower house.

As in most parliamentary systems, the Diet exists chiefly to legitimate decisions of the cabinet. Each chamber has a central nonpartisan career secretariat to provide most legislative services to both members and committees. Members receive only small allowances for staff and official expenses, thus perpetuating reliance on government bureaucrats for information and dependence upon party or faction leaders and on corporate contributors for both campaign and office management funds.

The prime minister is elected by the Diet and is always the president of the party with either an absolute majority in the 480-seat House of Representatives or of the senior party in a coalition that commands an absolute majority in the lower house. Although the prime minister may come from either chamber, every post–World War II prime minister has been a member of the House of Representatives.

The cabinet consists of the prime minister and not more than seventeen ministers of state who in theory serve at the pleasure of the House of Representatives but in practice at the pleasure of the ruling party. The prime minister and a majority of cabinet ministers must be members of the Diet, but nonmembers are occasionally appointed as ministers of health, environment, and even foreign affairs. Such nonmember ministers, however, suffer from the lack of a political base.

The prime minister has the power to appoint and dismiss ministers of state, who may not concurrently hold any other government office. This requirement, similar to the United States, bars serving military officers from holding a ministerial position. It was embedded in the 1946 constitution to prevent a recurrence of the military dictatorship that seized control of the civilian government during the 1920s and 1930s, when the ministers for war and navy were actively serving generals and admirals and the military regularly forced the resignation of civilian governments by refusing to supply officers to head those ministries.

The House of Representatives consists of 300 single-member districts with plurality voting, and 180 proportional representation seats, elected from closed party lists in 11 regions. A majority is not required and there are no runoffs. Members are elected for four-year terms but the prime minister and the ruling party can dissolve the House at any time for new elections and most often do.

Since the new mixed system of direct and proportional seats was introduced in 1994, no party has been able to win an absolute majority (241 seats) at the polls and voters have shown an increasing tendency to split their party votes between the single-member and proportional balloting, generally to the detriment of the dominant LDP and the smaller opposition parties (the Communist Party and the Social Democratic Party) and to the advantage of the larger non-LDP parties (the Democratic Party of Japan and the New Komeito Party).

The House of Councilors has 247 seats, of which 98 are elected nationwide from proportional representation party lists and 149 are directly elected by plurality from multiple-member prefecture-level districts. As a result of the reforms introduced in the 1994 elections, the upper house is moving toward the model of the U.S. Senate in providing geographical representation for prefectures, much as the Senate does for states. Prior to the 1946 constitution, the upper house was the House of Peers and was similar to the hereditary British House of Lords prior to Prime Minister Tony Blair's reforms.

Councilors are elected for six-year terms, like U.S. Senators, with half the members elected every three years, unlike the Senate where one-third are elected every two years. In July 2004 membership in the upper house dropped from 247 to 242, a staged reduction mandated by the 1993 election reforms. Because of the national and large prefectural constituencies, many Councilors are former television and radio personalities, actors, and athletes, including retired baseball and sumo stars who are well known throughout Japan.

In Japanese, the title of the monarch is literally "Son of Heaven," historically—but inaccurately—translated as "emperor." Under the 1946 constitution, drafted during the American occupation and largely influenced by General Douglas MacArthur's headquarters staff, the emperor was stripped of any claim to divinity and all political authority and transformed into the "symbol of the state," a hereditary monarch with no power who accepts the "will of the people" and decisions of the Diet and the cabinet.

The emperor has far less influence in national affairs than other contemporary monarchs in, for example, the United Kingdom, Thailand, Malaysia, Belgium, or the Netherlands. The Imperial Household Agency scrupulously avoids any political involvement and trains young members of the imperial family accordingly. Even when being formally briefed by government officials, the imperial family is careful to avoid asking any question that might reveal a political point of view.

Japanese policy, laws, and regulations historically originated in the powerful ministerial bureaucracies, not in the Diet. However, over the past decade, younger parliamentarians in the dominant LDP discovered that they could draft legislation as well or better than the bureaucrats, whose reputation for omniscience had been steadily undermined by events for the previous twenty years.

Career bureaucrats are competitively recruited directly after university graduation and generally serve thirty to thirty-five years, until retirement. Because the average tenure of cabinet members, including the prime minister, is less than two years, cabinet members are often slavishly reliant on their bureaucrats to tell them what to do and say. This symbiosis prevents Japanese politicians from making mistakes because of inexperience, so long as they stick to the script, but at the cost of being able to move forward initiatives or reforms that are not favored by the conservative bureaucracy.

Likewise, Japanese ministers involved in international negotiations have in the past been at a disadvantage because ministers fear altering positions the bureaucracy had previously endorsed. This deference not only annoys foreign negotiators but also deprives Japan of tactical and transactional benefits that can only occur at the bargaining table.

The prime minister has a small personal staff, far smaller that the heads of government of most Organization for Economic Cooperation and Development (OECD) nations. Most of this staff is seconded from the career bureaucracies of various ministries and agencies.

The prime minister submits proposed laws to the Diet after they are considered in the cabinet, brought to that level by ministers who receive the final drafts from their own ministry's bureaucrats. The Diet generally approves such bills, after formal debate that permits opposition views during debate, by a party-line vote; the majority party or ruling coalition invariably wins.

From 1990 to 2004, the grip of the institutional bureaucracy on both the Diet and the economy has weakened following the burst of the bubble economy, progressive loss of confidence in bureaucratic omniscience (e.g., the Ministry of International Trade and Industry once advised Toyota against trying to become a global automaker), greater assertiveness by Japanese politicians, and by partially successful economic reforms. In addition, reform-minded elements of the bureaucracy in various ministries quietly formed informal ad hoc alliances with political leaders to achieve change. These trends have accelerated because of the post–1990 influx of foreign investment—accompanied by new foreign management ideas and business executives—in the distressed automobile, real estate, banking, and insurance sectors.

Internal Security Environment

Internal security focuses on prevention and punishment of crime and terrorism. Citizens are forbidden to own handguns. Illegal drugs are a problem, particularly metamphetamines. Japanese take pride in their country's being safe, far safer than the United States. But that feeling of safety has been undermined over the past decade.

Japan's respected national police force has an extensive street presence, resulting in low rates of crime in what is normally a law-abiding society. The top priority of the police is to be trusted by the citizenry. Resident foreigners are required to register periodically with the police and carry their residence permit at all times. In one of the most ethnically homogeneous nations on earth, it is difficult for any foreigner, terrorist or tourist, to pass unnoticed.

Japan is no stranger to terrorism, domestically called "radicalism." Japanese prosecutors and police have adopted a containment policy in dealing with both organized crime and terrorist groups, which are constitutionally difficult to proscribe. The police watch and monitor groups dangerous to society, cutting off their sources of funding if possible.[1]

Many domestic and foreign critics, however, are alarmed by the "emergency antiterrorism measures" the Japanese government has adopted since 2001 granting the national government the broadest new authority it has had since 1945 over freedom of the press, the independence of local governments, and, potentially, individual freedoms. Fears of these measures extends to the creation of "domestic intelligence operations" within the Self-Defense Force (SDF) that revive memories of the notorious wartime *kempeitai* ("thought police").

No terrorist cells linked to al Qaeda or other related Middle East terrorist organizations have yet been discovered in Japan, but authorities are on guard against the possibility of foreign groups forming an alliance with domestic "radical" or criminal organizations for terrorist services on contract. The investigation of the Aum Shinrikyo (Aum Supreme Truth) sarin gas attack of 1995 uncovered substantial evidence of foreign links.

There are documented Middle East links to the Japanese Red Army (JRA) terrorist group, formed around 1970 and, although much diminished, still active. The group's fugitive leader is believed to be hiding in Syrian-controlled areas of Lebanon. Between 1970 and 1988, the JRA mounted terrorist attacks in Israel, the United States, Italy, and Malaysia and hijacked two Japanese airliners. The group is suspected of organizing cells in Asian cities, including Manila and Singapore.

The national police categorize criminal organizations into four major groups: (1) traditional organized crime organizations analogous to the Mafia (*bouryokudan*), popularly known in the West as *yakuza*, which are well-organized, disciplined, and tend to be established in the open (neighborhoods in the vicinity of various yakuza headquarters buildings are known to be especially safe); (2) racketeering groups (*sokaiya*), often blamed for local "protection" rackets and for extorting money from corporations to avoid disruption of stockholder meetings; (3) right-wing movements (*uyoku*); and (4) extreme left-wing movements (*kyoku-sa*).

Japanese experts say this taxonomy reveals police "indulgence" toward right-wing movements: while left-wing movements are characterized as "extreme," the police term for right-wing movements omits that adjective. Some journalists and scholars speculate about covert connections between these underworld organizations and the legitimate business and political communities.[2]

In 1995, 5 members of the Aum Shinrikyo religious cult released deadly sarin gas into the Tokyo subway system during the morning rush hour, killing 12 people and injuring more than 5,500. In 1994 the cult had launched a smaller sarin attack in Matsumoto that killed 7 and injured 591. It had also been accused of kidnapping and murder. Japanese police and prosecutors were widely criticized for moving against Aum Shinrikyo only after the Tokyo sarin attack. Although authorities have since managed to neutralize the cult, repeated efforts to put it out of business have failed, underscoring the difficulties Japan and other democracies face in dealing with domestic terrorism. Japan has many lay religious organizations, most associated with Buddhism, and Japanese authorities are reluctant to target them for fear of appearing to violate rights of religion and freedom of assembly.

The Group Regulation Act of 1999 was directed at controlling organizations like Aum Shinrikyo. The law expanded upon the existing Anti-Subversive

Activities Law that critics say the government did not properly apply. In 2000 the police invoked these laws to put Aum Shinrikyo under intense surveillance for the maximum permitted term of three years.[3]

Aum Shinrikyo reportedly amassed more than US$1 billion in assets, hammered together links with the Soviet KGB and Japanese crime syndicates, built a huge chemical factory, and allegedly infiltrated the Japanese police and military. Aum Shinrikyo has renamed itself Aleph and still has about one thousand members, down sharply from the twelve thousand at its peak. The trial of the group's leader, Asahara, started in 1996. He was finally sentenced to death in 2004 for murder, kidnapping, and gun- and drug trafficking, but appeals in such high-profile criminal cases can drag on for a decade or more.

External Security Environment

North Korea—the Democratic Peoples Republic of Korea (DPRK)—is the most immediate threat to Japan, following years of provocative probing of Japanese sea and air defense perimeters by North Korean gunboats and fighter aircraft, admitted development of nuclear weapons, kidnappings of Japanese citizens, relentless espionage, and, most alarming to Japanese, the 1998 launch of a ballistic missile over Japan, which Pyongyang claimed was a failed satellite launch.

Japan's relations with both Koreas are colored by the bitter heritage of Japanese colonial occupation of Korea from 1905 to 1945, which Japan formally annexed in 1910. Both North and South Korea frequently play the "war guilt" card in dealings with Japan. After centuries of invasion and domination by its powerful neighbors, Koreans have an understandable paranoia about foreign intentions. Japan has never signed a treaty with North Korea ending World War II. Evidence of improved Japan-South Korea relations was the recent repeal by Seoul of the ban on importing any item relating to "Japanese culture."

Tokyo was leery of the Clinton administration's "charm offensive" toward North Korea but joined the United States, South Korea, and the EU in financing Washington's initiative to offer North Korea incentives to stop its nuclear program through oil shipments and development of energy-generating capacity through the Korean Peninsula Energy Development Organization (KEDO). Tokyo has strongly supported the six-party talks (United States, Japan, China, Russia, North Korea, and South Korea) with North Korea initiated by President George W. Bush.

In September 2002 Prime Minister Junichiro Koizumi visited Pyongyang for bilateral talks with Kim Jong-il, during which Kim admitted that North Korea had for years been abducting Japanese citizens to serve as "teachers" in intelligence training facilities. Although some abductees have since re-turned to Japan, North Korea had not permitted all families to join them, which outraged Japanese public opinion. In 2004 the Diet adopted economic sanction legislation against North Korea. Koizumi made another visit to Pyongyang in 2004 to seek repatriation of hostage families. Japan's allies fear that Koizumi's visits, during both of which he delivered commitments of "humanitarian assistance," could undermine the common front of the six-party talks and encourage Kim Jong-il to continue to expect *quid pro quo* payments in exchange for ceasing lawless behavior. Some conservative American critics of Koizumi accuse him of appeasement. However, Japanese and Chinese critics of alleged American intransigence in the six-party talks say that some form of engagement with Pyongyang, like Koizumi's visits, is necessary to make headway in persuading Kim to act more rationally and to deter him from further provocations.

Although Japan is wary of possible regional destabilization because of reunification friction between Taiwan and the People's Republic of China, fears of Chinese military ambitions have partially receded. Relations with Beijing have warmed since President Hu Jintao took office in 2003, but China, South Korea, and other Asian neighbors continue to be irritated by the Japanese prime minister's practice of making public visits to the Yasukuni Shrine in Tokyo, a Shinto memorial to Japan's war dead that includes memorial tablets of several war criminals. In 2004 Chinese President Hu Jintao made an "unpublicized" tit-for-tat visit to the memorial hall for the victims of the 1937–1938 "Rape of Nanjing," when Japanese troops under the command of Emperor Hirohito's uncle allegedly slaughtered over 300,000 Chinese sol-diers and civilians.

Japan's territorial disputes have been limited to four areas: the Northern Territories, a group of four islands off the coast of Hokkaido that were seized by the Soviet Union in the closing days of World War II; the potentially oil-rich Senkaku Islands, southwest of Okinawa (called the Diaoyu Islands by China and Taiwan, the other claimants); the tiny Takeshima/Tokdo Island in the Japan Sea, now occupied by South Korea; and the annoying but less significant South Korean initiative to rename the Sea of Japan the East Sea. Japan is pursuing peaceful negotiations in all cases, but there have been low-level nonlethal skirmishes between Japan and China in the Senkakus.

Terrorism Threat and Response

Japan has been a key U.S. ally in combating terrorism since the September 11 attacks, in which twenty-four Japanese died, and was the first nation to deploy in support of the United States against the Taliban. In 2001 Japan sent five naval ships to the Indian Ocean, including two military oil tankers, to provide logistical support. Those tankers carried 50 percent of the oil needed for the United States and its coalition partners in Afghanistan. The Air Self-Defense Force also provided transportation services. Reaction to these deployments by Japan's neighbors was generally mild.

The 2004 deployment of Japanese SDF troops in Iraq was the largest and most risky Japanese military mission since World War II. SDF forces previously participated in several United Nations (UN) sanctioned humanitarian and peace-keeping operations (PKO), following passage of a 1992 law allowing restricted PKO participation by the SDF. The Iraq dispatch is the farthest distance Japanese military forces have deployed into a theater of war since 1915, when Japan, as an ally of Great Britain, sent a naval squadron to the Mediterranean during World War I.

Japan made early multibillion dollar commitments of financial assistance to both Afghanistan and Iraq. Japan cochairs the International Conference on Reconstruction Assistance to Afghanistan and was the first major U.S. ally to offer reconstruction aid to Iraq, initially pledging more than US$1 billion. Japan was already the largest donor of global economic development assistance, and these additional obligations are expected to force reductions in Japanese overseas development assistance (ODA) elsewhere around the globe.

Consistent with U.S. initiatives, Japan is moving to provide its citizens with machine-readable biometric passports and is attempting to comply expeditiously with U.S. Department of Homeland Security (DHS) shipping security requirements. Japan and the EU expressed unhappiness with the arbitrary deadlines DHS has unilaterally established, and the U.S. government has proved to be somewhat flexible in making adjustments.

Japan's antiterrorism initiatives included a diplomatic offensive; passage by the Diet of the Anti-Terrorism Special Measures Law to allow the SDF to supply fuel and air support to U.S. and UK forces and permitting the SDF to protect "important facilities" in Japan, including U.S. bases and SDF facilities; adoption of the International Convention for the Suppression of Terrorist Bombings and the International Convention for the Suppression of the Financing of Terrorism; and measures to freeze assets of the Taliban, Osama bin Laden and other persons and groups related to terrorism.

Military Structure and Defense Policy

Stung by global criticism of its "checkbook diplomacy" during the Gulf War of 1990–1991, when Japan contributed US$13 billion in cash but no troops, Japanese leaders were motivated to avoid a repetition of that embarrassing episode. A 1992 law allowed the Japanese SDF forces to take part in UN-led PKOs, limited to providing medical, logistical, and engineering assistance, as well as rear area support and humanitarian aid. Japan annually contributes 20 percent of the UN PKO budget. Soon afterward, the first overseas deployment of SDF forces in a UN-sponsored Blue Helmet PKO was to Cambodia. Since then, the SDF has had limited deployments, mostly on humanitarian missions, to Angola, Mozambique, El Salvador, Zaire-Kenya, Israel-Syria-Lebanon, Bosnia-Herzegovina, and East Timor. In 1998 a major U.S.-Japan agreement provided for SDF logistical support to U.S. forces in Asia.

The need for an expanded military has been discussed openly in Japan since the early 1980s as Japanese leaders came to the view that it was unwise to assume an endless American military presence in East Asia, especially considering the weak U.S. economy and Japanese triumphalism at that time. In 1995 Japan contemplated developing its own nuclear capability because of the North Korea threat but quickly abandoned the idea to avoid frightening its Asian neighbors.

The U.S.-Japan Security Arrangements continue as the basis of Japanese defense policy. For most of the post–Korean War period, since Japan created the SDF in 1954, foreign military observers expressed the concern that SDF doctrine was so exclusively defensive as to be limited to the command "die in place." But Japanese military doctrines have evolved to a more sophisticated strategy over the past decade.

The SDF is firmly subordinated and committed to civilian control, a status unquestioningly embraced by SDF uniformed personnel, unlike many of Japan's Asian neighbors where a military coup is viewed as the equivalent of a "snap election." A cabinet-level minister heads the Self-Defense Agency (SDA), which is attached to the prime minister's office and is not an independent ministry. The SDF is composed of three services: Ground (GSDF), Air (ASDF), and Maritime (MSDF) plus a reserve force (RSDF). The Japan Coast Guard is part of the Ministry of Land, Infrastructure and Transport.

The SDF is heavily weighted toward high technology military applications, similar to the United States. Japan spends about the same amount on defense as China, but China has ten times the number of uniformed military personnel. Because of political sensitivity about Article 9 of the constitution, Japan has limited defense spending to 1 percent of gross domestic product (GDP). But Japan's US\$45.8 billion annual defense budget makes it the fourth largest military spender in the world, after the United States, Russia, and China.

The SDF now have 140 ships, 480 aircraft, and approximately 240,000 uniformed personnel, including 148,000 ground troops. Japan is participating in the U.S.-sponsored missile defense program. The SDA has also embarked on a program for restructuring the high command along the lines of the U.S. Joint Chiefs of Staff model, including restructuring its intelligence operations to include domestic intelligence gathering.

Defense equipment is expensive because of the lack of competition among Japanese contractors, who are prohibited from exporting most types of military equipment and therefore are deprived of economies of scale. The largest defense contractors are Mitsubishi Heavy Industries, producing the 50-ton Type 90 battle tank and armored vehicles; Ishikawajima-Harima Heavy Industry Company, which builds and repairs military aircraft, including the F-2 fighter-bomber, a modified version of the U.S. F-16 with advanced phased-array radar but lacking the stealth technology of warplanes like the U.S. F-22; and Mitsui Engineering & Shipbuilding and Hitachi Zosen Corporation, builders of the Osumi-Class Transport Ship, a helicopter-carrying assault ship. Japan is planning to build a new generation of 18,500-ton helicopter-carriers double the size of existing MSDF ships. The *Forrestal*-class of U.S. aircraft supercarriers is over 79,000 tons. Because full-size aircraft carriers are viewed as offensive weapons, Japan has limited the size of these new vessels.

The U.S. military presence in Japan is concentrated in Okinawa and in the naval ports of Yokosuka, north of Tokyo, and Sasebo, near Nagasaki. Publicity surrounding the rape of an Okinawa girl by U.S. Marines in 1995 reignited calls for the United States to reduce its forces in Japan, especially Okinawa. The United States agreed to some accommodations in the Status of Forces Agreement and in military use of Okinawa, which is strategically and geographically desirable as a platform for U.S. forward deployment after the loss of U.S. naval and air force bases in the Philippines in 1991. Sources indicate that none of Japan's forty-six other prefectures were eager to accept U.S. military installations.

Japan pays US$5 billion annually in host-nation support of the fifty thousand U.S. military personnel in Japan. Both American and Japanese critics of Japan's self-imposed limit on defense spending say it encourages dependence on the United States and allows Japan to evade political and military realities. U.S. critics say that since the Korean War, the United States has provided US$900 billion to subsidize Japanese defense. Comments of this nature have served to accelerate Japanese thinking about independent national security arrangements against the day the U.S. military presence in Japan and South Korea diminishes.

Conclusions and Outlook

Japanese politicians, bureaucrats, and journalists are robustly questioning the conventional wisdom about defense and security policies under the watchful eye of Japanese voters who accept a form of revived nationalism but are fearful of anything that smacks of the totalitarian military rule of the 1930s and 1940s. Amending Article 9 of the constitution is no longer the "third rail" of Japanese politics, similar to the sensitive issue of Social Security in the United States. Casualties from such overseas military peacekeeping deployments as in Iraq could produce a public backlash that might freeze reform temporarily. Nevertheless, most observers agree there is an all-party consensus in the Diet on the need for overall constitutional revision, including Article 9, a process that could stretch out for another five to ten years.

Visible changes in traditional patterns of decision making include a new willingness by bureaucrats to implement or at least not seditiously impede political decisions by the prime minister and the cabinet. The pressure of external events guarantees that security issues cannot simply be put on the shelf indefinitely. The ruling LDP has pledged to propose Article 9 amendments by 2005.

Yukio Okamoto, a former career Foreign Ministry official who served between 2002 and 2004 as chairman of the prime minister's Task Force on Foreign Relations, reflects the views of a significant part of the generation now moving into the senior ranks of the career bureaucracy who believe that the status quo is an intolerable choice for Japan. Arguing for greater independence in Japanese policy, he wrote in a prestigious Japanese foreign policy quarterly in 2002:

> Japan's usual line, "Our hands are clean, so we are the best suited to act as peace mediator," does not win sympathy in the international community. If our hands are clean, that is because we have not lifted a finger to help in concrete ways. The person who watches from the bench and then sides with the winner does not make many friends.[4]

Inevitably, more independent Japanese policies on security and foreign affairs will strain relations with the United States after fifty years of what critics on both sides of the Pacific call American paternalism. Some observers believe that Asian fears of Japanese remilitarization may gradually recede as Japan distances itself from the U.S. orbit and is no longer viewed as America's agent in the Pacific, a major change from the previous post–World War II perception by Japan's neighbors that tolerated Japan as an instrument of U.S. policy because the U.S. presence in Japan was a guarantee of Japanese good behavior. Ironically, because the U.S.-Japan Security Arrangements are popularly accepted in Japan, moves by the Japanese government to change defense policy and stretch Article 9 are always carefully packaged in terms of fulfilling those treaty obligations. Japanese leaders are seeking a middle road that preserves the U.S. alliance while pursuing a more independent policy. But some Koizumi critics say that the LDP is using Iraq and the War on Terrorism as an excuse to roll back many of the post–World War II limitations on the power of the central government.

The Japanese economy appears to be improving marginally, but Japan's banking system is still staggering under the weight of nonperforming loans and distressed assets after the collapse of the bubble economy in 1990. Following the rapid appreciation in the value of the yen in 1986 (*endaka*), Japanese banks lent companies extraordinary sums of money, at traditionally low Japanese interest rates, secured by grossly exaggerated values of real estate collateral. With borrowed money, not equity financing through the stock market, companies expanded operations to increase market share and went on a global shopping spree for real estate and other assets. Profitability was ignored.

At the peak of the bubble Japanese banks had imputed values of real estate so high that the value of all real estate in Tokyo alone was equal to the total value of real estate in the entire state of California. But when banks started calling in the loans, the collateral was insufficient. Japan has so far been reluctant to nationalize these nonperforming loans.

Party politics are in a transitional stage. Since 1946, all but four prime ministers have been members of the conservative LDP, a collection of rival, personality-oriented, nonideological factions. Most LDP prime ministers during the 1970s and 1980s were reliable senior party leaders who did not want to rock the boat and had few passionate policy goals; strong politically nimble personalities like Prime Ministers Eisaku Sato and Yasuhiro Nakasone were the exceptions.

Japanese voters had no incentive to complain; the economy was expanding, personal incomes were rising, Japan was the envy of the world, and the nation's international duties, primarily as an ally of the West against the Soviet threat, were manageable. But public sentiment toward the LDP and Japanese politicians turned sour in 1990 when the bubble burst, signaling a sudden end to twenty years of increasing Japanese prosperity, undermining the guarantee of lifetime employment that benefited half of Japan's workers, and, worse, damaging hard-won Japanese pride and self-confidence. The simultaneous but unrelated collapse of the Soviet Union ushered in a new set of international challenges for which the LDP leadership was equally unprepared. The LDP has not won a majority in the lower house since 1990. Japanese commentators note that the LDP steadily lost standing with voters thereafter because it revealed that its chief goal was remaining in power at any price. After being out of power between 1993 and 1994, the LDP shocked voters in 1994 by joining a coalition under the Japan Socialist Party, the

LDP's polar opposite in ideology, in exchange for cabinet seats. The LDP has been forced to form coalitions after every election since 1994.

Voters are deeply disappointed with the LDP but still tend to embrace the party at times of crisis, in large part because the LDP holds onto a near-monopoly of parliamentarians with significant government experience. The main opposition, the Democratic Party of Japan (DPJ), which opposed the SDF deployment to Iraq, is composed of such a wide range of ideologies that internal agreement on issues is difficult. The primary unifying factor within the DPJ is fervent opposition to the LDP. The DPJ has steadily gained seats in the last few elections but does not yet have a leader to equal Koizumi. The DPJ and other opposition parties have benefited from voter preference for "manifesto" elections, where parties offer a specific set of promises, instead of appeals to party loyalty or ideology.

Junichiro Koizumi was an unusual choice for the LDP in 2001, a reform-minded maverick with movie-star charisma and national popularity but perceived as a threat by many traditional LDP leaders. Nevertheless, faced with prolonged voter anger, the LDP elected Koizumi head of the party and subsequently prime minister. In Koizumi's reform efforts, he often confronts long-entrenched special interests within the LDP. But he is seen, at least for the time being, as the salvation of the LDP, and party leaders have no choice but to stick with him. Koizumi also benefits, despite fluctuations in his unusually high popularity, from the national consensus that, again for the time being, "there is nobody else but Koizumi." Recent minor political scandals affecting the next generation of LDP leaders appear to further cement the LDP's reliance on Koizumi. The LDP also has difficulty in recruiting fresh candidates because of the rise in the number of Diet seats transferred from father to son within political families.

During the heyday of "Japan, Inc." in the 1980s, some American policy makers called for the United States to emulate Japan's industrial policy system, with close ties between the government and the private sector. But following the burst of the Japanese bubble and the 1997 Asian financial crisis, those industrial policies are now dismissed as "crony capitalism," and Japanese CEOs look to the United States for entrepreneurial models and methods. Japanese corporate governance is undergoing order-of-magnitude changes.

Japan faces a variety of other economic challenges. Despite strong current account and trade surpluses, Japan suffers from chronically high budget deficits and the largest national debt of any OECD country. One of the world's greatest beneficiaries of the liberalized World Trade Organization (WTO) multilateral trading regime, Japan is still viewed by its trading partners as resisting trade liberalization in order to protect its inefficient domestic agriculture and other noncompetitive sectors. Like China, with its dollar-peg for the renminbi, Japan is criticized for intervening in currency markets to adjust the value of the yen, though not to the same degree as China.

Demographic time bombs include the largest percentage of elderly in the world, expected to reach 25 percent of the population in a few years, and one of the lowest birthrates. By 2025 there will be one elderly person for every two persons of working age, a higher old-age dependency ratio than any other major industrial country. If current trends continue, the population could shrink 28 percent to 50 percent by the year 2100, accompanied by a cumulative 20 percent reduction in real GDP.

Japan faces a daunting agenda. A nation with a peace constitution that for half a century fervently trusted in America, multilateralism, the United Nations, international consensus, and economic strength as its bulwark against global turmoil is struggling to adjust to a new world order that demands Japan "take sides," and act independently, that insists Japan cannot be all things to all nations. However, the Japanese genius in synthesizing foreign experience, ideas, and technology, and eventually developing a uniquely Japanese response is good reason for long-term optimism. The Japanese timetable for resolving problems has rarely been what the rest of the world would want, but the final result usually satisfies all but the most unreasonable expectations.

Notes

1. Naofumi Miyasaka, "Terrorism and Anti-Terrorism in Japan," in Michael Green, *Terrorism Prevention & Preparedness: New Approaches to US-Japan Security Cooperation* (New York: Japan Society, 2001).

2. Ibid.

3. Ibid.

4. Yukio Okamoto, "Across to the Indian Ocean: Japanese Aid to Afghanistan," *Gaiko Forum,* p. 18, vol. 2, no. 3, English Edition/Fall 2002.

Suggested Readings

Cha, Victor D. *Alignment Despite Antagonism: The United States-Korea-Japan Security Triangle.* Stanford, CA: Stanford University Press, 2000.

DiFillipo, Anthony. *The Challenges of the U.S.-Japan Military Arrangement: Competing Security Transitions in a Changing International Environment.* Armonk, NY: M.E. Sharpe, 2002.

Green, Michael. *Terrorism Prevention & Preparedness: New Approaches to US-Japan Security Cooperation.* New York: Japan Society, 2001.

Hook, Glenn D., Julie Gilson, Christopher W. Hughes, and Hugo Dobson. *Japan's International Relations: Politics, Economics and Security.* New York: Routledge, 2001.

Ikenberry, G. John, and Takashi Inoguchi. *Reinventing the Alliance: U.S.-Japan Security Partnership in an Era of Change.* New York: Palgrave Macmillan Press, 2003.

Inoguchi, Takashi. *Japan's Asian Policy: Revival and Response.* New York: Palgrave Macmillan Press, 2002.

Maniruzzaman, Talukder. *Japan's Security Policy for the Twenty-first Century.* Dhaka: University Press, 2000.

Okamoto, Yukio. "Across to the Indian Ocean: Japanese Aid to Afghanistan." *Gaiko Forum*, p. 13, vol. 2, no. 3, English Edition/Fall 2002.

Osius, Ted. *The U.S.-Japan Security Alliance: Why It Matters and How to Strengthen It.* Westport, CT: Praeger Publishers, 2002.

Tu, Anthony T. *Chemical Terrorism: Horrors in Tokyo Subway and Matsumoto City.* Ft. Collins, CO: Alaken Press, 2002.

—— 10 ——

Laos

Learning to Live with the Outside World

William M. Carpenter

Introduction

Although in the early 1990s there were trends within Laos suggesting a shift away from a communist-style political and economic structure, elections in the late 1990s reversed the trends. Old party members replaced young technocrats who had been trying to liberalize the economy. There has been some departure from full state control, toward a market economy—prices are set by the market, farmers are allowed to own their land—but this small land-locked nation still clings to the goal of remaining a communist state.

Virtually defenseless on its own behalf, Laos has for centuries been at the mercy of its neighbors, most of whom have had malign intentions. Illustrative of the vulnerability of Laos to foreign intervention is its geography—all of its sixteen provinces border a foreign country.

Political Framework

The present system of government was imposed on Laos during and after the Vietnam War years, mainly by the former Soviet Union but also by China and by North Vietnam (under Soviet domination). The only legal political party in Laos is the Lao People's Revolutionary Party (LPRP). There is a head of state and a prime minister. A 9-member Politburo and a 42-member Central Committee set government policies. A constitution was adopted in 1991, and in the next year the 85-member National Assembly was elected by secret ballot. The Assembly has since been expanded to 104 members.

The outside influences present at the founding of the current government have mostly departed, but the nation is still struggling to find the right formula for its political and economic structure. An economic downturn in the

late 1990s and alarm in the minds of old hard-liners about the influx of corruption, gambling, prostitution, and drug abuse prompted a return to stronger party control. Since then, national security and foreign relations have been in an evolving state. Although this fear of foreign influence continues, Laos recently began to emerge from international isolation by seeking and expanding relations with Australia, France, Japan, Sweden, and India. Relations with China suffered a downturn when China attacked Vietnam in 1979, but they have since improved. Pursuing its outreach to neighbors, in 1997 Laos gained membership in the Association of Southeast Asian Nations (ASEAN), and has since been accepted for membership in several international organizations, including the Asian Development Bank, the World Bank, the Food and Agriculture Organization (FAO), the International Civil Aviation Organization (ICAO), the International Labor Organization (ILO), and the World Health Organization (WHO) and observer status in the World Trade Organization (WTO) pending approval of its application for membership.

A decade earlier Laotian leaders had realized that the Soviet-style economic system adopted at the start of the communist government was preventing rather than helping national development, and in 1986 a "new economic mechanism" (NEM) was adopted, creating conditions for private activity. In 1989 Laos signed an agreement with the World Bank for additional reforms to promote private sector activity. Progress continues, but was slowed by the Asian financial crisis of the late 1990s.

Internal Security Environment

From the time the present communist government was formed at the end of the Vietnam War in 1975, Hmong tribesmen have fought the government in a war that is largely unknown outside the country. This ragtag army claims to be fighting for freedom as it carries on its battles, mostly in the far north of Laos, but sometimes in assaults on cities, such as attacks on buses in Vientiane. But their motives appear to be mixed. In their attempts to restrain the Laos government from improving trade relations with the United States, they may see a way to harm the government they wish to overthrow. Some Hmong refugees in the United States support the war yet may favor trade relations, but others oppose the war, bemoaning the "loss of Laos" to the Communists. Whatever their motives, the unrest is a problem that seems unlikely to go away. Tourism is affected, of course, reducing much-needed revenue.

External Security Environment

Laos seems not at present threatened by external military aggression—a fortunate circumstance because the nation is not well prepared to defend itself. Courting friendship with its neighbors is both necessary and wise. Laos must buy time to stabilize its internal situation and get on with economic growth, so that in time a respectable national defense may be feasible and affordable.

The geography of Laos makes it a transit route between its neighbors: east and west between Vietnam and Thailand, and north and south between China and Thailand (and Cambodia, Malaysia, and Singapore). The trade route between Singapore and China is most direct through Laos, and highways are being built there to accommodate the increasing traffic flow. The Mitraphap (Friendship) Bridge over the Mekong River near Vientiane carries a steady and growing flow of trucks and autos between Thailand and Laos. Highway 13 makes it possible to drive on a paved road from Singapore up the Malay Peninsula into Laos and on into China and, eventually, as far as Beijing. In 1994 agreement was reached between Laos and its neighbors to the north and west to build a 250-kilometer (155-mile) highway from the city of Ban Houay Sai on the Mekong River (across from north Thailand) to the Chinese city of Boten— an all-weather road linking Thailand and China, with Laos as the willing link.

This expanding roadway system creates both benefits and dangers to Laos. The benefit is hoped to be economic: gaining income from the trade route by providing services along the Laotian portion of the highway and by facilitating imports and exports over the truck routes. The negative side is being seen in the influx of foreign influences, bringing pollution, deforestation, corrupt practices, and exposure to AIDS and other diseases. National defense is likewise made more difficult—it is impossible to defend all the routes into Laos with the small Laotian military force. Nevertheless, travel through Laos is likely to continue, and the benefits may exceed the negative implications.

Terrorism Threat and Response

Terrorism seems far away from this small country, having no attractive targets for attack that would further a terrorist's cause. U.S.-Laos relations are generally good. Since the late 1980s, U.S. and Laotian teams have collaborated in the search for Americans missing in the Vietnam War, and there is similar cooperative action to curb the narcotics trade through a crop-substitution program and the training of Laotian workers in actions against narcotics. If counterterrorism were needed in Laos, it is probable that the Laotian government would cooperate with the United States in countermeasures.

Military Structure and Defense Policy

Laotian army strength at 25,600 is less than half the peak strength in the mid-1960s (the total force then was 60,000, now about 29,000). The army is deployed in four military regions and consists of five infantry divisions, seven independent infantry regiments, one battalion of armor, five artillery battalions, nine air defense battalions, and three engineer regiments. Their equipment is limited; it includes 30 main battle tanks, 25 light tanks and about 70 armored personnel carriers. There are about 100 howitzers (155 mm down to 75 mm), about 40 mortars and 85 antitank weapons. For air defense there are about 60 surface-to-air missiles and 150 light antiaircraft guns. Army aviation includes 9 light transport aircraft and 2 transport helicopters.

Laos is a landlocked country whose only water access to the sea is via the Mekong River. On the river, the army has a small force of some 500 men (sometimes called the Lao People's Navy or LPN) manning about 16 patrol craft, 4 medium landing craft and about 490 small boats.

The Laotian air force has 3,500 men, with limited equipment: about 12 Russian MiG-21s, 10 light transports, and 20 helicopters.

Beside the regular armed forces, Laos has a village "home guard" militia of about 100,000 men. There continue to be insurgent forces within Laos, notably the Hmong tribal fighters, who have resisted the country's communist government ever since it took power in 1975. There have been deaths in this continuing unrest, including deaths of a few tourists, resulting in some decrease in tourism, a source of revenue the country needs. The U.S. State Department from time to time issues warnings against visiting certain areas in Laos.

There is a military draft for all males between seventeen and twenty-six years of age, with an eighteen-month minimum tour of service. Women volunteers may serve in the Medical Corps, but, considering the low pay and limited career prospects, few women—or men—volunteer for service. Beside the basic training of draftees, Laos has an Advance and Intermediate Training School for officers up to company command level. The former training abroad, mainly in Russia and Vietnam, has ended, probably because Laos cannot afford to pay. The United States has provided training and equipment for efforts in Laos to clear and dispose of unexploded ordnance, and in public education about the dangers of such ordnance. There has been as well some instruction about the dangers of HIV/AIDS. There is also help from the United Nations, private U.S. groups, Germany, and Britain.

There is almost no armaments industry in Laos, and the government has little money for buying weapons. The Laotian military will have to make do with the equipment and weapons it now has and with the modest levels of proficiency from training that the limited funds can provide. The small river force on the Mekong will probably be sufficient for patrolling to control smugglers and sometimes to prevent insurgents from crossing into Laos from Thailand. Laos has accused Thailand of harboring and supporting such insurgent groups as the Hmong tribesmen, though this problem with Thailand seems to have diminished.

Laotian defense policy is focused on defense of the homeland and protection of the political dominance of the ruling Lao People's Revolutionary Party. The Lao People's Army (LPA) is the main force, with the much smaller Lao People's Air Force and the riverine unit of the LPA (or Lao People's Navy) very much in subordinate status. The air force defense role is growing however, as it has progressed from providing transport and support functions to taking on limited air defense and strike missions. In addition to its political role, the primary missions of the LPA are border security and containment of tribal insurgencies in the northern highlands—the latter is the most difficult and apparently prevails. Thee regular forces are under the command of the Ministry of Defense in Vientiane, while the loosely organized militia is under the command of provincial authorities.

Conclusions and Outlook

Because Laos is surrounded by countries with much larger armed forces, the obvious strategy for this vulnerable country is to make friends with its neighbors. In the main, this is happening. Friendly relations result in help from neighbors as, for example, in April 1994 when an agreement was signed for Malaysian training of Lao technicians to manage and service hydroelectric power stations. Laos's membership in ASEAN should add measurably to Laotian national security, because ASEAN expanded its charter beyond the original economic linkage to include mutual security cooperation. The opening of Laos to the outside world has probably been its best hope for security. As a crossroads of commerce and communications, and if foreign capital continues to flow into the nation, the overall benefits will exceed the negative impact on its culture and security. In spite of some security risks, international tourism continues, benefiting both Laos and the tourists.

Suggested Readings

Far Eastern Economic Review. *Asia 2003 Yearbook.* Hong Kong, December 2002.
International Institute for Strategic Studies. *The Military Balance, 2001–2002.* London: Oxford University Press, 2002.
Lintner, Bertil. "Never Say Die." *Far Eastern Economic Review,* July 17, 2003, p. 21.
United States Department of State. *Background Notes: Laos.* April 2002.
United States Pacific Command. *Laos Primer.* November 2002.

11

Malaysia

Security Begins at Home

Bridget Welsh

Introduction

As a founding member of the Association of Southeast Asian Nations (ASEAN) in 1967 and one of the most stable regimes in Southeast Asia, Malaysia has maintained a strong commitment to minimizing external threats and dampening internal challenges. Like most countries in the region, Malaysia historically has been concerned with internal security, particularly perceived threats to the incumbent government. Externally, its main attention has centered on its neighbors, where there are persistent yet nondivisive territorial disputes. These concerns have not significantly threatened the country's security, allowing the government to pursue military modernization at its own pace and maintain an internally oriented security focus.

The post–September 11 world, however, has radically affected Malaysia's security climate, bringing its role as a moderate Muslim democracy to the fore and institutionalizing a difficult but pragmatic relationship with the United States in the War on Terrorism. The change has slowly forced Malaysia to acknowledge the central role that Malaysian soil has played for terrorists, especially for Jemaah Islamiyah (JI) (Islamic group or Islamic community), the regional organization behind the Bali nightclub and the Jakarta J.W. Marriott Hotel and Australian Embassy bombings. This has forced a serious rethinking of security that extends far beyond the country's national borders. The appreciation of new transnational perils has led to a restructuring of the Malaysian security forces, which is likely to expand in the future.

The changes have taken place as the longest serving prime minister, Tun Dr. Mahathir bin Mohamad, retired from office by his own decision. By 2003 Mahathir had effectively weakened the reform-oriented opposition that formed after the 1997 Asian financial crisis, led by Anwar Ibrahim, that inadvertently

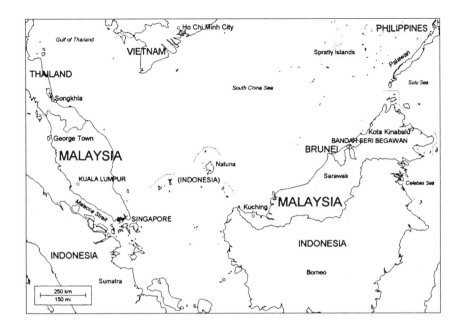

strengthened Malaysia's Islamic party, Parti Islam Se-Malaysia (Islamic Party of Malaysia, or PAS). When he retired in October 2003, he left an uneven legacy for his successor, Abdullah Ahmad Badawi, which included increasing the professionalism of the bureaucracy and security forces.

The new security environment poses a challenge for Abdullah. Yet the new prime minister will continue to rely on a multifaceted strategy of economic legitimacy, multiethnic harmony, United Malays National Organization (UMNO) Malay dominance, anticommunism, regional multilateralism, modernization of the country's defense forces and strategic bilateral ties. Malaysia's leader will harness his skills and resources to mitigate terrorism threats at home and cooperate internationally to offset threats to the region.

Political Framework

Malaysia is a parliamentary democracy with a constitutional monarchy. National elections are held every five years. The eleventh general elections were held in March 2004. Abdullah Badawi won a decisive political mandate, capturing over 90 percent of the seats in a campaign that distanced him from his predecessor. Abdullah is the leader of UMNO, the dominant party in the fourteen-party coalition known as the Barisan Nasional (BN, or National Front) that has effectively governed Malaysia since independence in 1957. UMNO supremacy was enhanced after the 1969 racial riots that led to eighteen months of emergency rule and politically further empowered the Malay majority. Malaysia is essentially a one-party state in which UMNO and defacto the Malays dominate decision making and the UMNO elite hold key cabinet positions, including the defense portfolio. The government is responsive to the electorate, however, with a capable bureaucracy and development-oriented policies that generate support for the regime.

The government is led by Prime Minister Abdullah, who took office on October 31, 2003, after five years as deputy prime minister. Abdullah was a former civil servant who entered politics in the 1970s and served in various offices, including the Ministry of Foreign Affairs, before assuming a leadership role in the UMNO hierarchy in 1998. He replaced Anwar Ibrahim, who was arrested, beaten, and tried for corruption and sodomy in proceedings that were highly politicized after he challenged the leadership of Mahathir. As deputy prime minister, Abdullah was careful not to alienate Mahathir and proved his loyalty by defending the treatment of Anwar, even in the face of high levels of criticism. Upon assuming office Abdullah, known affectionately as Pak Lah (Father Lah), engaged in populist measures to win his own mandate, including an anticorruption campaign, high levels of patronage to the rural areas and an anticrime initiative.[1] The most definitive measure was the acceptance of a September 2004 judicial appeal decision to overturn Anwar's sodomy conviction, which freed Anwar after six years in jail. These moves are part of an effort to step out of the shadow of his predecessor and strengthen Malaysia's political institutions.

One area that Abdullah will certainly try to follow his predecessor, however, is the area of economic performance. Mahathir was known as the "modernizer of Malaysia," stewarding the shift from an agricultural to an industrialized economy during his twenty-two-year tenure. Malaysia has the third highest per capita income in the region, US$3,540, and offers investors a modern infrastructure and an open and favorable business climate. Mahathir fostered these conditions and in the process attracted high levels of foreign investment. During his rule the economy expanded at an average rate of 7 percent annually, creating a robust middle class and a rapidly modernizing society, which in turn increased expectations from the new government. Abdullah will hope to build on the sound economic foundation he inherited.

Internal Security Environment

Protecting Incumbent Rule

The issue of economic strength is one of four consistent cornerstones of Malaysia's internal security priorities. Since the mid-1970s the need to maintain economic growth has been a driving force for the government, which recognizes the strong link between its pragmatic citizens and regime survival. Similar to Singapore, the BN relies heavily on economic legitimacy for popular support.

In this vein, the 1997 Asian financial crisis was a pivotal moment in Malaysia's history. The crisis threatened to erode years of economic development almost overnight. Not only did the crisis affect growth (growth rates plummeted from positive 7.5 percent in 1997 to a 7.5 percent contraction in 1998), the crisis undermined Malaysia's engine of growth, foreign capital. The country had strategically tapped into the favorable investment climate of the 1980s, attracting Japanese, Taiwanese, and American investment in light manufacturing.[2] In a decade the country of 23 million people became the United States' eleventh largest trading partner, largely through the export of semiconductors for computers. The diverse base of the economy, which includes oil, natural gas, palm oil and other agricultural exports, buttressed this performance. The contagion effects associated with the 1997 crisis cast a dark shadow over the Malaysian economy, whose fundamentals were much stronger than its neighbors, despite the presence of corruption and problems in the banking and regulatory markets. Initially, capital flight centered on portfolio capital, but the crisis also affected foreign direct investment as the cloud of economic failure rained on Mahathir's carefully constructed image of Malaysia as a development model.

Today, the Malaysian economy has recovered from the crisis through a combination of reforms and a reliance on key exports.[3] Mahathir claimed success for the recovery, highlighting the controversial introduction of capital controls in 1998 as the main reform measure that stabilized the economy. His effective crisis management was an integral part of the recovery, stabilizing exchange rates and stemming capital flight. While the crisis precipitated a political crisis, leading to the emergence of the Anwar challenge to Mahathir and a reform-oriented opposition movement, Malaysia's economic base remains on track.

The event, however, highlights the significance of the economy for the regime and the close link to international conditions. The government has focused on trade and investment missions overseas, especially the United States, and enhanced economic cooperation with its neighbors in such growth areas as the Indonesia-Malaysia-Thailand Growth Triangle. These strategies have been primarily reactive, following practices in the region, rather than proactive or pioneering. With investment flows in the region moving to China and investment from the United States receding, the Malaysian government has adjusted to the new conditions, fostering an expansion of trade with China to US$20.4 billion in 2003.[4] Abdullah will need to maintain Malaysia's competitiveness in the face of increasing competition and increasingly will have to formulate proactive strategies to deal with less favorable economic international conditions. Whether it involves a strategic slowdown on opening trade barriers to protect Malaysian industries like the national car or measures to tap into Chinese markets, economic legitimacy will be tied to the relationship with the international economy and the regime's domestic political fortunes. With legitimacy at stake, the government will continue to view the need to maintain and foster favorable economic international conditions as part of its internal security priorities.

The issue of economic legitimacy is closely tied to another cornerstone of internal security, ethnic harmony. Malaysia is comprised of nearly forty distinct ethnic groups, and the administration's efforts to promote their peaceful interaction have been an important rationale for internal security measures, from the early years of the anticommunist Emergency Period (1948 to 1962, although the Emergency officially ended in 1989) and pivotal 1969 race riots to the 2001 localized ethnic conflict near Kuala Lumpur. Today, the Malays comprise the majority with 57 percent, followed by the Chinese with 27 percent, Indians with 8 percent, and over thirty other indigenous communities. Despite its diversity, conflict among ethnic communities has been minimal, especially compared with Indonesia. Few incidents of ethnic violence unsettle the usually cordial relations among the groups, despite the persistence of strong distinct ethnic identities.

Not surprisingly, maintaining ethnic harmony has also been an integral part of Malaysia's internal security agenda. Interethnic cooperation among elites has been a defining feature of the political system since independence. The ruling coalition is based on the premise that it provides the most viable cooperation among ethnic groups, and the opposition's inability to forge a persistent multiethnic alliance has worked in the coalition's favor. The BN argues that it is the only political vehicle that can guarantee ethnic security and protect a minimum threshold of rights for the different communities, especially cultural autonomy in education and language. The perceived need to promote ethnic harmony has served to limit civil liberties in such areas as free speech and has led to the use of draconian laws, like the Internal Security Act, which allows two-years' detention without trial. Changes in the status quo are perceived by the regime to undermine ethnic harmony; thus, challenges to the existing order are not to be tolerated.

Criticism of the government is often defined as a threat to ethnic security. For example, the 1987 arrests of over a hundred activists for allegedly promoting ethnic tensions in Operation Lalang illustrates the extent to which the government uses this premise to subdue the opposition. Ethnic strife is strongly tied to the 1969 racial riots, which were a defining moment in Malaysian history. The creation in 2003 of a mandatory three-month National

Service program for the country's youth to promote ethnic integration demonstrates the government's commitment to manage this issue.

Ethnic harmony in Malaysia is based on the favored status of the Malay community, which has supreme political power and is given economic privileges in state policies through the New Economic Policy (NEP) that was introduced in 1971. This affirmative action policy has taken on different forms in the over thirty years of its existence, but the core of Malay special rights has persisted and become increasingly accepted in Malaysia, because the demographic dynamic of a greater birth rate in the Malay community shifts the balance away from non-Malay minorities. While Malays still lack dominance in the economy—due to the vibrant entrepreneurial businesses of the Chinese and the dependence of the Malay community on the state for patronage—Malaysia's political evolution has institutionalized an uneven playing field for the different communities. The ruling party, UMNO, relies on protecting the special rights of the Malays for its legitimacy. Challenges to these rights are especially sensitive.

Protecting and fostering Malay dominance stewarded by UMNO has been the third cornerstone of internal security. The overwhelming majority of the security forces are Malay, and little effort has been made to change the ethnic composition of the forces. Attention has focused on securing the support of the Malay community, and the security apparatus is often used to shore up support for the incumbent government. From 1999 onward, after the challenge from Anwar dented the support of the Malay community for UMNO, the regime worked to win back the support of the Malay majority and justified such measures as the arrest of opposition leaders in the Anwar-linked party KeAdilan (National Justice Party) on security grounds. At issue was the struggle for the "hearts and minds" of the Malay majority, who are Malaysia's most powerful political ethnic group.

In this regard, the challenge from the strongest opposition party, PAS, has been a persistent internal security concern. The opposition party has won state governments and held office, but operates in an environment of tight regulation. Circulation of the PAS newspaper, *Harakah,* has been capped and some political leaders in PAS have been arrested periodically, including most recently the son of the chief minister of Kelantan. The control of PAS has become increasingly significant in the post–9/11 context in that the party offers the most conservative form of Islamic governance, introducing *hudud* or Islamic laws in one of the states it governed from 2000. Efforts have also been made to tar PAS with the terrorist brush, although its leadership is careful to reject violence, with the exception of its support for the Palestinians. PAS argues for the need for strict Islamic governance, a position that was rejected by the overwhelmingly moderate Malaysian electorate in the 2004 national elections. UMNO in the BN coalition campaigned on the theme of Islamic moderation and builds on this image as part of the country's success.

Maintaining the mantle of Islamic moderation has been an important feature of UMNO governance beyond organized political challenges. This has been a difficult balance for the government, since it has used Islam for political legitimacy and engaged in its own Islamization drive since 1983.[5] The government has cracked down on groups that it perceives as violating accepted norms of Islam within Malaysia. In October 1980 eight Islamic militants were killed when they attacked a police station in the southern state of Johor. In November 1985 fourteen villagers and four police were killed in what is known as the "Memali incident." In 1986 the government banned the group Al-Arqam for "deviant" practices, and in 2000 the group arrested members of Al-Ma'unah for attacking a military outpost. Islamic extremism has been a long-standing security concern, even before the terrorism events of 2001. Eight of the twelve banned groups in Malaysia have been defined as "deviant" or "extremist" on religious grounds.[6]

Historically, other groups have directly threatened incumbent rule. The 1948–1962 Emergency Period was a response to the armed campaign of the Malayan Communist Party. The armed insurgency moved from the peninsula to East Malaysia in the 1970s. With the strong anticommunist orientation gained from its independence, the Malaysian government has consistently used the state to squash the political left. While this threat eased after the Cold War and the Emergency operations, protection of the incumbent elite remains an institutionalized priority of internal security, although a less salient one.

Malaysia's security priorities, like those of most Southeast Asian countries, have concentrated on domestic conditions. As the country has developed, the range of internal security challenges has expanded from managing the anticommunist threat to shepherding Islamic moderation and protecting economic legitimacy. The recent release of Anwar shows increasing confidence on the part of the new prime minister, although sensitivities to leadership challenges within the Malay community remain. Whether populist reform measures will extend into Abdullah's tenure remains to be seen. The supremacy of UMNO and the incumbent government will likely limit the ability to open the system.

External Security Environment

Multilateral and Bilateral Strategies at Work

Malaysia's focus on internal security stems from the fact that it has enjoyed a relatively benign and peaceful external security environment since it resumed its independence in 1957. Malaysia's security has not been significantly threatened by any external power. The greatest challenge occurred during a confrontation (*Konfrontasi*) with Indonesia in the early 1960s, in which Indonesia sponsored a guerilla invasion allied with the Communists into East Malaysia. When Soekarno was ousted from office in 1965 and ASEAN was formed in 1967, regional threats eased considerably. Soeharto's new leadership guaranteed that Indonesia would not attack its neighbors.

From its inception in 1967, Malaysia was committed to ASEAN.[7] The organization profoundly reduced the external threats from Malaysia's neighbors. This has led to a consistent commitment to the organization and harnessed Malaysia's diplomatic skills. These talents have been used to develop confidence-building measures and secure a position for Malaysia in regional security matters. After the 1998 regime transition in Indonesia, Malaysia tried to assume leadership of ASEAN. The government lobbied hard to set up the ASEAN Plus Three secretariat in Kuala Lumpur. This was inspired by the prominence of Mahathir in the region, whose vision of Southeast Asia was one of independence from Great Powers and strong regional cohesion. Mahathir was an avid advocate for the inclusion of Myanmar (Burma) in the organization in 1997 and a strong supporter of regional cooperation. Malaysia has yet to (and unlikely will due to its size) attain the leadership of the organization, but its effort has paid off in that it is a major trendsetter, shaping most recently the dialogue over terrorism with the signing of the Bali Concord on terrorism in 2003.

ASEAN has had an important impact on the most serious multilateral issue facing Malaysia—potential conflict in the Spratly Islands in the South China Sea, which are contested by six countries, including China. Of the fifty-one islands, forty-four are occupied. Malaysia occupies three islands and at least four rocks and has built a hotel on one of the islands. Currently Malaysia stations one hundred soldiers in the area to shore up its claim, which originated in 1979, on the grounds that the fishing and oil-rich islands are an extension of its continental shelf. Malaysia, along with China and Vietnam, is one of three countries that have aggressively protected their claims. Tensions among claimants were increasing in the 1990s, most obviously illustrated in the 1995 Mischief Reef conflict between China and the Philippines. Through dialogue within ASEAN, claimants signed the "Declaration on the Conduct of Parties in the South China Sea," committing to resolving conflict without violence in 2002. Although this document is not a legally binding code of conduct, the negotiations have reduced tensions and improved Malaysia's security environment.

Malaysia's involvement in ASEAN is part of a broad strategy of multilateralism for external security. Malaysia has played an important role in United Nations (UN) peace-keeping operations in Cambodia, Kuwait, Bosnia, and Somalia and has been an active member in the Organization of Islamic Conference and Non-Aligned Movement. In 2003 Malaysia assumed the chair of the latter two groups. The country's multilateral involvement includes economic organizations, including the Asia-Pacific Economic Co-operation forum and the World Trade Organization. While Malaysia closely defines its interests with the developing world, its prominence in these institutions has empowered Malaysia in international affairs and de facto enriched its interaction with countries worldwide. This active involvement cloaks Malaysia with international legitimacy and strengthens its position.

Behind the multilateral initiatives are strong strategic bilateral ties, especially with regional powers and neighbors. Mahathir set in place a pattern of dominating international affairs and set the tone for interaction with different countries.[8] He traveled widely and often, and his style provoked strong responses. Mahathir warmed to Japan and fostered a very robust tie with Tokyo, while his views of Australia and the United States were openly contentious, often prickly. Although relations with these countries were less overtly cordial, behind the rhetoric, economic and security ties were strong, with bilateral military exercises and steady flows of investment. The dominance of personality in these relations has led to uneven bilateral interactions over time. Despite this trend, Malaysia has used such relationships to address immediate security concerns.

The most pressing problems have been resource, labor, and territorial disputes. From 2000 onward relations between Singapore and Malaysia became increasingly strained, primarily over Malaysia's sale of fresh water to Singapore and land reclamation in Johor. The difficulties illustrate persistent competition between these rivals whose history is deeply intertwined from the colonial era. Strained relations crescendoed in 2003 with vicious verbal attacks. These died down immediately after Abdullah assumed office. The problem had less to do with security than personality conflicts among leaders. Malaysia's concern with resources extends to its relations with Brunei that has involved gunfire over the rich Kikeh oil field claimed by both countries. Here too, leadership style appears to be effective in reducing tensions.

Bilateral relations have also been affected by labor migration, which has become a transnational security problem for Malaysia closely tied to economic security. With a small population, Malaysia is highly dependent on cheap labor from its neighbors. The problems associated with recruitment and illegal labor flows from Indonesia in particular (estimated at one million) have become a persistent security concern because of the links to the illegal economy and transnational crime. The issue also has had an impact on crime within Malaysia, since Indonesian migrants have been closely associated with theft. Outside of Malaysia, the treatment of migrants by Malaysian authorities has led to an outcry by the human rights community, especially within Indonesia and the Philippines. Since 2000 Malaysian authorities have worked to diversify labor flows and mend relations. Unlike the issue of resources, the structural dependence of the Malaysian economy on labor has depersonalized this issue and resulted in a persistent problematic flash point for Malaysia's bilateral relations with its neighbors.[9] Abdullah has accorded priority to this, but the complex issues behind the problem are unlikely to offer any immediate resolutions. This difficulty will remain a security concern, although not a debilitating one.

Malaysia's territorial disputes have gradually eased through a reliance on multilateral organizations such as the International Court of Justice (ICJ) in The Hague and bilateral diplomacy. In 2001 the ICJ awarded Sipadan and Ligitan, also claimed by Indonesia, to Malaysia. The Singapore-occupied Pedra Branca/Pulau Batu issue is currently under arbitration. Bilateral talks have reduced concern over the claim of Sabah by the Philippines, of the border dispute over the Limbang River with Brunei, and the Kolok River contention with Thailand. These disputes are unlikely to go away but, similarly, are unlikely to foster armed conflict.

Part of the reason these smoldering disputes are unlikely to ignite is the fact that Malaysia also holds a wide range of bilateral military exercises with its neighbors, including Singapore, Thailand, the Philippines, Brunei, and India. Malaysia also participates in the Cobra Gold exercises with the United States. In 2004 it expanded its military exercises with the United States as part of the War on Terrorism. Malaysia is also part of a multilateral defense arrangement with Singapore, the UK, Australia, and New Zealand known as the Five-Power Defence Arrangement (FPDA). Formed in 1971, this loose alliance replaced the Anglo-Malayan Defense Agreement and provides for consultation of members in the event Malaysia is attacked.

Terrorism Threat and Response

The combination of multilateral and bilateral initiatives noted above has significantly improved Malaysia's traditional security position. Dominating the security scene now is the threat of terrorism.

Malaysia was closely tied to the 9/11 tragedy, as security cameras showed that some of the hijackers planned the bombings in Kuala Lumpur, the nation's capital. Subsequent research discloses that a small number of Malaysians have been active in regional militant organizations, especially the JI, which was responsible for the bombings in Bali and Jakarta, and the more ambiguous Kumpulan Militan Malaysia (Malaysian Mujahideen Group or KMM).

Two of the current leaders of the JI, Noordin Mohammed Top and Azahari Husin are Malaysian, and the previous leader, Hambali, had lived in Malaysia for a long time and married a Malaysian. In September 2003 the government admitted that it was actively looking for 273 JI members and estimated that there were 465 JI members in Malaysia.[10] Currently 79 alleged terrorists are imprisoned under the Internal Security Act.[11]

The nation's connection to terrorism has its roots in political and economic conditions.[12] The Malaysian government granted sanctuary to many Islamic dissidents, including the prominent Indonesian preacher Abu Bakar Bashir, who has been tied to the Bali bombing, and many of these were scholars who turned to *madrasas* or *pondoks* as they are known in Malaysia for recruitment. The close proximity to the southern Philippines and liberal response to the Muslim fighters in Mindanao allowed East Malaysia to become a sanctuary for both the Moro Islamic Liberation Front (MILF) and Abu Sayyaf Group rebels. Geographic proximity also fosters a connection to militant groups in southern Thailand that has reignited in 2004. The prominent Islamization drive that began in 1983 made Malaysia a more attractive location for a wide range of Islamists, including militants, and stimulated support for Islamic issues abroad. Many Malaysians visited Afghanistan and Pakistan, where they were exposed to al Qaeda operatives; they invested in sectarian conflicts in Indonesia, in Poso, and in the Malukus in 1999 in the name of promoting Islam. These initiatives were not openly supported by the government but not prevented either. Part of the difficulty for the Malaysian regime was the use of political Islam for legitimacy at home. The government used religion for support, and it was the country's success in the economic realm that deepened the interaction of Malaysian Muslims with the *umma* ("Muslim community"), including militant elements. These groups, however, make up only a small minority of Malaysian Muslims.

In the immediate aftermath of 9/11, the Malaysian government was very defensive, disavowing the country's links with international terrorism and rejecting the potent label of a terrorist center. Mahathir called for a broader study of the roots of terrorism and cautioned against an American militaristic response to 9/11. Malaysia has consistently opposed the invasion of Afghanistan and the war in Iraq, although it has quietly cooperated with the United States on terrorist issues, allowing the Federal Bureau of Investigation (FBI) to question suspects connected to 9/11, including Yazid Sufaat, who apparently met with the WTC hijackers. Malaysia's initial focus was on rooting out domestic militants and forging effective intelligence-sharing with countries concerned with regional terrorism. The government was careful not to openly align itself directly with the Bush administration, whose policies are negatively viewed throughout Malaysia. The government does not want a strong alliance with the United States that might domestically backfire.

By the end of Mahathir's tenure, Malaysia had gradually begun a more decisive approach to regional terrorism, even though this concern resonated more abroad than domestically. Malaysia began playing more of an enforcement role in addressing terrorist issues, which mirrored stronger regional enforcement, particularly in the Philippines and Thailand. The focus has zeroed in on the JI. In 2003 the government introduced four terrorist-related laws, including changes to the penal code and money-laundering measures. Malaysia also established a special naval police force to patrol its waters for terrorism. The patrols have been concentrated in East Malaysia, near the southern Philippines. In July 2003 the Malaysian government also set up a regional terrorism center in Kuala Lumpur. These steps show a commitment to addressing the issue of terrorism in Malaysia. As the former home affairs minister, Abdullah has maintained these efforts. In 2004 he established a new cabinet department specifically focused on the tie between terrorism and internal security.

Military Structure and Defense Policy

As structured, Malaysia's defense force, the Royal Malaysian Armed Forces (MAF), will not likely play a critical role in addressing the terrorist threat. Founded in 1933, the MAF has its roots in the colonial period and has a conventional structure. The MAF is led by the Chief of Defense and is subject to civilian authority. Unlike other militaries in the region, the MAF has always been subservient to civilian rule.

The armed forces underwent an extensive modernization program in the 1990s, which featured increasing the interoperability of the forces in UN peacekeeping exercises and military procurement. The reforms aim to reduce active manpower and improve the technological capacity of the forces. Currently, Malaysia's military has 104,000 active personnel and 51,600 reserves. The plan is to further streamline these forces by 2006. Since the 1990s, Malaysia has been actively purchasing military equipment. It was the first country to buy from both the United States and the former Soviet Union after the Cold War, purchasing the F/A-18D Hornet and C-130 Hercules aircraft from the United States and MiG-29MK Fulcrum from the former Soviet Union. The acquisition of equipment was constrained during the 1997 Asian financial crisis, but has rebounded since 2000. Malaysia plans to spend US$3–5 billion on weapons from 2002 to 2005. Most recently Malaysia purchased eighteen Sukhoi fighter jets from Russia in a US$900 million deal. These purchases are driven by a desire to strengthen Malaysia's offensive posture and thus narrow the gap with Singapore, whose military budget is roughly twice that of Malaysia.

Unlike Singapore, however, Malaysia has not purchased equipment that is compatible with each other. The range of items recently purchased included tanks from Poland, Russian and British surface-to-air missiles and mobile military bridges, Austrian Steyr assault rifles, and Pakistani antitank missiles. Some suggest that these purchases are impelled less by modernization demands than patronage.[13]

The upgrading effort has extended into a restructuring of the armed forces. Beginning in the 1990s Malaysia began strengthening the Royal Malaysian Navy (RMN) and Royal Malaysian Air Force (RMAF). Many purchases have been specifically geared toward these services. The balancing of services recognizes that conventional security threats no longer pose as significant a danger to Malaysia as formerly. Attacks are likely to come by sea or air, whether in the form of piracy or terrorism. In this vein, the new naval police is part of a restructuring program that recognizes the need to recast security forces to deal with nonconventional threats, especially small-scale attacks. Malaysia is committed to playing a leading role in addressing the threat of a maritime attack in the Straits of Malacca, working in close collaboration with the International Maritime Bureau based in Kuala Lumpur. This issue has become a major concern linked to terrorism, exacerbated by a surge of piracy incidents in 2004.

Conclusions and Outlook

The defense modernization effort reflects an appreciation of the changing international security climate. As the War on Terrorism continues to unfold in Malaysia, it is likely that these reforms will persist. Malaysia has proved to be adept at managing security issues. The focus will remain on internal issues, since the new challenge of terrorism is closely tied to Islamic militancy. Malaysia has a range of options that have proved successful. The greatest challenge will be curtailing Islamic militancy. Based on his history and positive performance to date, Prime Minister Abdullah will likely continue to effectively steward Malaysia through peaceful times.

Notes

1. Bridget Welsh, "Tears and Fears: Tun Mahathir's Last Hurrah," *Southeast Asian Affairs 2004* (Singapore: ISEAS, 2004).

2. K.S. Jomo, *Southeast Asia's Misunderstood Miracle: Industrial Policy and Economic Development in Thailand, Malaysia and Indonesia* (Boulder, CO: Westview Press, 1997).

3. K.S. Jomo, *The Malaysian Eclipse: Economic Crisis and Recovery* (New York: Zed Books, 2001).

4. Abdullah Ahmad Badawi, "China: Challenge and Opportunity." Speech by Deputy Prime Minister Abdullah Ahmad Badawi, Great Hall of the People, Beijing, China, September 16, 2003, printed in the *News Straits Times,* September 17, 2003.

5. Patricia Martinez, "Mahathir, Islam and the New Malay Dilemma," in Ho Khai Leong and James Chin, *Mahathir's Administration: Performance and Crisis in Governance* (Singapore: Times Books, 2001), pp. 120–60.

6. The eight groups include Koperasi Ankatan Revolusi Islam Malaysia (1972), Kumpulan Mohd Nasir Ismail (1980), Kumpulan Revolusi Islam Ibrahim Mahmood@Ibrahim Libya (1985), Kumpulan Mujahiddin Kedah (KMK) (1988), Kumpulan Perjuangan Islam Perak (KPIP) (1988), Kumpulan Al-Ma'unah (2000), Kumpulan Militan Malaysia (KMM) (2001), and Jemaah Islamiyah (2001). "Takeover Attempts by 12 Groups," *New Straits Times,* September 26, 2003.

7. Johan Saravanamuttu, *The Dilemma of Independence: Two Decades of Malaysia's Foreign Policy, 1957–1977* (Penang: Universiti Sains Malaysia for School of Social Sciences, 1983).

8. Joseph Liow, "Personality, Exigencies and Contingencies: Determinants of Malaysia's Foreign Policy in the Mahathir Administration," in Ho Khai Leong and James Chin, eds. *Mahathir's Administration: Performance and Crisis in Governance* (Singapore: Times Books, 2001), pp. 120–60.

9. Joseph Liow, "Malaysia's Illegal Indonesian Migrant Labour Problem: In Search of Solutions," *Contemporary Southeast Asia,* vol. 25, no 1, April 2003.

10. "Cops Still Looking for 273 JI Members," *The Star,* September 26, 2003.

11. U.S. Department of State, *Country Reports on Human Rights Practices 2003* (Washington, DC: Bureau of Democracy, Human Rights, and Labor), February 25, 2004.

12. Zachary Abuza, *Militant Islam in Southeast Asia: Crucible of Terror* (Boulder, CO: Lynne Rienner Publishers, 2003).

13. John Gershman, "US and Malaysia Now Best Friends in War on Terrorism," *Foreign Policy Focus,* at http://fpif.org/pdf/gac/0205malaysia.pdf, May 10, 2002.

Suggested Readings

Crouch, Harold. *Government and Society in Malaysia.* Ithaca, NY: Cornell University Press, 1996.

Welsh, Bridget. *Reflections: The Mahathir Years.* Washington, DC: Southeast Asia Studies. Johns Hopkins University-SAIS, 2004.

——— 12 ———

Mongolia

A Delicate Balancing Act

Michael J. Mitchell

Introduction

June 21, 1281

They appeared slowly at first. Faint spots low on the horizon.

Gradually the spots began forming into sails, and soon the outlines of ships, hundreds of ships, sent the coast watchers on the Japanese island of Kyushu scrambling to sound the alarm. For nearly a year they had been expecting the great armada, and now it was here! As the day drew on, over 900 warships with 25,000 soldiers and tens of thousands of sailors massed offshore.

The Mongols had arrived.

Kublai Yuan, the Great Khan, had finished subjugating China and Korea. Mongol horsemen, using speed, mobility, and a bow that was not only easy to handle on horseback but powerful and accurate, had vanquished those who stood in their way. People in the Middle East referred to them as the Scourge from God. A medieval chronicle in Europe wrote of the Mongol charge westward: "An immense horde of that detestable race of Satan, the Tartars, burst forth, like demons overrunning all who stand in their way, covering the earth like locusts, they ravaged the eastern countries with lamentable destruction, spreading fire and slaughter wherever they went."

Then at its political apogee, the Mongolian empire stretched from Central Asia, through Central Europe, Russia, most of the Middle East, and much of Asia. It was the greatest empire that the world had known. And now, the Great Khan had decided, his boundary of domination was to include Japan.

The Mongolians were furious with the Japanese emperor. Two delegations of Mongolian diplomats, each bearing terms for the emperor's surrender, had been executed on the emperor's orders, and their heads impaled on stakes. This insult would not be tolerated.

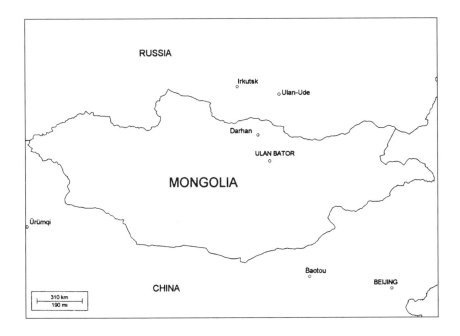

Mongol reinforcements arrived to support the attack. As the battle raged and thousands of samurai threw themselves at the invaders, Japanese military leaders knew they were in trouble. Across Japan, people turned to their gods and Shinto deities, begging for assistance and praying for deliverance from the evil horde that had set upon their land. Then a great wind began to blow. For two days, a tremendous storm battered the Mongolian fleet, sinking all but a handful of vessels. The invasion had been turned back, and the legend of the kamikaze, or divine wind, was born.

Japan was saved, but the Mongol empire was in trouble. Over time, their conquests bled away as rebellions and political upheavals took their toll. As fast as the Mongolian hordes rode across the world stage, they disappeared. Locked away in the harsh climate of Central Asia, it would take hundreds of years, several wars, including a Cold War, and the collapse of the Soviet Union for Mongolia to reemerge and make a far less bellicose encore presentation on the world stage.

Political Framework

For hundreds of years the country we know as Mongolia was part of the Chinese empire. Its small population made it ripe for cultural assimilation. The Mongolians kept their traditions and distinctive language alive, until they were able to overthrow the Chinese Han dynasty in 1921. The Mongolian general who led the uprising, Sukebaatar (Mongolians typically use only one name), realized quickly that the Chinese would be back soon with more soldiers than his dedicated force could handle. Sukebaatar had a losing hand, but he did have a trump card yet to play—the Soviet Union. He negotiated a deal with Vladimir Lenin that made Mongolia a Soviet protectorate, but the country was able to maintain its status as an "independent" state—albeit under full Soviet control. The Soviets wasted no time in constructing bases along the new Soviet-Sino border and Mongolia soon became a critical buffer state for the Soviet leadership. And that is how things stood until 1989.

A New Political Order

As the rumblings of democratic activism began to shake the foundations of Communist governments in Europe—Poland, the former Czechoslovakia, Hungary, and East Germany—Mongolians began to exert pressure on their politburo for more liberalization. When the Soviet premier, Mikhail Gorbachev, ushered in "glasnost," or openness, Mongolians were quick to seize the opportunity to challenge the ruling regime more openly.

In 1991 a group of democracy activists took to the main square outside parliament and went on a hunger strike until the politburo resigned. The dozen activists were just an oddity at first, but within days thousands of Mongolians poured into the streets and the square demanding an end to Communist rule and the creation of a democratic form of government.

"This was a dangerous period for us," stated Erdenine Bat-uul, a leader of the hunger strike. "We knew that there would be one of two outcomes: either jail or possibly death, or we would succeed and a new country would be born. Thankfully, the people won."

Taskhia Elbegdorj, another hunger striker, echoed Bat-uul's comments. "We had hundreds of thousands of people standing behind us. Every day there were more rumors that the military was going to take action," he stated. Half laughing, he remarked that "you should have seen the look on the faces of the old politburo members when they asked us what we wanted, and we told them we wanted them gone," he said. Elbegdorj went on to become Prime Minister in 1998.

After a demonstration of well over 400,000 people, the country reached a crisis point. If the politburo wished to stay in power, it would have to use force to clear the streets. The army was placed on alert. And to the everlasting credit of those former rulers, they announced that their governing body would resign and a new constitution would be written. There was to be no Tiananmen Square. Mongolia was now transitioning to a democratic process.

A new constitution was officially adopted on February 12, 1992. Elections soon followed that saw the former Communist Mongolian People's Revolutionary Party (MPRP), the only political party with a national infrastructure, sweep seventy of seventy-six seats in Parliament. During the next four years opposition political parties worked hard, and in the 1996 elections Central Asia witnessed an event unique to that part of the world: the peaceful transfer of political power from one party to another. The MPRP was defeated, and the Mongolian Democratic Union (MDU), winning fifty seats in Parliament, officially took over control of the government. The 2000 elections saw the political pendulum swing back the other way, and the MPRP recaptured Parliament.

In the July 2004 elections, Mongolia experienced a first for a young democracy. The Motherland-Democracy Coalition that challenged the MPRP was able to win control of 38 seats in Parliament. The MPRP held on to 38 of their seats. The result—divided government. As this chapter is being written, Elbegdorj has been sworn in for his second tenure as Prime Minister. The MPRP has been given control of the Speaker's position in parliament and ministries will be divided along a power-sharing agreement. It remains to be seen how long such a government can last. However, it is a fascinating exercise in governance. The government will face a host of challenges and its share of political internecine warfare as the two parties jockey for position and relevance within the government. It represents yet another chapter in the history of Mongolia's experiment in democracy.

Today, Mongolia stands apart as the only true democracy in all of Central Asia. There is a vibrant free press, commitment to human rights and individual liberties. The country's commitment to democratic ideals has strategic ramifications for its role in the region and the development of its foreign policy.

Internal and External Security Environment

Between the Bear and the Dragon

For all their historical conquests, Mongolians today find themselves landlocked between Russia to the north and China to the east, west, and south. The deep-water ports that brought trade and tribute and launched invasions to far shores are long gone. Mongolia is a massive country about the size of the United States east of the Mississippi River, with a population slightly larger than 2.5 million people. One worker for a nongovernmental organization said, "There's no one here." The country shares a 3,485 kilometer (2,166 mile) border with Russia and a 4,677 kilometer (2,907 mile) border with China. The topography of the country varies from the pancake-flat steppe in the east to the Gobi Desert, with its undulating sand dunes in the south, to the steep Altai mountain chain that bisects the country in a north-south direction in western Mongolia. All these elements have profound foreign policy and national security implications to the nation.

Mongolia is totally dependent on such imports as oil and much of its food for survival. There are only two seaports available to bring products into the country—Vladivostok in Russia and Tanjing in China. That gives these two countries enormous leverage over Mongolia. The Mongolian population is small with a per capita wage of about US$200/month. This makes its own economy very small and barely able to create the economic market synergies necessary for growth. Despite this, the Mongolian economy has recovered from the shock that accompanied the cutoff of Soviet subsidies in 1991 when one-third of the economy disappeared overnight.

Much of the Mongolian economy is agricultural-based. Figures vary, but it could be as much as 70 percent. Mongolian herdsmen raise sheep, yaks, horses, camels, and goats and move their herds according to the seasons to new pastures. Mongolian cashmere from goats is considered by the textile industry to be the best in the world. What should be a tremendous economic asset to Mongolians has proved only marginally fruitful. For example, cashmere prices remain depressed, and many Mongolians have begun to raise more goats, depressing prices further and creating serious overgrazing and erosion problems. During the past several years the country has been subjected to a climactic condition known as a *zud*—a summer of drought followed by an early winter. According to Mongolian sources, this has destroyed millions of animals and, according to agricultural experts, bankrupted most herdsmen. It will take years to rebuild economically viable herds.

"I always believed that we needed to look at other factors when we discussed Mongolia's national security," stated Elbegdorj. "For Mongolia, increased erosion and desertification is a national security issue."

Mongolia's national budget is, according to 2002 figures, approximately US$427 million, with taxation bringing in about US$386 million. Donor countries have been generous, contributing over US$300 million since 1999. The country is a net importer, with products entering the country worth an estimated US$659 c.i.f. (2002), and exports valued at US$501 f.o.b. (2002). The country's major trading partners are reflected in Table 5.

Among nonagricultural exports, Mongolia is rich in copper, with a massive mine located in the eastern part of the country. Recently gold deposits, and oil—shipped to China by tanker trucks—have fueled a miniboom that has seen many multinational mining and oil concerns sending geologists to the country's harsh Gobi Desert and to the vast eastern steppe. The problem with Mongolia's natural resources is that there is little or no transportation

Table 5

Mongolia's Major Trading Partners (2002 figures, by percent)

Exports	China	43.8	U.S.	33.6	Russia	9.6	
Imports	Russia	32.0	China	19.4	South Korea	12.1	U.S. 9.1

infrastructure to take them to market at competitive prices. The only major railroad is the Trans-Siberian line that runs north-south. Fearing that it could be used as an avenue for invasion, the Russians used a different gauge of track when the route crosses the China-Mongolian border. Freight trains have to stop, be unloaded, and then reloaded when they reach the border, delaying trade. Most roads in the country are little more than well-beaten trails. The Asian Development Bank, however, is helping fund a major east-west roadway (hard-packed dirt) that would be a quantum leap in the ability of people and products to move across the country if/when it is finished. Air service in Mongolia is good, though most airports feature unimproved landing strips.

The voracious appetite of China's economic engine is helping to turn the country into what one Mongolia-watcher has termed "the back door to China." Moreover, China is slowly turning to Mongolia to help supply resources to fuel her factories. This is good for Mongolia, but lax environmental laws have drawn increasing concern.

Looking for a Third Neighbor

Since Sukebaatar began choreographing Mongolia's diplomatic dance in 1921, the focus has been fixed on keeping the Chinese out and the Russians happy. This was true even during the 1990s. Despite the purges that took place during Soviet times, the threat of Chinese reoccupation always seemed to loom large over the population, producing a xenophobia that manifested itself in bizarre ways. For example, the Chinese government in Beijing donated hundreds of trees to Mongolia's capital, Ulaanbaatar (or Ulan Bator), in a gesture of friendship. Later, scores had to be dug up after they perished from the harsh climate. Also, rumors immediately began to circulate through the city that the Chinese had contaminated their trees with a lethal disease that would spread to Mongolia's trees, spurring many residents to cut down the Chinese gifts.

Following adoption of its new constitution, the MPRP realized they were, in a sense, squeezed between their neighbors and without a security guarantee. Mongolian policy makers realized that although they were a buffer between the two giant powers, new friends were desperately needed. Air links were quickly opened with Japan, and overtures were made to the United States and European countries. The former U.S. secretary of state, James J. Baker III, traveled to Mongolia in 1991 to encourage democracy and lay the groundwork for U.S.-Mongolian ties. Following the election of the MDU in 1996, this process was formalized in a policy coined The Third Neighbor.

"We realized that we needed to recruit a new 'neighbor' for Mongolia," stated Elbegdorj, the hunger activist turned prime minister. "When my cabinet was formed, we discussed foreign policy and national security in very specific terms," he said. "We were less concerned about traditional military threats than a sudden wave of economic or political refugees that would flood our country. Tiananmen Square still loomed large, and we watched on television as Russian tanks fired on their parliament building. With such a small population, we faced real fears that our country would be swamped with foreign refugees that could overwhelm our small population," he stated.

Living in such a potentially unstable neighborhood meant that the country had to work hard to establish cultural, social, political, economic, and military ties not only with other Asian states but principally to the West. "There was a careful balancing act that needed to be carried out," stated Amarjargal, a former member of Parliament and minister of foreign affairs. "Keep good relations between China and Russia, and build solid ties to other countries—especially the U.S. We had to sell ourselves and the way we did that was by demonstrating the need to support the only democracy in Central Asia," Amerjargal said.

The Clinton administration and the U.S. Congress responded to Mongolia's Third Neighbor outreach. In 1996 U.S. assistance to Mongolia totaled US$8 million. During a period of retraction in the foreign assistance budget, Mongolia saw increases in 1997 (US$10 million), and in 1998 the annual total was pushed up even further to US$12 million, where it has remained since.

Mongolia has also enjoyed political support, especially among several high-ranking Republican lawmakers. The former U.S. House Speaker, Newt Gingrich, was flattered when the MDU, taking a page from his playbook that allowed Republicans to take control of the House of Representatives, ran on the "Contract with the Mongolian Voter" slogan in 1996. The conservative politics articulated by the MDU leadership—fiscal restraint, elimination of trade barriers, and commitment to democracy and human rights—were welcomed in Washington, DC. Gingrich met twice with high-level Mongolian delegations. When Representative Dennis Hastert was voted Speaker, he too met a Mongolian delegation. Coincidentally, as a former wrestling coach, Hastert was familiar with Mongolia through its unique style of wrestling.

The MPRP has strengthened its ties with Washington through approving legislation that would prohibit any U.S. soldier serving in Mongolia to be turned over to the International Criminal Court for prosecution. These so-called Article 98 agreements have been a top priority of the George W. Bush administration.

It should be noted that although Mongolia has sought good relations with both Russia and China, the country will not be easily cowed by its neighbors. For example, despite strong protests from Beijing, the Mongolian government hosted the Dali Lama on an official visit, and the Republic of China (Taiwan) has opened an economic and cultural office in Ulaanbaatar. In late 2003 the Mongolians finally concluded an agreement on the amount of debt owed Russia as part of its communist past. The Russians were demanding repayment of US$11 billion. After difficult negotiating sessions, a deal was cut to pay Russia US$250 million over a thirty-year period.

The Mongolians place a premium on working within the structures of the UN and its associated bodies—such as the organization of landlocked nations—as well as the UN's health and social bodies.

North Korea

The number one security concern throughout Asia is the question of a nuclear North Korea. Pyongyang and Ulaanbaatar have always had good relations, and today Mongolian parliamentary delegations travel for meetings with North Korean officials. Mongolian businessmen have also visited North Korea at the invitation of Kim Jong-il's government to discuss business deals. "It is an amazing and sad place," stated Od, a Mongolian businessman. "There is nothing there, no electricity, no industry and the people live in poverty. It is as if the government officials we spoke to did not see any of this," he stated.

Mongolia has provided a small amount of food aid to North Korea as a goodwill gesture. Mongolia has an embassy in Pyongyang, and the North Koreans have a very small diplomatic presence in Ulaanbaatar. "We have urged them to discuss peace and reducing tensions with the U.S.," stated one Mongolian who has traveled several times to Pyongyang as part of official delegations. An American diplomat in Ulaanbaatar views the Mongolian overtures as helpful, but is realistic about the end results. "The North Koreans will not change course over what the Mongolians say, but at least it is an Asian country saying it," he remarked.

The North Koreans have returned the Mongolians' generosity by using their country as a gateway to launder tens of thousands of dollars in counterfeit U.S. currency. There was a problem with bogus U.S. $100 bills that suddenly appeared in the capital. Mongolian law enforcement officials traced it back to the North Korean embassy. This practice of using embassies to launder money has been a standard practice of the North Koreans for decades. Their printing presses are world-class and were a factor in the redesign of U.S. paper currency.

Terrorism Threat and Response

Mongolia was the first country in Asia to condemn publicly the September 11 terrorist attacks, and the MPRP government under Prime Minister Enkbayar has sent several hundred Mongolian soldiers to Iraq—not exactly unfamiliar turf as their ancestors did sack Baghdad.

Mongolia has no significant Muslim population and, because of its isolated location, is not considered a country with a high terrorist threat level. According to reports, however, there was an incident in the late 1990s when several Middle Eastern men were detained by Mongolian authorities for allegedly conducting surveillance on the U.S. embassy in Ulaanbaatar.

Military Structure and Defense Policy

The country has a small military force numbering just over eight thousand. Another seven thousand personnel are engaged in such paramilitary duties as border patrol, internal security, and civil defense.

In the late 1990s Mongolia and the United States began a series of military exchanges, with U.S. Special Forces training with their Mongolian counterparts. These exercises continue, and in 2003 a contingent of U.S. Marines were trained by the Mongolian military to—ride horses. Illustrating yet again that the past is the future. The lessons from Afghanistan where U.S. Special Forces had to adopt traditional means of transportation have been taken to heart.

Conclusions and Outlook

Mongolian foreign policy priorities should remain constant for the near future, unless there is a major change within China or Russia. The Mongolians have been aggressively reaching out from the isolation of their landlocked state to cultivate relationships with Western countries and their Asian neighbors to the south. To complement this effort, Mongolia will be seeking engagement through such bodies as the Association of Southeast Asian Nations (ASEAN) and various United Nations organizations.

Aside from traditional security threats, Mongolia's primary security goals will be to diversify its economic base and to develop programs to address the increasing desertification of the country. Establishing a healthy climate for foreign investment is critical to Mongolia's future. The country starts out handicapped by its location and lack of infrastructure. Addressing social problems that hamper business development—such as corruption—is crucial to growing the business sector.

As Mongolia enters its second decade of freedom and independence, its people have demonstrated that they are committed to a democratic process that links simultaneously economic development and human rights. One can only hope that Mongolia's immediate neighbors learn from that country's experiences and adopt the same commitment to political pluralism that has made Mongolia the only democracy in what is arguably a very tough neighborhood.

Note

The author has drawn on his own discussions with officials in Mongolia and in the United States for the quotes in this chapter.

Suggested Readings

Brooke, James. "Mongolians Return to Baghdad, This Time as Peacekeepers." *New York Times.* September 25, 2003, p. A10.
————. and Jargal Byambasuren. "In Mongolia, a Tilt Toward a Free Market." *New York Times.* October 21, 2003, p. W1.
Pomfret, John. "Restoring Their Good Names; After Nearly 80 Years, Mongolians Reclaim Identities—and a Past." *Washington Post.* July 11, 2000, p. A1.
Siv, Sichan. "Mongolia's Democratic Steppes." *Far Eastern Economic Review.* September 21, 2000, p. 39.

——— 13 ———

Nepal

Political Uncertainty amid the Maoist Threat

M.A. Thomas

Introduction

The Kingdom of Nepal, located in South Asia, is a landlocked country about the size of the U.S. state of Illinois. Nestled in the rugged Himalayas between two Asian giants, India and China, Nepal is the meeting point of the Indo-Aryan people of India with the Tibeto-Burmese people of the Himalayas. Popular culture views Nepal as a mystical and spiritual destination attracting the likes of tourists and trekkers. The stark reality is that Nepal, whose agriculture is the mainstay of its economy, is among the poorest and least developed countries in the world according to leading economic indicators. Forty-two percent of the population lives below the poverty line. This dismal economic condition, coupled with the country's weakened political institutions and rampant corruption, has paved the way for a Maoist insurgency to flourish in Nepal's rural areas since 1996. The ongoing Maoist insurgency has spread to more than fifty of Nepal's seventy-five districts and has claimed over eight thousand lives.

Nepal faces a looming challenge of national integration with its numerous ethnic, caste, and religious groups. Geography and, to a lesser extent, language, also pose obstacles to unifying its people. In many remote parts of the country, villagers are virtually cut off from the government, with no access to mass media or means of communication. Distances are measured by the number of days it takes to walk to a village, as public transportation and road construction is absent throughout much of the country. These conditions have made it easier for the Maoists to influence and terrorize the people.

Ethnicity and Caste

Nepal's numerous ethnic and caste groups can be categorized as either Indo-Nepalese or Mongoloid. Indo-Nepalese groups include upper-caste Hindus,

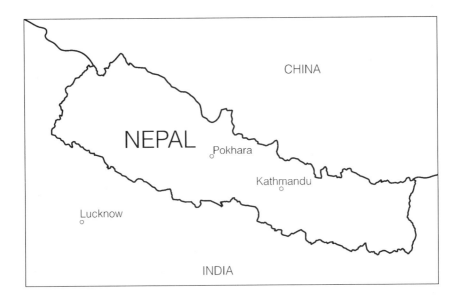

other Indian farmers and laborers, and Newaris. The upper-caste Hindus are the Brahmans and Chetris. Brahmans have traditionally constituted Nepal's intelligentsia and priests, and Chetris have conventionally served as the ruling elite. Indian farmers and laborers in Nepal have migrated from northern India, and their culture and traditions are therefore similar to those of that area. Newaris, primarily Hindu but also Buddhist, are highly literate and urbane; they tend to dominate Nepal's trade and commerce. Mongoloid groups include Magars, Gurungs, Kiratis, Thakalis, Sherpas, and Tamangs. The Magars and Gurungs are mainly Hindu and have produced Nepal's Gurkha soldiers. Kiratis constitute a distinct ethnic group, based upon their language and regional affiliation, and have sought autonomy within Nepal. Thakalis are of Tibetan origin and have recently adopted many Hindu practices. Sherpas are Buddhists well known for their mountaineering skills. Tamangs are Buddhists, also of Tibetan origin, who work mainly as porters and farm laborers.

Geography, Language, and Religion

Nepal's ethnic and caste groups are interspersed among north to south leading geographic zones of the country known as the Himalaya (mountains), the Pahar (midlands), and the Terai (Gangetic plain). These geographic zones can be further subdivided from east to west into the eastern, central, and western regions of each zone. Nepali, hailing from the Indo-European family of languages, is the official language of Nepal and is spoken by 90 percent of the country's population. About a dozen other languages and thirty dialects are also spoken among Nepal's multiethnic groups. English is used frequently in matters of government and business. Though Nepal is considered the world's only Hindu kingdom (86 percent Hindu), Buddhists (8 percent), Muslims (4 percent), and members of other religions (2 percent) are found throughout the country.

Political Framework

The political atmosphere in Nepal has witnessed numerous and sometimes drastic changes in its government during recent years. Coalitions of political parties have been forged and disbanded at alarming rates. Nepal's government is officially described as a parliamentary democracy and constitutional monarchy. At present, this description is misleading as the country's parliament has been dismissed and the king has controversially assumed executive power. To truly understand how Nepal has arrived at its current political situation, one must examine the unique circumstances of the country's political development, as well as the country's experimentation with various forms of government. The six main phases of Nepal's political development can be summarized as follows:

Phase 1: The Establishment of a Political State

In 1768 King Prithvi Narayan Shah, a member of the Shah dynasty, which continues to this day, unified the numerous small kingdoms existing at the time and established Kathmandu as the capital of Nepal. Shah is also credited with organizing the Nepali army along Western lines and with introducing a legal and administrative system for the country. Several decades later, armed conflict with the British led to the Sugauli Treaty in 1816, under which a significant amount of land was annexed to British India. Bitter about its loss to the British, Nepal shut off all foreign contact until 1951. The British restored some of the land to Nepal in 1858 as a reward for Nepali support during the Indian Mutiny (or First War of Independence as it is referred to by Indian nationalists). Nepal also gained British recognition of its sovereignty and has since been considered a buffer state between India and China. This is significant as Nepal did not share the same colonial experience as other South Asian nations.

Phase 2: The Rana Regime

Nepal experienced a feudalistic society during the Rana regime, in which the landed upper-caste Nepali noblemen held influential positions in the court, administration, and army. The Rana regime began in September 1846 when

Jung Bahadur Rana seized power through a decisive and violent coup. Rana assumed the title of prime minister and promulgated the position to be made hereditary. As prime ministers, the Ranas were able to exercise executive power with no room for democratic reforms. The king was relegated to a position of a pampered ceremonial figurehead. Although development during the Rana regime stagnated, the Rana regime remained intact for over a century.

Toward the end of their dominance, Nepal became politically unstable. Under the leadership of the charismatic Bishweshwar Prasad (B.P.) Koirala, the Nepali Congress Party (NCP) was established by many Nepalis and even members of the Rana family. At the same time, King Tribhuvan was being primed to overthrow the Ranas. In late 1950 King Tribhuvan fled and sought political asylum in neighboring India. The NCP demanded democracy for Nepal and launched an armed struggle against the Ranas. It set up a parallel government, thereby depriving the Ranas of their legitimacy as rulers of Nepal. This brought about an end to the Rana regime. The oligarchic system that existed under the Rana rule is often referred to today by detractors of the government. They claim that today's society is no better off as a few rich and powerful individuals are controlling the wealth and denying opportunities to the majority poor.

Phase 3: The Monarchy and Experimentation with Democracy

With Nepal in political turmoil, India exerted its influence and negotiated a solution where King Tribhuvan could return to Nepal. The king returned and set up a new government comprised of a coalition of both Ranas and members of the NCP under an interim constitution. Nepal also ended its isolation from foreign influences and began to establish diplomatic relations with the international community. King Tribhuvan died in 1955 and was succeeded by his son Mahendra.

Political instability became the hallmark of this era when the governing coalition disintegrated and the NCP became highly factionalized. This led Nepalis to look to the king for leadership, but King Mahendra was not an activist monarch. In 1959 a new constitution provided for a modified version of parliamentary government.

The 1959 elections brought victory to the NCP and B.P. Koirala became prime minister. In 1960 King Mahendra felt that Nepal was not prepared for such drastic changes as land reforms that were being proposed by Koirala. He also feared that a popular prime minister would erode his powers to a merely ceremonial position. The king dismissed the government, arrested Koirala and his cabinet members, banned political parties, and assumed executive power over the country. At the end of this phase Nepal remained a mainly feudal society with traditional ruling elites continuing to occupy influential positions within the administration and the army. The rivalry that existed between the king and politicians bears some semblance to the current situation. The only difference is that today, a third actor, the Maoists, have been thrown into the fray.

Phase 4: The Panchayat System

Even though King Mahendra felt that democratic and parliamentary forms of government were Western creations and would not be suited for Nepal's society, he felt that some form of representative element was required in the government. So in 1962 he issued a constitutional ordinance that established the panchayat (council) system—popular institutions based upon an indirect system of elections. The system was a pyramidal concept where the lowest councils would be elected directly by the people. Each higher council, in turn, would be elected by its preceding lower council. Finally, the highest council, the National Panchayat, would be elected by its preceding lower council as well as by members of professional and class organizations. A council of ministers would be selected from members of the National Panchayat and would serve as an advisory body to the king. Under this arrangement, the king acquired power to amend the constitution, as well as suspend it during periods of emergency. Most notably, political parties were not allowed to operate under the system.

In 1972 King Mahendra died and was succeeded by his son Birendra. The panchayat system failed to satisfy the demands of politicians, intellectuals, and students, leading to increased violent demonstrations against the government. In 1980 King Birendra acquiesced and held a nationwide referendum to determine what form of government Nepal should adopt. The choices were either a partyless panchayat system or a multiparty parliamentary type of government. The panchayat system won by a slim majority, and the king continued to hold sovereign power. The panchayat system, of which variations have been used elsewhere in South Asia, has been criticized by both sides of the political spectrum. For the majority who advocated direct elections, the panchayat system was not democratic enough. For the few who advocated a less representative form of government, the panchayat system was too liberal.

Phase 5: Parliamentary Democracy in Uncertain Times

In 1990 public pressure forced King Birendra to replace the panchayat system with a democratic parliamentary form of government. A new constitution provided for such a government, as well as for fundamental rights to citizens, a multiparty democracy based on universal adult suffrage, and a bicameral parliament where the lower house would be elected directly by the people and the upper house would be partly elected by the people and partly appointed. The prime minister would wield executive power, and the king would be the ceremonial head of state. The May 1991 elections brought the NCP to power with Girija Prasad (G.P.) Koirala, brother of the late B.P. Koirala, who died in 1983, as prime minister of Nepal.

Nepalis had great expectations from the government now that a new era of democracy had begun. Unfortunately, bitter infighting among politicians and a series of price hikes nullified any hope for a stable polity and economy. General strikes often became violent, and ultimately a no-confidence vote for Koirala forced Nepal to hold midterm elections in late 1994, which resulted in a hung parliament. The Communist Party of Nepal-Unified Marxist-Leninist (CPN-UML) cobbled together a coalition with the Rastriya Prajatantra Party (RPP) gaining tacit support from the NCP. Rarely has a communist government ever come to power by popular vote in a multiparty democratic system, with a monarch, and supporting a free-market economy.

The NCP formed a new government after it withdrew its support for the CPN-UML. Continuing political rife caused the government to change four times in 1998 alone. A renewed sense of hope emerged in May 1999 when the NCP secured a majority in parliament. However, Nepal quickly reverted to a state of political uncertainty as intraparty factionalism caused the NCP to split. It might be surprising to learn that the strong leftist and communist influence in Nepal did not result from neighboring China. Instead, most of Nepal's politicians were educated in eastern India, a communist hotbed at the time. Even the noncommunist NCP had strong leftist leanings.

Phase 6: Reemergence of the Monarchy?

In one of the most stunning events of Nepal's recent history, Crown Prince Dipendra took the lives of King Birendra, Queen Aishwarya, other close relatives, and then himself in a drunken shooting spree in June 2001. With unsubstantiated conspiracy theories running amok, Gyanendra, the younger brother of Birendra, was controversially crowned king of Nepal. King Gyanendra, expected by many to play a passive role in Nepal's government, declared a state of emergency in November 2001 after a spate of Maoist attacks, ordering the Royal Nepalese Army to quell the Maoist insurgency. Furthermore, he shocked Nepalis when he dissolved parliament over the Maoist problem in October 2002 and assumed executive power over Nepal while maintaining a caretaker prime minister.

King Gyanendra has made public statements justifying his actions and his role in administering executive power. He feels that most Nepalis want him to play a more proactive role in Nepal's affairs, and that the days of the monarch acting as a mere figurehead are over. The king states that neither the mainstream political parties nor the Maoists have addressed the people's concerns. King Gyanendra enjoys support from the Royal Nepalese Army, some segments of society (especially those on the right of the political spectrum), as well as some members of the international community.

Internal Security Environment

The Maoists: Nepal's Internal Threat

The goal of the Maoist insurgency in Nepal is to overthrow the constitutional monarchy and replace it with a communist republic. The Maoists have emerged as an increasing and brutal threat to Nepal since the Communist Party of Nepal-Maoist (CPN-M) went underground in 1996 and launched its self-proclaimed People's War. The number of hard-core well-trained Maoist cadre varies from source to source; however, most indications suggest about five thousand. Another ten thousand to fifteen thousand less-trained members constitute the Maoist militia and operate in a supporting role. The leader of the Maoists is Pushpa Kamal Dahal, popularly known as Prachanda ("the fierce one"). Dr. Baburam Bhattarai is second in command. The Maoist leadership has often used Indian territory as its base from which to plan operations.

A number of factors account for the rise of the Maoists in Nepal. Foremost among them are Nepal's widespread poverty and pervasive corruption. After Nepal democratized in the 1990s, political stability and economic development toward a viable free-market economy remained elusive. Raised expectations by the common Nepali were dashed away with partisan political infighting and a rising inflation rate. Endemic corruption among official quarters, bad governance, and lack of opportunity nullified any aspirations for the common man to enjoy a better standard of living. This provided fodder for the Maoists to gain support among the poor for their cause. Most Maoist guerillas hail from remote districts that lack roads, schools, and other economic infrastructure due to government negligence.

The modus operandi of the Maoists has been to conceal their combat units while operating politically through a number of front organizations and sympathetic groups. As Maoist affiliates, these groups operate openly and legitimately. They tend to extend political, financial, informational, and even military support to Maoist activities. These groups attempt to help the Maoists win the hearts and minds of the people. A sympathetic newspaper or magazine, for example, will publish an article instigating the public to rise against the state. In addition to creating confusion among the public, the Maoist media especially seek to demoralise the police by identifying certain front-line officials as torturers, rapists, and killers. These articles are ordered, crafted, and planted with a view of weakening and disintegrating the counter-insurgency thrust of the government.

Members of the public who oppose the Maoists or their mission have been brutally beaten or killed. There are several cases of recording the voice of a victim before an execution. As a means of discouraging those going against the terrorists, the Maoists would play the recording in front of others. Thus, the public is made to support the Maoists by dint of strength, fear, and indignation. Funding comes from criminal activity or extortion (referred to as "taxes") from the public.

In order to accomplish its goal of capturing power, the primary strategy of the Maoists is to build their strength by widening the class conflict. The Maoists control about 40 percent of Nepal and regularly launch guerrilla activities in their stronghold of the remote districts, especially in Rolpa and Rukum. They have declared the rich as the enemy of the people, and attack police stations and local government offices to cripple the government administration and exercise political control. They have deliberately created an environment of terror and insecurity to gather strength and gain control.

The Maoists have adopted the following strategies in attacking civilians, policemen, army, government installations, and nongovernmental organization (NGO) offices: use small arms that are easier to discard and allow for escape; move in groups of thirty-five to forty members; create an atmosphere of terror by attacking symbolic targets and exploding bombs; target foreign-funded projects, government staff, and public buildings to disrupt foreign and domestic development activities; capture weapons from the police and army to be used in future offensive operations; and target local infrastructure such as the Village Development Council (VDC) offices in order to cut the link between the government and the people, and hence fill in the resulting vacuum.

Long-term strategies of the Maoists are to increase the number of weapons among its members, to procure more sophisticated weapons, to conduct operations on a larger scale, to improve its human rights posture, to garner support of the people more from genuine solidarity rather than from fear tactics, and to utilize cease-fires and peace negotiations to consolidate domestic political gains and to woo international acceptance.

The Maoists have also established relationships with a number of foreign terrorist and radical political organizations. They are members of the Revolutionary Internationalist Movement (RIM), a radical organization whose guiding ideology is Marxism-Leninism-Maoism. The Maoists have a close affinity toward the Sendero Luminoso (Shining Path) of Peru, which was used as a model when the Maoists first organized. As of this writing, the Maoists have no open office in the West. The main international support base of the Maoists is primarily in neighboring India. They have links with the People's War Group (PWG) and the Maoist Coordination Centre (MCC), which are active in the Indian states of Andhra Pradesh, Madya Pradesh, and Bihar. The Maoists have also established ties with the United Liberation Front of Assam (ULFA) and other insurgent groups in India's northeast. It is also believed that the Maoists have ties with the Liberation Tigers of Tamil Eelam (LTTE) of Sri Lanka.

Owing to Nepal's porous border with India, the Maoists have successfully used Indian territory as a safe haven. Maoists have been gathering, assembling, and meeting in strength in western Nepal and in the bordering areas of India. From these sheltered areas, the Maoists have built a robust support network supplying trained manpower, weapons, and finances into midwestern Nepal.

External Security Environment

Sandwiched between India and China, Nepal has always attempted to balance its relations between the two most populous nations in the world. Nepal formally established relations with China in 1956, and since then bilateral relations have generally been very good. China provides considerable developmental aid to Nepal, especially in the area of road construction. It should be noted that despite adopting the ideology of Mao Zedong, there is no evidence that the Maoists have received any support from China. Conversely, China feels that the term "Maoist" is unjustified for the insurgency in Nepal. In addition, China has expressed concern of the possible use of Nepal as sanctuary for Tibetan refugees. Much to China's chagrin, Nepal has been used as a transit point for Tibetan refugees on their way to India, a country where they have been granted political asylum. Moreover, about thirty thousand Tibetans have remained in Nepal.

Nepal has been economically and culturally closer to India, a country with which it shares an open border, allowing for the free movement of people. India and Nepal restored trade relations in 1990, after a break caused by India's security concerns over Nepal's relations with China. By far Nepal's most important trading partner, India signed a bilateral trade treaty with its smaller northern neighbor in 1996. India, which often acts in a proprietary manner over the smaller South Asian nations, usually makes its resentment known when Nepal concludes economic or security-related deals with China or any Western countries. India has promised Nepal increased support in denying the Maoists sanctuary in Indian territory. It views increased support to Nepal as decreasing outside and Western influences in the region.

Terrorism Threat and Response

In the wake of September 11, 2001, the United States, Nepal's second largest trading partner, added the Maoists to its comprehensive list of terrorist organizations. The United States, which has traditionally enjoyed favorable relations with Nepal, has provided the Royal Nepalese Army with 8,400 M-16 automatic rifles as part of a two-year, US$17 million aid package that also includes training in small-unit tactics and human rights law. The United States views continued professionalization of the Royal Nepalese Army as necessary for Nepal to combat its terrorist problem. The United States and Nepal view such assistance as part of the global War on Terrorism. Nepal has declared its unqualified support for the U.S.-led coalition against international terrorism, although some communist opposition parties have criticized this stance as a violation of the principles of nonalignment. Of immediate concern to the United States is the Maoist threat to American citizens, property, and interests in Nepal. A longer-term concern is that a failed state in Nepal could increase regional instability and become a sanctuary for international terrorists.

Nepal and the United Kingdom have traditionally enjoyed close relations. The only outstanding issue involves the demands of the Gurkha soldiers who have retired from British military service. Gurkhas, elite warriors from Nepal, have served in the British armed forces for almost two centuries. They feel that they should be accorded the same treatment as soldiers who are British nationals.

Germany, Nepal's third largest trading partner, is one of Nepal's most important development cooperation donors, along with Japan, the United States, the United Kingdom, Norway, and Denmark.

Nepal has played an active role in the formation of the economic development-oriented South Asian Association for Regional Cooperation (SAARC) and is the site of its secretariat. On international issues, Nepal follows a nonaligned policy and often votes with the Nonaligned Movement in the UN. Nepal participates in a number of UN specialized agencies and is a member of the World Bank, International Monetary Fund, Colombo Plan, and the Asian Development Bank.

Military Structure and Defense Policy

The organizational structure of the Nepalese defense establishment reflects the country's indigenous military traditions, its long association with the

British military, and reforms introduced by Indian military advisers in the 1950s and 1960s. Following the British pattern, there is a Ministry of Defense, which, in conjunction with the king and the parliament (when functional), is responsible for overseeing the military establishment.

Patterned after the British and Indian armies, Nepal's sole regular armed force is the Royal Nepalese Army, long regarded as the bulwark of the king. Although there is no separate air force, the army operates a small air wing, primarily to transport troops within the country and to aid the civilian population during natural disasters. Because Nepal is landlocked, the country has no naval capabilities beyond a few small launches used by the army to patrol lakes and ford rivers.

Conclusions and Outlook

With such daunting economic challenges lying ahead, Nepal can ill afford to remain mired in highly partisan politics, feeble coalitions, and power struggles between the politicians and the monarch. Many Nepalis have welcomed the king's decision to dissolve parliament. Politicians in Nepal are viewed with disdain, and are regarded as corrupt, self-serving, and obstructionist by failing to bring about a better quality of life for the common man. On the other hand, political party supporters, student activists, and groups sympathetic to the Maoists have engaged in massive street agitation campaigns to restore parliament and curtail the executive powers of the king.

The idea of making Nepal a republic is one trump card political party supporters are threatening to play against the king. The concept of a republic would relegate the king to a ceremonial position, portraying him merely as a figurehead. Furthermore, the term "republic" has connotations that would satisfy a demand of the Maoists, who would view a republic as a stepping-stone toward the ultimate establishment of a communist republic.

Nepal will endeavor to balance relations between its two overshadowing neighbors, India and China. Its short-term external objectives are to secure India's help in combating the Maoists with military assistance, and to urge India to be more proactive in denying the Maoists territory to be used as sanctuary. Nepal will continue to assuage China's concerns of Tibetan refugees using Nepal as a base and as a transit point for onward travel to India. Nepal will keep a watchful eye on China to make sure that no links are established with the Maoists in retaliation for Nepal's acquiescence toward Tibetan refugees.

The Maoists, who are anti-American due to stark ideological differences, pose a continuing threat to American citizens, property, and interests in Nepal. In 2003 the Department of State designated the Communist Party of Nepal

(Maoist) as a terrorist organization under Executive Order 13224. This stigma bars most transactions with the Maoists, including the contribution of funds, goods, or services that would benefit the organization.

A communist takeover in Nepal would have grave implications for the country and the region. A Maoist regime would be autocratic and totalitarian in nature with no room for dissension. Moreover, its leadership has rhetorically made statements that a communist state of Nepal would be one step closer toward the globalization of Maoism. For India, a Maoist Nepal would provide moral and military support to India's northeast insurgencies and other radical groups that aim to destabilize the government in New Delhi. India might be pressured to intervene if such a scenario arose. China would view the occupation of Nepal by India as a serious security threat, and both nuclear rivals would be pushed to the brink of conflict.

The geographic and cultural isolation of many ethnic groups in remote villages has made it easier for the Maoists to influence and terrorize the rural poor. However, even though the Maoists have succeeded in eliminating government functionaries and supporters, disrupted government and foreign-funded development projects, and gained control over vast stretches of territory, they are still far from their goal of seizing political power in Nepal. Whether it remains a monarchy or reverts to a parliamentary system, the government of Nepal will continue to have the surmounting challenges of political stabilization, economic development, winning the hearts and minds of Nepalis, and defeating the Maoists for years to come.

Notes

The views presented in this chapter are those of the author and do not necessarily represent the views of the Department of Defense or any of its components.

The author would like to thank Dr. Rohan Gunaratna of the International Centre for Political Violence and Terrorism Research, Singapore, and Dr. Thomas A. Marks, Adjunct Professor, U.S. Joint Special Operations University, Hurlburt Field, Florida, for their invaluable insights into the Maoist insurgency in Nepal.

Suggested Readings

Bhattarai, Baburam. *The Nature of Underdevelopment and Regional Structure of Nepal: A Marxist Analysis.* Delhi: Adroit Publishers, 2003.

Gregson, Jonathan. *Massacre at the Palace: The Doomed Royal Dynasty of Nepal.* New York: Hyperion, 2002.

Hoftun, Martin, William Raeper, and John Whelpton. *People, Politics, and Ideology: Democracy and Social Change in Nepal.* Kathmandu: Mandala Book Print, 1999.

Hutt, Michael. *Nepal in the Nineties: Versions of the Past, Visions of the Future.* London: Oxford University Press, 2002.

Karki, Arjun, and David Seddon, eds. T*he People's War in Nepal: Left Perspectives.* Delhi: Adroit Publishers, 2003.

Kumar, Dhruba, ed. *Domestic Conflict and Crisis of Governability in Nepal.* Kathmandu: Center for Nepal and Asian Studies (CNAS), Tribhuvan University, 2000.

Marks, Thomas A. *Insurgency in Nepal.* Carlisle, PA: Strategic Studies Institute, U.S. Army War College, December 2003.

———— 14 ————

New Zealand

A Small Nation's Perspective

Bruce Vaughn

Introduction

New Zealand's perspective on defense and security is, to a large extent, shaped by its history, geography, and emerging identity as a small country committed to multilateral peace operations and to the promotion of international norms that seek a peaceful settlement of disputes. New Zealand is a small state of 3.8 million people. New Zealand is also an island state situated on the periphery of the Asia-Pacific region. It has no close neighbors, nor any threatening ones, in its quarter of the Pacific. By the year 1000 New Zealand had been populated by a Polynesian people known as the Maori. In the early nineteenth century Europeans, largely from the United Kingdom, called Pakeha by the Maori, began to settle New Zealand. New Zealanders, Maori, Pakeha, and other islanders have a strong warrior tradition and military history. The Maori had frequent intergroup conflicts before the arrival of Europeans, though the lethality of this conflict grew greatly with the introduction of European firearms. The Musket Wars of the early nineteenth century between various Maori groups, and to a lesser extent the subsequent New Zealand Wars between Maori and Pakeha, so decimated the Maori people that it was not until 1960 that the Maori population attained its pre–Musket War level.[1] The 1840 Treaty of Waitangi continues to serve as the bedrock for relations between the two communities.

New Zealand was an active supporter of the British Empire. It first sent troops abroad to fight for Britain in the Boar War in 1899. Its most heroic contribution came during World War I. For the most part, New Zealand did not distinguish British interests from its own interests at that time. The Battle of Gallipoli figures prominently in the national ethos of war and sacrifice. New Zealand forces suffered an 87 percent casualty rate on the Gallipoli

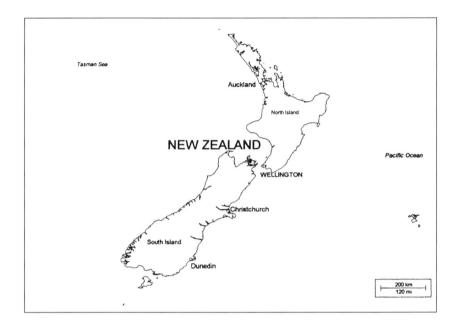

Peninsula. By the end of World War I, 48 percent of New Zealand's male population between the ages of nineteen and forty-five had served, with an overall casualty rate of 58 percent.[2] Gallipoli was also where the Australia-New Zealand Army Corps (ANZAC) legend was largely forged. New Zealand was more reluctant to shed its loyalty to Britain than was Australia, who shifted more readily to an alliance with the United States after the fall of Singapore in World War II. New Zealand's contribution to the United Kingdom's imperial strategy continued through World War II and the Malayan Emergency. New Zealand also contributed troops to the Korean War and fought alongside the Americans in Vietnam. New Zealand forces remained part of Britain's Middle East defense structure until 1955, when they were pulled back to take a place closer to New Zealand in Britain's Commonwealth Strategic Reserve Force in Southeast Asia. New Zealand is also a member of the 1971 Five-Power Defence Arrangement with Australia, the United Kingdom, Singapore, and Malaysia.

Despite this military tradition, New Zealand's defense force today is to a large extent, measured only by its recent deployments, focused on peace operations. The island's geographic isolation has given it a benign security environment. Its closest and largest neighbor, Australia, is closely bound to New Zealand by a shared history, language, and culture and by their close relationship in economic and security issues. These relationships were articulated in the Canberra Pact and subsequently, in 1951, in the ANZUS alliance between Australia, New Zealand, and the United States. The Closer Defense Relations and the Closer Economic Relations agreements both extended and regularized this early cooperation and have the effect of preserving and enhancing the very close relations between New Zealand and Australia.

Political Framework

New Zealand is a unicameral, mixed-member proportional, representative parliamentary democracy. There are several key political parties, of which the Labor and National parties are the two most important. The current prime minister, Helen Clark, is of the Labor Party. New Zealand was reluctant in seeking full independence from the United Kingdom. Indeed the queen of England remains the formal head of state. New Zealand received Dominion status in 1907 and full independence in 1947 under the Statute of Westminster Adoption Act. Today Maori comprise some 14.5 percent of the population, while Pacific Islanders are 6.5 percent, giving New Zealand a South Pacific character, particularly as Pakeha New Zealanders come to accept more of a Pacific identity for the nation.

In the post–World War II era New Zealand wanted to keep the United States involved in the security dynamics of the Pacific. As a result, New Zealand drew closer to the United States as a key ally.[3] By the mid-1980s, however, New Zealand and the United States had a falling out over New Zealand's adoption of antinuclear policies. France's nuclear testing in the South Pacific did much to mobilize New Zealanders' impulses against nuclear weapons. Legislation was passed in New Zealand prohibiting nuclear-powered or nuclear-armed ships from visiting its ports. This precipitated a de facto split in 1986 in the New Zealand-United States side of the trilateral ANZUS alliance. America and New Zealand, while they remain close, are no longer formal allies. Limited cooperation with significant caveats does continue in the area of intelligence sharing and in such programs as providing support to the U.S. Antarctic program.

Despite its ongoing tradition of contributing to international security efforts, there is a lack of support in New Zealand to sustain what is viewed by many as a costly defense establishment. For this reason, it is thought that there are few votes to be had for increasing the defense budget. This largely stems from a sense of security from traditional menaces that comes from geographic isolation and a sense that a threat—to the extent that there is one—is an economic one, stemming from the forces of globalization. New Zealand is a heavily trade-dependent nation. The economic aspects of its security are paramount over more traditional security concerns, which in

New Zealand's case has largely meant maritime and regional security as well as peace operations. The perception that more long-established security concerns are second to economic security concerns could change if New Zealand were to experience an attack on a scale similar to that which Australia suffered in the October 2002 bombing in Bali, Indonesia.

New Zealand has been seeking new markets for its largely agricultural exports since its preferential access to the United Kingdom ended. The United Kingdom entered the European Common Market (now the European Union) in 1973. This search for markets manifests itself today in New Zealand's push for a free trade agreement (FTA) with the United States. The United States and Australia completed negotiations on a FTA in early 2004. New Zealand's stance on Iraq, which preferred UN-sponsored action, as well as lingering tensions over New Zealand's antinuclear policy, as compared with Australia's willing contribution to the war in Iraq, may be the reason why New Zealand was lagging behind Australia in its FTA negotiations in 2004. That said, U.S. president, George W. Bush, has stated that the nuclear issue, while complicating the previous alliance relationship, does not at present represent an impediment to a strong trade relationship. Fifty United States Representatives and nineteen Senators wrote to President Bush to support movement on an FTA with New Zealand in 2003.

Internal Security Environment

While Maori-Pakhea conflict over land rights and sovereignty led to the New Zealand wars in the nineteenth century, there is no longer a significant internal security problem in the nation. Nevertheless, New Zealand recognizes that the War on Terrorism is increasingly a global phenomenon that has the potential, even if not likely, of reaching out to its remote part of the world. New Zealand's reluctance to be involved in the invasion phase of operations in Iraq makes it less of a target than Australia or Britain, which contributed forces to the United States-led coalition. New Zealand is developing its ability to prevent an attack against its land or to use it as a staging area for operations elsewhere.

External Security Environment

The geography of New Zealand's most immediate external security environment is maritime. With the exception of Australia, all of New Zealand's closest neighbors are small Pacific island states with little or no military capability. Papua New Guinea and Fiji do have small armed forces, while France retains interests in New Caledonia and French Polynesia. The region is increasingly beset by "cumulative stresses arising from population growth, ethnic tensions, widening socioeconomic disparities, governance failures, and the impact of global trends."[4] Within this neighborhood New Zealand is perceived as a largely positive influence. Many Pacific islanders migrate to New Zealand, making Auckland the world's largest Polynesian city. New Zealand's special relationship with the Pacific has led it to play a constructive role in ameliorating conflict in the region. This has been most notable in the recent conflicts in Papua New Guinea, East Timor, and the Solomon Islands. New Zealand has constitutional responsibilities for the security of the Cook Islands, Niue, and Tokelau.

For its size, New Zealand has played a very active role in international peace operations both within its region and beyond. It carried out a leading position in initiating the peace process in the Bougainville conflict.[5] New Zealand was also a key contributor in East Timor under both multilateral and UN auspices. In 1999 New Zealand contributed forces under the Australian-led International Force East Timor (INTERFET) that later became the UN Transitional Authority East Timor (UNTAET). New Zealand also contributed land forces to the UN Protection Force (UNPROFOR) and has continued to contribute to Peace Support Operations in the Balkans, often with British forces. More recently it contributed troops to multilateral peace operations in the Solomon Islands that arrested growing chaos there. New Zealand also has soldiers involved with peace operations in Bosnia, Kosovo, Sierra Leone, Mozambique, Cambodia, and elsewhere. New Zealand has, in the ways described above, been an active supporter of the United Nations and such other multilateral groupings as the Pacific Islands Forum. In keeping with this focus, the New Zealand Defence Force (NZDF) is increasingly configured to carry out peace operations missions.

Terrorism Threat and Response

New Zealand became aware of the potential dangers of terrorism before 9/11. A New Zealand police raid in March 2000 in Auckland found maps detailing entry and exit routes to a nuclear reactor in the southern suburbs of Sydney, Australia, where the Summer Olympics were held in 2000.[6] A number of New Zealanders were subsequently killed in the World Trade Center in New York on 9/11 and also in the Bali, Indonesia, attack in October 2002.

In January 2002 New Zealand announced its intentions to expand and enhance intelligence agencies, police for airport security, intelligence gathering resources, and immigration and customs interception capabilities. New Zealand also announced plans to set up chemical and biological terrorism teams within the armed forces and to post police intelligence specialists in

Washington and London to keep New Zealand informed of counterterrorism intelligence.[7] New Zealand also passed the Terrorism Suppression Act that seeks to develop the tools to deal with terrorists, while balancing this against the need to protect civil liberties.[8] New Zealand has also moved to stop terrorist financing.

New Zealand has increased resources allocated for intelligence activities in the wake of 9/11. For example, the Security Intelligence Service (SIS) annual budget of NZ$16.5 million was increased 22 percent. Other arms of the New Zealand intelligence community include the Government Communications Security Bureau, which handles electronic signals intercepts, including those from the Waihopai facility, the External Assessments Bureau, which provides analysis to the Prime Minister's Office, and the Directorate of Defense Intelligence and Security, which provides military intelligence.[9] The Waihopai intercept facility is part of the Echelon system that provides signals intelligence to a collaborative effort between the United States, the United Kingdom, Canada, Australia, and New Zealand.[10]

New Zealand's contribution to the international War on Terrorism has included a small number of peacekeeping and reconstruction forces on extended deployment to Afghanistan and Iraq. New Zealand assisted the United States in establishing a number of joint civilian-military Provincial Reconstruction Teams (PRT) to establish areas of stability across Afghanistan. New Zealand has played a leading role with the Bamian PRT, which it assumed leadership of in September 2003. Its contribution was demonstrated further in December 2003 when one of its P-3 aircraft spotted two suspicious ships in the Arabian Sea that were later found to be smuggling US$11 million worth of heroin and methamphetamines for al Qaeda.[11] Elements of the New Zealand Special Air Service were deployed to Afghanistan in 2002 and took part in combat operations against the Taliban and al Qaeda forces alongside American Special Forces in Operation Enduring Freedom. New Zealand is party to all twelve United Nations conventions on terrorism. Prime Minister Clark also provided some diplomatic support to President Bush for his effort to get the Asia-Pacific Economic Cooperation (APEC) organization to focus on security matters. New Zealand also sent a small contingent of soldiers to assist with reconstruction in Iraq. This deployment earned New Zealand the status of "force contributing nation," which qualified it to compete for American reconstruction contracts in Iraq. While the country has supported United States reconstruction efforts in Afghanistan and Iraq and has cooperated with terrorist interdiction efforts in the Gulf area, it is more comfortable participating in such activity when the international community sanctions it, particularly if it is done through the United Nations.

The New Zealand foreign minister, Phil Goff, urged greater cooperation at a region-wide counterterror meeting in Bali, Indonesia, in February 2004. Goff focused on the need for regional states to sign on to all twelve United Nations legal frameworks for countering terrorism and to develop mechanisms to facilitate extradition, obtaining evidence for prosecutions, enhancing law enforcement, and sharing intelligence. Fiji's foreign minister, Kaliopate Tavola, welcomed Goff's offer of assistance to help Fiji adopt various international counterterror conventions.[12]

Like other Western democracies, New Zealand is grappling with civil liberties issues as it takes measures to defend itself against a terrorist attack. SIS head Richard Woods issued a security-risk certificate against Ahmed Zaoui that put Zaoui in prison. The New Zealand government has not publicly made a case why Zaoui is a threat. Zaoui was previously arrested and charged with heading the Armed Islamic Group, receiving a four-year suspended sentence in France in 1995. Zaoui was subsequently deported from Switzerland and fled Malaysia to avoid extradition to Algeria. The New Zealand Refugee Status Appeal Authority previous to the certificate had found Zaoui to be a refugee. As a result, there is some debate in New Zealand over whether he is being legally imprisoned.[13]

Military Structure and Defense Policy

The New Zealand Armed Forces are not large. There are a total of 12,904 members of the New Zealand Armed Forces, of which 8,660 are active, 2,338 are reservists, and the balance civilians. The army has 105 LAV III light armored vehicles that are replacing forty-one M-113 armored personnel carriers. This is part of a significant upgrade of army equipment, including antiarmor and communications capability upgrades. It also has twenty-four 105 mm towed artillery and fifty 81 mm mortars. The navy has three frigates. Two are ANZAC class and the third is the *Canterbury,* which is the former British Leander class. The New Zealand Navy also has four patrol and coastal combatant ships. The New Zealand Air Force has six P-3K Orion aircraft, five C-130H and two Boeing 727 transport aircraft.[14]

New Zealand has remained hesitant to fund defense, even as its ability to afford it has risen. The New Zealand defense budget has declined as a percentage of gross domestic product (GDP) from 1.83 percent in 1988/1989 to 0.88 percent of GDP in 2003/2004. This represents a 52.27 percent decrease in defense expenditure since 1988.[15] It has been reported that the Defense Long Term Capital Plan is only partially funded.[16] This decrease in defense spending occurs at a time when the New Zealand economy is doing well, the regional security situation is faltering, and the need for peace operations and the threat of terrorism are on the rise. New Zealand GDP rose 4 percent in

2002 and 3.9 percent in 2003. Unemployment at the end of 2003 was at a 16-year low. The New Zealand dollar rose 22 percent against the U.S. dollar, retail sales increased 7.4 percent, and the share market was up 23 percent in 2003.[17]

There are five key factors influencing New Zealand's national security posture, and its worldview.

1. New Zealand is a small nation.
2. It has adopted a staunch antinuclear stance.
3. There is increasing instability in New Zealand's neighborhood.
4. The War on Terrorism.
5. Economic security.

As discussed above, New Zealand's worldview as a small state leads it to play an active role in the UN and to promote a rules-based international system. Its antinuclear policies have complicated its relations with the United States. The increasing uncertainty in what is becoming an arc of instability to the north of New Zealand would point to the need to develop defense capabilities. At present force structure levels, it is very difficult for New Zealand to take the lead in promoting peace and stability in its region even with small island states like the Solomons. New Zealand is taking the War on Terrorism seriously and is making a significant contribution relative to its size. Nevertheless, the War on Terrorism has not been the basis for an increase in defense spending—indeed, defense spending has declined since 9/11 when measured in constant dollars. In this way economic security remains a key factor in its defense policy.

New Zealand defense policy is described in the *2003/04 Output Plan* as largely being based on the *Defence Policy Framework* and the *Defence Beyond 2000 Report* issued by the New Zealand government in 2000. The *2003/04 Output Plan* also points to *Strategic Assessment 2000,* from the External Assessment Bureau, and *New Zealand's Foreign and Security Policy Challenges,* from the Ministry of Foreign Affairs and Trade, as key policy documents that set the policy framework within which the NZDF outputs are defined. The policy framework defined by these documents leads to five key official policy objectives for the NZDF. They are meant to:

1. Defend New Zealand and to protect its people, land, territorial waters, Exclusive Economic Zone, natural resources, and critical infrastructure;
2. Meet our alliance commitments to Australia by maintaining a close defense partnership in pursuit of common security interests;
3. Assist in the maintenance of security in the South Pacific and to provide assistance to our Pacific neighbors;

4. Play an appropriate role in the maintenance of security in the Asia-Pacific region, including meeting our obligations as a member of the Five-Power Defence Arrangement; and
5. Contribute to global security and peacemaking through participation in the full range of UN and other appropriate multilateral peace support and humanitarian operations.[18]

Conclusions and Outlook

In light of the above identified defense policy goals, it appears that the resources being made available to the NZDF in order to be able to fulfill its various missions are not sufficient to meet all objectives robustly. The budget is able only to sustain a small force with little left over for future procurement and upgrades of aging existing systems. Further, the trend line in defense funding indicates that an increase in funding is not likely. This will mean that the NZDF's capability to carry out all its policy objectives will likely be limited. New Zealand will more likely uphold it ability to provide politically significant contributions to various peace operations led by other states in the future, even as its ability to act independently in its large South Pacific locality and in high-intensity operations continues to erode. New Zealand may also find increasingly that its air and naval assets are insufficient to meet espoused objectives in its maritime environment and South Pacific neighborhood.

Notes

The views expressed in this chapter are the author's own and do not necessarily reflect the views of the Congressional Research Service. The author would like to thank Military Attaché Lieutenant Colonel Collett of the New Zealand embassy in Washington, DC, for his views and background information, as well as Dr. Patty O'Brien of the Center for Australian and New Zealand Studies at Georgetown University in Washington, DC.

1. Ian McGibbon, ed., *Oxford Companion to New Zealand Military History* (London: Oxford University Press, 2002).

2. Barry Gustafson, "If You Ever Need a Friend, You Have One," Center for Australian and New Zealand Studies, Georgetown University, April 1997.

3. W. David McIntyre, *Background to the ANZUS Pact* (Christchurch, NZ: Canterbury University Press, 1995). See also Jacob Bercovitch, *ANZUS in Crisis: Alliance Management in International Affairs* (Basingstoke, UK: Macmillan Press, 1988).

4. Air Marshal B.R. Ferguson, *Report of the New Zealand Defence Force: Te Ope Kaatua o Aotearoa,* for the year ended June 30, 2003.

5. Bede Corry, "The Bougainville Peace Process: The 'Pacific' Settlement of Disputes?" in Bruce Vaughn, ed., *The Unraveling of Island Asia? Governmental, Communal, and Regional Instability* (Westport, CT: Praeger Publishers, 2002); and

Rebecca Adams, *Peace on Bougainville: Truce Monitoring Group* (Wellington, NZ: Victoria University Press, 2001).

6. Council on Foreign Relations, "Have International Terrorists Been Active in Australia and New Zealand?" at www.cfrterrorism.org.

7. "New Zealand Boosts Counter-terrorism Spending," *Radio Australia News*, 1/30/02.

8. John Smith, "New Zealand's Anti-terrorist Campaign: Balancing Civil Liberties, National Security, and International Responsibilities," at www.fulbright.org.nz.

9. Colin Espiner, "State of Our Spies," *Christchurch (NZ) Press*, February 7, 2004.

10. Jeffrey Richelson, "Desperately Seeking Signals," *Bulletin of Atomic Scientists*, March/April, 2000.

11. "Concern Growing that Some Asian States Are not Pulling Their Weight," *New Zealand Herald*, February 7, 2004.

12. Dona Chisholm, "Top Spy's Zaoui Fury," *Sunday Star Times*, February 8, 2004.

13. Mathew Dearnaly, "Orion Patrol Finger Dhows Linked to Al Qaeda," *New Zealand Herald*, December 22, 2003.

14. The International Institute for Strategic Studies, *The Military Balance 2003–04* (London: 2003).

15. New Zealand Defence Force and Ministry of Defence Statistics, various years.

16. David Dickens, "New Zealand: Wanting to do a Lot with a Little," *Asia-Pacific Defence Reporter*, December 2003.

17. "Goldilocks Economy Continues for a Second Year," *New Zealand Press Association*, December 28, 2003.

18. New Zealand Defence Force, *2003/4 Output Plan Between the Minister of Defence and the Chief of the Defence Force*, June 30, 2004, pp. S1–3/S1–4.

Suggested Readings

Adams, Rebecca. *Peace on Bougainville: Truce Monitoring Group*. Wellington, NZ: Victoria University Press, 2001.

Ferguson, Air Marshal B.R. *Report of the New Zealand Defence Force: Te Ope Kaatua o Aotearoa*. For the year ended June 30, 2003.

McGibbon, Ian, ed. *Oxford Companion to New Zealand Military History*. London: Oxford University Press, 2002.

New Zealand Defence Force. *2003/4 Output Plan Between the Minister of Defence and the Chief of the Defence Force*. June 30, 2003.

New Zealand Department of Defence. *Defence Long-term Development Plan, Update*. June 2003.

Rolf, James, *The Armed Forces of New Zealand*. St. Leonards, NZ: Allen and Unwin, 1999.

Vaughn, Bruce, ed. *The Unraveling of Island Asia? Governmental, Communal, and Regional Instability*. Westport, CT: Praeger Publishers, 2002.

15

North Korea

Continued Advancement of Weapons of Mass Destruction Programs

Larry A. Niksch

Introduction

North Korea, officially the Democratic People's Republic of Korea (DPRK), stands out as a state that poses a significant threat to regional and international peace and stability. This threat derives principally from the regime's continued development of weapons of mass destruction (WMD) and its exportation of WMD systems and components to other rogue governments in geopolitically sensitive regions of the world. A one-man dictatorship under the control of Kim Jong-il, North Korea faces a future of uncertainty with regard to how its brazen pursuit of WMD will eventually play out and is dealt with in the face of strong international opposition. This high-stakes diplomatic and political-military situation is taking place against the background of continued economic hardship for the people of North Korea.

North Korea today is in a stronger overall position with regard to its nuclear and other WMD programs: stronger in terms of advances in these programs and in a stronger position diplomatically in relation to the United States. This diplomatic gain is surprising, given North Korea's seeming isolation in early 2003 after it withdrew from the Nuclear Non-Proliferation Treaty (NPT) and reopened the nuclear facilities at Yongbyon that had been shut down under the U.S.-North Korean Agreed Framework of 1994.

The reopened installations are the heart of North Korea's plutonium-based nuclear program, which Pyongyang constructed and began to operate in the late 1980s. The plutonium program represented a long-standing commitment by the late North Korean dictator Kim Il-sung to a nuclear weapons program. The rationale for the program appeared to shift with the changes in the country's military and economic fortunes in the 1990s. Kim Il-sung seemed

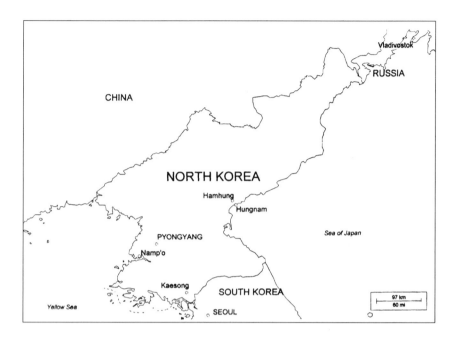

to view the development of nuclear weapons as strengthening North Korea's military position in relation to South Korea and the United States and giving North Korea more aggressive military options on the Korea Peninsula. However, in the 1990s North Korea faced the collapse of the Soviet Union, its chief patron, which triggered a sharp deterioration of North Korean conventional forces and a virtual collapse of its economy. WMD, especially nuclear weapons and missiles, now were viewed as an alternative to conventional forces and Soviet backing and as necessary to limit the adverse shift in the military balance on the Korea Peninsula. It also became a component to the stability of the North Korean regime after Kim Il-sung died in July 1994 and his son, Kim Jong-il, took power.

WMDs satisfied the politically powerful North Korean military, which Kim Jong-il has emphasized as the chief pillar of his rule. Earnings from overseas sales of missiles, as much as US$500 million in individual years, has provided crucial foreign exchange for Kim Jong-il to finance his nuclear programs and satisfy the economic needs of the military and the political elite in the midst of mass malnutrition, acute energy shortages, and industrial decline. Kim Jong-il is estimated to expend around US$100 million annually to purchase luxury goods overseas, which he distributes to a broad swath of top military, Communist Party, and government officials in order to secure their loyalty.[1]

North Korea's main problem in advancing WMD programs has been opposition from the United States. North Korea agreed to shut down its plutonium program in the 1994 Agreed Framework, but it retained the physical facilities and the weapons-grade plutonium, which experts believe it produced prior to 1994. By 1996, probably even earlier, the country was working secretly on a uranium-enrichment program, an alternative way to produce nuclear weapons. It entered into an agreement with Pakistan under which Pakistan supplied uranium-enrichment technology and components to North Korea and Pyongyang sold technology and components of medium- and intermediate-range ballistic missiles to Pakistan. North Korea's end of this agreement illustrated the continuing advance of its missile program in the 1990s. It tested the Taepo Dong 1, a long-range ballistic missile in August 1998, which shocked the Clinton administration and American opinion.

Post–September 11 Challenges and Terrorism Linkages

The challenge from the United States reemerged after the September 11, 2001, terrorist attacks on the United States. President George W. Bush labeled North Korea part of an international Axis of Evil and demanded that North Korea stop proliferating and shut down its WMD programs. The public disclosure of Pyongyang's secret uranium-enrichment program in October 2002 initiated a new round of North Korean-U.S. confrontation. The Bush administration moved to end U.S. obligations under the Agreed Framework and forge a multilateral coalition of countries to force North Korea to dismantle its nuclear programs. North Korea struck back hard, reopening its plutonium facilities at Yongbyon and withdrawing from the NPT.

A related danger that has taken on much great significance in the aftermath of 9/11 is that North Korea could undertake a brazen act of proliferation that would place WMDs in the hands of a terrorist group like al Qaeda. As of this writing, there is no evidence of North Korean links with al Qaeda. However, the country has military links with governments and elements within governments that have links to al Qaeda and other terrorist groups. North Korea and Iran have intimate ties in the development of missiles and nuclear weapons. The same kinds of links have existed between North Korea and Pakistan. North Korea has dealt with Pakistani intelligence services, which play a key role in Pakistan's nuclear program. The intelligence services contain individuals and groups that support al Qaeda and the Taliban. Elements of Iran's Revolutionary Guards may have similar ties to al Qaeda. North Korea also has extensive military ties with Syria, another terrorist-supporting state.

North Korea certainly has the kind of WMDs that al Qaeda wants. Much speculation of this kind has centered on nuclear weapons and nuclear materials; but an al Qaeda interest in North Korea could focus on Pyongyang's chemical and biological weapons such as sarin gas, anthrax vials, and small-pox vials.[2] Especially disturbing is evidence that, for a number of years, North Korea has supplied the technology for producing chemical agents to Syria, Iran, and possibly Libya.[3]

North Korea already is more comfortable and confident in its dealings with the United States than it was when the United States attacked Iraq. North Korean fears of being the "next target" appear to have dissipated because of its diplomatic successes and the problems of the United States in Iraq. This confidence will grow if diplomatic successes continue. It will grow immeasurably if North Korea creates a credible nuclear deterrent without suffering international penalties. If such confidence transforms into overconfidence, North Korea might be tempted to provide WMDs to a terrorist group, especially chemical or biological weapons. Temptation likely would grow under three conditions: (1) if a buyer offered North Korea a considerable amount of money for WMDs, (2) if North Korea believed that it had a good prospect of not being discovered as the ultimate source of WMDs in the hands of a terrorist group, and (3) if it had reasonable confidence that the United States would not retaliate militarily (such confidence could come from possessing a nuclear deterrent).

Weapons of Mass Destruction and Military Capabilities

The reopening of the Yongbyon installations illustrated overall advances in North Korea's WMD programs in 2003. The extent of these advances is uncertain; North Korean secrecy presents major problems for U.S. intelligence agencies. However, U.S. intelligence officials and Bush administration officials have indicated that a number of these programs are advancing. The reopening of the Yongbyon facilities led to a North Korean claim that it had reprocessed eight thousand nuclear reactor fuel rods into weapons-grade plutonium. In January 2004, a visiting U.S. nuclear expert saw evidence that North Korea had the technology to produce weapons-grade plutonium. U.S. officials acknowledged that North Korea appeared to have reprocessed most of the rods into enough plutonium for four to six atomic bombs. The Central Intelligence Agency (CIA) also informed the U.S. Congress in August 2003 that North Korea had completed the design and triggering mechanism of atomic bombs without having to conduct a nuclear test.[4] When asked if North Korea has produced plutonium or nuclear weapons in 2003, a "senior administration official" replied: "I would mean both. But I can't be specific because I don't think we know" the quantities.[5] Potentially more disturbing, the CIA reported to the Japanese government in mid-2003 that North Korea was close to developing nuclear warheads that it could mount on its missiles.[6] (Some analysts believe that Pakistan's warhead technology was part of the North Korean-Pakistani deal.)

The state of North Korea's uranium-enrichment program was an even bigger mystery to the U.S. intelligence community. Information indicated that North Korea had accelerated its overseas procurements of materials and components for a uranium-enrichment infrastructure. U.S. intelligence estimates reportedly varied from late 2004 to 2006,[7] in estimating when North Korea would be able to produce an atomic bomb through uranium enrichment, but they also indicated, again, that North Korea was advancing this program.

The same was true of North Korea's missile program. U.S. intelligence estimates in 2003 and 2004 cited a new intermediate-range ballistic missile that has a longer range and greater accuracy than the No Dong model that North Korea began deploying after 1993. The new missile is believed capable of striking Okinawa, the site of major American military bases, and Guam, the home of over 100,000 Americans and key American military facilities. These new estimates also cited advances in North Korea's program to produce a long-range, intercontinental ballistic missile that could reach Alaska, Hawaii, and the U.S. West Coast.[8]

U.S., South Korean, and Russian intelligence estimates have cited for years growing development and stockpiles of chemical and biological agents by North Korea. U.S. and South Korean estimates place the size of those stockpiles of chemical agents at between 2,500 and 5,000 tons. North Korea produces about twenty chemical agents, including sarin gas, V-agents, mustard gas, phosgene, and hydrogen cyanide. North Korean also is known to have the biological agents cholera, bubonic plague, anthrax, smallpox, typhoid, and typhus.[9]

U.S. estimates were not greeted with universal acceptance by other concerned governments. This clearly reflected the credibility problem stemming from apparently inaccurate U.S. intelligence estimates and White House claims regarding Iraq's WMD programs, especially the nuclear program. Japanese officials expressed some skepticism over the CIA's estimate of North Korea's advances in nuclear warheads. Chinese and Russian officials in early 2004 voiced doubts over the existence of a secret uranium-enrichment program in North Korea. Nevertheless, the differences between U.S. intelligence estimates of North Korean WMDs and Iraqi WMDs are significant, and the evidence and history of North Korea's programs leads to a credible conclusion that key programs are advancing. Unlike the Iraq situation, the Bush administration voiced skepticism over North Korea's claim that it reprocessed eight thousand nuclear fuel rods; but frequent North Korean test explosions in recent years were of the type used to develop the design and triggering mechanism of atomic bombs. Moreover, the bulk of the U.S. intelligence community's evidence of North Korea's secret uranium-enrichment program appears to be information of substantial North Korean overseas procurements (and attempted procurements) of materials and components that would go into such a program.

It also has been reported that Pakistan has provided the United States with information regarding its nuclear-missile deal with North Korea, although Pakistan is now only beginning to disclose publicly the details of its widespread proliferation activities. The evidence behind the U.S. claims of North Korean advances in intermediate and intercontinental missiles is unknown, but the U.S. claims come against the background of substantial evidence over fifteen years of a steadily advancing North Korean missile program.

Surprising Diplomatic Strength but Uncertain Future

If North Korean advances in WMD programs have been a consistent trend in the last decade, the strength of its diplomatic position in 2004 was nothing short of astonishing. When Pyongyang withdrew from the NPT and reopened its plutonium facilities at the beginning of 2003, the international community universally condemned North Korea and called on it to fulfill its international nuclear agreements and end its nuclear programs. The Bush administration concluded communiqués with Japan, South Korea, China, and Russia containing such statements of concern. The U.S. government rejected North Korea's demand of bilateral negotiations with the United States and instead gained agreement from these countries for a multilateral, six-party negotiation. White House officials expressed the view in 2003 that the other parties to the six-party talks would join the United States in insisting that North Korea dismantle its nuclear programs "completely, verifiably, and irreversibly." If North Korea did not meet such a demand, dubbed CVID (for "complete, verifiable, and irreversible dismantling"), the other participants would join the United States in imposing stringent sanctions against North Korea. Some administration officials viewed such sanctions as needed to bring about a collapse of the Kim Jong-il regime. U.S. officials were quoted as predicting that North Korea would behave so obnoxiously in six-party talks and in touting its nuclear program that the other governments would become alienated from Pyongyang and would join the U.S. camp. Officials from President Bush down stressed confidence that China would cooperate with the United States, given China's official position that Korea should be free of nuclear weapons. China seemed to move toward alignment with the United States when it organized three-party talks in April 2003 and six-party talks in August 2003 in Beijing.

The Six-Party Talks

The status of the six-party talks in 2004 was very different from the scenarios laid out by the Bush administration. North Korea had established a strong position in the talks. It was succeeding in advancing its negotiating proposals despite their vagueness, likely hidden agenda, and demands for sweeping U.S. concessions. Its demand for a security guarantee from the United States stood at the top of the negotiating agenda of the talks. The U.S. government was offering North Korea a security guarantee, albeit a multilateral one; but it would include a guarantee against a U.S. conventional attack as well as a nuclear attack. It would take effect when North Korea committed to or provided "benchmarks" to a dismantling of its nuclear programs. In contrast, in the 1994 Agreed Framework, the Clinton administration promised a guarantee against a U.S. nuclear attack (not conventional) after North Korea had dismantled its nuclear programs. North Korea also made progress in placing its December 2003 proposal of a nuclear "freeze" at the top of the negotiating agenda. This "reward for freeze" proposal would defer dismantlement indefinitely. It would not include the enriched uranium program or apparently even the 8,000 fuel rods removed from storage in early 2003 or any plutonium reprocessed from the fuel rods. It thus would be more limited in scope than the freeze North Korea agreed to in the 1994 Agreed Framework. The "reward for freeze" proposal also called for U.S. benefits and concessions that were not in the Agreed Framework, such as immediate electricity to North Korea and removal of Pyongyang from the list of terrorism-supporting countries. Nevertheless, China, Russia, and South Korea spoke favorably of the proposal.

North Korea was receiving increased financial aid (US$50 million reported in October 2003), fuel, and food from China and significant food aid and, likely, secret financial aid from South Korea.[10] The White House announced 60,000 tons of new food aid to North Korea in December 2003. Like the Clinton administration, the Bush administration denied that it was "buying meetings" with North Korea. However, it was evident from several statements on food aid in late 2003 that Washington was weakening and/or abandoning the specific conditions regarding monitoring, geographical access, and nutritional surveys that U.S. foreign aid director, Andrew Natsios, had laid down in June 2002 for continued U.S. food aid to North Korea.

On June 23, 2004, at a six-party meeting, the United States issued a comprehensive settlement proposal, the first such proposal since the talks began in April 2003. The proposal called for a freeze of short duration—three months—followed by a verified dismantlement of all North Korean nuclear programs. North Korea would receive heavy oil and an interim security guarantee during the freeze. Other benefits would be negotiated when the process of dismantlement was a fait accompli. North Korea's initial response to the proposal was mixed; but on July 24, 2004, Pyongyang's Foreign Ministry issued a statement labeling the U.S. proposal as a "sham proposal." North Korea followed up this statement with a concerted propaganda campaign against the proposal and U.S. policy generally. It also resisted proposals for a six-party meeting in September 2004, hinting that it would not agree to another meeting until after the U.S. presidential election of November 2004. Clearly, North Korea had decided to kill the U.S. proposal as an active basis of negotiations prior to the U.S. elections. Neither the United States nor the other six-party governments adopted concerted measures to counter Pyongyang's strategy, leaving the U.S. position in the six-party talks weakened and uncertain on the eve of the U.S. election.

What accounts for this surprising North Korean success? Part of this was the result of a North Korean negotiating strategy that played upon the commitment of other governments to the six-party talks and a propaganda campaign that portrayed Pyongyang's proposals as benign and peace-seeking. Beginning with the Beijing meetings in April and August 2003, North Korea frequently criticized the meetings, criticized the U.S. position at the meetings, criticized Japan, and warned that it saw no usefulness in the meetings and likely would not participate in another meeting. Other governments, especially China and South Korea, reacted with apprehension to these warnings, fearing that the talks would collapse. The Bush administration, the author of multilateral talks, also expressed concern. Then, after issuing repeated warnings, North Korea made "new" proposals or gave priority to older proposals. After the April 2003 meeting, it hammered away on its proposal for a North Korea-U.S. nonaggression pact or formal U.S. "security guarantee." In December 2003, in the aftermath of the second Beijing meeting, North Korea issued its "reward for freeze" proposal. North Korean propaganda asserted that such a nonaggression pact was necessary to prevent the United States from staging a unilateral attack on North Korea, similar to the U.S. attack on Iraq. Pyongyang's propaganda organs contended that a freeze, coupled with substantial U.S. concessions, was a logical "first stage" in a settlement process. North Korea warned that a U.S. rejection of these proposals would give Pyongyang no choice but to "strengthen our nuclear deterrent."[11]

Other governments, apprehensive over the future of the talks, sought to react positively to North Korea's proposals in order to persuade Pyongyang to agree to another six-party meeting. China, South Korea, and Russia came out in favor of a security guarantee for North Korea, and they pressured the United States to offer a guarantee. President Bush acceded to China's overtures in October 2003. Beijing and Seoul also spoke positively regarding North

Korea's "reward for freeze" proposal. Knowledgeable Chinese sources admitted that their government placed great emphasis on avoiding offending North Korea in word or deed. Public and elite opinion in South Korea and China reacted favorably to North Korea's proposals, clearly influenced by North Korean propaganda. This "say only positive things about Pyongyang" response carried over into the absence of positive responses from the other six-party governments to the U.S. proposal of June 23, 2004. By the time the Bush Administration issued the proposal, North Korean tactics had so conditioned Beijing, Moscow, and Seoul that they dared offer no endorsements of the U.S. proposal lest they offend North Korea.

North Korea, too, was able to exploit weaknesses in the U.S. strategy. The first was the lack of a comprehensive U.S. negotiating proposal for a settlement with North Korea until June 2004. The U.S. administration consistently refused to present a comprehensive proposal at the six-party talks that would detail the steps that North Korea must take to dismantle its nuclear programs and detail U.S. policy responses to positive North Korean actions. Administration officials rejected the concept of U.S. reciprocal responses until North Korea had dismantled its nuclear programs. Moreover deep divisions within the U.S. government throughout 2003–2004 prevented the formulation of concrete proposals. So-called "engagers," mainly in the State Department, sought to negotiate actively with North Korea. They were opposed by an antinegotiation bloc composed of Vice President Richard Cheney and his advisers, Secretary of Defense Donald Rumsfeld and his advisers, and Undersecretary of State John Bolton. This coalition opposed negotiations and advocated a strategy of relying exclusively on sanctions and pressure on North Korea. They expressed the view that the Kim Jong-il regime would collapse if the United States and other countries did this. At a U.S. initiative, directed by Undersecretary Bolton, eleven nations formed the Proliferation Security Initiative (PSI) in 2003, aimed at interdicting the proliferation of WMDs by North Korea and other rogue states. The Bush administration thus had a potential instrument to shrink North Korea's crucial foreign exchange earnings from such sales and other illicit exports like drugs.

The antinegotiation bloc did not succeed in preventing negotiations, but did succeed in limiting the leeway of Assistant Secretary of State James Kelly, the chief U.S. negotiator. Kelly was ordered by President Bush to follow a tight script at the Beijing meeting and not to engage in any exchanges of views or positions with the North Koreans.[12] Moreover, the factions within the U.S. government were reported to be divided over the kind of details on such future issues as the timing of offering a security guarantee and the strength of a U.S. proposed verification system.[13] There also appeared to be a lack of full support from within the Administration to the June 23 proposal, which the State Department had pushed within the government. This undoubtedly contributed to the lack of an effective follow-up strategy to advertise and promote the proposal, which North Korea took advantage of.

This, however, opened the way for other governments to press the Bush administration for exceptions to this position. The U.S. offer of a security guarantee and new food aid seemed to represent a chipping away of this hard-line front by the beginning of 2004. The absence of a detailed, comprehensive, and balanced U.S. settlement proposal gave the Bush administration little opportunity to establish the U.S. negotiating agenda as the dominant position in the six-party talks. A negotiating agenda dominated by a U.S. comprehensive settlement proposal would force North Korea to respond to the United States and make a clear policy choice between continuing its present policies and altering policies toward abandoning WMDs and fundamentally improving relations with the United States and other countries. In the absence of this, North Korea was able to push its proposals forward relatively unhindered. A U.S. comprehensive settlement proposal would give other governments an instrument to compare with North Korea's proposals and thus put Pyongyang's proposals in a more unfavorable light. Without it, North Korea's proposals stood uncontested as the only detailed solutions offered in the talks. Without it, too, South Korea, China, and Russia displayed growing unhappiness with the U.S. position at the talks.

The U.S. proposal of June 23 did produce these results. North Korea did make a choice, to reject the proposal and seek to kill it diplomatically. The other six-party governments also made a choice against supporting the U.S. proposal. This was unfortunate, but it at least showed the Bush administration the totality of the obstacles it faced in multilateral negotiations. It also demonstrated that Russia, China, and South Korea especially were not willing to press for a settlement based on dismantlement of North Korea's nuclear programs but instead preferred a settlement based on a long-term freeze that excluded the uranium enrichment program.

The U.S. administration's heavy reliance on China also contributed to the defensive position it found itself in early 2004. Both the so-called engagers and the antinegotiation bloc saw China as essential to their objectives. China would influence North Korea to accede to U.S. diplomatic terms, or China would join the United States in applying heavy sanctions against North Korea that would bring down the regime. President Bush spoke glowingly of China's cooperation whenever he issued public pronouncements on North Korea. This optimism was influenced by several Chinese actions. China supported the U.S. proposal for multilateral talks and worked hard to arrange the Beijing meetings. China joined the United

States and other governments in calling for a nuclear-free Korean peninsula. China reportedly cut off oil shipments to North Korea for several days in March 2003, which U.S. analysts interpreted as a sign of Beijing's displeasure with Pyongyang. Members of China's influential think tanks issued statements proposing that China reevaluate its long-standing alliance with and support of North Korea. Nevertheless, even as these actions occurred, China began to display a tilt toward North Korea on substantive issues between North Korea and the United States. China quickly endorsed the proposal of a U.S. promise not to attack North Korea, arguing that the United States needed to address North Korea's "legitimate security concerns." Chinese pressure was the key factor in President Bush's offer of a security guarantee to North Korea at the Bangkok Asia-Pacific Economic Cooperation summit in October 2003.[14] China also made clear in April 2003 that it would oppose any U.S. move to take the North Korean problem to the United Nations Security Council. Chinese officials indicated during this early period that China favored a settlement that would restore key elements of the Agreed Framework. This indication came to fruition in China's November 2003 proposal of a draft statement by the six parties,[15] its favorable response to North Korea's nuclear freeze proposal, and its escalating expressions of skepticism over the existence of a North Korean enriched uranium program in January 2004. By this time, Chinese think tank criticism of North Korea had ended for several months. Chinese Communist Party newspapers such as Xinhua praised North Korea for its flexibility in the talks and called on the United States to offer meaningful concessions.[16] Of major importance, China voiced criticism of the PSI soon after its proclamation and warned the United States against a policy of pressure against North Korea. China's payoffs of money, oil, and food to North Korea to "buy" Pyongyang's attendance at six-party meetings only encouraged North Korea to continue its strategy and delaying tactics.

There is no doubt that China's stance in early 2004 reflected growing frustration with the Bush administration's unwillingness to lay comprehensive proposals on the negotiating table. Nevertheless, China's rule of not offending North Korea resulted in its silence toward the U.S. proposal of June 23, 2004. U.S. policy had not obtained an answer to a fundamental question: What does China really want to see as an outcome to the diplomatic process? Does China give high priority to attaining a complete termination of North Korea's nuclear program? Or does China seek to "put the cork back in the bottle," meaning a restoration of the situation before the Kelly visit to Pyongyang in October 2002? Until the Bush administration secures a credible answer to this question, its reliance on China likely will prove an unstable foundation in these complex negotiations.

The failure of the U.S. government to respond effectively to North Korea's concerted propaganda campaign also contributed significantly to U.S. diplomatic defeats. Pyongyang employed propaganda constantly to implement its strategy of spreading fear that it would end participation in the six-party talks and then promoting its proposals as benign and peace seeking. In pushing its proposal for a nonaggression pact and formal U.S. security guarantee, it used the Iraq war and the Bush administration's own tough rhetoric against the United States. Chinese, Russian, and South Korean leaders all expressed concern that the United States was planning to attack North Korea. In initiating the nuclear freeze proposal, North Korea was aware that China, South Korea, and Russia had misgivings over the collapse of the Agreed Framework. North Korea also employed enticing captions, such as "nonaggression," "nuclear freeze," "simultaneous actions," and "noninterference in our economic development" to appeal to elite and public opinion in these countries. These seemingly attractive diplomatic formulations also overshadowed in overseas perceptions the lack of substance in these proposals and the likely hidden North Korean agenda in them. South Korean opinion, in particular, appears to have been influenced heavily by Pyongyang's propaganda strategy.

It is doubtful that the U.S. government has a clear recognition that a key part of the diplomatic interaction with North Korea in the six-party talks is a propaganda struggle. Its reaction to North Korea's proposals after each Beijing meeting was to state a rejection of them and restate the U.S. position that North Korea first commit to a "complete, verifiable, and irreversible dismantling" of its nuclear programs. Administration officials did not challenge the substance of North Korea's proposals in order to point out their negative features and bring into the open Pyongyang's hidden agenda in them. U.S. officials failed to make a basic point that North Korea's proposals offered less than the obligations Pyongyang accepted in the 1994 Agreed Framework but demanded more benefits and concessions from the United States than Pyongyang had received in the 1994 accord. The U.S. government's only substantive response to the nonaggression proposal was to contend that the U.S. Senate would not ratify it. In short, while Washington's demand that North Korea commit to the CVID formula is a legitimate requirement for the start of any settlement process, it has been a limited, one-dimensional, and inadequate response to North Korea's sophisticated diplomatic and propaganda strategy. The administration's failure to comprehend the importance of propaganda (i.e., "public diplomacy") resulted in the absence of a U.S. strategy to promote and advertise the June 23 U.S. proposal during the summer of 2004. This gave North Korea another open playing field to propagandize against the proposal in its strategy to kill the proposal as a basis for six-party negotiations.

The U.S. response to North Korea's constant denials of a uranium-enrichment program also has been limited. Its responses have been infrequent and only argue that North Korea admitted to the program during the Kelly visit to Pyongyang. North Korea's denial of such an admission presented to the other involved countries a "he said-she said" situation in which the attractiveness of North Korea's negotiating proposals and the controversy over the administration's justification of war with Iraq weakened the U.S. position. There was no public assertion from Washington that the United States, itself, had firm evidence of the uranium-enrichment program, and there was no offering of evidence. This despite many reports that U.S. intelligence agencies had accumulated considerable information of North Korean overseas procurements and attempted procurements of equipment and materials that could be used in uranium enrichment; North Korean attempts at procurement had occurred even in the open societies of Western Europe and Japan.

Conclusions and Outlook

By late 2004 there was no sign that North Korea had self-destructed in the six-party talks, contrary to predictions by Bush administration officials. North Korea's advantage in the talks going into 2004 created a prospect that the negotiations will drift into 2005 with no agreed-upon settlement or may break down entirely. The most likely agreement would be to North Korea's advantage: a limited nuclear freeze that would cover the nuclear installations at Yongbyon but would allow Pyongyang to retain the fruits of its reprocessing of the eight thousand fuel rods and would leave unresolved the highly enriched uranium program, plutonium, and/or atomic bombs produced prior to 1994, and North Korea's nuclear cooperation programs with Iran and possibly other countries. In the future, the United States can expect pressure from China, Russia, and even from South Korea to accept such a freeze agreement that would be designated as a "first phase" of a settlement, but in reality would stand alone, with other phases of a settlement to be determined later through an undefined diplomatic process. The Bush administration undoubtedly would reject such entreaties, and the result likely would be an erosion and eventual end of the six-party talks similar to the death of the four-party talks over a Korean peace agreement in 1997–1999. In the four-party talks, too, the Clinton administration (and South Korea) chose not to present a comprehensive proposal for a Korean peace treaty and rejected any discussions over the U.S. military presence in South Korea. North Korea was able to dominate the agenda of the talks with its proposals, however, unsatisfactory they were.

Throughout the nearly fifteen years in which the North Korean nuclear issue has occupied the United States, there have been arguments for diplomatic "drift" and not to bring the issue to a major point of decision. Such a situation avoids a crisis and heightened dangers of war on the Korea Peninsula. Another argument for "drift" has been that the U.S. occupation of Iraq and the War on Terrorism are priorities that exceed the importance of North Korea and that U.S. military resources are already stretched too thin to risk a military crisis on the peninsula. The Bush administration has given off signs since October 2002, if not before, that it was influenced by these considerations and wanted to keep North Korea on a second tier of priorities. Moreover, the view within the U.S. government that North Korea is headed toward a political collapse and regime change argued for U.S. policy of waiting until North Korea self-destructed. Ten years ago, U.S. officials predicted a near-term North Korean collapse in order to justify the weaknesses in the Agreed Framework.

Diplomatic drift and stalemate could have new, serious consequences for the United States. First, the critical attitudes of China, Russia, and even South Korea toward the United States in the event of stalemate and collapse of the talks would remove any opportunity for the U.S. to gain their support in a policy of economic sanctions and interdiction of North Korea's sea and air traffic.

Second, if these governments blamed the United States for the collapse of the talks, North Korea would gain a wider opening to demonstrate that it possesses nuclear weapons with less risk of penalties from China, Russia, South Korea, and other countries. Thus North Korea's threats in 2004 to develop its "nuclear deterrent" further if the U.S. administration did not accept its freeze proposal should not be taken lightly. Going forward, Pyongyang might calculate that it needs to demonstrate a nuclear weapons capability in order to bolster deterrence against the United States in 2005 and beyond. Again, if North Korea produced six to eight atomic bombs through reprocessing of the fuel rods, it would have a minimal but genuine nuclear deterrent against the United States.

Both the Bush administration and the Kim Jong-il regime have expressed that "time is on our side." It is doubtful that both are correct. But real danger could be the result if North Korea is correct.

Notes

The views expressed in this chapter are the author's own and do not represent the views of the Congressional Research Service.

1. "New N. Korea food aid pledges only a beginning—WFP," Reuters, March 4, 2003. The estimate came from U.S. military officials in Seoul.

2. Kevin Johnson, "Official: Al-Qaeda plans something big," *USA Today*, November 28, 2003, p. 3A. U.S. intelligence estimates reportedly cite a high-level interest by al Qaeda in acquiring chemical and biological weapons.

3. Kin Kyoung-soo, "North Korea's CB Weapons: Threat and Capability," *The Korean Journal of Defense Analysis*, Spring 2002, p. 78.

4. David E. Sanger, "Visitors see North Korea Nuclear Capacity," *New York Times*, January 11, 2004, p. 9; and David E. Sanger, "North Korea's Bomb: Untested but Ready, C.I.A. Concludes," *New York Times*, November 9, 2003, p. 4.

5. David E. Sanger, "Bush Lauds China Leader as 'Partner' in Diplomacy," *New York Times*, December 10, 2003, p. A6.

6. Ikuko Higuchi and Junichi Toyoura, "North Korea's Nuclear Threat Growing," *The Daily Yomiuri* (Tokyo, Internet version), June 21, 2003.

7. Thomas Omestad, "The Art of the Deal," *U.S. News and World Report*, September 1, 2003, p. 21; and Barbara Slavin and John Diamond, "N. Korean Nuclear Efforts Looking Less Threatening," *USA Today*, November 5, 2003, p. 18A.

8. Carol Giacomo, "N. Korea Has More Capable Missiles," Reuters, September 10, 2003; and Andrew Feickert, *North Korean Ballistic Missile Threat to the United States*, CRS Report 21473, Washington, DC: Congressional Research Service, October 1, 2003.

9. Kim Kyoung-soo, "North Korea's CB Weapons: Threat and Capability," pp. 69–96.

10. The author exposed in March 2001 secret payments of several hundred million dollars to North Korea by affiliates of the Hyundai Corporation. After two years of denials, a South Korean special prosecutor found in June 2003 that several Hyundai affiliates, supported by the South Korean Kim Dae-jung administration, made secret payments of US$500 million to North Korea in 2000. There is evidence that North Korea used the money to help finance accelerated overseas procurements of components for its secret uranium-enrichment program. Reports persist of a pattern of secret cash payments by South Korean firms to the North Korean regime.

11. Ambassador Li Gun, "Requisites for Resolving the Nuclear Question," December 16, 2003. Li Gun, deputy chief of the Bureau of U.S. Affairs in North Korea's Foreign Ministry, submitted this detailed statement of North Korea's negotiating proposals to the Washington, DC-based Center for National Policy.

12. Glenn Kessler, "U.S. has a shifting script on N. Korea," *Washington Post*, December 7, 2003, p. A25; and Joshua Kurlantzick, "Look Away," *The New Republic*, December 15, 2003, p. 14.

13. Joel Mowbray, "North Korea's Nukes: Taking a Hard Line against Pyongyang," *Washington Times*, December 11, 2003, p. A23; and Glenn Kessler, "Run-up to Talks on N. Korea Falters," *Washington Post*, December 3, 2003, p. A24.

14. David E. Sanger, "Bush Proposes North Korea Security Plan to China," *New York Times*, October 20, 2003, p. A4.

15. "China's Lost North Korea Plan," *Far Eastern Economic Review*, December 25, 2003–January 1, 2004, p. 9; and Nobuyoshi Sakajiri, "The U.S. Rejects Two Points of the Chinese Proposed Document of the Six-Party Talks on North Korea," *Asahi Shimbun* (Tokyo), December 18, 2003, p.1.

16. Xinxua editorial, January 2, 2004; and Glenn Kessler, "Chinese Not Convinced of North Korean Uranium Effort," *Washington Post*, January 7, 2004, p. A16.

Suggested Readings

Feickert, Andrew. *North Korean Ballistic Missile Threat to the United States.* Congressional Research Service (CRS) Report RS21473, October 1, 2003.

Kessler, Glenn. "U.S. Has a Shifting Script on N. Korea." *Washington Post.* December 7, 2003, p. A25.

Kim, Young C. "North Korea's Strange Quest for Nuclear Weapons." *Problems of Post-Communism*, March–April 2003, pp. 3–11.

Kurlantzick, Joshua. "Look Away." The New Republic. December 15, 2003, pp. 14–16.

Niksch, Larry. *Korea: U.S.-Korean Relations-Issues for Congress.* CRS Issue Brief, December 18, 2003.

———. *North Korea's Nuclear Weapons Program.* CRS Issue Brief, December 18, 2003.

Noland, Marcus. *Korea After Kim Jong-il.* Washington, DC. Institute for International Economics, January 2004.

Oh Hassig, Kongdan. *Confronting North Korea's Nuclear Ambitions: US Policy Options and Regional Implications.* Washington, DC, Institute for Defense Analysis, September 2003.

Sanger, David E. "Intelligence Puzzle: North Korean Bombs." *New York Times.* October 14, 2003, p. A7.

——— 16 ———

Pakistan

Hanging in the Post–9/11 Balance

K. Alan Kronstadt

Introduction

The events of September 11, 2001, transformed almost overnight the security circumstances of the Islamic Republic of Pakistan. In fact, it can be argued that no country's security orientation was more drastically altered in the period following the terrorist attacks on the United States. This dynamic has historic roots. Born of the same colonial entity as the Republic of India, Pakistan began as a geographical oddity at both the northeastern and northwestern reaches of British India, created as a homeland to the Muslims of the Asian subcontinent. Partition became official on August 14, 1947, and the ensuing communal turmoil brought about the violent deaths of up to one million people and the forced migration of millions more. Within two months the new countries were fighting a war over the disputed princely state of Jammu and Kashmir in the northwest. Nearly six decades later, bitter ethnonational, communal, and territorial conflicts remain unresolved and continue to haunt South Asia and the global community. These conflicts also have shaped Pakistan's strategic choices and involvement with regional Islamic militancy in ways that have direct bearing upon the new century's global War on Terrorism and upon Pakistan's leading and controversial role within that framework.

Political Framework

Pakistan is a federal republic comprised of four provinces (Punjab, Sindh, Baluchistan, and the Northwest Frontier Province, or NWFP), along with a territory known as the Federally Administered Tribal Areas (FATA), and the Islamabad Capital Territory. Among the key considerations in Pakistan's

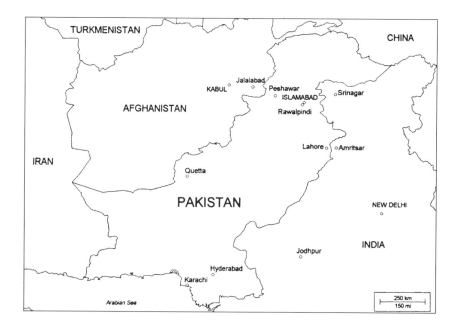

security orientation has been the dominant political role played by the country's military. The history of parliamentary democracy in Pakistan is a troubled one and has been marked by an ongoing tripartite power struggle among presidents, prime ministers, and army chiefs. Military regimes have ruled Pakistan for more than half of the country's existence and there is no sustained history of effective constitutionalism. From the earliest, bloody days of independence, Pakistan's armed forces have thought of themselves as "saviors of the nation," a perception that has received significant, though limited, public support. The military, usually acting with the president, has engaged in three outright seizures of power from civilian-led governments: General Ayub Khan in 1958, General Zia ul-Haq in 1977, and General Pervez Musharraf in 1999. Since 1970, five successive governments have been voted into power, but not a single one has been voted out of power—all five were removed by the army through explicit or implicit presidential orders. Of Pakistan's three duly elected prime ministers, the first (Zulfikar Ali Bhutto) was executed, the second (Benazir Bhutto) was exiled and her husband jailed on corruption charges, and the third (Nawaz Sharif) has been in exile under threat of imprisonment for similar abuses should he return.

Given this inauspicious record with democratic processes, many observers lauded Pakistan's most recent president-general, former army commando Musharraf, for the mere act of holding October 2002 elections as promised soon after he seized the reins of power from Nawaz Sharif in October 1999. Those elections did seat a new National Assembly and, by the end of 2002, the military-friendly Pakistan Muslim League-Quaid-e-Azam (PML-Q), or "king's party" had used its plurality presence to elect a new prime minister, former Baluchistan chief minister and Musharraf ally, Mir Zafarullah Jamali.

Jamali's tenure ended nineteen-months later, when Musharraf requested his resignation and "shuffled" the prime ministership. By September 2004, a new cabinet was seated under prime minister Shaukat Aziz. Aziz, Musharraf's finance minister since 1999, is seen as an able, pro-Musharraf technocrat with almost no political base in the country. Some two years after national elections and the re-establishment of civilian political institutions, the parliament could boast of only scant concrete accomplishments, and few deny that the military was still making national policy in the person of Musharraf, who retained the posts of both chief of army staff and president (a vote of confidence legitimized his presidency through 2007). Musharraf made a December 2003 pledge to resign from the military by the end of 2004, but it appears likely that he will instead retain the post "in the national interest," and at the behest of his cabinet and numerous parliamentarians, and the reported support of the Pakistani public.

Pakistan's 1973 constitution envisaged a sovereign parliament where powers primarily rested with the prime minister, but subsequent changes under the military-dominated regime of General Zia shifted power to the presidency. A surprise accommodation between Musharraf and the newly empowered Muttahida Majlis-e-Amal (MMA or United Action Front)—a coalition of six Islamist parties formed for the 2002 elections—included what essentially was a restoration of the president's constitutional authority to dissolve Parliament. The December 2003 Musharraf-MMA deal served to end a thirteen-month-long deadlock in Parliament that had prevented passage of any legislation except for a single budget bill.

The MMA had spent most of 2003 vociferously denouncing Musharraf as an "illegitimate" president, and they demanded he resign his military commission. In this effort they found common cause with the country's moderate secular parties. The most important of these, the Pakistan People's Party (PPP) led by the former prime minister, Benazir Bhutto, had in fact won the most votes at the 2002 polls, but election rules awarded them runner-up status only, and a number of key defections to the PML-Q had further reduced their representation in Parliament. In fact, Bhutto and the deposed prime minister, Nawaz Sharif—by all accounts Pakistan's leading civilian politicians—had been barred by Musharraf from running in the 2002 elections regardless of the status of pending criminal cases against them. A "mullah-military alliance" has, for the time being, squeezed Pakistan's moderate secular political parties into powerlessness. Despite re-establishment of the institutions of civilian governance in Pakistan, military rule substantively continues, and military agencies are criticized for abusing human rights. Most analysts suggest that only by allowing the country's secular political parties fully into the system can Pakistan realize stable and enduring democracy.

Internal and External Security Environment

The persistent and generally dominant role of the military in Pakistan's political framework is to a great extent the result of the country's core identity as a homeland for South Asia's "persecuted" Muslim population. The two-nation theory that gave rise to the idea of Pakistan also entailed the perception and conception of what many in Pakistan consider to be an eternally-threatening Other—Hindu-dominated India. The need to defend against the real or imagined threats posed by Pakistan's far larger and more populous neighbor has been a central and consistent theme of Pakistani political life. It also has provided the key raison d'être for the Pakistani military, which continues to deploy more than 80 percent of its active troops along the border with India.[1] Many an observer has suggested that Pakistan's preoccupation with India as a looming menace goes beyond what the historic record will support, but there can be no doubt that the view from Islamabad identifies no other meaningful and existential threat to Pakistan's security. Lengthy borders with the sometimes troubled states of Iran and, especially, Afghanistan have brought both upheaval and violent conflict, but have not altered the consistently India-centric security worldview of Pakistanis.

The painful and costly Partition of British India remains unfinished business. The Indian state of Jammu and Kashmir has a Muslim majority. The decision of its Hindu maharaja to accede to India spurred the first Pakistan-India war, and left India in possession of some two-thirds of Jammu and Kashmir's land area, including the territory's main prize—the fertile and heavily Muslim-populated valley around the city of Srinagar. Pakistan denounces the Instrument of Accession as fraudulent and three UN Security Council resolutions urged the holding of a plebiscite to determine the wishes of the Kashmiri people. The perception of India as having illegitimately and forcefully snatched what was rightfully a part of the new Muslim homeland in South Asia persists and sustains a Pakistani identity as ever-vulnerable victim of Indian aggression and even efforts at total absorption. A brief but furious 1965 war with India began with a covert Pakistani thrust across the Kashmiri cease-fire line and ended with the city of Lahore threatened with encirclement by the Indian army. Another UN-sponsored cease-fire left borders unchanged, but Pakistan's vulnerability had again been exposed. Pakistan's sense of insecurity was much more fully reinforced by the outcome of its 1971 civil war, which pitted the West Pakistan army against the Bengali Muslims of East Pakistan who sought greater autonomy and an end to Punjabi political-military domination of the country. The fighting forced many millions of East Pakistani refugees into India, triggering New Delhi's intervention. Within weeks, Indian troops had captured some ninety thousand Pakistani soldiers and East Pakistan became the newly independent nation of Bangladesh. The 1972 Simla Accord between Pakistan and India, which many Pakistanis believe was made under duress, sealed Pakistan's national defeat. Fully two years passed before New Delhi formally recognized the new Bengali state and released the Pakistani prisoners.

Even Pakistan's relations with neighboring Afghanistan have largely been colored by the overarching theme of India-centrism. An effort to gain "strategic depth" against India by cultivating a friendly regime in Kabul had long shaped Islamabad's policies toward its western neighbor. This became an especially important motivator for General-President Zia ul-Haq in his support for the mujahideen "freedom fighters" who were battling the Soviet invaders during the 1980s. During this period Pakistan's identity as a Muslim state was most heavily tilted toward an extremist conception, as Zia made use of Islamic extremists to balance against the influence of mainstream Pakistani political parties that opposed his rule.[2] With significant U.S. financial support, Pakistan's powerful Inter-Services Intelligence agency (ISI)—itself increasingly rife with a sometimes militant Islamist ideology—covertly coordinated an anti-Soviet war in Afghanistan. More than three million Afghan refugees fled into Pakistan. In 1988 the frustrated Soviet army finally began withdrawing from Afghanistan, allowing Islamabad the opportunity to see a friendly regime replace the Communists in Kabul but also leaving Pakistani society infected with a virulent strain of militant Islam that President Musharraf later came to identify as the single greatest threat to Pakistani security.

In 1989 a full-blown separatist rebellion erupted in Kashmir, where Islamic militant veterans of the Afghan war would soon continue their "jihad." By the mid-1990s Pakistan was both actively supporting a bloody separatist rebellion in Kashmir and sponsoring the Taliban regime of radical Sunni Muslims that took Kabul in 1996. The powerful and largely autonomous ISI is widely believed to have provided significant support for militant Kashmiri separatists after 1993 as a proxy war against India. Although Pakistan did not launch the uprising, it fanned the flames throughout the 1990s, and the ISI employed guerrilla warfare expertise gained in Afghanistan to "bleed" India in the mountainous region.[3] Islamabad's militarized Kashmir policy may have peaked with the 1999 incursion at Kargil, which led to an embarrassing withdrawal and the ensuing overthrow of Nawaz Sharif. Also during the 1990s, Afghan Taliban leaders who had been educated at Pakistani religious seminaries (madrasas) seemed for a time to be providing Islamabad with a manageable ally on its western flank. General Zia had died in a mysterious 1988 plane crash, but successive civilian-led governments of Prime Ministers Benazir Bhutto and Nawaz Sharif continued to provide material support to the radical Islamic elements that Zia had strengthened both within the Pakistani polity and in neighboring Afghanistan.[4]

This strategic shift toward increased reliance on radical elements to carry out Pakistani foreign policy would come back to haunt Islamabad's leadership with new external and internal security threats. The proliferation of madrasas under Zia included the establishment of some that have been implicated in teaching militant anti-Western, anti-American, and anti-Hindu values. Moreover, they are known to teach militant opposition toward other Islamic sects, mainly Shiite (about three-quarters of Pakistan's Muslims are Sunnis). Many of these madrasas are financed and operated by influential Pakistani Islamist political parties such as Jamaat-e-Ulema Islam (JUI, closely linked to the Taliban), as well as by multiple unknown foreign entities. One result of the growth of Islamic militancy thus has been an increase in sectarian violence that plagued Pakistan throughout 2003 and into 2004. While President Musharraf has in the past pledged to crack down on the more extremist madrasas in his country, there is little concrete evidence that he has done so.[5] Similarly, Musharraf's efforts to end the operations of known radical militant groups in Pakistan has met with only halting success to date, with some calling the efforts cosmetic and the result of international pressure rather than a genuine recognition of the threat posed.[6]

Strategic Alliances

Unable to ensure its long-term political-military security by approximating India's material advantages, Pakistan's leaders have continuously sought external balancers. The country's strategically important setting has provided its leaders with geopolitical currency in this effort. In the 1950s these leaders were able to exploit their country's cartographic position within the new global Cold War framework. The United States viewed Pakistan as a valuable "frontline ally" in its efforts to encircle and contain the Soviet Union; Pakistan saw the United States as a powerful guarantor of its security vis-à-vis India. By the close of 1955, Pakistan had become embedded in two U.S.-led security pacts: the Central Treaty Organization (or "Baghdad Pact") and the

Southeast Asia Treaty Organization. Two key results were the institutionalization of close Pakistan-U.S. ties and the provision to Pakistan of large assistance packages, including sophisticated weaponry.

Despite this early establishment of security ties with the United States, Pakistan has never felt fully confident in this alliance. Following the 1965 war, the United States banned arms sales to both Pakistan and India. Likewise, although the U.S. tilted toward Pakistan in 1971 by sending the USS Enterprise carrier task force into the Bay of Bengal to deter an Indian attack on West Pakistan, the United States again imposed a general arms embargo, and the disheartened Pakistanis turned increasingly toward China as a counterweight to Indian power. Beijing would become Pakistan's most important strategic ally, with the relationship blossoming most rapidly in the 1970s, following Pakistan's role as a vital conduit in the establishment of U.S. diplomacy with China in 1973.

An apparent theme of American tactical engagement followed by strategic abandonment was played out more distinctly in the late 1980s. Coming on the heels of the humiliating loss of East Pakistan, India's "peaceful nuclear explosion" of 1974 had been a sharp blow to Pakistan's sense of security, and Prime Minister Z.A. Bhutto responded by vowing that Pakistanis would "eat grass" if necessary in order to match India's nuclear capability. Thus began the South Asian nuclear proliferation dyad, and also U.S. scrutiny of Pakistan's proliferation efforts. The United States imposed proliferation-related sanctions on Pakistan in 1979. Only six months later, the Soviets invaded Afghanistan, the sanctions were waived, and Pakistan again became a frontline ally, this time in the largely U.S.-funded effort to push the Red Army back across the Soviet-Afghan frontier. Yet a decade later, when U.S. tactical goals in the region had been met, it appeared to many Pakistanis that the United States was all too ready to punish its erstwhile ally merely for seeking what Islamabad called "nuclear parity" with India. In 1990 all nonhumanitarian U.S. assistance to Pakistan was halted, including a shipment of twenty-eight F-16 fighter aircraft for which Islamabad had already paid. The May 1998 nuclear tests by Pakistan and India triggered sweeping U.S. aid restrictions on both countries, and an October 1999 military coup in Pakistan brought added U.S. sanctions on aid to Islamabad. Pakistan's sense of abandonment was acute.

After 1971 Beijing proved to be what seemed a more reliable ally with which Pakistan could balance against India's greater material power. China's strategic rivalry with India, its expressions of support for Islamabad's Kashmir policy, and its willingness to provide Pakistan with major weapons platforms provided clear benefits. No less important was Beijing's assistance to Pakistan's nuclear weapons and ballistic missile programs, which caused significant consternation in both Washington and New Delhi.[7] After the 1990 imposition of U.S. sanctions on Pakistan, the Islamabad-Beijing arms relationship was further strengthened and, over the course of the next decade, China is believed to have provided Pakistan with ring magnets used in uranium enrichment, M-11 missiles, blueprints and equipment for missile factories, and medium-range missile components, along with numerous conventional weapons systems.[8] China continues to be Pakistan's leading source of armaments. However, in the first years of the twenty-first century it would again be pointed U.S. attention to South Asia that has "tipped the balance" and has strongly influenced Pakistan's security perceptions.

Terrorism Threat and Response

Terrorist attacks in New York and Washington in September 2001, New Delhi in December 2001, and Rawalpindi in December 2003 had major impacts on Pakistan's security perceptions and policies. The September 2001 terrorist attacks suddenly transformed U.S. relations with Pakistan, which again became a frontline U.S. ally, this time against radical Islamic terrorists and their supporters. Under immense diplomatic pressure from Washington, President Musharraf made a swift decision to end his government's support for the Taliban regime in Afghanistan and join the U.S.-led antiterrorism coalition. Remaining restrictions on U.S. aid to Pakistan were quickly lifted by the U.S. Congress and President George W. Bush, and a small trickle of funds in fiscal year (FY) 2001 (US$3.5 million) became a prodigious flow of US$1.16 billion in FY2002, including nearly US$400 million in security-related aid. The Pakistani economy also benefited from U.S. debt forgiveness and U.S. support for Pakistan's position in the major international financial institutions. In return, Pakistan provided basing and overflight permission for all United States and coalition forces engaged in Afghanistan, and deployed some 70,000 of its own troops along the rugged Pakistan-Afghanistan border region in support of U.S.-led efforts to capture Taliban and al Qaeda fugitives. The 180-degree policy reversal by Musharraf, however, apparently was made out of necessity and without the full support of the country's citizens or its military and intelligence organizations (Musharraf has engaged in wholesale replacements of top-level, Islamist-sympathizing generals).

Despite Pakistan's "crucial" cooperation with the United States, the complex and murky links between some elements of Pakistan's security forces and Islamic political parties on the one hand, and known terrorist groups on the other hand, have clouded the new Pakistan-U.S. alliance, as well as causing trepidation in New Delhi, where Pakistan has often been viewed as the "epicenter of global terrorism."[9] As noted above, Pakistan's tolerance of and support for radical Islamists in both the country and in neighboring regions has been rooted in ethnic Pashtun ties that traverse the Afghan-Pakistani border, in its manipulation of Kashmiri separatism, and perhaps most directly in Zia's moves to strengthen Islamists during the 1980s. President Musharraf's sweeping policy shift away from Islamic extremism began with the severing of all official ties to the Taliban, but was consummated with a landmark January 2002 speech in which he vowed to end Pakistan's use as a base for terrorism of any kind, and criticized religious extremism and intolerance in the country (some Pakistanis will quip that Zia may have died in 1988, but he was finally buried in 2002). In the wake of the speech, several thousand extremists were arrested and detained, though most were later released.[10]

The December 2001 terrorist assault on the Indian Parliament complex in New Delhi had done much to trigger Musharraf's clarion call for Pakistan to choose moderation over radicalism: suicide attackers identified as members of the Sunni militant Lashkar-e-Tayyiba (LT) (Army of the Pure or Army of the Righteous), a U.S.-designated Foreign Terrorist Organization (FTO), killed nine people and spurred an outraged India—which held Pakistan responsible for supporting LT—to fully mobilize its military along the India-Pakistan frontier. An ensuing ten-month-long standoff involved one million Indian and Pakistani soldiers and was viewed as the closest the two countries had come to full-scale war since 1971, causing numerous governments to become concerned that a conventional war could escalate into a nuclear confrontation.

A further complication was that U.S. military operations in eastern Afghanistan in 2001–2002 sent several thousand al Qaeda fighters fleeing into Pakistan, and these elements continued to conduct hit and run attacks on U.S.-led coalition forces in Afghanistan. They established bases in such Pakistani cities as Karachi, Peshawar, and Quetta in collusion with indigenous Pakistani radicals.[11] Top al Qaeda and Taliban leaders may themselves have taken refuge in a remote area of Pakistan near Afghanistan. Al Qaeda reportedly was linked to numerous anti-Western terrorist attacks in Pakistan during 2002, although the primary suspects in most attacks were members of indigenous Pakistani groups. Such attacks included the kidnapping and ensuing murder of *Wall Street Journal* reporter Daniel Pearl; a car bombing that killed fourteen outside a Karachi hotel, including eleven French defense technicians; and a June car bombing outside the U.S. consulate in Karachi that killed twelve Pakistani nationals.

With Islamist parties in control of Pakistan's two western provinces, and with the Pakistan army's focus still on India, Islamic militants were able to continue operating from the historically-autonomous Federally Administered

Tribal Areas populated by conservative ethnic Pashtuns who share intimate religious and tribal linkages with their counterparts in Afghanistan. Similarly, and despite a warming trend in Pakistan-India relations after April 2003, New Delhi and Washington were demanding that Pakistan end its support for Kashmiri separatist militants and close their training camps in Azad Kashmir. Throughout 2003 pressures mounted on Islamabad to take decisive measures that would halt the "exfiltration" of Islamic militants into neighboring regions.

Insofar as the global War on Terrorism represented a new (U.S.-defined) organizing principle for international relations, it had the effect of shaking the foundations of Pakistan's security policies. With a seemingly resolute United States seeking to stabilize neighboring Afghanistan—in part, through the empowerment of ethnic Tajiks and Uzbeks—Islamabad's narrow backing of Afghan Pashtuns appeared untenable. Likewise, the definitional tensions between "freedom fighter" and "terrorist" in the Kashmir dispute heightened and had the effect of undermining the perceived legitimacy of Islamabad's support for militancy on its northeastern frontier. Without fanfare, the Musharraf government quietly accepted an April 2003 "hand of friendship" offer from New Delhi, and by November this had produced a formal cease-fire agreement along the entire Pakistan-India frontier, including the Kashmiri Line of Control. Musharraf's later suggestion that Pakistan might be willing to "set aside" its demands for a UN-sponsored plebiscite in Kashmir brought waves of criticism from his secular and Islamist opponents alike, who accused him of abandoning the cause.[12] Moreover, just days after the U.S. ambassador expressed particular concern over the continuing activities of banned organizations, Musharraf moved to arrest members of these groups and shutter their offices. Up to 25,000 Pakistani troops were sent into the tribal areas in an unprecedented show of federal force there.

Islamic militants expressed their animosity toward the Pakistani president not with press releases, but with high explosives. A December 14, 2003, remote-controlled bombing attempt on Musharraf's motorcade in Rawalpindi and dual suicide car bomb attacks on his convoy eleven days later were blamed mainly on members of the Jaish-e-Mohammed (JEM, or Army of Mohammed), another U.S.-designated FTO, with some officials suggesting an al Qaeda link. With his governance status solidified through accommodation with the Islamic parties, Musharraf made some bold policy decisions. First, while hosting the Indian prime minister in Islamabad, Pakistan agreed to launch a "composite dialogue" with New Delhi to bring about "peaceful settlement of all bilateral issues, including Jammu and Kashmir, to the satisfaction of both sides." Musharraf also reassured the Indian prime minister that he would not permit any territory under Pakistan's control to be used to support terrorism. On the western front, Musharraf launched major military operations in the tribal areas to root out remaining foreign militants and their Taliban hosts. The offensive, run in tandem with U.S. and Afghan forces across the frontier, led to fierce fighting in 2004 and vehement criticism from the MMA, but Musharraf insists that religious extremism has no place in Pakistani society, and he has requested that Islamic clerics join him in his efforts to stamp out the threat posed by militancy.[13]

Military Structure and Defense Policy

The Pakistan army is firmly rooted in the traditions of its British progenitor. An offspring of the British Indian army, Pakistan's military was from the start dominated by ethnic Punjabis and Pashtuns who had fought for the British crown during World War II. The official history of the Pakistan army opens with references to succeeding invaders of the Indian subcontinent, beginning with the Aryans. The officer corps traced its roots to "the men who fought Alexander the Great" and who "established the first Mogul stronghold in India." Such claims reflect the urgent search for an institutional identity separate from that of the Indian military, a search that continues to the present day. Still, the Pakistan army remains "visibly and substantively more British than Mogul, and will continue to be so as long as it remains a professional army."[14]

Pakistan's 1973 constitution makes the president the commander in chief of military forces, and the army itself dominates these. Nine regional corps include 2 armored divisions and 19 infantry divisions totaling about 550,000 active-duty soldiers, more than 2,000 tanks, and 1,300 towed artillery tubes. The Pakistan navy operates 10 submarines—including 2 new French-built Agostas—and 8 frigates. The air force fields more than 350 combat aircraft, but most of these are Chinese-built with 1970s-era avionics. Some French-built Mirages provide ground-attack capability; two squadrons of American-built F-16s are often grounded for want of spare parts.[15] Along with these regular forces, Pakistan's Interior Ministry oversees a 65,000-man Frontier Corps and the 30,000-man Pakistani Rangers. The ISI has a total strength of about 10,000.[16]

Pakistan's defense spending and interest on public debt together consume 70 percent of total government revenues, and the military budget has remained static at about US$3 billion per year for some time. As India's spending and access to sophisticated weaponry has increased, many analysts believe Pakistan has become more dependent on its nuclear weapons arsenal to balance against and deter India. Islamabad's nuclear program is shrouded in secrecy, but some thirty-five to fifty nuclear warheads are believed to exist.

Pakistan maintains an extensive ballistic missile program that includes current development of at least three medium-range platforms and possibly an intermediate-range missile capable of traveling up to 3,500 kilometers (2,170 miles). Still, F-16s are considered the most likely delivery system for Pakistan's nuclear weapons.[17]

Pakistani military leaders view India's growing defense budget with much alarm, especially the growth of the Indian Navy (acquiring aircraft carriers and submarines) and Air Force (acquiring sophisticated airborne radars). No less critically, New Delhi's 1998 nuclear tests are seen to have posed grave security challenges to Pakistan and to have drastically altered the strategic balance in South Asia. With regard to nuclear doctrine, the Pakistani government has produced no document comparable to India's Draft Nuclear Doctrine, and it provides only ambiguous statements regarding its own nuclear weapons policies. Thus far, these have mostly been ad hoc responses to Indian actions. A hint of this reactive position can be found in the words of President and Chief of Army Staff Musharraf:

> The rationale behind our nuclear policy is purely security and we only want to retain a minimum credible deterrence to deter any aggression against our homeland. Pakistan, unlike India, does not harbor any ambitions for regional or global status. We would not enter into a nuclear arms race with India and would never subject our people to economic deprivation.[18]

This statement reflects Islamabad's key concern with deterring a full-scale Indian attack or, if this fails, to use nuclear weapons to offset India's conventional force advantage. The Pakistani leadership—both civilian and military—has emphatically rejected a no-first-use pledge and suggested that Pakistan would consider using nuclear weapons first if attacked by conventional forces. This is not unexpected from the party seen to be at a numerical disadvantage in conventional forces (U.S./NATO nuclear policy similarly avoids such a pledge).

Conclusions and Outlook

In evaluating Pakistan's security outlook, it is important to understand that the Pakistani idea—centered as it is around the vision of a Muslim homeland in South Asia—has been and continues to be a essentially contested one. While the rift in Indian nationalism can in simple terms be called one of secularists versus communalists, in Pakistan the issue is the degree of communalism and emphasis on religion that is appropriate. To wit: how shall "Muslim nationalism" be defined? For "nationalists," the goal has been the establishment of a stable and democratic nation-state, one that is Muslim, but that does not take an expansive view of religion's role in nationhood. In this expression, Pakistani nationalism is indistinguishable from others in the region. For "Islamists," however, the goal has been the expansion of Islamic law and customs to many, if not most spheres of Pakistani life, including the constitution, legal system, and civil society. It can also be expressed as animosity toward Western liberal ways of organizing society, and so can and does entail hostility toward Western nation-states, as well. While "Father of the Nation" Mohammed Ali Jinnah himself is widely considered to have been a more moderate brand of nationalist, early leaders were not conclusive with respect to the meaning of Muslim nationalism, and the ongoing debate continues to occupy many column-inches of Pakistani editorial pages. Thus, Pakistan's triumphant Islamic communalism has stood in the way of prospects for secular nationalism: "In Pakistan, constitution and law sanctifies unicommunal, that is, Muslim preponderance. . . . The exaltation of religion as the only basis of national identity has created an abnormality and imbalance in the Pakistani body-politic."[19]

Clearly, Pakistan's essentially contested identity needs to become a matter of consensus before the country's future path can be plotted. President Musharraf apparently has committed himself to establishing in Pakistan a moderate Islamic state. His policy reversals of 2001 and 2002 have set him and his supporters on a perilous course, but the rewards thus far have included international recognition of and support for his previously ostracized military regime. Pakistan's new course has also earned it huge amounts of U.S. foreign assistance and a designation as Major Non-NATO Ally of the United States. No longer are "potential failed state" references to Pakistan so common as they were during the 1990s.

Yet Pakistan is set in a dangerous region. India's perceived "hegemonic intent," the Kashmir dispute, turmoil in the western Pashtun-majority regions, and domestic radicalism continue to preoccupy Pakistani security planners, some of whom hold Islamist sympathies. Evidence of Pakistani nuclear proliferation activities undercut Islamabad's standing. A spike in Afghanistan's post-Taliban opium production has raised anew concerns that Pakistan's western neighbor may become an unstable "narco-state," with potentially dire results for Pakistani security. Questions about political succession in Islamabad, which became sharper after the December 2003 attempts on President Musharraf's life, are far from settled. However, if Musharraf and his supporters remain on a path of "enlightened moderation," have success in efforts to reform Pakistan's governance and education systems, put a final halt to the activities of militant groups operating on its soil, find accommodation with India, and make effective use of renewed alliance with the United

States to bolster their international standing, the outlook for Pakistan's future security may yet turn positive.

Notes

The views expressed in this chapter are the author's own and do not necessarily reflect the views of the Congressional Research Service.

1. "Pakistan: External Affairs," *Jane's Sentinel Security Assessment—South Asia*, November 4, 2003.

2. Stephen P. Cohen, "South Asia," in Richard Ellings and Aaron Friedberg, eds., *Strategic Asia 2002–03: Asian Aftershocks* (Seattle: National Bureau of Asian Research, 2002).

3. Dennis Kux, *The United States and Pakistan 1947–2000: Disenchanted Allies* (Washington, DC: Woodrow Wilson Center Press, 2001), p. 305.

4. Ahmed Rashid, *Jihad* (New Haven, CT: Yale University Press, 2002), pp. 214–15.

5. Author interviews with Pakistani government officials and scholars, Islamabad, January 19–23, 2004; "Unfulfilled Promises: Pakistan's Failure to Tackle Extremism," International Crisis Group Report 73, January 16, 2004.

6. Husain Haqqani, "Skepticism Over Crackdown," *Nation* (Lahore), November 19, 2003; and Najam Sethi, "Writing On the Wall," *Friday Times* (Lahore), November 21, 2003.

7. See Ashok Kapur, *Pakistan's Nuclear Development* (New York: Croom Helm, 1987). Declassified U.S. State Department documents show that U.S. concerns about China-Pakistan security cooperation began in the late 1960s and increased with evidence of Beijing's assistance to Pakistan's nuclear weapons program in the 1970s (National Security Archive, "China, Pakistan, and the Bomb," March 5, 2004, at www.gwu.edu/~nsarchiv/NSAEBB/NSAEBB114/press.htm).

8. U.S. Department of Defense, Office of the Secretary of Defense, *Proliferation Threat and Response*, November 1997; U.S. Department of State, "Report on Nuclear Nonproliferation in South Asia," March 17, 1998; and U.S. National Intelligence Council, "Foreign Missile Developments and the Ballistic Missile Threat to the United States Through 2015," September 1999.

9. "Advani Talks Tough Again, Says Pak Hotbed of Al Qaeda," *Hindustan Times* (Delhi), June 23, 2003.

10. Paul Watson, "Revolving Doors for Pakistan's Militants," *Los Angeles Times*, November 17, 2002.

11. Tim McGirk, "Al Qaeda's New Hideouts," *Time*, July 29, 2002; *U.S. Department of State, Patterns of Global Terrorism 2002*, April 30, 2003; Howard French, "Officials Warn of Links Between Al Qaeda, Pakistanis," *New York Times*, May 29, 2002; Hasan Mansoor, "Karachi Killings Reveal Sectarian-Jihadi Nexus," *Friday Times* (Lahore), October 10, 2003.

12. Simon Denyer, "Pakistan Ready to Meet India Halfway on Kashmir," *New York Times*, December 17, 2003.

13. Rana Qaisar, "Clerics Asked to Help Fight Terror," *Daily Times* (Lahore), February 18, 2004.

14. Stephen P. Cohen, *The Pakistan Army* (New York: Oxford University Press, 1998), p. 8.

15. International Institute for Strategic Studies, *The Military Balance 2003–2004* (London: International Institute for Strategic Studies, 2003).

16. "Pakistan: Security and Foreign Forces," *Jane's Sentinel Security Assessment—South Asia*, November 4, 2003.

17. See Andrew Feickert and K. Alan Kronstadt, *Missile Proliferation and the Strategic Balance in South Asia* (Congressional Research Service Report 32115), October 17, 2003.

18. Faraz Hashmi, "Deterrence Main Aim of Nuclear Policy: CE," *Dawn* (Karachi), June 27, 2000.

19. Rasheeduddin Khan, "Pakistan's Communal Muslim Path," *New Perspectives Quarterly*, Spring 1994, pp. 42–43.

Suggested Readings

Ahmed, Feroz. *Ethnicity and Politics in Pakistan*. Karachi: Oxford University Press, 1998.

Bose, Sumantra. *Kashmir: Roots of Conflict, Paths to Peace*. Cambridge, MA: Harvard University Press, 2003.

Burki, Shahid Javed. *Pakistan: Fifty Years of Nationhood*. Boulder, CO: Westview Press, 1999.

Cohen, Stephen P. *The Pakistan Army*. New York: Oxford University Press, 1998.

Kux, Dennis. *The United States and Pakistan 1947–2000: Disenchanted Allies*. Washington, DC: Woodrow Wilson Center Press, 2001.

Rashid, Ahmed. *Taliban*. New Haven, CT: Yale University Press, 2000.

Rizvi, Hassan Askari. *Military, State, and Security in Pakistan*. New York: St. Martin's Press, 2000.

Talbot, Ian. *Pakistan: A Modern History*. London: Hurst, 1998.

Weaver, Mary Ann. *Pakistan: In the Shadow of Jihad and Afghanistan*. New York: Farrar, Straus, and Giroux, 2002.

Wirsing, Robert. *Kashmir in the Shadow of War*. Armonk, NY: M.E. Sharpe, 2003.

Wolpert, Stanley. *Jinnah of Pakistan*. New York: Oxford University Press, 1984.

17

The Philippines

Searching for Stability

David G. Wiencek

Introduction

By the late 1990s, it appeared that the Philippines had finally put behind it the political turmoil of the Marcos years and the bumpy transition to democracy associated with Corazon Aquino's People Power revolution. Two consecutive peaceful presidential elections in 1992 and 1998 seemed to augur well for future stability. The economy was rebounding from the severe 1997 Asian financial crisis. At the same time, long-running internal security threats showed signs of manageability. The country then began looking outward and at coping with the potential external security threats it was facing, most notably, stemming from territorial disputes in the South China Sea.

But the stability and forward momentum proved transitory. In January 2001 a corruption scandal enveloped then President Joseph Estrada, forcing him from office. His vice president, Gloria Macapagal-Arroyo, assumed the presidency. President Arroyo's term saw a sharp increase in internal security and law and order challenges, continued problems with corruption at high levels, a serious coup attempt in 2003, crushing budget deficits, and a range of new pressures stemming from the War on Terrorism. Such continuing political and security risks and economic turmoil have undercut investor confidence and stymied the economy.

Growth rates are positive but simply not strong enough to relieve the intense poverty suffered by wide segments of the population. Indeed, by September 2004, President Arroyo acknowledged the country was in an economic crisis. Experts similarly warned that the Philippines faced an Argentina-like economic collapse unless widening public deficits are brought under control.[1] The poor investment climate and lack of sustained economic development has its roots in political instability, structural weaknesses, and a deteriorating law-and-order and security situation.

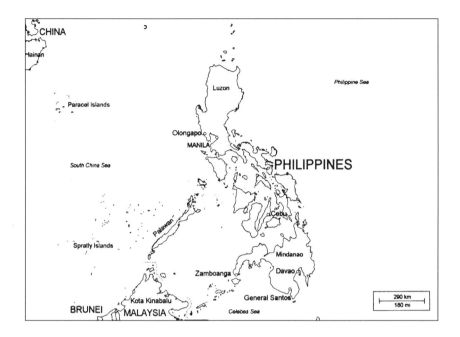

Though presenting new challenges, the War on Terrorism initially led to a strengthening of relations between the Philippines and the United States. Since 9/11, the two allies have worked closely on counterterrorism, with Washington providing increased aid and military assistance to Manila in an effort to stem the threat from Islamic radicals operating in the country or through links with affiliates in the region and beyond. But a critical setback occurred arising from President Arroyo's decision in July 2004 to remove Philippine troops from Iraq in the face of a threat to kill a Philippine truck driver taken hostage by Iraqi terrorists. This decision caused a disruption in relations with Washington, undoing much of the progress made since 9/11 and leading the United States to question the reliability of its ally in Manila.

Political Framework

The Philippines is regarded as one of Asia's most vibrant democracies, with freedom of speech, press, and other civil liberties guaranteed by the 1987 constitution; yet within this context a relatively small group of elites dominate politics and business and, despite efforts to curb it, corruption is a problem. The Philippines follows a presidential system of government. Under the constitution, the president, elected by direct popular vote, is the head of the government and commander in chief of the armed forces. A bicameral legislature and an independent judiciary form the two other branches of government. There has been talk of moving away from the presidential system to a parliamentary model, but such a fundamental change appears unlikely any time soon.

To help prevent a recurrence of past abuses, the constitution specifies a single presidential term of six years and that the president is not eligible for reelection. This provision took on new importance during the political crisis surrounding former President Estrada in late 2000–early 2001. Two-and-a-half years into his term, Estrada faced impeachment proceedings over charges that he received nearly US$12 million in kickbacks from illegal gambling and tobacco revenues. Opposition intensified and mass protests took place in Manila, dubbed People Power II, a virtual replay of the events that ended the rule of Ferdinand Marcos fifteen years earlier. On January 19, 2001, the military establishment (including Chief of Staff of the Armed Forces of the Philippines [AFP] General Angelo Reyes and Defense Secretary Orlando Mercado) withdrew support for Estrada and placed its support behind Vice President Arroyo. The next day the Philippine Supreme Court declared the office of the president effectively "vacant," paving the way for Arroyo to be sworn in as president. Shortly thereafter, Estrada stepped down though he did not officially resign. Several months later he was placed under arrest on charges of economic plunder and has remained under detention ever since. President Arroyo finished out Estrada's unexpired term and won reelection in May 2004 to serve a six-year term of her own.

Although the Philippines surmounted an important challenge in the 2001 political crisis by achieving a peaceful transfer of power, it was not a healthy development for the country's democracy. The resort to extra-constitutional measures to effect a change in national leadership—the People Power II popular revolt—showed that government institutions are weak and incapable of withstanding serious tests. These events indicate that long-term institution building will be required to reestablish confidence in the country's political framework.

The July 2003 Coup Attempt and Oplan "Andres"

But political turmoil in Manila continued in the aftermath of the leadership change and reached a peak with a coup attempt on July 27, 2003. This serious challenge to President Arroyo's administration flared when disgruntled junior officers and enlisted men took over a commercial center in the capital, rigged it with explosives, and then demanded that the government resign. The tense situation lasted for nineteen hours before the rebellious troops agreed to stand down. Subsequent investigation indicated the involvement of some 498 military personnel, with 356 active participants, 136 supporters, and 6 other officers identified as leaders of the uprising.

The initial objective of the disgruntled troops was to air grievances related to high-level military corruption and to low pay. In particular, they accused senior commanders of selling weapons to Islamic terrorists in Mindanao. However, evidence later emerged that opposition politicians sought to use the uprising as a pretext to seize power through a well-funded operational plan known as Oplan "Andres." This plan involved a military takeover of the presidential palace, the Manila airport, broadcast and media outlets, and other strategic points in the capital. Plans also called for the assassination of President Arroyo and the installation of a 15-man ruling junta.[2]

Importantly, the coup attempt reignited concerns about the military's role in politics and respect for civilian authority. Previous reforms aimed at instilling greater professionalism and curbing the military's political intervention tendencies appeared to have floundered and will need to be reexamined in light of these events.

Internal Security Environment

The Philippines suffers from internal security problems that have ebbed and flowed over many years. Recent trends have seen a deterioration in the internal security environment and an upturn in law-and-order threats. As such, internal security challenges are now the primary focus of Philippine security policy. The most important challenges stem from terrorists associated with the Communist Party of the Philippines (CPP) and its military arm, the New People's Army (NPA), and from Muslim secessionists in the southern part of the country, primarily the Abu Sayyaf Group (ASG) and the Moro Islamic Liberation Front (MILF). Kidnap-for-ransom gangs also have become increasingly active. This form of criminality poses specific threats to the business community and is deterring foreign investment.

A new mission-specific internal security requirement relates to defense of the Malampaya gas field, a multibillion U.S. dollar energy project operated by a consortium of foreign companies led by Royal/Dutch Shell Group. The project, located offshore of Palawan, is the country's single largest foreign investment and involves natural gas reserves that could generate power for decades and contribute significantly to the country's self-sufficiency in energy. The project's offshore platform could be vulnerable to attacks from the air or from the sea.

The CPP-NPA

The NPA is operationally active in several provinces, including in central Luzon and in the metro Manila area. It has been gaining in strength in recent years and is currently assessed to field approximately twelve thousand members. This number is double the membership level of the mid-1990s. Theoretically, the CPP-NPA still advocates a Maoist strategy of protracted armed struggle as a means to gain power. The leadership is split among three factions, the largest of which is led by Jose Maria Sison, operating in exile out of the Netherlands. An out-of-touch Sison, the communist movement's longtime figurehead, has recently even held up North Korea as a potential political model. Empty revolutionary rhetoric aside, the movement's impact on the internal security situation cannot be taken lightly. It has managed to survive for more than thirty years and is able to stay relevant through successful exploitation of political uncertainty and widespread poverty in the country coupled with violent actions and intimidation tactics.

On the ground, the NPA specializes in armed attacks on business interests and governmental facilities, and in hostile engagements with Philippine armed forces. Its intimidation efforts also extend to extortion, kidnapping, propaganda and protest, and demonstration activities. Reports also indicate that the group may take in US$30 million per year from a gold-mining operation in Mindanao.[3] NPA extortion receipts (known as "revolutionary taxes") are estimated at over US$5 million per year.[4]

In 2002 the United States designated the CPP-NPA a Foreign Terrorist Organization (FTO), signifying its growing capabilities and threats to American interests. After the United States announced the FTO designation, a CPP-NPA spokesman issued a threat against multinational corporations and said "U.S. companies will realize just how much a U.S. war of aggression in the Philippines will disadvantage them." Sison also called for a revival of "armed city partisan warfare," a reference to assassination squads that targeted local officials in the 1980s and which also carried out attacks on U.S. military personnel. In addition to trying to defeat the CPP-NPA on the ground, the government of the Philippines is attempting to engage the Communists in peace talks hosted by Norway as a parallel means of conflict resolution.

Islamic Terrorism and Its International Linkages

Islamic extremism is a significant factor in the internal security environment of the Philippines. The roots of this problem run deep and stretch back hundreds of years. From the time of Magellan's landing in Cebu in 1521 up until the American colonial period began in 1898, the Spanish were never able to conquer the long-established Muslim population (called Moros by the Spanish) or integrate them fully into the emerging Philippine nation. The situation improved little during the American colonial period and, as early as 1905, Moro leaders called for a jihad against American troops.

Today's Muslim secessionist movement thus directly traces its lineage to this historical clash between Christianity and Islam in the Philippines. The movement's grievances have been passed down for generations and remain highly problematic in a nation that is overwhelmingly Catholic (85 percent) and only 5 percent Muslim. Yet for the Muslim minority in the Philippines, the search for greater autonomy, if not an independent and separate homeland in Mindanao, remains the focal point of the struggle. While there has been some progress over the years toward autonomy, the groups that continue the struggle have resorted to terrorist tactics and methods. A new dimension to this long-running conflict emerged in the aftermath of 9/11. It became clear that Islamic extremists in the southern Philippines had clandestinely established extensive ties to international terrorist groups, specifically to al Qaeda and Jemmah Islamiyah (JI) (Islamic group or Islamic community), and that they had linked their own grievances with those of the international jihad network. These external linkages with international extremists complicate efforts at conflict resolution with domestic-based groups.

The Abu Sayyaf Group (ASG)

In the early 1990s an Islamic preacher, Ustadh Abdurajak Abubakar Janjalani, formed the ASG and took the name "Abu Sayyaf" (or Swordbearer) as a nom de guerre and in tribute to an Afghan fighter, Abdul Rasul Sayyaf. The name Abu Sayyaf was later adopted by the group as a whole. Janjalani studied in Saudi Arabia and Libya and fought alongside the mujahideen forces in Afghanistan in the 1980s. He was killed in an ambush in the Philippines in 1998. ASG elements are led today by his younger brother, Khadaffy Janjalani.

Initially, ASG professed a radical form of Islamic fundamentalism and sought to establish a separate homeland in the southern Philippines, although today ideology has taken a backseat to purely criminal and terrorist activities that primarily emphasize making money. Early on the group received funding from a variety of sources, but importantly became linked with Osama bin Laden and the al Qaeda network.[5] Ramzi Yousef, another Afghan war veteran and the mastermind of the first World Trade Center (WTC) attack in New York, in 1993, reportedly first traveled to the Philippines in 1991 and in 1992 held a meeting with Abdurajak Janjalani. According to an informed ex-ASG member, Yousef sought to use the Philippines as a "launching pad" for a worldwide terrorist campaign—and in this he nearly succeeded.

Following the 1993 WTC attack, Yousef fled to Pakistan. He subsequently traveled back to the Philippines and in 1994 planted a bomb on a Tokyo-bound Philippines Airlines flight, killing one passenger and injuring ten others. The attack was a dress rehearsal for a series of planned in-flight bombings of eleven U.S. passenger aircraft across Asia. The arrest of a Yousef colleague at a safe house in Manila in 1995 led Yousef to flee the Philippines and thwarted his various planned attacks known by the code name Operation Bojinka. Bojinka included plans to crash an explosives-filled plane into CIA headquarters in Virginia—a precursor to the attack method used by al Qaeda on September 11, 2001. Yousef's terrorist plotting in the Philippines also included plans to assassinate visiting dignitaries Pope John Paul II and the U.S. president, Bill Clinton, possibly using the chemical agent phosgene in an attack on the latter.

In 1995 Yousef was captured in Pakistan and extradited to the United States. Upon his arrest, U.S. investigators found letters in his possession threatening to kill the president of the Philippines and poison the country's drinking water or conduct attacks on vital installations with chemical weapons. Today Yousef is imprisoned in the United States.

In recent years ASG has shifted its tactics to kidnap-for-ransom as a way of gaining funds. Many kidnap victims over the past decade have been Christian or from Western countries. But it was the kidnapping on April 23, 2000, of twenty-one people from a diving resort on Sipadan Island, Malaysia, that catapulted the group into the international spotlight. Some eighteen heavily armed ASG members used two small boats to reach Sipadan. There were ten Western nationals among the victims (three Germans, two French, two Finns, two South Africans, and a Lebanese), in addition to nine Malaysians and two Filipinos who worked at the resort. Two American citizens, who were present when the kidnappers arrived, managed to escape. The kidnap victims were transported over twenty hours back to Philippine territory. [6]

The victims languished in captivity under harsh jungle conditions on Jolo Island in the Sulu Archipelago. The first hostage was released some two months later, and all but one victim was released within a period of five months. Libya (and to a lesser extent perhaps Malaysia) reportedly provided the substantial sum of US$15–20 million in ransom money under the guise of "developmental aid" for Mindanao.

The group struck again in May 2001 when it conducted another high-profile kidnapping at a beach resort on Palawan Island. Twenty hostages, including three U.S. citizens, were captured and transported from Palawan to the group's stronghold on Basilan Island approximately three hundred miles away. One of the Americans was beheaded after begging for his life. The two other American victims were a missionary couple, Martin and Gracia Burnham. Martin Burnham was killed during a rescue attempt, while his wife was liberated from the ASG's clutches after 376 days in captivity.[7]

At this time, the ASG appears to be comprised of at least two different factions, with Khadaffy Janjalani serving as titular leader. The group's current membership is assessed to be less than five hundred, down from several thousand after the Sipadan incident. Nevertheless, ASG remains a threat to Philippine national security, conducting bombings and assassinations and engaging in kidnapping and extortion. This activity continues to undermine the country's stability and deter much-needed foreign investment. The ASG also poses a clear threat to U.S. interests through its continued targeting of American civilians, as well as U.S. military personnel in-country assisting the Philippine armed forces. Ransom money may have also flowed back to al Qaeda to support the wider jihad movement. Indeed, operational alliances with the MILF, JI, al Qaeda, or other parts of the Islamic extremist network—carried out for the sake of ideology or for profit—place the ASG among the key groups to be neutralized in the War on Terrorism.

The Moro Islamic Liberation Front (MILF)

For more than twenty years, the MILF has sought to carve out a separate and independent Islamic state operating under sharia law in the southern Philippines and has resisted previous autonomy proposals. Today the group fields about twelve thousand members, mostly deployed in central Mindanao. The MILF's longtime leader, Salamat Hashim, died of natural causes in 2003. Salamat's deputy, Al Haj Murad Ebrahim, assumed the chairmanship of the group and vowed to continue the struggle.

Through the years, the MILF has demonstrated its capability for terrorist bombings and infrastructure destruction. It also has used cease-fire periods with the government as a means to regroup and reconstitute its capabilities. After a get-tough military campaign under the Estrada administration, President Arroyo held out the possibility for fresh talks and a peaceful resolution to the conflict. In 2003 the MILF and Philippine government entered into negotiations hosted by Malaysia, with additional diplomatic facilitation offered by a group of senior retired U.S. officials working with the United States Institute of Peace (USIP) from Washington. The situation on the ground has been relatively quiet as a result of the peace process. But the future outlook for a possible political, military, and economic settlement remains uncertain. Bridging the large gap between the MILF's stated goal of an independent homeland and the government's willingness to offer the group some form of expanded autonomy or other political formula to bring an end to the conflict is the key negotiating hurdle.

Unlike the CPP-NPA and ASG, the MILF has so far successfully avoided the official "terrorist" designation by the United States as an FTO. This has been done at the request of Philippine authorities who fear that such a label would hinder the peace process and lead to a resumption of major hostilities.

But the evidence, especially after 9/11, is all too clear that the MILF is an integral part of the Southeast Asian terror network and has forged deep links with al Qaeda. Although the group denies ties to bin Laden and other Islamic extremists, newly uncovered evidence points to a different conclusion. Thousands of Islamic radicals have trained at MILF camps; others have offered training to new MILF recruits.[8] The MILF also received funding from al Qaeda, as money from its other state sponsors, Malaysia and Libya, dried up.

An important link to the wider regional terrorist network was Fathur Rahman Al-Gohzi, a key JI personality and liaison between the JI and the MILF. An expert in explosives and bomb making, Al-Ghozi was a former student of Abu Bakar Bashir, the JI founder and its emir. In the early 1990s Al-Ghozi went to Afghanistan where he trained at an al Qaeda camp. He later participated in a combined MILF-JI bombing operation in Manila in December 2000, was closely involved in JI plots to bomb Western targets in Singapore in late 2001, and was assembling large quantities of explosives in the Philippines for further attacks when he was arrested in Manila in January 2002. Al-Ghozi was sentenced to a long prison term in the Philippines, but managed to escape from prison in Manila. He made his way back down to Mindanao, where he was killed in 2003 by authorities.

As noted in the introduction to this book, JI also attempted to solidify its regional relationships through an alliance known as the Rabitatul Mujahideen (Mujahideen League). This alliance comprised the MILF, a southern Thailand-based jihadist group, and others. JI had its own training facility within the MILF's main base in Mindanao and operated an interlinked Philippine-based cell.

External Security Environment

The previous trend in Philippine security policy placed a growing emphasis on external defense. However, this posture has now been reversed and the armed forces have reverted to a primary focus on internal security and law and order threats. As described above, the current focus encompasses domestic terrorism, as well as linkages with regional and international terrorist elements.

This policy shift notwithstanding, the country must still keep a watchful eye on the external security environment. The principal concern in this connection relates to the territorial disputes in the Spratly Islands in the South China Sea and China's growing military buildup. The Spratly disputes are lying dormant for the moment but could easily be rekindled and spark a new security crisis affecting Philippine interests.

Located in the southern reaches of the South China Sea, the Spratlys are claimed by China, Taiwan, and Vietnam; Malaysia and Brunei, meanwhile, assert smaller claims. For its part, the Philippines claims fifty-three islands and islets in the South China Sea as the Kalayaan (Freedomland) Island Group (KIG), administratively part of the province of Palawan and not considered by the Philippines to be associated with the Spratly archipelago. The Philippines has occupied eight islands in the KIG and stationed troops on some of them since the early 1970s; Pag-asa (Thitu) Island has the largest garrison and a 1,300–1,800 meter (1,421–1,969 yards) airstrip.

In 1995 China seized Mischief Reef, located only 150 miles (241 kilometers) west of Palawan Island, in the heart of Philippine-claimed waters and well within the country's 200-mile (322-kilometers) exclusive economic zone (EEZ). In late 1998 and early 1999, with the region distracted by the Asian financial crisis, China upgraded its outpost on Mischief Reef. This Mischief Reef II episode resulted in the building of new permanent, multistory structures on concrete platforms. These developments dramatically underlined China's strategic push into the South China Sea. Beijing is intent on expanding its sphere of influence with the ultimate goal of dominating the vital sea-lanes of Southeast Asia. The cumulative objective of this Chinese activity is to develop strategic waypoints in the Paracel Islands in the northern portion of the South China Sea (particularly Woody Island) down through the Spratlys. This Chinese strategy is closely linked with its enunciated goals of moving away from a coastal defense orientation and more toward a blue-water navy capable of power projection.

Manila's lack of credible military options limits its capability to respond effectively to these moves or to protect its interests in the South China Sea. The Philippines has periodically raised the possibility that a military encroachment on its territories in the South China Sea would invoke a U.S. response under the 1951 Mutual Defense Treaty. U.S. authorities, however, have not endorsed such an interpretation and have stated that the treaty would not trigger an automatic response but rather consultations in accordance with "constitutional processes" (per Article IV of the treaty). In short, the United States has emphasized that ambiguity is important as a deterrent to an act of aggression in the Spratlys. But were a conflict to break out, Washington would be compelled to become involved and could not stand by and permit China to dominate this vital maritime region.

Some observers have heralded a 2002 nonbinding joint Association of Southeast Asian Nations (ASEAN)-China statement, the "Declaration on the Conduct of Parties in the South China Sea," as an important breakthrough for conflict prevention. ASEAN worked hard for years on the diplomatic front to get China to agree to confidence-building language on the Spratlys dispute. But unfortunately the declaration is simply a statement of purpose that could be subject to differing interpretations, ignored, and/or broken at any time. In short, it does not address the deeper underlying political, economic, and military issues involved.

ASEAN is in essence pursuing a holding action in hopes that China will somehow back off its broad claim to the entire South China Sea. But this is unlikely. By all appearances Beijing is biding its time until it has sufficient military capabilities to back up its expansive claim through the use of force. China's strategy thus appears to be one of wearing down the other claimants through endless diplomacy combined with an effort to exert de facto control through continuing occupations and reinforcement of existing outposts.

The Philippines also has reported that Chinese vessels have been increasingly frequenting Scarborough Shoal. This disputed area is within the Philippines's EEZ and lies in the northern portion of the South China Sea off the western coast of Luzon Island, well north of the Spratlys. Such probing could be a prelude to China establishing a new military outpost in the vicinity of Scarborough Shoal.[9]

Terrorism Threat and Response

The terrorist events of September 11, 2001, in the United States reverberated loudly in the Philippines, where Islamic terrorists had long been active. The network of ties between al Qaeda, JI, and Philippine Islamic groups led to an intense focus by the United States on working with its Philippine ally to counter these threats as part of the War on Terrorism.

One of Washington's very first strategic moves after Operation Enduring Freedom began in Afghanistan in October 2001 was to turn its attention to al Qaeda surrogates and affiliates in the Philippines. Under the framework of annual training exercises called Balikatan (which means standing "shoulder to shoulder" in the Filipino language), the U.S. initially dispatched some 660 special forces and support troops beginning in January 2002 to assist Philippine forces with counterterrorism missions in Mindanao and Basilan. These activities were specifically geared toward the ASG. The deployment later grew to 1,200 U.S. forces. In tandem, various civil affairs, education, health, and infrastructure support projects also were undertaken to help win the hearts and minds of the local population. Bowing to a specific provision in the Philippine constitution, as well as to nationalist sensitivities, the American troops were technically barred from engaging enemy forces and only could act in self-defense in any hostile encounters. A larger U.S. deployment to Mindanao scheduled for 2003, prior to the start of Operation Iraqi Freedom, was put on hold after an expanded combat role for U.S. troops raised public controversy. A subsequent Balikatan exercise in 2004 took place and was geared toward defending the offshore Malampaya gas field against terrorist attack.

As a result, the War on Terrorism initially strengthened bilateral ties. President Arroyo shared President George W. Bush's assessment of the global terrorist threat. Manila also supported Washington on the question of taking military action against Iraq. As a steadfast ally, President Arroyo was given the honor of an official state visit in May 2003—one of the very few such visits accorded a foreign leader during the Bush presidency. High-level contact between the two leaders continued when President Bush visited the Philippines in October 2003. Amid the deepening ties, the Philippines sent a contingent of personnel to serve on a humanitarian and medical mission in Iraq.

In 2003 the United States promised fresh military and other assistance and aid amounting to approximately US$100 million. The assistance covered counterterrorism training and equipment, funds to support economic development in Mindanao and the peace process with the MILF, and money for defense articles. Washington also took the symbolically important step of designating the Philippines as a Major Non-NATO Ally, which opens up the possibility of future bilateral military research, as well as special access to U.S. defense equipment. (Close U.S. partners such as Australia, Japan, Israel, and Thailand also share this designation.)

But the relationship experienced a critical setback in 2004. Iraqi terrorists kidnapped Angelo de la Cruz, a Philippine civilian truck driver and threatened to kill him unless the Philippine government withdrew its humanitarian and medical contingent from Iraq. Faced with what it judged to be serious domestic pressure, the newly elected Arroyo government complied with the terrorists' demand. This decision was bitterly criticized by the United States and other Coalition partners in Iraq on the basis that it was a capitulation to the terrorists and would only lead to more threats. This incident led to a chill in relations between Washington and Manila. The United States questioned the reliability of its Philippine ally. Aid and assistance to the Philippines not yet in the pipeline was effectively frozen pending further assessment by U.S. policymakers.

On the issue of terrorist financial flows, the Philippines signed and ratified the International Convention for the Suppression of Terrorism Financing. The government also has been taking steps on combating money laundering, but the need for stronger legislation still remains.

Military Structure and Defense Policy

National security policy formulation occurs at the cabinet level through the National Security Council and at the agency level through the Department of

National Defense headed by the Secretary of National Defense. The Secretary of National Defense supervises the country's defense program and exercises executive control over the military, known collectively as the Armed Forces of the Philippines and composed of the army, navy, and air force. The chief of staff commands the AFP and serves as the president's chief military adviser. The AFP encompasses approximately 106,000 active duty forces.

The Philippines is allied with the United States under the 1951 Mutual Defense Treaty, which constitutes the country's main pillar of deterrence from foreign attack. Military-to-military relations were substantially affected by the Philippine Senate's historic vote on September 16, 1991, rejecting an agreement that would have provided for continued United States use of Subic Bay Naval Base for ten years. With that decision, the Senate brought to a close almost a century of major U.S. military presence in the Philippines. As a result, meaningful defense cooperation between the two sides ground to halt. It was not until the mid-1990s that the situation began to change. This shift was spurred in large measure by China's moves in the South China Sea. By 1998 Washington and Manila had concluded the Visiting Forces Agreement (VFA), the first step in revitalizing their defense ties. The VFA provides legal protection for U.S. military personnel participating in exercises on Philippine territory, and as such updates a previous Status of Forces Agreement, which had lapsed, effectively suspending bilateral military exercises. The Philippine Senate officially approved the VFA in 1999, paving the way for resumed military contacts, ship visits and military exercises, and helping breathe life back into the Mutual Defense Treaty.

Following 9/11, the Philippines became a primary theater in the War on Terrorism. Bilateral ties with the United States expanded greatly. In 2002 the two sides created a bilateral Defense Policy Board to enhance defense and military interaction.

With respect to military capabilities, an extensive defense modernization program has been under discussion for the better part of a decade. But lack of funding has effectively hampered any real progress toward upgrading AFP capabilities. The United States is also providing assistance in this area. The two countries are jointly assessing and identifying Manila's key defense requirements, and Washington also is helping to fill some urgent shortcomings by offering excess defense articles, such as UH-1H helicopters, as they become available. Additional equipment, such as M-16 rifles and night-vision equipment, also were transferred to Philippine forces to support counterterrorism goals. It will likely be some time however before the AFP can address other critical deficiencies, such as in air power and naval patrol vessels. Fallout from the Philippines' early withdrawal from Iraq in 2004 puts into question elements of future U.S. military assistance.

Conclusions and Outlook

The Philippines is situated strategically at the crossroads of the Pacific. With its own revived Muslim insurgency and positioned as it is at the edge of Southeast Asia's arc of Islamic instability, the country also figures prominently as a likely theater in the ongoing War on Terrorism. This has created new pressures for policy makers in Manila and diverted attention away from other pressing social and economic priorities. Sustained terrorist threats, coupled with growing criminality, also have led a number of nations, including the United States, Australia, and Japan, to issue periodic travel warnings advising their citizens to defer travel to the Philippines. Although reflecting an accurate assessment of the internal security situation, these international reactions have had a further negative impact on the country's investment climate and economic development.

With a hard-working, English-speaking population, the Philippines in fact offers many opportunities for foreign investors. But the country's progress has been hamstrung by its inability to achieve real political stability and a failure to contain law-and-order and security threats. Until confidence is restored, the country will continue to face important economic challenges to its national development. This will come at great cost. With a population of nearly 80 million (some estimates are as high as 84 million), the Philippines is the fourteenth most populous country in the world. Poverty is widespread, and the pressure exerted by overpopulation is great. The new Arroyo administration thus faces a crucial challenge in getting the country moving forward to better realize its full potential.

Notes

1. See "GMA Explains Chasm Between Revenues, Foreign Debt," News Headline, September 19, 2004, Office of the President, Republic of the Philippines, at www.op.gov.ph and Juan Sarmiento, "UP economists warn of RP crash in 2 years," *Philippine Daily Inquirer*, August 23, 2004, p. A1. For further analysis, see the August 2004 study by a prominent group of economists with the faculty of the University of the Philippines School of Economics: "The Deepening Crisis: The Real Score on Deficits and Public Debt," Discussion Paper DP2004-09, August 2004, at www.econ.upd.edu.ph/home/index.php.

2. Karl B. Kaufman, "Slay Plot on President Declassified," *Manila Times*, August 12, 2003, at www.manilatimes.net; James Hookway, "Genuine Grievances," *Far Eastern Economic Review*, August 7, 2003, pp. 16 and 18; and Ellen Nakashima, "Army Loyalty Saves Leader In Philippines," *Washington Post*, July 29, 2003, pp. A9 and A14.

3. Arnaud de Borchgrave, "Resurgent Marxist Rebels Pose Big Threat," *Washington Times*, October 17, 2003, p. A17.

4. James Hookway, "The Business of Terrorism," *Far Eastern Economic Review,* January 16, 2003, p. 50.

5. The bin Laden/al Qaeda/Ramzi Yousef-ASG links are described well in Zachary Abuza, *Militant Islam in Southeast Asia: Crucible of Terror* (Boulder, CO: Lynne Rienner Publishers, 2003), esp. pp. 99–115; Maria A. Ressa, *Seeds of Terror: An Eyewitness Account of Al-Qaeda's Newest Center of Operations in Southeast Asia* (New York: Free Press, 2003), chap. 2 and chap. 6; and in earlier reporting by the *Washington Post* in David B. Ottaway and Steve Coll, "Retracing the Steps of a Terror Suspect," *Washington Post,* June 5, 1995, pp. A1 and A15; and Matthew Brzezinski, "Bust and Boom," *The Washington Post Magazine,* December 30, 2001, pp. 15–17, and 27–28.

6. Based on the account of one of the German victims as related in his subsequent book about the incident. See Werner Wallert, *Horror im Tropenparadies* (Munich: Wilhelm Goldman Verlag, December 2000).

7. The account of this incident is told in Gracia Burnham with Dean Merrill, *In the Presence of My Enemies* (Wheaton, IL: Tyndale House Publishers, 2003).

8. For background, see Ressa, *Seeds of Terror: An Eyewitness Account of Al-Qaeda's Newest Center of Operations in Southeast Asia,* esp. pp. 7–10 and chap. 7; Abuza, *Militant Islam in Southeast Asia: Crucible of Terror,* esp. pp. 90–91 and 136–38; Ministry of Home Affairs, Republic of Singapore, *White Paper: The Jemaah Islamiyah Arrests and the Threat of Terrorism,* January 7, 2003, at www2.mha.gov.sg/mha/index.jsp, esp. pp. 3–4 and 7–8; Alan Sipress and Ellen Nakashima, "Al Qaeda Affiliate Training Indonesians on Philippine Island," *Washington Post,* November 17, 2003, pp. A18-A19; and John McBeth, "Across Borders," *Far Eastern Economic Review,* July 22, 2004, p. 27.

9. For more information on the South China Sea disputes, see John C. Baker and David G. Wiencek, eds., *Cooperative Monitoring in the South China Sea: Satellite Imagery, Confidence-Building Measures, and the Spratly Islands Disputes* (Westport, CT: Praeger Publishers, 2002); and David G. Wiencek, "South China Sea Flashpoint Revisited," in *China Brief* by the Jamestown Foundation, December 2002, at www.jamestown.org.

Suggested Readings

Burnham, Gracia, with Dean Merrill. *In the Presence of My Enemies.* Wheaton, IL: Tyndale House Publishers, 2003.

Buss, Claude A. *Cory Aquino and the People of the Philippines.* Stanford, CA: Stanford Alumni Association, 1987.

Dolan, Ronald E., ed. *The Philippines: A Country Study.* 4th ed. Washington, DC: U.S. Government Printing Office, 1993.

Rasul, Amina, ed. *The Road to Peace and Reconciliation: Muslim Perspective on the Mindanao Conflict.* Makati City, The Philippines: Asian Institute of Management, 2003.

Wiencek, David G. "Mindanao and Its Impact on Security in the Philippines," in Bruce Vaughn, ed., *The Unraveling of Island Asia? Governmental, Communal, and Regional Instability.* Westport, CT: Praeger Publishers, 2002, pp. 47–59.

18

Singapore

Stability and Prosperity

William M. Carpenter

Introduction

Singapore owes much of its success as a stable and prosperous nation to its separation from Malaysia in 1965 to become a fully independent city-state. Given internal self-government by Britain in 1959, Singapore then became part of the newly formed Malaysia in 1963. It was a union that was not to be, however, because of fundamental differences with the regime in Kuala Lumpur. By 1965 separation was necessary. Since that time, Singapore has prospered more rapidly than it would have by remaining a small part of Malaysia. Strategically situated as an influential entrepôt of foreign trade, it has in addition built up a strong industrial base and has seen an economic growth rate better than most of its East Asian neighbors. Like all nations in the region, Singapore was affected by the Asian financial crisis of the late 1990s—and also by the severe acute respiratory syndrome (SARS) scare of 2003—but overall, Singapore continues to be one of the strongest economies in East and Southeast Asia. Its strong economy enables this nation to afford a respectable armed force for its own protection and, importantly, for the security of the sea-lanes in and near the Malacca Strait. The new century had hardly begun when the worldwide threat of terrorism arose, and, again, Singapore rose to the task of doing its part to cope with the threat.

Political Framework

Shortly after independence in 1965, Singapore became a republic headed by a president, but in fact it was led from that time until 1990 by the strong leader of the People's Action Party (PAP), Prime Minister Lee Kuan Yew. On November 29, 1990, Lee handed over the prime ministership to Goh Chok Tong, but Lee remained a potent force in the government as a senior minister. Goh took a surprising risk in 1992 by resigning his seat in Parliament to contest a by-election—he won by a large majority. The leading party, the

259

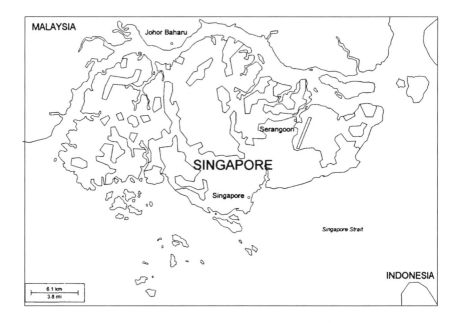

PAP, seems to be in no danger of losing its government role, and in 2004 the nation seemed ready for its second leadership change in its forty years of independence. The third prime minister is Lee Hsien Loong, son of Lee Kuan Yew, Singapore's legendary first prime minister. In the new leadership configuration, Goh Chok Tong became Senior Minister and Lee Kuan Yew took on the newly created position of Minister Mentor. Upon assuming office in August 2004, Lee Hsien Loong said it was time for a change in Singapore. He and the younger generation had come to see their nation as overly protective. They wanted to loosen the government's strict control of daily life to allow for greater participation by the people in national affairs. Change will inevitably come, but it is likely to be in slow and measured steps, because the established record of the forty-year-old national system gives it a deserved reputation as the engine of success. The PAP will remain dominant, but there are opposition parties in Singapore. The Workers Party and the Barisun Socialis (Socialist Front) continue to try for a place in the government, but by 2004 there had never been more than four opposition members in Parliament (now numbering eighty-four members).

Internal Security Environment

Until the fateful date of September 11, 2001, when al Qaeda terrorist attacks on New York City and the Pentagon shocked the world, Singapore seemed not to have a serious internal threat to its security. Tensions between Singapore and Malaysia have persisted over the years since their separation, but they were not likely to incite any domestic unrest within either country. Even the sharp bickering in 2002 over Singapore's land reclamation projects near the channels leading to Malaysian ports did not cause any demonstrations by Malaysian or Singaporean sympathizers in the other's capital. But the coming of the global threat of terrorism (see below) prompted Singapore to prepare to cope with this new factor in its internal security environment.

External Security Environment

Most observers of the East Asian region would agree that the risk of invasion of Singapore by a foreign power has been negligible—that is, until September 11, 2001, when terrorists, organized and directed by a foreign enemy, attacked the United States. It was at once apparent to those responsible for its security that Singapore was, indeed, vulnerable, for two main reasons: first, it is one of the world's most important trade and manufacturing centers, and second, Singapore is widely known for its strong support of the United States—the archenemy of al Qaeda and probably other terrorist networks. Singapore's reaction to this new threat (see below) was swift and effective, and the responses will without doubt continue. There is one other significant external threat, and that is the new order of piracy, which has been a serious threat to the world's sea-lanes for more than a decade. Singapore, a major shipping port, sits next to the critical Strait of Malacca and is thus vulnerable to attacks on shore or at sea.

Terrorism Threat and Response

The al Qaeda attacks on the United States were a wake-up call for Singapore; the nation's leaders realized immediately how vulnerable Singapore was and began to act in response to the threat. Not only could this major trade and manufacturing center be subject to great damage as a result of any terrorist attack but this vulnerability is heightened by Singapore's record of strong support of the United States. Singapore's armed forces, already strong for a nation its size, were ordered to increase readiness and training to counter terrorism. The people were alerted to the dangers of terrorism from within and without, by a high-profile campaign of information and instruction on the theme of "total defense."

This new awareness of the terrorism threat was confirmed when, in late 2001, thirteen members of Jemaah Islamiyah (JI) (Islamic group or Islamic community) were arrested in Singapore. They were accused by the government of plotting bomb attacks on the American embassy, against U.S. Navy ships, and on a bus carrying American troops.

As an example of Singapore's awareness of the threat of terrorism and its willingness to engage in international cooperation, the Singapore Police Force in 2003 trained a new Iraqi Facility Protection Service by sending a police task force to Baghdad. Other opportunities for cooperation may arise to which Singapore will be ready to respond.

Military Structure and Defense Policy

Enabled by its strong economy, Singapore has in recent years been pressing ahead with a military buildup, spending about 5 percent of gross domestic product (GDP) on defense. Singapore bought fighter aircraft from the United States, submarines from Sweden, and in its own shipyards has built fast-attack naval craft, equipped with state-of-the-art electronics. The career military force of 15,900 is supplemented by 44,600 on active National Service—compulsory for able-bodied young men—and another 225,000 reservists. The armed forces participate in joint training exercises with the United States, Australia, Taiwan, and India. Singapore's active role in the Association of Southeast Asian Nations (ASEAN) encourages further defense cooperation with the members of ASEAN.

Singapore is a member of the Five-Power Defence Arrangement (FPDA) with the United Kingdom, Australia, New Zealand, and Malaysia. This pact obligates members to consult in the event of external threats and authorizes the stationing of Commonwealth forces in Singapore. In furtherance of Singapore's support of a strong U.S. military presence in the region, the United States and Singapore in 1990 signed a Memorandum of Understanding (MOU) providing for access by U.S. forces to Singapore's port facilities and military bases.

The Singapore Armed Forces (SAF) are integrated into an effective unified force: the army the largest with 50,000, a navy of 4,500, and an air force of 6,000. The army has some 80 main battle tanks, about 350 light tanks and 75 towed artillery pieces. The navy has two submarines, six corvettes and six missile craft, equipped with Harpoon missiles, and five amphibious craft. The air force has 40 F-5s, 25 F-16s and 28 armed helicopters. For air defense, aircraft are equipped with Sparrow, Sidewinder, Harpoon, and Shrike missiles. There are 12,000 in the Singapore Police Force and 84,000 in the Civil Defense Force, which includes reservists and volunteers. Singapore's defense policy relies heavily on its own defense, and with ready cooperation with friends and allies.

Conclusions and Outlook

Singapore, like its ASEAN allies, does not have the military force to cope, by itself, with an attack by a major power, but its confidence in defense is strengthened by two factors: the continued strategic presence of the United States and the preservation of the FPDA. Britain maintains that the FPDA is still relevant and useful for enhancing security and stability, and is not likely to change. The U.S. Department of Defense issued a position paper in 1998 that reaffirmed U.S. intentions to maintain forward deployment of forces in East Asia and the Western Pacific region. In the present era of awareness of the global threat of terrorism, Singapore is prepared to cooperate fully with the U.S. objective of defeating terrorism wherever it may threaten. Full access to Singapore by U.S. forces is ongoing evidence of Singapore's supportive policy. This was confirmed in 2004 when the U.S. Pacific Command announced a new operation, the Regional Maritime Security Initiative (RMSI), to send U.S. forces to join with forces of local nations to cope with pirates and seaborne terrorists in the Pacific and Indian Oceans, and Singapore readily agreed to cooperate.

Given the prospect of confidence in the American presence and the retention of the FPDA, Singapore's upgraded military structure should be adequate for the country's security for some years to come. This nation of 4.2 million people—with an area of 683 square miles (1,700 square kilometers)—has a GDP of US$91 billion (2002) and spends about 5 percent of GDP on defense. Given Singapore's strong economy and the recent upgrading of its armed forces, this level of defense expenditure should be sustainable and adequate.

Suggested Readings

Lee Kuan Yew. *Memoirs: The Singapore Story.* Singapore: Prentice Hall, 1998.

Ministry of Home Affairs, Republic of Singapore. *White Paper: The Jemaah Islamiyah Arrests and the Threat of Terrorism.* January 7, 2003, at www2.mha.gov.sg/mha/index.jsp/.

The Straits Times. "PM Goh: We Will Soar Again." August 8, 2003.

U.S. Department of State. *Background Notes: Singapore.* October 2003.

——— 19 ———

South Korea

An Emerging Power in the Pacific

Dennis Van Vranken Hickey

Introduction

In recent years the Republic of Korea (ROK or South Korea) has experienced a dramatic political transformation. On the domestic front, the nation has made the transition from authoritarianism to democracy. On the international front, the ROK has been embraced by many of its former adversaries—including the People's Republic of China (PRC). Perhaps equally significant, Seoul has adopted a new approach toward relations with its archrival on the Korea Peninsula—the Democratic People's Republic of Korea (DPRK or North Korea). These developments hold important implications for the ROK's security policy and the nation's armed forces.

Political Framework

As World War II came to a close, the United States and the Soviet Union agreed to temporarily partition the Korea Peninsula at the 38th parallel. This division ultimately sparked the Korean War—a major international conflict that ended with an armistice (not a formal peace treaty) in 1953. The armistice was only supposed to last several months. But peace talks broke down in 1954 and never resumed. For over half a century, the Korea Peninsula has remained divided with the ROK in the south and the DPRK in the north.

Today, the ROK is a lively democracy with powers shared between a popularly elected president and a unicameral legislature (the National Assembly). For much of its history, however, the ROK could perhaps best be described as an authoritarian regime. Throughout the 1960s, 1970s, and 1980s, the ROK military played an important role in ROK politics. Indeed, until relatively recently, a series of strongmen with close ties to the armed forces and security agencies ruled the country.

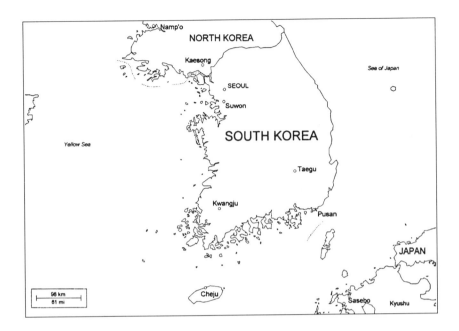

In May 1960 Major General Park Chung Hee seized control of the government shortly after demonstrations forced Syngman Rhee, the ROK's first president, to resign. Park ruled the country with an iron fist until he was assassinated by the Korean Central Intelligence Agency (KCIA) in October 1979.

Park's successor, Major General Chun Doo Hwan, proved to be an unpopular leader. His administration was marked by numerous demonstrations, repression, and violence. In 1980 the government attempted to restore order and silence the opposition by declaring martial law. This move, however, led to a critically important event in South Korea's modern political history—the 1980 Kwangju uprising, in which government troops killed hundreds of civilians.

In 1987 Chun turned over the government to his handpicked successor, General Roh Tae Woo. Massive demonstrations, however, convinced Roh that the time had arrived to restore civilian rule. In what were generally considered to be fair and open elections, he was succeeded by President Kim Young Sam in 1992.

In 1997 Kim Dae-jung, a former political prisoner, was elected ROK president. This election marked the first time that an opposition party candidate had been elected to the presidency since the country was established in 1948. It was also noteworthy because Kim had campaigned on a platform calling for a new approach to North Korea—the so-called Sunshine Policy. In December 2002 Roh Moo-hyun won election as president largely on a platform of continuing the Sunshine Policy.

According to the 1987 ROK constitution, the military must observe "political neutrality." The president is commander in chief of the armed forces and appoints a prime minister and all members of the State Council or cabinet—including the minister of defense. He may also appoint and remove the nation's leading military officers. When crafting defense policy, the president is most often assisted by the National Security Council (an advisory group), the National Intelligence Service (successor to the KCIA), and the Foreign Affairs and Trade Ministry. In some instances, other agencies and officials may be invited to play a role in decision making.

Internal Security Environment

Since 1987 South Korea has experienced profound political liberalization. The new constitution revitalized the National Assembly, restored freedoms of expression and assembly, and led ultimately to free and fair elections. Power is now shared between the president and the National Assembly. Consequently, the violent antigovernment demonstrations and civil disturbances that characterized much of South Korea's political landscape during the authoritarian era are largely a thing of the past.

In addition to political liberalization, the ROK economy has recovered from the Asian financial crisis of the late 1990s. Some had feared that the country would experience a complete financial meltdown in 1997 or 1998. But the ROK now enjoys economic growth that is conducive to democracy and political stability.

Despite its participation in the global War on Terrorism, the ROK has not suffered any recent terrorist attacks (in the past, the DPRK had launched terrorist attacks in the ROK). According to some reports, agents linked to al Qaeda have journeyed to South Korea to study the feasibility of conducting terrorist attacks against U.S. and/or ROK forces. However, U.S. officials contend that the potential for such an attack is relatively low because of the country's rigorous internal security measures that are in place to cope with the DPRK threat.

To be sure, most trends appear to favor political stability in the ROK. But South Korean politics is anything but tranquil. In presidential elections in December 2002, Roh Moo Hyun promised voters that he would seek greater independence from the United States. However, his postelection efforts to maintain cordial relations with Washington—including his support for deploying ROK troops to Iraq—have enraged many South Koreans. The president also has little to show for his efforts to engage North Korea. Rather than respond to Seoul's peace overtures, Pyongyang has ratchetted up tensions by violating the terms of the 1994 Agreed Framework and flouting its nuclear ambitions. Domestically, Roh promised to rein in the ROK's *chaebols*—the country's gigantic corporate conglomerates. But he has accomplished very little. Finally, the Roh administration appears to be plagued by corruption, sometimes described as "the Korean disease." There are allegations that some of his top advisers have received bribes from the chaebols.

In sum, the Roh administration has been characterized by a series of disappointments. The matter reached a crucial point in early 2004 when legislators voted to impeach President Roh. This decision created further political turmoil and uncertainty in the country. The impeachment was later overturned by the Korean Constitutional Court and President Roh was restored to power on May 14, 2004. Unfortunately, it appears that domestic political stability remains an elusive goal for the ROK.

External Security Environment

The ROK government acknowledges that there are numerous "security flash points" in East Asia. Moreover, the emergence of the threat of international terrorism has complicated the region's security equation. But the North Korean threat continues to be the most immediate concern for South Korean defense planners.

The ROK employs several tactics in an effort to maintain peace and stability on the Korean peninsula. In addition to improving relations with the DPRK and working toward a permanent peace on the peninsula, Seoul hopes to deter a war by maintaining a robust military capability and a strong alliance with the United States.

The Sunshine Policy

In 1998 the government of the ROK launched a new approach toward relations with the DPRK—the Sunshine Policy. In his inaugural address, President Kim Dae-jung announced three principles on which the South's policy toward the North would be based:

- The ROK will not tolerate armed provocations from the DPRK;
- The ROK has no intention to either destroy or absorb the DPRK; and
- The ROK hopes to press ahead with a policy of reconciliation and cooperation with the DPRK.

The Sunshine Policy employs a mixture of both carrots and sticks. For example, the Hyundai Corporation has been permitted to ferry South Korean tourists to the North's culturally important Mount Kumgang. The giant corporation is paying the DPRK nearly US$5 billion for this privilege over five years. But programs such as the Mount Kumgang tours could be suspended or terminated if the North engages in provocative behavior. Indeed, some fear that the apparent resumption of North Korea's nuclear program will ultimately derail Seoul's peace initiatives. Not surprisingly, the ROK is determined to continue beefing up its military capabilities. In other words, the ROK hopes to be prepared to handle a military crisis should the policy of engagement fail.

A Strong ROK Military Capability

The ROK boasts a thoroughly modern military arsenal. The ground forces are armed with new tanks, infantry combat vehicles, and surface-to-air missiles. The navy is seeking to graduate from a coastal patrol force to a blue-water navy. In 2002 it agreed to purchase Aegis combat defense systems that will be installed on three domestically built destroyers. The air force is armed with modern license-built F-16 fighters and is developing an indigenous trainer (the T-50). In 2002 Seoul also agreed to purchase forty new F-15K fighters from the United States

U.S.-ROK Defense Alliance

In addition to its impressive military muscle, the ROK relies upon the 1954 U.S.-ROK Mutual Defense Treaty to deter a DPRK attack. The United States stations roughly 37,000 troops in South Korea, including the U.S. Army's Second Infantry Division and several air force tactical squadrons. Along with the ROK military, these forces maintain a high state of readiness—an essential element in the strategy of deterrence.

Security ties between the ROK and the United States remain strong. The relationship continues to be dogged, however, by contentious issues. Perhaps most significant, Seoul and Washington appear to differ in their perceptions of the threat posed by Pyongyang. But the two sides have also quarreled over the level of ROK host-nation support, the future of U.S. troops in Korea after unification, U.S. pressure on the ROK to purchase only American arms, the ROK missile program, and the Status of Forces Agreement.

These tensions have contributed to some adjustments in the alliance. For example, the Status of Forces Agreement was modified in 2001. According to the revised terms of the pact, certain offenses by off-duty American soldiers may now be tried in civilian courts. Furthermore, the United States is consolidating its forces in fewer bases and moving the Second Infantry Division away from the border to bases south of Seoul. Finally, President George

W. Bush announced in August 2004 that up to 12,500 American troops would be removed from the ROK as part of a major restructuring of United States forces prompted by the end of the Cold War and the beginning of the War on Terrorism.

Terrorism Threat and Response

The ROK is no stranger to terrorist attacks. Since the armistice in 1953, DPRK agents have engaged in numerous acts of terrorism. In some instances, the intended targets were located in South Korea. In other cases, DPRK agents attacked ROK officials while traveling abroad. In keeping with the Sunshine Policy, however, the ROK has resisted American efforts to brand the DPRK as a terrorist state. In fact, the inclusion of the DPRK in what President George W. Bush described as an Axis of Evil is reported to have sent shock waves throughout Korean political circles.

Despite the differences over the nature of the DPRK regime, the ROK has generally supported the United States-led War on Terrorism. In early 2002 President Kim Dae-jung declared: "Terrorism has no face. Terrorism kills innocent civilians. It is the most cowardly and cruel act of provocation. It is a heinous and barbaric crime that cannot be justified under any pretext. . . . It must be rooted out at all cost."

Domestically, South Korea's intelligence services reportedly monitor the activities of thousands of foreign workers and foreign students from Muslim countries. Moreover, antiterrorism drills have been conducted to prepare authorities to cope with an emergency. Furthermore, after years of debate, in 2003 the National Assembly passed controversial legislation designed to combat terrorism. The new law will enhance the government's powers to control the entry and exit of foreigners suspected of engaging in terrorist activities and establish special military units to handle any terror-related incidents. Civic groups oppose the legislation on the grounds that it might lead to human rights abuses.

On the international front, the ROK has agreed to work with other nations to curb the spread of terrorism. For example, the ROK has joined together with China, Japan, and the ten-member states of the Association of Southeast Asian Nations (ASEAN) to cooperate in the War on Terrorism. Perhaps most significant, however, is the ROK deployment of military forces overseas.

In 2002 South Korea's air force flew cargo missions in support of Operation Enduring Freedom in Afghanistan. In 2003 the ROK sent roughly four hundred medics and engineers to Iraq. In February 2004, after almost five months of debate, the National Assembly voted overwhelmingly to dispatch more than three thousand troops to Iraq. The contingent is the third largest serving in Iraq after the United States and the UK.

ROK officials realize that support for the War on Terrorism may come with a price. The deployment of troops to Iraq sparked antiwar demonstrations in Seoul and fears that the country may itself become the target of an al Qaeda attack. The decision also contributed to strains with the DPRK. Pyongyang describes the deployment as "a rash act to be always cursed by history and the generations to come" and claims that the South Koreans will serve as "bullet shields" for U.S. forces.

Military Structure and Defense Policy

Numbering roughly 560,000 troops, the ROK ground forces form the core of South Korea's defense. In order to maintain current force levels, the government employs a universal conscription system. All male youths fit for military service enter active duty at the age of twenty (service may be postponed to attend college). Most men serve in the army for a total of twenty-six months. Those who opt to enlist in the other services (the navy and air force rely upon volunteers) will serve a longer tour of duty.

During peacetime, the ROK military's chief mission is to help deter a DPRK attack. Should deterrence fail, the overall goal of the ROK ground forces is to help ensure a victory over the DPRK invaders. Two of the ROK army's three field armies—the First ROK Army and the Third ROK Army— are charged with the responsibility of defending the region that stretches from the Demilitarized Zone (DMZ) to the greater Seoul metropolitan area. Each of these units consists of an army command and several corps commands, divisions, and brigades. The ROK Second Army is responsible for defending rear areas. Like the forward-deployed armies, it consists of an army command and several corps commands, divisions, and brigades. In addition to combating DPRK infiltration forces in rear areas, the Second Army guards the coastlines, defends the sea lines of communication (SLOCs) and mobilizes materials and reserve forces.

The ROK has launched a number of programs to modernize the army and provide it with new tanks and other equipment. There are also plans to downsize the army and merge some field commands as the army begins to realize the technological advances resulting from the revolution in military affairs (RMA). The RMA has also required the army to take steps required to raise the education level and technological training among the troops.

Like the ground forces, the chief duty of the ROK Navy is to deter a DPRK attack. Unlike the army, however, the 67,000-man navy (which includes the ROK Marines) relies entirely upon volunteers who serve for a period of twenty-eight months.

The ROK Navy Operations Command consists of three fleets, with one based in the East Sea, another in the Yellow Sea and the third in the Korea Strait. Each fleet possesses a variety of surface combatants (destroyers, escorts, speedboats, etc.), submarines, and aircraft. The Marine Corps Command is divided into two divisions and one brigade. It possesses amphibious vehicles (including amphibious tanks), landing equipment, and its own means of fire support to assist in amphibious operations.

The ROK Navy operates roughly 190 vessels including submarines and 70 aircraft. In recent years the ROK has sought to put more muscle into its navy by domestically producing its own warships and submarines. It has also enhanced its antisubmarine warfare (ASW) capability with the acquisition of imported ASW helicopters and maritime patrol aircraft.

Like the naval forces, the ROK Air Force relies entirely upon volunteers. Recruits who opt to join the air force must serve for thirty months. At the present time, roughly 63,000 personnel serve in the air force.

The ROK Air Force consists of the Air Force Headquarters, Operations Command, and Support Commands. Two flight wings belong to the Air Force Headquarters (the Air Defense Artillery Command and the Aircraft Control and Warning Wing), while the Operations Air Command possesses nine flight wings. One training wing operates under the Training Command. The Theater Air Control Center retains direct control over all air operations.

In order to maintain air superiority in a conflict, the air force possesses more than 800 modern aircraft. The mainstay of the air force is its chief fighter plane—the license-built F-16 C/D or KF-16 warplane. Thus far, Seoul has acquired 120 of the fighters and has placed a follow-up order for 20 more. All of these aircraft are armed with precision-guided mid-range air-to-air missiles, air-to-surface missiles and air-to-ship missiles. Problems associated with older F-4 E/F and F-5 D/E aircraft ultimately led Seoul to open bidding for a new fighter in 2001. After stiff (and controversial) bidding by four international competitors, the ROK announced that it would purchase 40 F-15K warplanes from Boeing for US$4.5 billion in April 2002. It is noteworthy that the air force also possesses a wide variety of transports, helicopters, reconnaissance planes, and other aircraft.

Finally, mention should be made of the roughly three million-strong ROK reserve forces. After completing their obligatory military service, all troops are required to serve an additional eight years in the reserves. During peacetime they engage in training exercises on a regular basis. Should war break out on the Korea Peninsula, however, the reservists will be called up for duty. Many will be assigned to combat units, while others may serve in a support capacity.

Conclusions and Outlook

Given the uncertain strategic environment that exists on the Korea Peninsula, it is understandable that defense planners in the ROK agree that the country must be prepared for conflict. But careful deliberation and thoughtful diplomacy may also play an increasingly important role in South Korea's relations with the DPRK. Indeed, the question of war or peace in Korea may ultimately hinge on the ability of the participants in the six-party talks (ROK, DPRK, Japan, Russia, China, and the United States) to persuade the DPRK to shelve its nuclear weapons program.

Despite the North Korean nuclear crisis, it is becoming increasingly clear that the ROK is looking beyond the traditional DPRK threat in its defense calculations. The ROK Ministry of National Defense (MND) now refers to the need to maintain "a strong omni-directional defense posture" as its "foremost" defense priority. Indeed, the MND stresses that the military's stated goal of defending the nation "means protecting it from *any* possible external military threat as well as those immediate threats from North Korea, which, as the nation's main enemy, could endanger our survival [emphasis added]."[1] Whether the ROK will be able to achieve this goal remains a matter of speculation—particularly given the rise in the military capabilities of China and Japan.

Note

1. See Ministry of National Defense, *Defense White Paper, 2000* (Seoul: Ministry of National Defense, 2000), at www.mnd.go.kr.

Suggested Readings

Hickey, Dennis V. *The Armies of East Asia: China, Taiwan, Japan and the Koreas.* Boulder, CO: Lynne Rienner Publishers, 2001.
———. "Reaching for Regional Power Status: A Net Assessment of the Military Capabilities of the Republic of Korea." *The Journal of East Asian Affairs,* vol. XVII, Spring/Summer 2003, pp. 93–120.
Ministry of National Defense, Republic of Korea. *Participatory Defense Policy 2003,* at www.mnd.go.kr.
Park, Kyung-Ae and Dalchoong Kim. *Korean Security Dynamics in Transition.* New York: Palgrave, 2001.

20

Sri Lanka

Political Uncertainty Under the Threat of Insurgency

M.A. Thomas

Introduction

The Democratic Socialist Republic of Sri Lanka, a small teardrop-shaped nation located off the southern coast of India, is a tropical paradise that has been mired in a two-decade-old internal conflict. The island nation is often overshadowed in world affairs by its larger and more prominent South Asian neighbors, India and Pakistan. Sri Lanka has remained a two-party-dominated democracy since it gained independence from British rule in February 1948. The country's bitterly contested politics and its struggle to defeat the Liberation Tigers of Tamil Eelam (LTTE) have caused considerable hardship among its war-weary population of 20 million. Nevertheless, Sri Lanka, formerly known as Ceylon, continues to enjoy one of the highest standards of living among South Asian countries.

Two rival political parties currently lead Sri Lanka under a unique and often confrontational power-sharing agreement. Both the Sri Lanka Freedom Party (SLFP), led by President Chandrika Bandaranaike Kumaratunga, and the United National Party (UNP), headed by former Prime Minister Ranil Wickremasinghe, continue to engage one another in highly partisan politics, often to the detriment of the country. The April 2004 national elections in Sri Lanka reaffirmed the rancorous nature of politics in the country.

The LTTE, designated as a Foreign Terrorist Organization (FTO) by the United States, has waged a protracted insurgency against the Sri Lankan government that has claimed some 65,000 lives since July 1983. The group, also known as the Tamil Tigers, espouses an ideology of Tamil nationalism toward the establishment of an independent homeland carved out of the northern and eastern portions of the country. Since December 2001, however, the LTTE has downplayed its key demand of secessionism to engage the Sri

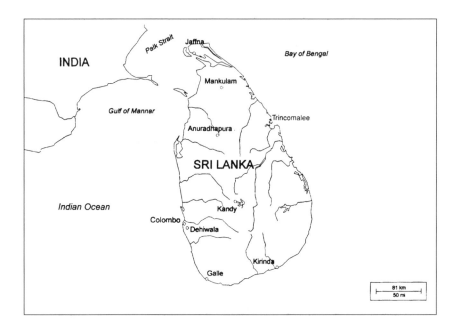

Lankan government in a series of peace negotiations brokered by Norway under an ongoing cease-fire agreement.

Ethnicity, Language, and Religion

Ethnicity is a highly divisive issue in Sri Lanka. Ethnic discrimination has led to the emergence of Tamil militancy and thus to many of Sri Lanka's problems. The Sinhalese constitute the majority (74 percent) in the country with the Tamils forming the largest minority (18 percent, of which Sri Lankan Tamils make up 12 percent and Indian Tamils 6 percent). Muslims (7 percent) are categorized as both an ethnic and a religious group in Sri Lanka. Other ethnic groups (1 percent) include Burghers, Malay, and Veddahs.

Sinhala, belonging to the Indo-European family of languages, is spoken by the Sinhalese majority. Tamil, a Dravidian language hailing from southern India, is spoken by the ethnic minority of the same name. Most Muslims speak both Tamil and Sinhala, while English is commonly used by all ethnic groups in matters of business and government.

Buddhism (70 percent), practiced by most Sinhalese, is the dominant religion in Sri Lanka. Hinduism (15 percent) is the religion of most Tamils. Both Sinhalese and Tamils follow Christianity (8 percent), and Muslims practice Islam (7 percent).

Political Framework

Sri Lanka has maintained a steady democratic tradition since its independence in 1948. In its search for finding the best form of democracy to suit its polity, the country has experimented in the past with a British Westminster type of parliamentary government with both bicameral and unicameral legislatures and with the prime minister exerting executive power.

Currently, Sri Lanka has a French quasi-presidential form of government with a unicameral legislature as per the country's third constitution, adopted in 1978. The president, elected for a six-year term, is both the chief of state and head of government. The exact relationship between the president and the prime minister varies according to their respective political affiliations. Members of the 225-seat parliament are elected by universal adult suffrage to serve six-year terms.

UNP-SLFP Rivalry

Upon achieving independence in 1948, largely as a by-product of the Indian independence movement, Sri Lanka was led by the UNP until 1956. Don Stephen (DS) Senanayake, the country's first prime minister, was a conservative nationalist whose agenda was one of continuity. UNP members were stigmatized as Westernized elite and accused of retaining British habits well after independence. After his accidental death, DS Senanayake was succeeded first by his son, Dudley Senanayake, and then by his cousin Sir John Kotelawala.

In 1956 Solomon West Ridgeway Dias (SWRD) Bandaranaike, father of current President Chandrika Bandaranaike Kumaratunga, formed the SLFP and campaigned on the slogan, "We are not brown Englishmen." He emphasized the importance of Sinhalese culture and language in the country and advocated giving a special status for Buddhism in Sri Lanka's society. This initiated the rivalry between the two parties, based on Sinhalese nationalism.

The SLFP espoused a socialist economic policy as opposed to the UNP's pro-business approach. Bandaranaike began to moderate his nationalistic policies once he was elected prime minister in 1956. In order to placate the Tamils, he abandoned the conditions of the "Sinhala Only" Language Act (described below) after massive violent protests. Viewed by Sinhalese hardliners as becoming soft on Sinhalese nationalism, Bandaranaike was assassinated by a militant Buddhist monk in 1959. The SLFP retained power with Srimavo Bandaranaike, widow of SWRD Bandaranaike, becoming the first female prime minister in the world in Sri Lanka's 1960 national elections. A poor economy led to the UNP's Dudley Senanayake regaining power in 1965 only to lose it again to Mrs. Bandaranaike in 1970.

Sinhalese-Tamil Antagonism

Under British "divide and rule" tactics, the minority Tamils were assigned influential positions in the administration during colonial rule. This created a backlash against Tamils at independence when the majority Sinhalese began to govern the country. For decades, UNP and SLFP administrations competed against one another on platforms of Sinhalese nationalism, which often led to discriminatory practices against Tamils.

One of the most controversial issues was that of language. Under the "Sinhala Only" Language Act of 1956, Tamils in government and administrative positions were given three years to learn Sinhala or relinquish their positions. Although the law was never implemented, it emphasized the prevailing atmosphere of Sinhalese nationalism at the expense of the Tamils.

Paranoia emerged among the Sinhalese that Sri Lanka's Tamils would join with their Hindu cousins in India and threaten the existence of Sinhalese culture. Conversely, Tamils began to view themselves as a threatened minority. Tamils began to demand regional autonomy to handle their own affairs in the northern and eastern parts of the country where their numbers were large. When these demands were not being met, a number of Tamils abandoned the democratic process and turned to militancy to address their needs. A number of Tamil militant groups formed in the 1970s. Most prominent amongst them was the LTTE.

The LTTE caught the attention of the Sinhalese-dominated government after it ambushed and slaughtered fifteen Sri Lankan soldiers on an army patrol in 1983. A violent Sinhalese backlash by hard-liners against Tamil civilians in July 1983 led to mass rioting, murderous rampages, and an exodus of hundreds of thousands of Tamils abroad.

Politics amid Insurgency

After the UNP's Junius Richard (JR) Jayewardene became prime minister in 1977, he changed the constitution to its current form and was subsequently reelected as president. Though he attempted to placate Tamils by declaring their language as a "national" language, he was unable to contain the escalating violence between the LTTE and the security forces, which culminated in the July 1983 riots and the beginning of a full-scale insurgency. Jayewardene's administration had to contend with the LTTE insurgency, India's intervention in Sri Lanka, and a Sinhalese Marxist rebellion by the Janatha Vimukthi Peramuna (JVP, or People's Liberation Front). The UNP continued to govern under President Ranasinghe Premadasa after Jayawardene retired. Premadasa was assassinated by the LTTE in May 1993.

Partisan Politics

Chandrika Bandaranaike Kumaratunga, leader of the SLFP, assumed power in August 1994 on the platform of bringing peace to the country. Though peace remained elusive, Kumaratunga won a second term in December 1999, just days after she survived an LTTE assassination attempt in which she lost the sight of one eye during a car bomb explosion. UNP leader Ranil Wickremasinghe became prime minister of Sri Lanka in the December 2001 national elections, negotiating a cease-fire between the LTTE and security forces. A power struggle between the UNP prime minister and the SLFP president led to political instability, with President Kumaratunga dismissing key UNP ministers and suspending parliament in February 2004. Though not able to command a clear majority in Parliament, President Kumaratunga and her SLFP-led coalition won 45 percent of votes over the UNP's 37 percent in the April 2004 national elections. This has resulted in the ousting of Ranil Wickremasinghe as leader of Parliament, and the installation of Mahinda Rajapakse as prime minister, a move that has consolidated President Kumaratunga's power base.

Politics and Buddhism

Theravada (or Hinayana—"Lesser Vehicle") Buddhism, the dominant form of the religion found in the country, tends to be highly politicized and to manifest itself through political activism in Sri Lanka. Theravada Buddhism places considerable emphasis on the role of the monk and of monk organizations. As a result, leaders of monk organizations are extremely influential in Sri Lanka's politics. Politicians often get blessings from influential monks before running for elections. Most monk organizations in Sri Lanka tend to espouse Sinhalese nationalistic views and tend not be sympathetic to the plight of Tamils. They are apt to be against the government negotiating with the LTTE, and view peace talks as leading to concessions for the terrorist outfit. The assassination of SWRD Bandaranaike in 1959 by a militant Buddhist monk is an example of religious extremism used for political purposes. In addition, Buddhist monks are thought to have incited rampaging Sinhalese mobs to attack Tamil establishments during the July 1983 riots in Colombo, the capital.

Internal Security Environment

The LTTE remain Sri Lanka's main internal security concern. The group has waged a prolonged insurgency against the government since 1983. Throughout much of the past two decades, the LTTE, estimated to have ten thousand armed combatants with a core of five thousand trained fighters, has administered its stronghold of the Jaffna Peninsula in the north as a de facto government. Championing itself as the true representative of the Tamil people, the LTTE has routinely eliminated rival more moderate Tamil personalities through intimidation and assassination.

A key success of the LTTE has been the simplicity of its ideology. The group's ideology has been one of Tamil nationalism toward the establishment of an independent homeland (Eelam). Other Tamil militant groups that emerged alongside the LTTE have often complicated their ideologies with Marxist rhetoric, making it difficult for the Tamil commoner to find solidarity with their movements.

Another success of the LTTE is the group's emphasis on discipline and organization. Tamil Tigers are not permitted to drink, smoke, or engage in sexual relations. They can marry only with permission and are allowed only limited contact with their families. The most indoctrinated and skilled cadres are chosen among volunteers to become Black Tigers, an elite, well-trained subset of the LTTE who engage in suicide missions.

Sinhalese discrimination against Tamils in the past and the events of July 1983 led to an increased polarization between Sinhalese and Tamils in Sri Lanka, and to a surge of moral and financial support for the LTTE. The LTTE members were initially viewed as freedom fighters by many Tamils against a hostile Sinhalese-dominated society.

Fewer in number than the Sri Lanka security forces, the LTTE has often outmaneuvered the security forces by staving off army advances. In addition, the group has successfully employed guerilla warfare tactics, and at times has even challenged the government forces in conventional confrontations. Even though the LTTE has maintained a cease-fire since December 2001, it continues to engage in forcible recruitment (especially among children), in political assassinations of rival Tamil individuals, and in skirmishes with the security forces. The group has adopted a "wait and see" posture regarding the current government impasse.

Velupillai Prabhakaran, leader of the LTTE, exerts authoritarian control over the organization. Described as a megalomaniac, Prabhakaran leaves no room for dissent in the organization and has not groomed anyone as his successor. Potential rivals inside the LTTE have been tortured and/or killed in the past. In an unprecedented move in March 2004, Vinayagamoorthy Muralitharan, the eastern military commander of the LTTE popularly known as Karuna, splintered from the group with his followers, accusing Prabhakaran of unfairly drawing resources from the east and funneling them to benefit the north. Prabhakaran has downplayed the split, which has further complicated the peace negotiation process.

A lesser-known internal security concern involved the JVP, a Sinhalese radical group. It launched a violent insurrection against the government in 1971 and during the late 1980s. Espousing a Marxist ideology, the group attempted to overthrow the government and replace it with a socialist state through tactics of mass agitation and political assassination. In a controversial government crackdown, the Sri Lankan security forces arrested or killed most of the group's top leadership in 1989, which ultimately led to the JVP's disintegration. In recent years, however, the JVP has made a resurgence into Sri Lanka's politics. The group, whose support base consists of students, laborers, and farmers, has pledged to remain nonviolent and to adhere to the democratic process. Forming the third largest political party in Sri Lanka, the JVP has entered into alliances with the SLFP.

External Security Environment

Externally, Sri Lanka enjoys cordial relations with all its South Asian neighbors, as well as with a number of countries throughout the world. Sri Lanka particularly enjoys excellent political and military bilateral relations with the United States. The Sri Lankan government continues to win favor with the United States and the West by considerably improving its human rights record among its security forces over the past decade, as well as by proposing measures to find a political solution that would accommodate Tamils. Sri Lanka has earned more assistance and respect from Western powers, which have come to view the Tamil Tigers as terrorists rather than as freedom fighters. Both the Sri Lankan government and the LTTE have agreed upon Norway's role in mediating the negotiations.

Sri Lanka's international relations have been strongly influenced by India, its giant South Asian neighbor 20 miles (32 kilometers) across the Palk Strait. During the early 1980s India, pressured by its own 60 million Tamils in its southern state of Tamil Nadu, covertly assisted the LTTE in training and arms procurement. At the time, the LTTE cadres were widely regarded as freedom fighters for Tamils in Sri Lanka, who were facing human rights abuses perpetrated by the security forces. As India began to experience its own terrorist problems, it changed its policy toward the LTTE and withdrew its support (even though the LTTE continued to receive support from Tamil Nadu). India brokered a deal with the UNP-led government to send a peacekeeping force to Sri Lanka to disarm the LTTE in exchange for the government granting more autonomy for Tamils in the north and east. As this was not acceptable to the LTTE, the LTTE began to turn its sights on the Indian Peacekeeping Force. India's involvement in Sri Lanka from 1987 to 1990 has often been compared to America's involvement in Vietnam. The Indian

Peacekeeping Force left Sri Lanka, failing to accomplish its mission and with an alarming number of Indian casualties.

The LTTE has continued to lobby foreign governments for its cause against the Sri Lankan government. The organization has used its international contacts to procure weapons and material for waging its war. It has exploited the Tamil expatriate community in North America, Europe, and Asia to finance its activities. The group is thought to have been involved in international narcotics trafficking, alien smuggling, extortion, and various forms of fraud. With an improved human rights record, the Sri Lankan government has also lobbied foreign governments to ban the LTTE and to assist in curtailing its fundraising activities.

Terrorism Threat and Response

The LTTE has posed a unique threat to Sri Lanka. The organization has confronted the government on a conventional level as well as using guerrilla warfare tactics. It has conducted a number of terrorist bombing campaigns against Sri Lanka's economic infrastructure. The group is regarded as one of the pioneers in suicide bombings and has more suicide bombings than all other terrorist organizations combined. The LTTE has targeted foreign and domestic commercial vessels in Sri Lankan waters. Since 1996, the group has targeted Sri Lanka's economic infrastructure such as banks, trains, buses, oil tanks, and power stations. Also, it has carried out organized-crime-like operations throughout Europe, North America, Asia, Africa, and Australia, maintaining a large number of Tamil front organizations for assistance in garnering moral and financial support.

The LTTE has been designated as an FTO by the United States. This is a sensitive point of contention for the organization, which is striving to attain legitimacy in governing the Tamil people. The LTTE has a litany of terrorist incidents attributed to its actions. Some of the most prominent terrorist attacks conducted by the organization include the 1991 assassination of former Indian prime minister Rajiv Gandhi in a suicide bombing while he was campaigning for reelection in southern India; the 1993 assassination of President Premadasa during a May Day rally; the 1996 bombing of the headquarters of Sri Lanka's central bank; the 1997 bombing of the Colombo World Trade Center; the 1998 bombing of the Temple of the Tooth, one of the most sacred Buddhist temples in Sri Lanka; the 1999 car bombing targeting President Kumaratunga that led to her loss of sight in one eye; and the 2001 attack on Sri Lanka's international airport, destroying half the fleet of the country's national airline.

Military Structure and Defense Policy

The 130,000-strong security forces in Sri Lanka consist of the army, navy, air force, and police force, and are subordinate to civilian political control. The Sri Lankan Army is the largest of the country's armed forces, comprising 83 percent of the security forces. Formerly established as the Royal Ceylon Army in 1949, the Sri Lankan Army was ill prepared to handle the LTTE insurgency as under British rule it was traditionally regarded as a ceremonial army. Like other South Asian armies, the Sri Lankan Army has retained the British regimental system where individual regiments operate independently and recruit their own members. Assistance by the United Kingdom, India, Pakistan, Australia, Malaysia, Israel, and the United States has led to increased professionalization and counterinsurgency skills among the security forces.

Conclusions and Outlook

Despite President Kumaratunga's recent victory over her long-term political rival Ranil Wickremasinghe, the SLFP-led administration will face daunting challenges in deciding what form of government is best suited for Sri Lanka. Highly partisan politics has thus far prevented any viable resolution of the Tamil question, and it is likely that the SLFP and UNP will continue their political bickering for years to come.

After the World Trade Center and Pentagon attacks of September 11, 2001, the LTTE has been particularly sensitive of its designation as an FTO by the United States. Battlefield fatigue and domestic politics have factored into the group's decision to declare a unilateral cease-fire and enter into Norwegian-brokered peace negotiations (though often tenuous and stalled) with the government. Though the group has toned down its rhetoric of establishing an independent homeland, the LTTE has not abandoned its cause. It would view any form of regional autonomy in the north and east as a stepping-stone toward its ultimate goal of achieving Eelam.

Despite the cease-fire, the LTTE continues to recruit, arm, and fortify its positions. Sinhalese hard-liners, including large segments of the Buddhist clergy, are against the peace talks. They feel that the government is granting too many concessions to the LTTE in its bid to bring about a lasting peace. For Sinhalese and Tamil skeptics of the peace process, it is a matter of when, and not if, hostilities resume. Nevertheless, a large number of war-weary Sri Lankans as well as members of the international community are optimistic toward a lasting peace.

Note

The views presented in this chapter are those of the author and do not necessarily represent the views of the Department of Defense or any of its components.

Suggested Readings

Dissanayaka, T.D.S.A. *The Agony of Sri Lanka.* Colombo: Swastika (Private), 1983.
Gunaratna, Rohan. *International and Regional Security Implications of the Sri Lankan Tamil Insurgency.* Colombo: Taprobane Bookshop, 1997.
Munasinghe, Sarath. *A Soldier's Version.* Colombo: Market Information Systems (Private), 2000.
Narayan Swamy, M.R. *Tigers of Lanka.* Colombo: Vijitha Yapa Bookshop, 2002.
Pratap, Anita. *Island of Blood.* New Delhi: Penguin Books India (Private), 2003.
Rotberg, Robert. *Creating Peace in Sri Lanka: Civil War and Reconciliation.* Cambridge, MA: World Peace Foundation and Belfer Center for Science and International Affairs, 1999.

——— 21 ———

Taiwan

Deterring a Rising China

Dennis Van Vranken Hickey

Introduction

In recent years the Republic of China (ROC or Taiwan) has experienced an extraordinary metamorphosis. It has managed to transform itself from a backward, authoritarian state into a multiparty democracy and an economic powerhouse. But Taipei has also alarmed both Beijing and Washington by inching closer and closer to declaring itself independent of China—a move that could ignite a major conflict in East Asia. These fears escalated with the election of Chen Shui-bian, a former independence activist, as ROC president in March 2000 and again in the closely contested March 2004 presidential election.

Political Framework

In 1949 the ROC government retreated from mainland China to Taiwan. From that time until his death in 1975, Chiang Kai-shek ruled the island with an iron fist and promised to take back the mainland by force. Opposition parties were banned, dissidents were jailed, the press was muzzled, and parliamentary elections were restricted to a small proportion of the seats. In short, the ROC was an authoritarian regime.

In 1987 the generalissimo's son, President Chiang Ching-kuo, lifted martial law and paved the way for the democratization of Taiwan. Shortly after this move, lawmakers legalized opposition parties and elections were held to elect a new legislature and National Assembly (a body that amends the ROC constitution). Restrictions on the broadcast and print media also were lifted. With its first direct presidential election in 1996, Taiwan completed its transition from an authoritarian, one-party state to a full-fledged democracy. The ROC is now described officially by the U.S. Department of State as a "multiparty democracy."

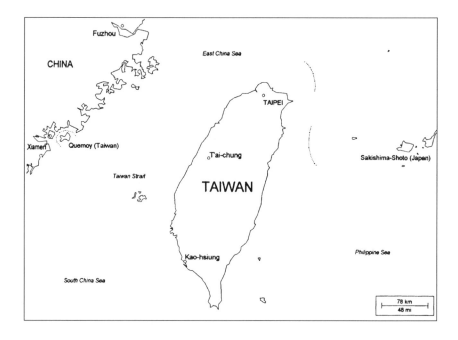

According to Article 36 of the ROC constitution, the president of the ROC has "supreme command of the land, sea and air forces of the whole country." But day-to-day administration of the military is carried out by the Ministry of National Defense (MND). The MND is headed by a minister "who directs and oversees the national defense system formed by the three systems responsible for military administration, military command, and military armament."[1] The defense minister (who must be a civilian by law) may potentially exert significant "influence over the setting of both national security strategy and defense policy through his interactions with the president (as commander in chief and head of state) and the premier (as head of the executive branch)."[2] The MND as a whole, however, does not play a leading role in shaping the island's overall national security strategy. Rather, this is a responsibility of the president.

The General Staff Headquarters (GSH) is housed within the MND and functions as its "military command staff and the command institution for joint operations of the ROC armed forces."[3] Like the MND, the GSH's influence in the decision-making process is wielded primarily by the individual in charge of the organization—the Chief of the General Staff (CGS). The CGS may make recommendations to the president about force levels, the allocation of defense resources, the defense budget, and other matters related to national defense. But these responsibilities pale in comparison to the powers wielded by the CGS prior to passage of the National Defense Law and the Defense Organization Law in 2000. As a result of Taiwan's recent military reforms, the defense minister is now the most powerful figure in the military, and the CGS serves as his chief of staff.

For more than four decades, questions and concerns pertaining to Taiwan's security remained shrouded in mystery. With the lifting of martial law, however, questions began to be raised about Taiwan's security policy. Defense issues are now subject to widespread discussion and debate, and the island's voters hold decision makers accountable for their actions. Furthermore, many new actors have been brought into the policy-making process. In addition to the president, the "players" in Taiwan's defense policy-making "game" now include a handful of ministries and councils, the legislature, political parties, interest groups, the news media, and an assortment of other actors. Indeed, it is now a common practice for Taiwanese to discuss and debate *all* of the major defense issues confronting Taiwan. These include questions about (1) military strategy, (2) relations with the United States, (3) the need for costly new weapons systems, (4) a proposed theater missile defense system, (5) conscription policies and exemptions from traditional military service, (6) sexual harassment, (7) political warfare classes, (8) armed forces morale, (9) the possible establishment of confidence building mechanisms with the mainland, and (10) Taiwan's de jure independence from China.

Internal Security Environment

On March 18, 2000, Taiwanese voters went to the polls to elect the tenth president of the ROC. The result of the election was especially significant because it marked the first time that a candidate outside the ruling Kuomintang (KMT) party had been elected president of the country. As expected, the armed forces remained neutral during the election.

Following his election in 2000, Chen initially toned down his proindependence rhetoric. Perhaps most significant was his inaugural address on May 20, 2000. In the speech, the new president referred to himself as the president of the Republic of China (not Taiwan or the Republic of Taiwan as some feared he might) and outlined what has become known as the "Five No's." Chen proclaimed that, as long as the People's Republic of China (PRC) did not use military force against Taiwan:

- He would not declare Taiwan independent of China;
- He would not support changing the national title of the Republic of China;
- He would not push for the inclusion of former president Lee Teng-hui's "state-to-state" description of the ROC-PRC relationship in the ROC Constitution;

- He would not promote an island-wide referendum on the island's status;
- He would not abolish the National Reunification Council or the National Reunification Guidelines.

These pledges and a number of other initiatives—particularly the authorization of the three "minilinks" between the two offshore islands of Kinmen and Matsu and the Chinese mainland—led some to believe that Chen might be able to improve the cross-strait relationship and thereby enhance Taiwan's security. But this did not occur.

Throughout the first Chen administration, cross-strait negotiations—talks that had been terminated in the early 1990s—remained suspended. Beijing insisted that Taipei must return to the "one China principle" as a precondition for any talks. However, Taipei claimed that the issue of "one China" was a legitimate topic for discussion. Rather than negotiate, the two sides engaged in provocative behavior. The PRC continued to purchase a variety of sophisticated weapons systems from Russia and deploy missiles directly opposite Taiwan. For its part, Taiwan authorities described the PRC and Taiwan as "separate countries," proclaimed their intention to draft a new constitution and pushed for a series of popular referendums. President Chen's critics charged that he was ramping up cross-strait tensions in an effort to distract attention from record unemployment and his administration's clumsy handling of the economy.

Despite cross-strait tensions, partisan bickering, and the bizarre showmanship that has come to characterize the island's domestic politics, Taiwan might best be described as a stable multiparty democracy. The military maintains strict neutrality during the island's political quarrels, and the island does not suffer from the scourge of domestic and/or international terrorism. Not surprisingly, very few Taiwanese want to return to the days of authoritarian rule. They appear to agree with Winston Churchill's observation that "democracy is the worst form of government, except for all the rest." Moreover, the quarrels about Taiwan's defense policy should not be exaggerated. After all, a consensus exists among a majority of Taiwanese, irrespective of political party affiliation, with respect to the maintenance of a strong military, and public opinion polls reveal that almost no one supports Beijing's "one country, two systems" unification scheme.

External Security Environment

On May 1, 1991, President Lee Teng-hui terminated the Period of National Mobilization for Suppression of the Communist Rebellion. This move formally signified the ROC's willingness to renounce the use of force to achieve the unification of China, and Taipei began to profess a desire to ultimately unify the country peacefully through a three-stage unification process outlined in the *Guidelines for National Unification*. The PRC suspected, however, that Taiwan's leadership cohort actually supported the island's permanent separation from China. The election of Chen Shui-bian as president in 2000, and his reelection in 2004, served only to reinforce these fears.

Although Taipei has renounced the use of force to unify China, Beijing has not reciprocated. The PRC has long embraced, as a basic policy, the position that it may use all means necessary, including military means, to achieve unification. Consequently, ROC military authorities assert that the PRC is the greatest menace to Taiwan's security.

Taiwanese security analysts have identified various situations that might lead Beijing to resort to military action. They contend that the PRC would employ force against the island under the following circumstances:

- If Taiwan declared independence;
- If massive disturbances break out in Taiwan;
- If the comparative fighting strength of Taiwan's military weakens significantly;
- If foreign forces interfere in Taiwan's affairs;
- If Taiwan continues to reject reunification talks; and
- If Taiwan develops nuclear weapons.

Some have warned that an attack most likely would be between the years 2005 and 2010—after China has completed its military modernization program and before the deployment of America's theater missile defense (TMD) system in East Asia.

Should the PRC opt to use force against Taiwan, the MND believes it would resort to one of three actions:

- A sea and/or air blockade of Taiwan,
- A raid on Taiwan's outlying islands, or
- A full-scale assault on the island.

The ministry warns that these moves could be undertaken independently, sequentially or simultaneously.

Many defense analysts believe that a paralyzing blockade intended to bring Taiwan to its knees would be Beijing's most likely form of military action. In order to achieve this objective, the PRC might employ missile tests (it has deployed hundreds of missiles in coastal provinces facing Taiwan), mines, submarines and surface ships to blockade certain shipping routes and/or announce that waters surrounding Taiwan are in an area in a state of civil war. Any of these moves could lead many foreign ships to steer clear of Taiwan and make shipping prohibitively expensive.

In addition to the threat of a blockade, Taiwanese defense officials are increasingly nervous about other coercive applications of force short of a full-scale invasion. Many now warn of the dangers of an information warfare attack. Others caution that Beijing is determined to undercut Taiwan's international support—particularly its friendship with the United States. Still others argue that China might attempt to provoke a severe economic downturn in the economy. After all, Taiwan's investments in the mainland now exceed US$66 billion and exports to China exceed US$40 billion. The two societies are becoming increasingly intertwined. In short, it appears that Taiwan must be prepared for a wide range of potential threats and military scenarios.

Terrorism Threat and Response

Taiwan has supported the global War on Terrorism. Following the September 11, 2001, attacks on the World Trade Center and the Pentagon, Taipei quickly condemned the terrorists and offered its sympathy and support. In subsequent months, Taiwan authorities voiced support for U.S.-led interventions both in Afghanistan and in Iraq.

Taiwan has taken concrete steps to bolster its counterterrorism laws and regulations. Security has been stepped up at all of the island's major transportation hubs (Taiwan is one of the world's major trading nations) and at the island's official and unofficial embassies (particularly at the American Institute in Taiwan). Moreover, lawmakers have passed legislation to enhance anti-money-laundering laws and to examine suspicious bank accounts. Finally, the government has established an antiterrorism command center and conducted a series of antiterrorist training drills in an effort to upgrade the island's capability to confront a terrorist attack. These exercises include the armed forces, local police, and a variety of other relevant agencies.

In one critical respect, the War on Terrorism represents a unique threat to Taiwan. The sneak attacks on the World Trade Center and the Pentagon effectively moved China off America's "enemies list." Gone are the descriptions of China as a "strategic competitor." President George W. Bush now praises the PRC as "an emerging marvel" and "the most important country" in the Asia-Pacific region. Although he has stopped short of designating the country as a "strategic partner," the president claims to pursue a "constructive, cooperative, and candid" relationship with China.

The War against Terrorism and the North Korean nuclear crisis have helped push Washington and Beijing closer together. As relations have warmed,

Chinese officials have expressed hopes that Washington might agree to concessions on the Taiwan issue. They have called on the United States to "stand by its commitment, properly handle the issue of arms sales to Taiwan and do more things that are beneficial to the peaceful reunification of China."[4] During discussions with the author, Taiwanese officials acknowledged that such comments raise concerns in Taipei.[5] Victor Chin, director-general of the Department of North American Affairs in the ROC Ministry of Foreign Affairs, contends that "China's strategy is that they want to use the antiterrorist [campaign] and also other opportunities to exert pressure on the US government to alienate Washington from Taipei and at the same time increase relations with them."[6] American officials, however, insist that there will be no linkage between China's cooperation in the United States War on Terrorism and Washington's relations with Taipei. Richard Armitage, deputy secretary of state, contends that "China is operating under the mistaken assumption that the war against terrorism and Iraq will get them something in return on Taiwan, that the U.S. will make concessions on Taiwan. *This won't happen* [emphasis added]."[7]

The United States has not sacrificed Taiwan to gain China's friendship and support. However, all available evidence suggests that the Bush administration will not risk Beijing's wrath by endorsing any radical adjustments in Taiwan's international status. In fact, President Bush has declared that the United States is opposed to any action that "might unilaterally change the status quo" across the Taiwan Strait. It seems that Taipei's drive to obtain Washington's support for de jure independence from China has hit a brick wall.

Military Structure and Defense Policy

For roughly three decades, the ultimate goal of the ROC military was to take back by force the Chinese mainland. Military planners concentrated on building an army capable of fielding forty or more divisions. The structure of the armed forces reflected this mission: the ROC maintained one of the world's largest land armies. But this policy has changed.

According to official MND documents, the ROC military's current strategy might best be described as "effective deterrence and resolute defense." The ROC hopes that its military strength will deter an attack on its territory. Should deterrence fail, however, the military is prepared to defend the country. In order to achieve these objectives, the island maintains a formidable military force and a close relationship with the United States.

A Formidable Military

Taiwan hopes that its military muscle and a series of military reforms will help deter PRC aggression. Weapons systems are being upgraded to cope with the mainland's growing military might, and training programs are being redesigned to meet the requirements of combined services operations and to familiarize personnel with the high-tech elements of modern warfare. Primary emphasis is being placed on building a more effective navy and air force. At the same time, the armed forces are being reorganized and downsized into a smaller defensive force.

The ROC military has been downsized into a defensive force of roughly 385,000 troops. A majority of the recent cuts have affected the army. But the army continues to make up almost 50 percent of Taiwan's total armed services (the navy and air force each comprise roughly 25 percent). The MND plans for a second stage of downsizing that will lead to additional cuts. Force levels could ultimately drop as low as 270,000 troops.

The ROC Army's current mission is "to defend [the] state's territory and to ensure the integrity of sovereignty."[8] Although intended primarily to serve as a fighting force, Taiwan's military also helps farmers harvest their crops and provides relief and rescue operations during natural disasters. Army combat units are being both modernized and restructured. MND plans call for incorporating traditional army divisions into "combined services brigades." The ultimate objective is to make Taiwan's three military branches interoperable and able to function as a team within ten years.

Weapons systems in the ROC Army's inventory include M48 and M60H tanks; M109 and M110 self-propelled artillery; M113, V-150, and CM-21 armored personnel carriers; UH-1H helicopters; AH-1W attack helicopters; Kung-feng 6A rocket systems; TOW-type antitank guided weapons; Chaparral SP, Hawk, Tien-kung (Sky Bow), and Tien-chien (Sky Sword) air defense missile systems; vehicle-mounted Avenger missiles and man-portable Stinger missiles; and Hsiung-feng I and Hsiung-feng II antiship missile systems. The ROC Army also operates the island's Patriot Air Defense System. In June 2003 the MND announced that it would move forward with plans to purchase three Lockheed-Martin Patriot Advanced Capability (PAC)-3 units and upgrade two PAC-2 Plus units to PAC-3 standards.

Looking to the future, there are unconfirmed reports that Taiwan plans to resume production of ballistic surface-to-surface missiles in response to China's provocative 1995 and 1996 missile tests and the growing arsenal of missiles that Beijing has deployed directly opposite Taiwan. The Taiwanese missiles—which could be armed with conventional or nuclear warheads— would be capable of striking targets in southern and southeastern China (although Taiwan does not possess nuclear weapons, it admits that the MND has the capability to produce them). Officials reason that deployment of the missiles might help deter a PRC attack.

During peacetime the ROC Navy is responsible for patrolling the Taiwan

Strait and ensuring that Taiwan's sea-lanes remain open. It also provides aid to Taiwanese fishing boats requiring assistance and conducts reconnaissance missions. If attacked, the ROC Navy will play a critical role in the island's defensive strategy. The navy would take part in joint operations together with the army and air force to counter a PRC naval blockade, engage in surface warfare in the waters surrounding Taiwan, and attack an invading enemy. Like other branches of the ROC military, the navy is being restructured and streamlined. The number of admirals is being cut and the mission of the elite marine force—whose training focused largely on seizing beachheads as the vanguard of an invasion force—has been revised. The marines will now defend naval bases and the offshore islands and engage in other unspecified combat missions.

Taiwan's navy is acquiring technology and equipment designed to enhance its ability to engage in warfare at three levels—air, sea, and below the ocean surface. It also has formed an antisubmarine command to study ways to counter a possible PRC blockade. In order to enhance its naval forces, Taipei has purchased American minesweepers, antisubmarine helicopters, Knox-class destroyers, MK-46 torpedoes, and Harpoon antiship missiles. It also has acquired La Fayette-class frigates from France and a variety of domestically manufactured frigates, fast-attack craft, and sophisticated missiles. Due to budgetary constraints and domestic political considerations, Taiwan has not moved forward with plans to purchase eight conventional submarines, four Kidd-class guided missile destroyers, and twelve submarine-hunting PC-3 Orion aircraft from the United States. U.S. officials have emphasized that these weapons systems would play a critical role in any effort to counter a PRC blockade. Many analysts agree that Taiwan will eventually purchase the items.

Finally, Taiwan is putting more muscle into its air force. In January 1994 the armed forces began to take delivery of 135 domestically manufactured Indigenous Defense Fighters (IDF), a new warplane designed originally to replace Taiwan's aging stock of 80 Lockheed F-104G and 300 plus Northrop F-5E/F aircraft. Perhaps most significant, Taiwan has acquired 150 F-16A/B warplanes from the United States and 60 Mirage 2000-5 fighters from France. It also has purchased 4 American-built Grumman E-2T Hawkeye early-warning planes.

American Military Support

With the abrogation of the U.S.-ROC Defense Treaty in 1979, the United States terminated its formal security commitment to Taiwan. However, the United States continues to play a critical role in Taiwan's defensive strategy. American military equipment, technological assistance, and an informal or "tacit alliance" augment the island's defenses.

According to the Taiwan Relations Act (TRA)—the legislation that guides official American policy toward Taiwan—the United States will "make available to Taiwan such defense articles and defense services in such quantity as may be necessary to enable Taiwan to maintain a sufficient self-defense capability." Recent sales of American-built military equipment have included missiles, advanced fighter aircraft, sophisticated antisubmarine helicopters, and the Patriot Anti-Missile System. As described, the United States has also offered to sell conventional submarines, guided-missile destroyers, and submarine-hunting aircraft to Taiwan. As might be expected, the PRC opposes the arms transfers. It is especially nervous about Taiwan's possible inclusion in a TMD system or the acquisition of Aegis-equipped warships.

In addition to arms sales, the United States has transferred critical technologies to Taiwan. This technological assistance has enabled Taipei to domestically manufacture a wide range of military hardware—including advanced warplanes, missiles, warships, and tanks. The United States also shares intelligence with Taiwan, and, despite the lack of formal diplomatic ties, U.S.-ROC military-to-military contacts remain intact. Indeed, American military teams—specialists removed in 1979 as a precondition for establishing relations with China—have returned to Taiwan. U.S. military personnel now regularly observe Taiwanese defense exercises and offer military advice.

The U.S. security commitment to Taiwan is discussed in the TRA and three joint communiqués with the PRC. Some argue that the TRA mandates an American military response to a PRC attack. But these individuals are mistaken. The TRA provides the United States only with an *option* to defend Taiwan; it does not necessarily commit the United States to Taiwan's defense. On April 25, 2001, however, President Bush was asked whether the United States had an obligation to defend Taiwan if China attacked. The president replied, "Yes, we do and the Chinese must understand that. Yes I would." When asked if this meant protecting the island "with the full force of the American military," Bush replied, "Whatever it took to help Taiwan defend theirself[*sic*]." No other president has made such a sweeping commitment to Taiwan's defense during the postnormalization era.

To be sure, the Bush administration has moved Washington closer to Taipei. Arms sales have escalated, high-level military contacts have accelerated, America's security commitment to Taiwan has been bolstered, and political ties have been strengthened. But there do appear to be some limits to American support. On December 9, 2003, President Bush warned the Taiwanese government about a series of referendums timed to coincide with the island's presidential election—referendums guaranteed to infuriate China. The White

House apparently feared that Taiwan was moving too close to declaring itself independent of China—a development that could ignite a major conflict in East Asia at a time when U.S. forces were tied down in the Middle East. Not surprisingly, Bush's statement provoked a furious response from America's "anti-China lobby." Despite Bush's warning about the referendum issue, however, most analysts agree that the prospect of American intervention in a cross-strait crisis continues to play a key role in Taiwan's defense.

Conclusions and Outlook

The ROC has abandoned its past strategic objective of having a massive military that, beyond defending Taiwan and the offshore islands, would also be capable of liberating mainland China. Military strategy now focuses almost exclusively on defense and deterrence. In order to achieve these objectives, the ROC is seeking to streamline its military and acquire a new generation of military forces based on the principles of smaller force levels, higher quality weapons systems, and enhanced operational capabilities. The ROC also is seeking to strengthen its military ties with the United States. In addition to the acquisition of arms and technology, Taipei is interested in enhancing military exchanges with the United States. Finally, Taiwan has initiated a series of military reforms to address what the U.S. Department of Defense describes as "deficiencies." These measures are intended to enhance the educational level of recruits, raise the percentage of professional soldiers within the armed services, guarantee civilian control over the military, and boost the ability of the three military branches to function as an integrated unit.

It is likely that these moves will bolster Taiwan's security. They also help to make the cost of a PRC invasion prohibitively high. In the final analysis, however, more than military equipment and U.S. support will be needed to protect Taiwan. As one U.S. official explained some years ago, "In the end, stability in the Taiwan Strait will be contingent on the ability of the two sides of the strait to come to terms with each other on a political basis."[9] Despite the passage of time, this fact has not changed.

Notes

1. Republic of China (ROC), Ministry of National Defense, *2002 National Defense Report, Republic of China* (Taipei: Ministry of National Defense, 2002), p. 75.

2. Michael D. Swaine, and James C. Mulvenon, *Taiwan's Foreign and Defense Policies: Features and Determinants* (RAND Corporation: Santa Monica, CA, 2001), p. 84.

3. ROC Ministry of National Defense, *2002 National Defense Report, Republic of China*, p. 231.

4. "Armitage Discusses Taiwan with Chinese Military Official," *Agence France Presse,* December 11, 2002, in *Lexis/Nexis.*

5. During an interview with the author, an official acknowledged that "we want to be very, very careful and be very observant to the conduct of business between Washington and Beijing because we don't want our interests to be at the expense of this relationship. So, we've been watching U.S. relations with Beijing very closely." Author's interview with Victor Chin, Director-General of the Department of North American Affairs, Ministry of Foreign Affairs, Republic of China, Taipei, Taiwan, November 7, 2002.

6. Ibid.

7. "Armitage Discusses Taiwan with Chinese Military Official."

8. ROC Ministry of National Defense, *2002 National Defense Report: Republic of China,* p. 127.

9. Jay Chen and Sofia Wu, "Roth Reaffirms US Commitment to Taiwan's Security," *Central News Agency,* June 19, 1998, in *Lexis/Nexis.*

Suggested Readings

Copper, John F. *Taiwan: Nation-State or Province?* 4th ed. Boulder, CO: Westview Press, 2003.

Edmonds, Martin, and Michael Tsai, eds. *Defending Taiwan: The Future Vision of Taiwan's Defense Policy and Military Strategy.* New York: Routledge, 2003.

Hickey, Dennis Van Vranken. *Taiwan's Security in the Changing International System.* Boulder, CO: Lynne Rienner Publishers, 1997.

———. *The Armies of East Asia: China, Taiwan, Japan and the Koreas.* Boulder, CO: Lynne Rienner Publishers, 2001.

Ministry of National Defense, Republic of China. *2002 National Defense Report: Republic of China.* Taipei: Military History and Translation Office, Ministry of National Defense, 2002.

U.S. Department of Defense. *The Annual Report on the Military Power of the People's Republic of China.* Washington, DC: The Pentagon, July 28, 2003.

───── 22 ─────

Thailand

Resurgent Extremism and Other Challenges

David G. Wiencek

Introduction

Thailand weathered difficult financial and political storms brought on by the 1997 Asian financial crisis, which was triggered when Bangkok devalued the baht after a decline in exports and the stock market. Political stability was initially restored under the administration of Prime Minister Chuan Leekpai, who held power from October 1997 through January 2001. A new government, led by businessman Thaksin Shinawatra and his Thai Rak Thai (Thais Love Thais) Party, was formed in February 2001 and at this writing is firmly in control of the country's political landscape.

In the economic sphere, after years of hardship Thailand repaid in 2003 its obligations to the International Monetary Fund and other creditors stemming from the 1997 crisis, amounting to some US$14 billion. Growth rates for 2002–2003 were at healthy levels of 5–6 percent, and Prime Minister Thaksin set an ambitious target of achieving even higher growth levels in 2005 and beyond. While such improved rates would be reminiscent of economic achievements of decades past, high oil prices, lingering debt, and other financial system weaknesses could derail this projected strong recovery.

At the same time as grappling with political and economic fundamentals, Thai leaders have been forced to come to terms with the War on Terrorism and the challenges arising from resurgent extremism in its Muslim-majority provinces in the south. Thailand's Muslims are principally ethnic Malays and represent 3–5 percent of the country's total population. Muslims in the south have long resented their domination by Thailand's Buddhist authorities. They also chafe at the region's impoverishment relative to the rest of the country and its persistent lack of socioeconomic development. The August 2003 arrest of Hambali, a pivotal figure in the international jihad network,

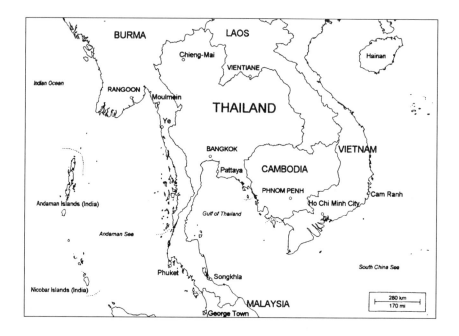

highlighted Thailand's potential vulnerabilities to international terrorism. A flare-up in the south in 2004 further underlined internal security concerns associated with Islamic extremism.

The Thaksin government also faces an important national security challenge in the form of methamphetamines flowing into the country from Burma. An aggressive policy was implemented in 2003 to combat illegal drugs. Results to date are mixed. Government credibility was likewise tested during an outbreak of avian influenza (or bird flu) in 2004. Initially played down by authorities, the bird flu outbreak devastated poultry exports, had a negative impact on economic prospects, and created a health crisis. Strong leadership will thus be required to deal with the periodic crises that are sure to impact Thailand's interests in the years ahead.

Political Framework

Thailand is a democracy with a constitutional monarchy. King Bhumipol Adulyadej, the world's longest-serving monarch, has now ruled for nearly sixty years. The king has little direct power under the constitution but is a symbol of national identity and unity. He has subtly exercised authority in past political crises, and his influence will be missed when he eventually passes from the scene.

The prime minister is head of the government. Thailand's legislature, the National Assembly, is bicameral, with a House of Representatives and a Senate. The current government assumed office in February 2001 under the leadership of Prime Minister Thaksin. Thaksin was a successful telecommunications executive and perhaps the country's wealthiest individual. His election, however, was marred by corruption charges that he concealed assets worth millions of U.S. dollars. He was later acquitted of those charges. The prime minister and his party hold an absolute majority in the House of Representatives and also maintain a tight grip on such other levers of power as the media. Prime Minister Thaksin has pursued a populist agenda built around economic revival. He appears well positioned to retain power through the next election cycle in 2005 and should be a dominating influence in the country's politics for many years to come.

Internal Security Environment

Thailand's main internal security preoccupation today stems from Islamic extremism in its southernmost provinces of Songkhla, Pattani, Yala, and Narathiwat. A long-running Muslim separatist movement in southern Thailand appeared to have basically withered by the end of the 1990s. The activities of this movement that were taking place were more criminal than ideological in orientation. But since 9/11, it has become clear that Islamic extremism remains alive and that local elements are cooperating with the wider regional and international jihad network of Jemaah Islamiyah (JI) (Islamic group or Islamic community) and al Qaeda.

Following the breakup of plots to mount significant terrorist attacks in Singapore in late 2001, authorities in Singapore connected a JI-inspired regional alliance to Thailand and reported that the Rabitatul Mujahideen (Mujahideen League) was comprised of the Moro Islamic Liberation Front (MILF) in the Philippines, an unnamed southern Thailand-based jihadist group, and others.[1] One of JI's main operational cells also covered southern Thailand. Although Bangkok initially played down such information, subsequent developments confirmed linkages with the Southeast Asian terror network.

In May–June 2003 three local JI accomplices were arrested in Narathiwat and a senior Singaporean JI member was arrested in Bangkok. The four were reportedly planning attacks on Western diplomatic establishments in Bangkok, as well as the kidnapping of Western diplomats and businessmen. Other potential targets of this group were tourist locations in Phuket and Pattaya in attacks designed to coincide with the October 2003 Asia-Pacific Economic Cooperation (APEC) summit meeting held in Thailand. Also, in May 2003 two Thai Muslims and an Egyptian were arrested in Cambodia for alleged connections with JI and an al Qaeda front.

These arrests were followed by a major counterterrorism breakthrough—the capture of Asia's most wanted man, Riduan Isamuddin (also known as Hambali) in August 2003 in Ayutthaya, about 50 miles (80 kilometers) north of Bangkok. Hambali was a pivotal figure in the international jihad network with ties to Osama bin Laden, al Qaeda plotting throughout the 1990s, and the September 11, 2001, attack itself. As an Indonesian, he was the only non-Arab member of the al Qaeda inner circle and reportedly was the organization's fourth highest-ranking leader.[2] Hambali developed the 2002 Bali attack plan at a meeting on Thai soil and, upon his arrest, was believed to be involved in fresh targeting of Western diplomatic establishments in Thailand. Hambali appeared to have moved in and out of the country with relative ease on a number of occasions over the years.

In early 2004 the situation in the south flared anew and led to the imposition of martial law in parts of the region. On January 4, 2004, armed men raided an army depot in Narathiwat and stole hundreds of weapons. During the raid four Thai soldiers were killed. Elements of the same group also conducted a series of arson attacks on twenty state schools in a simultaneous action that served as a diversionary tactic for the depot raid. A day later bombings in Pattani province killed two police officers.

Thailand's national security adviser, retired General Kitti Rattanachaya, linked the events of January 2004 to a local separatist group called Mujahideen Pattani (MP) and noted that the MP possibly was aided by the JI-linked Kumpulan Militan Malaysia (Malaysian Mujahiddin Group, or KMM) operating from Malaysia.[3] The defense minister subsequently stated that the attacks were part of an attempt by Islamic separatists to take over Narathiwat province.[4] The violence escalated on April 28, 2004 with coordinated strikes against police and army posts across the provinces of Songkhla, Yala, and Pattani. Security forces repulsed the attackers, killing 107, including 32 that had taken positions inside the historic Krue Se mosque near Pattani city.[5]

In October 2004, seventy-eight people died after a protest in Tak Bai in Narathiwat. These developments point to significant tensions in the Muslim-majority provinces of southern Thailand, and to continued counterterrorism challenges ahead. The government reports that some five thousand Thai-Muslim students have studied in the Middle East, and the defense minister publicly estimated that 10 percent of these have been recruited by extremist organizations.[6]

As for other issues related to internal security, economic improvements in the aftermath of the 1997 Asian financial crisis have helped to stabilize gradually the overall crime situation in Thailand. Crime rates are relatively low today. But international crime syndicates pose a concern. African criminal gangs, for example, are present in Bangkok and engage in drug and diamond smuggling and other scams.[7]

In 2003 authorities thwarted the attempted sale of cesium-137, a material that could be used by terrorists in a radioactive dispersal device (or "dirty bomb"). The material, which the seller, a local man, incorrectly believed was uranium, had been smuggled into Thailand from Laos and possibly originated in Russia. Meanwhile, Thai authorities were investigating a March 2004 theft of a large quantity of explosives from a mine. Strong evidence points to Muslim extremists, and it may be only a matter of time before this stolen material is used for terrorist purposes.

External Security Environment

The most pressing external security issue facing Thailand is the insidious threat of illegal drugs originating in neighboring Burma. In particular, methamphetamines, known locally as *yaa baa* or "mad medicine," have flooded into Thailand from laboratories across the border in Burma. Originally destined for export elsewhere, these drugs (in tablet form) have flowed through the country and found a vast market among young people and workers. They now pose a critical national security challenge. It is estimated that approximately 4–5 percent of the population is hooked on methamphetamines, making Thailand the largest consumer of these drugs in the world and indicating a level of drug abuse on par with the cocaine epidemic of the 1980s in the United States.[8]

Burma's rebel United Wa State Army (UWSA) is the region's biggest methamphetamine trafficker. Efforts by Thai authorities to stem the flow of pills, which are easily transportable, have proved futile, and this has created a tense situation along the Thai-Burma border with periodic military clashes. The UWSA has promised to make the territory that it controls opium-free by the end of the 2005 poppy harvest. But the UWSA's heavy continued involvement in methamphetamine production and distribution would likely offset any gains made by ending its opium trafficking.

Prime Minister Thaksin launched a controversial war on drugs in 2003. The no-holds-barred offensive targeted drug dealers and others believed to be involved with illegal narcotics. In 2003 police reportedly killed over two thousand people. This led to complaints by civil rights groups that innocent people were being inadvertently caught up in the government's crackdown. The U.S. government weighed in and criticized Thailand in its annual 2003 human rights report. Thailand took umbrage at the pointed criticism and an exasperated Prime Minister Thaksin referred to Washington as a "useless friend." Thailand stated that many of the deaths in the drug war were the result of acts of self-defense by police or caused by drug gang infighting. Undeterred by the criticism,

Thailand relaunched its drug offensive in 2004, focusing on relapsed addicts and drug peddlers in major cities and along the Burmese border.

There are also other lingering problems along the Thai-Burma, as well as the Thai-Cambodian, borders. Long areas of these borders are poorly demarcated—or not demarcated at all. In the past Thailand has experienced armed conflict as Burmese soldiers have shot down a Thai helicopter, purportedly for violating airspace believed to be their own, and fired on Thai military trucks and equipment. On the Thai-Cambodian border, some areas are not under the direct control of the government in Phnom Penh but groups have reached quid pro quo agreements with the Cambodian prime minister, Hun Sen, to stay out in exchange for tribute payments. This has led to large-scale smuggling of logs, gems, sex workers, and drugs into Thailand. Voices within the Thai military want to take a harder line, especially with the Burmese regime, but the prime minister has so far rejected these calls, instead pursuing a strategy that in essence puts business development over security.

Prime Minister Thaksin and the Region

With the retirement in 2003 of the Malaysian prime minister, Mahathir Mohamad, long looked to as a leader within the Association of Southeast Asian Nations (ASEAN), Prime Minister Thaksin is positioned to be his replacement as a leading regional figure. Thaksin has taken a high-profile role in trying to mediate a transition to democratic rule between the Burmese military junta and that country's democracy movement. According to Burmese political activists, however, Thaksin's actions have not been balanced. "Thaksin is more interested in building stability and business development than a transition to democratic rule," stated Aung Din, a former political prisoner and activist. "Thaksin has placed tremendous pressure on Burma's ethnic groups along the border to reach a cease-fire with the regime, is organizing the repatriation of Burmese refugees back to conflict areas in Burma, and shut down offices of Burmese democracy groups in Thailand," he said.[9]

In some cases, Thaksin's foreign policy priorities appear focused more on regional economic integration than national security concerns. For example, the prime minister is a leading proponent of the Greater Mekong Subregion Development Plan that aims to build an east-west road between ports in southern Vietnam and Burma that would link Vietnam, Cambodia, Thailand, and Burma. There is also an energy-generation component that would provide increased power to China, Cambodia, Burma, Thailand, and Vietnam through new dams on the Mekong River and a lake in Burma. Prime Minister Thaksin has used Thai government spending as a catalyst for economic growth. In order to keep up debt payments, the economy must flourish. This backdrop may explain why the prime minister has taken a hard line on political activists in exchange for increased economic growth.

Whether he will emerge as the next leader of the ASEAN region remains to be seen. But his ability to dominate Thai politics should give him a longevity that other regional leaders will be hard-pressed to match.

Terrorism Threat and Response

Initially Thailand appeared reluctant to embrace U.S. strategy in the War on Terrorism. In the face of early post–9/11 calls to boycott American products and major pro-Muslim rallies in Bangkok, the government adopted a low profile. This was done perhaps to assuage domestic constituencies critical of U.S. policies and to protect Thai economic interests, for example, jobs in the Middle East being performed by overseas workers. Such calculations were carried forward as the Thaksin government repeatedly denied that Islamic terrorists were present in the country. Support at a public level for American actions in Afghanistan and Iraq was correct, if cautious. Such posturing appeared aimed at insulating the country's valuable tourist industry from the fallout of a more realistic assessment of the threat and the country's true vulnerabilities. As a result, early on Bangkok did not walk in lockstep with Washington as others in the region such as Singapore and the Philippines, were doing.

But events, such as the arrest of Hambali on Thai soil, eventually forced the hand of the government and helped create the basis for greater cooperation. Defense Minister Thammarak Isarangura reflected this sentiment when he stated in July 2003:

> The world situation has changed. We are afraid terrorists will try to use Thailand as a place to launch their activities against international targets. We have to ensure security.[10]

Thailand sent engineers to Afghanistan and deployed a small humanitarian mission to Iraq. The country is now a full partner in the War on Terrorism and bilateral security ties with the United States are deepening. President George W. Bush paid a state visit to Thailand in October 2003 and took the symbolically important step of designating Thailand as a Major Non-NATO Ally. This designation opens up the possibility of future bilateral military research, as well as special access to U.S. equipment. (Close U.S. partners such as Australia, Israel, Japan, and the Philippines also share this designation.)

Military Structure and Defense Policy

The king is the commander in chief of the Royal Thai Armed Forces. Policy is formulated at the cabinet level. The defense establishment follows an overall policy of comprehensive security that encompasses traditional defense missions, new forms of transnational threats, and strategies aimed at conflict prevention and confidence building. Reforms are being pursued to transform a military force largely structured for conventional warfare missions of the past into a more versatile institution responsive to today's changing threat environment. The 1997 economic crisis took a toll on defense budgets and armed forces modernization efforts today are described as "incremental."[11]

The military has three branches: the Royal Thai Army (RTA), the Royal Thai Navy (RTN), and the Royal Thai Air Force (RTAF). The RTA is divided into four regions, covering Bangkok and the central plains, the northeast, the north and the south, and has approximately 190,000 members. Thailand's naval fleet is based at Sattahip, southeast of Bangkok. The navy maintains a small fleet, including the carrier *Chakri Naruebet,* with seven AV-8B Matador (Harrier) aircraft. The 68,000-man navy includes a marine corps, based on the American model, with a strength of 18,000 members trained in amphibious and jungle operations. The RTAF has its main base at Don Muang airport in Bangkok and has a strength of 48,000 personnel. In 2003 the United States furnished eight sophisticated Advanced Medium Range Air-to-Air Missiles (AMRAAMs) to Thailand to help the RTAF counter imminent threats from regional air forces.

U.S.-Thai security ties derive from a 1962 communiqué signed by the then U.S. secretary of state Dean Rusk and the Thai foreign minister Thanat Khoman. The Rusk-Thanat arrangement obligates Washington to come to Thailand's aid if attacked. The two allies thus have strong military ties dating back decades. Although, the United States maintains no bases in Thailand, Bangkok regularly grants the United States important air transit rights and quietly provides other logistical support to American forces. Military-to-military relations are built on a vigorous joint training program and, in particular, the annual Cobra Gold exercise, which is the largest joint training opportunity in Southeast Asia. In recent years forces from Singapore also have participated in Cobra Gold.

Thailand has taken an interest in peacekeeping operations and has provided a force commander and troops for the United Nations Transitional Authority in East Timor (UNTAET).

Conclusions and Outlook

Prime Minister Thaksin appears firmly in control of the country's political future, at least through the end of this decade. Economic performance will remain a key variable to future national stability, and Thaksin's position will be further enhanced should he continue to deliver strong growth. Illegal drugs will plague Thailand for some time and cause turmoil in relations with neighboring Burma. But the greatest wild card facing the country, and its political and economic stability, is the threat of resurgent Islamic extremism in the south. The full extent of the relationships between local extremists and the wider regional and international jihad network is not entirely clear. However, a number of indicators, including the presence of Hambali in the country, point to growing Islamic-inspired threats. Faced with this and other challenges, Bangkok will deepen its ties with Washington in the continuing War on Terrorism.

Notes

1. See "Singapore Government Press Statement on Further Arrests under the Internal Security Act," September 19, 2002, at www2.mha.gov.sg/mha/index.jsp/; Ministry of Home Affairs, Republic of Singapore, *White Paper: The Jemaah Islamiyah Arrests and the Threat of Terrorism,* January 7, 2003, p. 7, at www2.mha.gov.sg; and Zachary Abuza, *Militant Islam in Southeast Asia: Crucible of Terror* (Boulder, CO: Lynne Rienner Publishers, 2003), p. 171.

2. Don Greenlees, "Still a Force to be Feared," *Far Eastern Economic Review,* January 22, 2004, p. 14.

3. Associated Press, "Thai Attackers Said Regional Terrorists," January 8, 2004. An earlier report by Thailand's National Security Council pointed to a new clandestine umbrella group in the south consisting of remnants of three former insurgent groups: the Pattani United Liberation Organization (PULO), New PULO, and the Barisan Revolusi Nasional (BRN), and that this new grouping had foreign connections. As quoted in Shawn W. Crispin, "Strife Down South," *Far Eastern Economic Review,* January 22, 2004, p. 13.

4. Reuters, "Militants Want to Capture Province, Minister Says," January 13, 2004.

5. Local sources indicated a BRN splinter group was responsible for organizing the clashes of April 28, 2004. See Piyanart Srivalo and Panya Thiewsangwal, "Muslim Militants: Rebels Expected to Mount More Attacks," *The Nation,* April 29, 2004, at www.nationmultimedia.com. Also see special section "The South is on Fire" at the same Web site.

6. See "Part II: Thailand Joins the Global War on Terrorism," *The Nation,* July 30, 2003, at www.nationmultimedia.com.

7. Shawn W. Crispin, "Out of Africa," *Far Eastern Economic Review,* May 24, 2001, pp. 60–63.

8. "The 'Speed' Fix," *Far Eastern Economic Review,* September 26, 2002, p. 6; Alan Sipress, "Thailand's Drug War Leaves Over 1,000 Dead," *Washington Post,* March 9, 2003; and Rajiv Chandrasekaren, "U.S. Forces Train Thai Unit to Block Traffic from Burma," *Washington Post,* July 17, 2001, p. A11.

9. Interview with author, Washington, DC, May 2004.

10. Shawn W. Crispin, "Targets of a New Anti-Terror War," *Far Eastern Economic Review,* July 10, 2003, p. 12.

11. Gen. Teerawat Putamanonda (Ret.), "Thailand's Defense Concept and

Transnational Threats." Paper delivered at 2002 Pacific Symposium, U.S. National Defense University, February 20–21, 2002, p. 11.

Suggested Readings

Brook, Micool. "Drugs, Thugs: US Army Ups Ante Against Narco Insurgents." *Armed Forces Journal International.* February 2001, pp. 10–11.

Che Man, W.K. *Muslim Separatism: The Moros of Southern Philippines and the Malays of Southern Thailand.* Manila: Ateneo de Manila University Press, 1990.

Crispin, Shawn. "Thailand's War Zone." *Far Eastern Economic Review.* March 11, 2004, pp. 12–14.

Putamanonda, Gen. Teerawat (Ret.). "Thailand's Defense Concept and Transnational Threats." Paper delivered at 2002 Pacific Symposium, U.S. National Defense University, February 20–21, 2002.

United States Department of State, *International Narcotics Control Strategy Report.* (Annual.)

———— 23 ————

Vietnam

Focused Domestically, Adrift Internationally

Mark Manyin

Introduction

Ever since communist North Vietnamese forces defeated U.S.-backed South Vietnam in 1975, reunified Vietnam has been struggling with how to maintain a balance between two often contradictory goals: maintaining ideological purity and promoting economic development. For the first decade after reunification, the emphasis was on the former. By the mid-1980s, disastrous economic conditions led the Vietnamese Communist Party (VCP) to adopt at its sixth National Party Congress in 1986 a more pragmatic line, one that evolved into a three-pronged national strategy followed by Vietnam ever since:

1. Prioritize economic development through market-oriented economic reforms dubbed *doi moi* ("renovation") that can support improved living standards and military modernization.
2. Pursue good relations with Southeast Asian neighbors that provide Vietnam with economic partners and diplomatic friends.
3. Repair and deepen the relationship with China, while simultaneously buttressing this with a great power counterweight to Chinese ambition.[1]

Political Framework

Economic Developments

For the first decade after the *doi moi* reforms were launched, Vietnam became one of the world's fastest-growing countries, averaging around 8 percent annual gross domestic product (GDP) growth from 1990 to 1997, as the

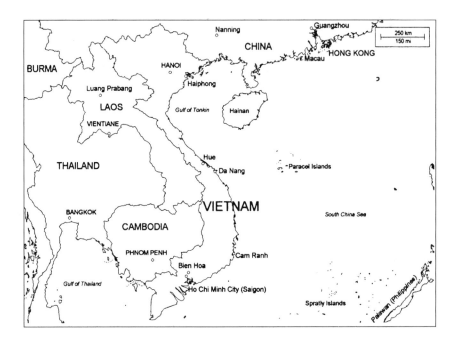

country adopted a "socialist-orientated market economy." Agricultural production doubled, transforming Vietnam from a net food importer into the
world's second-largest exporter of rice and third-largest producer of coffee.
The move away from a command economy also helped reduce poverty levels from nearly 60 percent of the population in 1992 to around 33 percent a
decade later.

Policy-making Paralysis

By the time of the eighth Party Congress in 1996, however, the reformist
momentum had dissipated, in large measure due to perhaps the worst infighting and political deadlock Vietnam had experienced since reunification.
The Asian financial crisis deepened the policy-making crisis, as real GDP
growth in 1999 fell below 5 percent in 1999, and foreign direct investment
(FDI)—the engine for much of Vietnam's growth in the 1990s—plummeted
to US$600 million in 1999, the lowest level since 1992. The deadlock can be
simplified as disagreements between reformers and conservatives over how
far to continue the economic reforms and concomitant integration into the
international community. Both groups felt their own prescription was crucial
for the party to maintain its legitimacy. The former group called for a steady
rollout of market-oriented reforms and increased integration into the global

economy, if for no other reason than to find employment for the over one million new entrants to the labor force every year. In contrast, many conservatives feared that economic rationalization would *increase* unemployment, in particular by forcing the government to curtail subsidies to state-owned enterprises (SOEs). Conservatives also felt that economic reform would impinge on Vietnam's sovereignty and undermine the "socialist foundations" of the country's economic and political systems and thereby erode the VCP's monopoly on power. Vietnam's consensus-based decision-making style, combined with the absence of any paramount leader, only exacerbated the effect of these divisions.

Breaking the Logjam

In 1999 and 2000 the economic reform debate became inextricably tied up with consideration of a sweeping bilateral trade agreement (BTA) that had been negotiated, but not yet signed, with the United States.[2] After over a year of deliberations, Vietnam's leaders finally decided to sign the agreement. Under the BTA, the United States granted Vietnam temporary most-favored nation (MFN) status, a move that significantly reduced U.S. tariffs on most imports from Vietnam. In return, Hanoi agreed to undertake a wide range of market-liberalization measures, including improving the transparency of the economic policy-making process, phasing out many differences in the treatment of foreign and domestic companies, reducing tariffs on goods, easing barriers to U.S. services (such as banking and telecommunications), committing to protect certain intellectual property rights, and providing additional inducements and protections for foreign direct investment. After the BTA went into effect, Vietnam's exports to the United States rose nearly five-fold, to over US$4 billion in 2003, largely due to an explosion of textile exports to the U.S. market.

The decision to sign the BTA appears to have broken the policy-making logjam by fashioning a consensus in favor of a new reformist push that was effectively endorsed by the leadership changes at the ninth Party Congress in 2001. In short order after signing the BTA, the government enacted a series of measures, including passing a new Enterprise Law, passing a constitutional amendment giving legal status to the private sector, reducing red tape, creating unprecedented transparency rules for prior publication of new rules and regulations, and for the first time giving party members the green light to engage in private business. Adhering to the BTA's implementation deadlines and achieving the government's goal of joining the World Trade Organization (WTO) by the end of 2005 have helped galvanize the Vietnamese bureaucracy toward enacting many of these steps. Vietnam's economy appears to have responded to these moves. Since 2001, growth has rebounded to the 7 percent level for the past several years. In contrast with the boom of the 1990s, a significant portion of the current growth has been driven by Vietnam's newly energized private sector.

An Open Market Industrialization Strategy

As a result, Vietnam has effectively committed itself to an "open market industrialization" strategy.[3] By entering into the BTA, by pushing to join the WTO, and by participating in the ASEAN Free Trade Area (AFTA), Vietnam is attempting to achieve its goal of becoming an industrialized country by 2020 without the benefits of protectionism and subsidization that the East Asian Tigers employed in an earlier era. Additionally, because it expelled much of its ethnic Chinese population in the 1970s, Vietnam will not have the advantage of tapping into the overseas Chinese community.

Assessing the Economic Reforms

Rapid growth since the mid-1980s has transformed Vietnam's economy, which has come to be loosely divided into three sectors: the state-owned, the foreign-invested, and the privately owned, which make up roughly 50 percent, 30 percent, and 20 percent of industrial output, respectively. For much of the 1990s, Vietnam's foreign-invested enterprises (FIEs) were among the country's most dynamic. Since the 1997 Asian financial crisis, the private sector has also made impressive gains, to the point where privately owned firms employ nearly a quarter of the workforce. Most of the giant SOEs, meanwhile, are functionally bankrupt and require significant government subsidies and assistance to continue operating. In 1990 state firms employed 2.5 million people. In 2001 this figure was down to 1.6 million. The economic reforms have also integrated Vietnam into the global economy. In 2000 exports constituted over 50 percent of GDP, double the percentage a decade earlier, and imports have grown faster than exports. Also impressive is Vietnam's strides in diversifying its exports beyond primary products (such as oil, rice, coffee, and seafood) into light manufacturing (particularly textiles and footwear).

Despite these dramatic changes, however, economic problems abound. Vietnam remains one of East Asia's poorest countries. Per capita GDP is estimated at around US$400, equivalent to approximately US$2,250 when measured on a purchasing power parity basis—placing Vietnam 167 out of 231 countries surveyed by the U.S. Central Intelligence Agency. Growth continues to be impeded by Vietnam's failure to tackle its remaining structural economic problems—including the unprofitable SOEs, a weak banking sector, massive red tape, and bureaucratic corruption—major impediments to continued growth.

Formal Structure

Vietnam's experiments with political reform have lagged behind its economic changes. Vietnam is a one-party, authoritarian state. In practice, the VCP sets the general direction for policy, while the details of implementation generally are left to the four lesser pillars of the Vietnamese polity: the state bureaucracy, the legislature (the National Assembly), the Vietnamese People's Army (VPA), and the officially sanctioned associations and organizations that exist under the Vietnamese Fatherland Front umbrella. The VCP's major decision-making bodies are the Central Committee, which has 150 members, and the Politburo, which currently has 15 members. In recent years, membership on the Politburo generally has been decided based upon maintaining a rough geographic (north, south, and central) and factional (conservatives and reformers) balance. The three top leadership posts are the VCP general secretary, followed by the prime minister, and the president. Since the death of Vietnam's last "strongman," Le Duan, in 1986, decision making on major policy issues typically has been arrived at through consensus within the Politburo, a practice that often leads to protracted delays on contentious issues.

The VCP holds National Party Congresses every five years to set the direction for Vietnam's economic, diplomatic, and social policies. They often are the occasion for major factional battles and leadership realignments. At the last Party Congress, the ninth, in April 2001, the conservative General Secretary Le Ka Phieu was ousted in favor of the more moderate Nong Duc Manh, the influential speaker of the National Assembly who represents the ideological center of the Communist Party. Thus far, Manh appears to be much more apt at consensus building than his predecessor, as the policy immobilism of Phieu's tenure appears to have been broken, particularly on economic reform. Manh's motivation for pushing a reform agenda appears to be maintaining the VCP's monopoly on power. As such, he is not expected to be a transformative figure.

Professionalization of the Government

In subtle ways the VCP's decision to prioritize economic development above ideological orthodoxy has led the party to loosen gradually its former stranglehold on the decision-making process, so that policy making has become more organic and pluralistic relative to the past. When it drafted the 1992 constitution, for instance, the VCP created a more powerful executive branch because of a general recognition that party cadres often were ill suited to implementing VCP policy directives. The new constitution also gave more influence to the legislative branch, the National Assembly, in part because the VCP realized that it needed to make the organs of government more responsive at the grassroots level in order to preempt domestic opposition. Over the past decade, despite the fact that more than 90 percent of its members are VCP members, the Assembly has increased its influence to the point where it can no longer be dismissed as a mere rubber stamp. For instance, the Assembly occasionally has rejected the nomination of cabinet-level officials, forced the VCP to redraft legislative proposals, and in 2003 for the first time was given the authority to examine line by line the government's budget proposal. In 2004 the National Assembly plans to send full-time officials to serve in Vietnamese embassies in Washington, Brussels, and other foreign capitals to observe the how Western legislatures operate. How far the National Assembly expands its purview will be an interesting development to watch over the coming years.

Internal Security Environment

Corruption

Although Vietnam's political situation is highly stable, the public's support for the VCP and the government is dwindling because of anger over official corruption, which thrives due to a high degree of governmental regulation, opaque decision making, low government salaries, and rapid economic growth.[4] In surveys of foreign executives, Vietnam regularly is ranked among the most corrupt societies in Asia. Since assuming his post in April 2001, General Secretary Manh has intensified the country's long-running anticorruption campaign. In the high-profile trial of Ho Chi Minh City gangster Nam Cam, two Central Committee members and dozens of other party officials were dismissed from their posts for their involvement with Nam Cam's network, though there is evidence that higher level officials have been shielded. Manh also has taken such other lower-profile steps that could have an impact as requiring party officials to declare their financial and property interests.[5]

Human Rights

Vietnam's willingness to crack down on organized expressions of dissent has become a thorn in its relations with the United States and certain European states. For the past several years, the VCP appears to have followed a strategy of permitting most forms of personal and religious expression while selectively repressing individuals and organizations that it deems a threat to the party's monopoly. A moderately vibrant press has sprouted and is more or less tolerated so long as it keeps criticism of the government to "safe" issues like low-level corruption, environmental pollution, and trafficking of women and children. However, the government has cracked down harshly on anti-government protests by various ethnic minority groups, most prominently the Montagnards in the country's Central Highlands and the Hmong in the Northwest Highlands. Although there is evidence that some of the protests were affiliated with expatriate groups that seek to overthrow the Communist Party, in the main the complaints were against local government corruption and against encroachment of ancestral lands by recent ethnic Vietnamese settlers. Religious groups who refuse to register with the government also have been targeted for harassment and repression. Furthermore, in its effort to control the Internet, the government also has stepped up repression of so-called cyber dissidents for criticizing the government's record on fighting corruption and the signing of land-border agreements with China, and for calling for greater political accountability and political competition. To many observers the government's unwillingness to countenance most independent criticism or dissent seems to border on paranoia, since there is little evidence to suggest that any group might emerge to threaten the one-party system in the near future.[6]

External Security Environment

Vietnam largely has achieved the goals outlined in the landmark Politburo Resolution no. 13 of May 1988, which stressed that a "multi-directional" foreign policy orientation—in other words, turning away from its reliance on the Soviet Union—was necessary to secure economic development over the coming ten to fifteen years. In that time, Vietnam has withdrawn its troops from Cambodia and Laos, restored relations with China and the United States, joined the Association of Southeast Asian Nations (ASEAN), and expanded contacts with virtually all countries. Most of Vietnam's relationships, however, are either highly conflicted (e.g., China, the United States, Cambodia) or formal, rather than warm. They also have tended to be heavily weighted toward the economic dimension. Thus far, a favorable international environment has not tested this imbalance. However, China's increased economic presence and diplomatic assertiveness in Southeast Asia has begun to challenge Vietnam's traditional interests with its neighbors. If this development continues, it may push Vietnam to develop a new foreign policy paradigm beyond "diversification."[7]

Vietnam-China Relations

Since reorienting its foreign policy, Vietnam has placed primacy on fully restoring its relationship with China. Sino-Vietnamese relations had been severed during the brief but bloody conflict the two countries fought in 1979. Relations were formalized in 1991, but progress was slow for most of the 1990s, due in part to Chinese opposition to Vietnam's joining ASEAN and to Chinese military actions in the South China Sea, where Vietnam and China are two of several countries with competing claims. Since the late 1990s, when China began espousing its "new security concept" of emphasizing cooperation with its neighbors, improvements in Sino-Vietnamese relations have accelerated, most notably with a number of successful summits and the signings of a land border treaty in 1999 and a sea border treaty for the Gulf of Tonkin in 2000.

For Vietnamese leaders, this process has been fraught with ambivalence. On the one hand, maintaining stable, friendly relations with its northern neighbor is critical for Vietnam's economic development, and Hanoi does not undertake large-scale diplomatic moves without first calculating Beijing's likely reaction. China's ruling Communist Party is an ideological bedfellow, as well as a role model for a country that seeks to marketize its economy without threatening the Communist Party's dominance. China also has become an increasingly important economic partner.

On the other hand, China represents Vietnam's most significant rival for influence in Southeast Asia. Beijing's outreach to Cambodia and Laos in recent years has rekindled internal battles between pro-Hanoi and pro-Beijing camps in both countries, and has spurred countermoves by Hanoi. Vietnam and China still have overlapping claims to the Spratly Island chain in the South China Sea, differences that led to military clashes in the late 1980s. In 2002 ASEAN and China signed a "Declaration on the Conduct of Parties in the South China Sea," a nonbinding agreement to resolve disputes diplomatically, exercise restraint, and respect the freedom of navigation and overflight. Significantly, Vietnam did not succeed in its efforts to have the agreement specifically include the Paracel Islands, claimed by both Vietnam and China. Instead, the declaration is vague on its geographic scope. Like other countries in the dispute, Vietnam has continued to expand its presence in the island chain. China also represents an economic rival, as both compete for foreign direct investment and for markets in many of the same low-cost manufacturing products. Imports from China have been surging, to over US$2 billion in 2002, up from US$60 million in 1995.

One sign of the sensitivity of China relations is that it remains a delicate political issue inside Vietnam. Many "cyber-dissidents" have been arrested for criticizing the government for being too compliant in the land-border negotiations, a charge that also played a role in the 2001 ouster of Le Ka Phieu as VCP general secretary. Indeed, the two countries continue to snipe over demarcating the land border that was agreed upon in 1999.

Vietnam-U.S. Relations

The signing of the U.S.-Vietnam BTA in 2000 marked the effective end to the incremental process of normalizing relations between the two countries that began in the early 1990s.[8] For years to come, the two countries will share a special interest in one another by virtue of the Vietnam War and the over one million ethnic Vietnamese and their descendents who are now U.S. citizens. Yet as far as the two governments are concerned, so-called "legacy issues"—including American POW-MIAs, refugee resettlement programs, and compensation for Vietnamese affected by Agent Orange defoliant—have either been more or less resolved or set aside.

Economically, Vietnam has benefited greatly since the United States ended its trade embargo in 1994. Total bilateral trade in that year was only US$223 million, less than a twentieth of the nearly US$5 billion recorded in 2003. Almost overnight after the BTA went into effect, the United States leap-frogged Japan, China, and other countries to become Vietnam's largest export market. U.S. aid to Vietnam has risen from under US$2 million in 1996 to nearly US$50 million in 2004, spread among HIV/AIDS care, aid to children (particularly victims of the Vietnam War), educational exchange programs, food assistance, and trade promotion programs to help Vietnam prepare for and implement the U.S.-Vietnam bilateral trade agreement. By dollar amount, the U.S.-Vietnam Fulbright exchange program is the Fulbright program's largest.

The transformation of Vietnam from a war to a country in the American mind over the past several years has had some negative consequences for Vietnam. Recently, trade friction and clashes over Vietnam's human rights record have soured relations somewhat since the heady days after the BTA was signed. In the mid- and late 1990s the intensity of such tensions often was diluted by the push for normalization. Now, however, in the absence of a single principle guiding the relationship, issues are often evaluated discretely, rather than balanced against one another. Additionally, the rise in Vietnamese exports has made Vietnamese enterprises a target for import-competing industries in the United States, most notably catfish and shrimp farming, both of which have filed antidumping suits against their Vietnamese competitors. In April 2003 the United States required Vietnam to sign a textile agreement establishing quotas that appear to have dampened the growth in

Vietnam's garment industry. Vietnam's record on human and religious rights have become much more prominent on the congressional agenda, ensuring that U.S. scrutiny of Vietnamese domestic situation is likely to increase in the coming years, particularly if the Vietnamese government continues its crackdown against dissidents and ethnic minorities. In 2004, for the third time in the past four years, the U.S. House of Representatives passed legislation that would make increases in nonhumanitarian U.S. aid to the Vietnamese government contingent upon improvements in Vietnam's human rights situation. The 2004 version of the measure awaits a decision in the U.S. Senate, which rejected the earlier versions of the bill.

For all the improvements in the bilateral relationship, Vietnam is still highly ambivalent toward the United States. Whereas China represents perhaps the greatest threat to Vietnam's national interests, the protracted debate over the BTA showed that many Vietnamese leaders see engagement with the United States and the West as perhaps the most dangerous to the VCP through "peaceful evolution," which is viewed as the equivalent of a Trojan horse designed to erode the Party's hold on power. These suspicions have only been heightened by reports that the 2001 protests against local government corruption in the Central Highlands were partially funded by American expatriate groups. It was only in early 2003 that Vietnam's leadership made the decision to upgrade its political and strategic relations with Washington, perhaps as a response to China's outreach to ASEAN members. Hanoi's efforts culminated in November 2003 when the Vietnamese defense minister, Pham Van Tra, visited Washington and the guided missile frigate USS *Vandergrift* and its two hundred sailors made a four-day call at the port of Saigon. Both events were firsts since the end of the Vietnam War, and have been followed by additional visits in 2004. It is still unclear how far, how fast, and in what form any new security relationship will develop.

Vietnam-ASEAN Relations

During the 1990s Vietnam's leaders sought to improve relations with its ASEAN neighbors, with the result that the country increasingly is integrating into the region's economy. Vietnam now buys electricity from China and Laos and sells it to Cambodia, for instance.[9] Vietnam has signed a cross-border agreement with Laos and Thailand to harmonize and simplify regulations governing flows of goods, vehicles, and people. The deal is part of a 240 mile (386 kilometer) East-West Transport Corridor highway project designed to link areas of Laos and Thailand to the port of Da Nang in central Vietnam. The highway has raised fears that trafficking in drugs, contraband, and humans—already on the rise—will increase further.

Despite these improvements, a number of trouble spots exist in Vietnam's relations with its neighbors. Vietnam has tried to preserve its "special relationship" with Laos, where Vietnamese troops remained until 1989. There have been reports that Vietnamese troops have assisted the Laotian regime in combating an insurgency by Hmong ethnic minorities. However, amid reports of a split in the Lao leadership between pro-Hanoi and pro-Beijing factions, China also has increased its military and development assistance to Laos. Sino-Vietnamese rivalry in Vientiane was on evidence in 2001 when, following a 2001 visit to Laos by the Chinese defense minister, Vietnam's defense minister, Pham Van Tra, flew in to offer military assistance that Vietnam earlier had declined.[10]

Although government-to-government relations between Vietnam and Cambodia have warmed considerably, relations outside the official level remain problematic. In Cambodia's 2003 National Assembly elections, both major opposition parties (FUNCINPEC and the Sam Rainsy Party) campaigned on anti-Vietnamese platforms. Vietnam's relations with Cambodia also were tested by the April 2001 protests in the Vietnamese Central Highlands. Following the government's crackdown, hundreds of Montagnards fled into Cambodia, where many applied for asylum. A repatriation agreement signed in January 2002 by Vietnam, Cambodia, and the United Nations High Commissioner for Refugees (UNHCR) crumbled after Vietnam refused to abide by its agreement to allow the UNHCR access to the Central Highlands to monitor refugee returns. To settle the dispute, Cambodia in late March 2002 accepted an offer from the United States to resettle the more than nine hundred Montagnards who remained in Cambodia. There is speculation that Vietnam's acquiescence to the plan was obtained by Cambodia's pledge to close its borders to future asylum-seekers from Vietnam.

In ASEAN, which Vietnam joined in 1995, Hanoi has had a reputation for working closely with other new members Cambodia and Burma to block efforts to increase ASEAN's institutional clout. Shortly after assuming the chairmanship of ASEAN in 2001, Vietnam rebuffed United Nations secretary general Kofi Annan's suggestion that it convene a troika of ASEAN ministers to help start a dialogue between Burma's military government and dissident Aung San Suu Kyi. A Vietnamese official said that Hanoi had rejected the idea because it constituted an unwarranted "interference" in Myanmar's affairs. In the previous year, ASEAN foreign ministers had agreed that the organization should form a troika of officials to resolve political and security problems of common concern in the region.

Terrorism Threat and Response

The War on Terrorism has not had a direct effect on Vietnam because the country's small Muslim population, relatively tight internal security presence, and undeveloped financial markets mean that it has few of the conditions necessary for there to be either a homegrown terrorist threat or a country of opportunity for outside groups to use as a point of attack, transit, or finance. Thus, Vietnam has little to offer in terms of counterintelligence. That said, the presence of corruption and the increased activity of Vietnamese and foreign criminal networks inside Vietnam could represent potential problems for the future. The U.S. embassy in Hanoi was closed for a period of time in September 2002 after a captured Jemaah Islamiyah (JI) (Islamic group or Islamic community) leader reported that U.S. interests in Vietnam—as well as several other countries—were being targeted.

Vietnam has given the United States modest support in the antiterrorism campaign. As of January 2004, Hanoi had granted overflight rights to U.S. military planes, provided US$300,000 in supplies to the Afghanistan reconstruction effort, and instituted name and asset checks on suspected terrorists and terrorist organizations. Although Vietnam opposed the U.S.-led invasion of Iraq in 2003, after the war it sent US$500,000 in rice aid, no doubt in an attempt to maintain its place as Iraq's largest supplier of rice. An additional motivation for cooperating on counterterrorism may be to try to secure U.S. support for combating what Hanoi describes as "terrorist" groups that operate within Vietnam—such as the Montagnard tribes in the Central Highlands—and expatriate groups in the United States that have been giving the Montagnards assistance, occasionally through violent means.

The War on Terrorism has had at least four indirect effects on Vietnamese interests. First, the war has marginalized Vietnam from discussions of major security issues in the region because it has little to offer in combating terrorist organizations. Additionally, Vietnam's low tolerance for outside interference in its internal affairs has led Hanoi to oppose or water down U.S. and Singaporean attempts to fashion a more robust antiterrorism response in ASEAN. Second, the War on Terrorism may be contributing to the increased focus on Vietnam's human rights record, which has become a major issue of U.S. congressional interest. Unlike such countries as China, Indonesia, and Pakistan, Vietnam has few examples of current security cooperation it can use to offset human rights criticisms. Third, the United States prioritizing the War on Terrorism has accelerated the expansion of China's influence in Southeast Asia, a development that in turn has given Vietnam the motivation for increasing its political-security ties with the United States. Finally, increased U.S.-China cooperation on North Korea, terrorism, and Iraq has provided Hanoi with an opportunity to reach out to Washington without causing undue alarm in Beijing.

Military Structure and Defense Policy

Size and Posture

Vietnam has the largest standing armed forces in Southeast Asia, with just over 400,000 personnel, down from over a million in the late 1980s. Rapid downsizing in the 1990s has been accompanied by a modernization push; after years of neglect in the 1980s, defense spending increased to US$1.1 billion in 1992 and to over US$2 billion five years later.[11] Even so, Vietnam's military capabilities are widely believed to have deteriorated significantly since the 1970s. China's assertiveness in the South China Sea led Vietnam in the 1990s to shift its defense posture from maintaining large ground forces to prioritizing the modernization of its naval and air forces, which are thought to be in the forty thousand- and thirty thousand-man range, respectively.

Policy-making Role

Like most communist countries, Vietnam has an iron triangle of party-army-state relations, where military elites occupy positions at top of the military and the party. Since the late 1980s, the VPA has increased its influence in the policy-making process, simultaneously becoming more involved in policy making and more autonomous vis-à-vis other institutional actors. The 1992 constitution enlarged the military's role (Article 12) by giving it the duty of defending the socialist regime and, for the first time, by placing it in the same legal position as other state organs. In large part this move was a reaction to the changing external environment. The collapse of socialist regimes in the Soviet Union and Eastern European countries, where various parties were deemed to have lost control over the military, led Vietnamese leaders to integrate the military into the party in exchange for the VPA's agreement to keep its own house in order. Also, VPA leaders' acquiescence to the *doi moi* reforms and the withdrawal from Cambodia enabled them to demand an overt role in the policy process. That said, the opaque nature of Vietnamese policy-making process in general, and the Politburo in particular, makes it impossible to know how the military makes its influence felt and, indeed, whether it speaks in a unified voice.

Commercialization

As in China, the Vietnamese military has become increasingly commercialized. The process first began in the late 1980s as a response to dire budgetary conditions in aftermath of *doi moi,* when the situation was so bad that there were reports that military salaries were insufficient for some soldiers to purchase food. By 1995 there were over three hundred army-run enterprises, reaching into virtually every corner of the Vietnamese economy. Reforms in the mid- and late-1990s cut back on the number of military enterprises by more than a third, but they also were designed to upgrade the efficiency. By the Defense Ministry's estimates, up to 80 percent of the output of these enterprises goes to the civilian sector, not the military.[12] The VPA was said to have been among the staunchest opponents of the U.S.-Vietnam BTA because of concerns that the deal would threaten its commercial interests, particularly in the telecommunications sector.

Conclusions and Outlook

In 2004 Vietnamese leaders appear surer of their county's domestic policy direction than at any time in the past decade. In retrospect, the decision to sign the BTA with the United States in 2000 and the VCP's ninth Party Congress in 2001 appear to have been watershed events, breaking the logjam that for years had stalled economic policy making. For the foreseeable future, Vietnam unambiguously has embraced deeper integration into the global economy as key to the country's economic policy. Indeed, it perhaps is the key to the vibrancy of the VCP, as economic growth increasingly becomes its main source of legitimacy. Additionally, the push to enter the WTO, combined with the reform deadlines in the BTA, should provide the discipline and focus Vietnamese leaders will need to overcome domestic opposition to the painful reforms that are sure to come. Meanwhile, on domestic political matters, the VCP is likely to continue emulating its Chinese brethren by relaxing restrictions on personal freedoms generally but selectively and by harshly clamping down on organized and individual expressions of dissent.

In contrast to the domestic situation, Vietnam's foreign policy orientation remains far more muddled, largely because of the uncertainties over how to respond to China's economic and diplomatic resurgence. Relations with Beijing, still Vietnam's most important diplomatic partner, remain conflicted and are likely to become even more so if China continues to expand its trade with, aid to, and diplomatic presence in Indochina. Increased Chinese influence also is likely to heighten Sino-Vietnamese rivalry in Cambodia and Laos, further clouding Hanoi's relations with those two neighbors.

Yet Vietnam at present is ill suited to turn elsewhere if it wished to find a counterweight to China. ASEAN has been weakened, perhaps terminally, by domestic turmoil in Indonesia, and Vietnam's extreme sensitivity to foreign "interference" in its domestic affairs makes it highly unlikely it would countenance a more interventionist role for the organization. For two reasons, embryonic security ties with the United States are unlikely to do more than expand incrementally. First, establishing some sort of strategic partnership would be highly distasteful for many ideological conservatives in Hanoi, who worry about U.S. attempts to democratize Vietnam through "peaceful evolution." A counterargument to this position is that the more strategically important Vietnam becomes in Washington's eyes, the less important human rights and political reform will be to U.S. policy makers. Second, Vietnamese leaders must tiptoe carefully along the tightrope between Washington and Beijing, so that improved relations with one capital not be perceived as a threat in the other. The situation in 2004, in which Sino-American relations are relatively positive, thus may represent a window of opportunity for Vietnam to expand further its security ties with the United States.

Notes

The views in this chapter are Dr. Manyin's and do not necessarily represent those of the Congressional Research Service.

1. Marvin Ott, "The Future of US-Vietnam Relations." Paper presented at "The Future of Relations Between Vietnam and the United States." (SAIS, Washington, DC, October 2–3, 2003.)

2. Carlyle A. Thayer, "Political Developments in Vietnam: The Rise and Demise of Le Kha Phieu, 1997–2001," in Lisa B.W. Drummond and Mandy Thomas, eds., *Urban Culture in Contemporary Vietnam,* (New York: Routledge Curzon Press, 2003).

3. I am indebted to Steve Parker, of the U.S.-Vietnam STAR Project, for this insight.

4. Economist Intelligence Unit, *Vietnam Country Report,* October 2003, p. 12.

5. Carlyle A. Thayer, "Vietnam: The Stewardship of Nong Duc Manh," in Daljit Singh and Chin Kin Wah, eds., *Southeast Asian Affairs 2003,* (Singapore: Institute of Southeast Asian Studies, 2003).

6. Carlyle A. Thayer, "Vietnam: The Stewardship of Nong Duc Manh."

7. Carlyle A. Thayer, "Vietnamese Foreign Policy: Multilateralism and the Threat of Peaceful Evolution," in Carlyle A. Thayer and Ramses Amer, eds., *Vietnamese Foreign Policy in Transition,* (New York: St. Martin's Press, 2000).

8. The only significant legal step remaining is the United States granting permanent MFN status to Vietnam, a move that is likely to come as part of Vietnam's joining the WTO.

9. Lyall Breckon, "A New Strategic Partnership Is Declared," *China-Southeast Asia, Comparative Connections,* 4th Quarter 2003, at www.csis.org.

10. Carlyle A. Thayer and Gérard Hervouet, "The Army as a Political and Economic

Actor in Vietnam," in Christopher Goscha and Benoît de Tréglodé, eds., *Le Viet Nam Depuis 1945: Etat, Marges Et Constructions Du Passe,* (Paris: L'Harmatan, 2004), pp. 97–98.

11. Thayer and Hervouet, "The Army as a Political and Economic Actor."
12. Ibid.

Suggested Readings

Abuza, Zachary. *Renovating Politics in Contemporary Vietnam.* Boulder, CO: Lynne Rienner, 2001.

Chanda, Nayan. *Brother Enemy: The War after the War.* New York: MacMillan Publishing Co., 1986.

Dalpino, Catharin. "Finding a New Balance: Positives and Negatives in US-Vietnamese Relations." Paper presented at "The Future of Relations Between Vietnam and the United States," SAIS, Washington, DC, October 2003.

Dapice, David. "Vietnam's Economy: Success Story or Weird Dualism?" Cambridge, MA: Harvard University Press, 2003.

Ott, Marvin. "The Future of US-Vietnam Relations." Paper presented at "The Future of Relations Between Vietnam and the United States," SAIS, Washington, DC. October 2–3, 2003.

Stromseth, Jonathan, ed. *Dialogue on U.S.-Vietnam Relations: Domestic Dimensions.* Washington, DC: The Asia Foundation, 2003.

Thayer, Carlyle A. "Vietnam: The Stewardship of Nong Duc Manh," in *Southeast Asian Affairs 2003.* Daljit Singh and Chin Kin Wah, eds. Singapore: Institute of Southeast Asian Studies, 2003.

———. "Vietnamese Foreign Policy: Multilateralism and the Threat of Peaceful Evolution," in *Vietnamese Foreign Policy in Transition.* Carlyle A. Thayer and Ramses Amer, eds. New York: St. Martin's Press, 2000.

Thayer, Carlyle A., and Gérard Hervouet. "The Army as a Political and Economic Actor in Vietnam," in Christopher Goscha and Benoît de Tréglodé, eds., *Le Viet Nam Depuis 1945: Etat, Marges Et Constructions Du Passe.* Paris: L'Harmatan, 2004.

Van Arkadie, Brian, and Raymond Mallon. *Viet Nam—a Transition Tiger?* Canberra: Asia Pacific Press at the Australian National University, 2003.

"U.S.-Southeast Asia" and "China-Southeast Asia," in *Comparative Connections,* various issues. Center for Strategic and International Studies (CSIS), Washington, DC, at www.csis.org.

Glossary of Abbreviations and Acronyms

ABRI	Angkatan Bersenjata Republik Indonesia (Indonesian armed forces)
ADF	Australian Defence Force
AFP	Armed Forces of the Philippines
AFTA	ASEAN Free Trade Area
AID	Agency for International Development
AIDS	acquired immunodeficiency syndrome
ANZAC	Australian and New Zealand Army Corps
ANZUS	Australia-New Zealand-United States
APEC	Asia-Pacific Economic Cooperation organization
ARF	ASEAN Regional Forum
ASCM	Anti-Ship Cruise Missile
ASDF	Air Self-Defense Force
ASEAN	Association of Southeast Asian Nations
ASG	Abu Sayyaf Group
ASW	Anti-Submarine Warfare
AWACS	Airborne Warning and Control System aircraft
BJP	Bharatiya Janata Party
BN	Barisan Nasional (National Front)
BNP	Bangladesh Nationalist Party
BRN	Barisan Revolusi Nasional
BTA	Bilateral Trade Agreement
CBRN	Chemical-Biological-Radiological-Nuclear
CCP	Chinese Communist Party
CDS	Chief of Defense Staff
CGS	Chief of the General Staff
CIA	Central Intelligence Agency
CHT	Chittagong Hill Tracts

CMC	Central Military Commission
CPN-M	Communist Party of Nepal-Maoist
CPN-UML	Communist Party of Nepal-Unified Marxist-Leninist
CPP	Cambodian People's Party; Communist Party of the Philippines
CVID	complete, verifiable, and irreversible dismantling
DHS	Department of Homeland Security
DoA	Defense of Australia
DPJ	Democratic Party of Japan
DPRK	Democratic People's Republic of Korea
EEZ	Exclusive Economic Zone
EU	European Union
FPDA	Five-Power Defence Arrangement
FTA	Free Trade Agreement
FTO	Foreign Terrorist Organization
FUNCINPEC	United Front for an Independent, Neutral, and Peaceful Cambodia
GAM	Gerakan Aceh Merdeka (Free Aceh Movement)
GDP	gross domestic product
GMD	Ground-based Midcourse Defense
GNP	gross national product
GSDF	Ground Self-Defense Force
GSH	General Staff Headquarters
HIV	human immunodeficiency virus
HUJI	Harakat ul-Jihad-i-Islami
HUJI-B	Harakat ul-Jihad-I-Islami/Bangladesh (Movement of Islamic Holy War)
HUM	Harakat ul-Mujahidin (Movement of Holy Warriors)
IAEA	International Atomic Energy Agency
ICBM	Intercontinental Ballistic Missile
ICJ	International Court of Justice
ICM	Islami Constitution Movement
IJO	Islami Jatiya Oikya
IMB	International Maritime Bureau
IMF	International Monetary Fund
INC	Indian Congress Party
INP	Indonesian National Police
IO/IW	Information Operations/Information Warfare
IOJ	Islami Oikya Jote (Islamic United Front)
IRBM	Intermediate-Range Ballistic Missile
ISA	Internal Security Act

ISD	Internal Security Department
ISI	Inter-Services Intelligence agency
JDC	Joint Commission of Defense Cooperation
JEM	Jaish-e-Mohammed (Army of Mohammed)
JI	Jama'at-e Islami (Islamic Society)
JI	Jemaah Islamiyah (Islamic group or Islamic community)
JRA	Japanese Red Army
JUD	Jamaat ud-Dawa
JVP	Janatha Vimukthi Peramuna (People's Liberation Front)
KCIA	Korean Central Intelligence Agency
KEDO	Korean Peninsula Energy Development Organization
KIG	Kalayaan (Freedomland) Island Group
km	kilometer
KMM	Kumpulan Militan Malaysia (Malaysian Mujahideen Group)
KMT	Kuomintang Party
KNU	Karen National Union
LACM	Land-Attack Cruise Missile
LDP	Liberal Democratic Party
LJ	Laskar Jihad
LOC	Line of Control
LPA	Lao People's Army
LPN	Lao People's Navy
LPRP	Lao People's Revolutionary Party
LT	Lashkar-e-Tayyiba (Army of the Pure or Army of the Righteous)
LTTE	Liberation Tigers of Tamil Eelam
MAF	Malaysian Armed Forces
MDU	Mongolian Democratic Union
MEC	Myanmar Economic Corporation
MFN	Most-Favored Nation
MIA	Missing in Action
MIB	Melayu Islam Beraja (Malay Islamic Monarchy)
MILF	Moro Islamic Liberation Front
MMA	Muttahida Majlis-e-Amal (United Action Front)
MMI	Mujahideen Council of Indonesia
MND	Ministry of National Defense
MOD	Ministry of Defense
MOGE	Myanma Oil and Gas Enterprise
MP	Mujahideen Pattani
MPRP	Mongolian People's Revolutionary Party
MRBM	Medium-Range Ballistic Missile
MSDF	Maritime Self-Defense Force

NACD	National Authority for Combating Drugs
NAM	Non-Aligned Movement
NATO	North Atlantic Treaty Organization
NCP	Nepali Congress Party
NGO	Non-Governmental Organization
NLD	National League for Democracy
NPA	New People's Army
NPT	Nuclear Non-Proliferation Treaty
NWS	Nuclear Weapons State
NZDF	New Zealand Defence Force
ODA	Overseas Development Assistance
OECD	Organization for Economic Cooperation and Development
OEF	Operation Enduring Freedom
OIC	Organization of Islamic Conference
OIF	Operation Iraqi Freedom
PAC	Patriot Advanced Capability
PAP	People's Action Party; People's Armed Police
PAS	Parti Islam Se-Malaysia (Islamic Party of Malaysia)
PCJSS	Parbatya Chattagram Jana Sanghati Samiti
PKDB	Partai Kebangsaan Demokratik Brunei (Brunei National Democratic Party)
PKO	Peace-Keeping Operation
PLA	People's Liberation Army
PLAAF	People's Liberation Army Air Force
PLAN	People's Liberation Army Navy
PLANAF	People's Liberation Army Navy Air Force
PML-Q	Pakistan Muslim League-Quaid-e-Azam
POW	prisoner of war
PPKB	Parti Perpaduan Kebangsaan Brunei (Brunei National Solidarity Party)
PRB	Partai Ra'yat Brunei (People's Party of Brunei)
PRC	People's Republic of China
PRT	Provincial Reconstruction Teams
PSI	Proliferation Security Initiative
PULO	Pattani United Liberation Organization
QDR	Quadrennial Defense Review
RAMSI	Regional Assistance Mission to the Solomon Islands
RBAF	Royal Brunei Armed Forces
RCAF	Royal Cambodian Armed Forces
RM	Rabitatul Mujahideen (Mujahideen League)
RMA	Revolution in Military Affairs

RMAF	Royal Malaysian Air Force
RMN	Royal Malaysian Navy
RMSI	Regional Maritime Security Initiative
ROC	Republic of China
ROK	Republic of Korea
RPC	Regional Piracy Center
RSDF	Reserve Self-Defense Force
RTA	Royal Thai Army
RTAF	Royal Thai Air Force
RTN	Royal Thai Navy
SARA	ethnicity, religion, race, and intergroup conflict (in Indonesia)
SARS	severe acute respiratory syndrome
SCO	Shanghai Cooperation Organization
SDA	Self-Defense Agency
SDF	Self-Defense Force
SEATO	Southeast Asia Treaty Organization
SIS	Security Intelligence Service
SLFP	Sri Lanka Freedom Party
SLORC	State Law and Order Restoration Council
SLV	Space Launch Vehicle
SPDC	State Peace and Development Council
SRBM	Short-Range Ballistic Missile
SRP	Sam Rainsy Party
TMD	Theater Missile Defense
TNI	Tentara Nasional Indonesia (Indonesian armed forces)
TRA	Taiwan Relations Act
UAV	Unmanned Aerial Vehicle
UMEH	Union of Myanmar Economic Holdings
UMNO	United Malays National Organization
UN	United Nations
UNHCR	United Nations High Commissioner for Refugees
UNP	United National Party
UNTAET	UN Transitional Authority in East Timor
USINDO	United States-Indonesia society
UWSA	United Wa State Army
VCP	Vietnamese Communist Party
VFA	Visiting Forces Agreement
VPA	Vietnamese People's Army
WMD	weapons of mass destruction
WMEAT	World Military Expenditures and Arms Transfers
WTC	World Trade Center
WTO	World Trade Organization

Appendix 1

Comparative Country Data

This appendix shows in table form comparative data on the countries surveyed in this book. The data provide a snapshot and summary of key geographic, population, political, economic, and military indicators.

Country	Total geographic area (sq km, sq miles)	Population and population growth rate	Labor force (millions)	Government type	Economy: gross domestic product (GDP), real growth rate, and product per capita (purchasing power parity) (U.S. dollars)	Military manpower availability males ages 15–49, those fit for military service	Military expenditures (U.S. dollar figure, percent of GDP)
Australia	7,686,850, 2,967,893	19,731,984 0.93%	9.2	Democratic; federal-state system recognizing the British monarch as sovereign	$525.5 billion, 3.6%, $26,900 (2002 est.)	5 million males, 4.3 million fit	$11.39 billion, 2.9% (FY02)
Bangladesh	144,000, 55,598	138,448,210 2.06%	64.1[1]	Parliamentary democracy	$238.2 billion, 4.8%, $1,800 (2002 est.)	38.4 million males, 22.8 million fit	$559 million, 1.8% (FY96)
Brunei	5,770, 2,228	358,098 2%	143,400[2]	Constitutional sultanate	$6.5 billion, 3%, $18,600 (2002 est.)	110,888 males, 63,966 fit	$329.7 million, 5% (FY02)
Burma	678,500, 261.969	42,510,537 0.52%	23.7 (1999 est.)	Military regime	$73.69 billion, 5.3%, $1,700 (2002 est.)	12.3 million males and 12.3 million females, 6.5 million males fit, 6.5 million females fit	$39 million, 2.1% (FY97)

(continued)

Appendix 1 *(continued)*

Country	Total geographic area (sq km, sq miles)	Population and population growth rate	Labor force (millions)	Government type	Economy: gross domestic product (GDP), real growth rate, and product per capita (purchasing power parity) (U.S. dollars)	Military manpower availability males ages 15–49, those fit for military service	Military expenditures (U.S. dollar figure, percent of GDP)
Cambodia	181,040, 69,900	13,124,764 1.8%	6	Multiparty democracy under a constitutional monarchy established in September 1993	$20.42 billion, 4.5%, $1,600 (2002 est.)	3.2 million males, 1.8 million fit	$112 million, 3% (FY01 est.)
China	9,596,960, 3,705,386	1,286,975,4 68, 0.6%	744	Communist state	$5.989 trillion, 8%, $4,700 (2002 est.)	375 million males, 206 million fit	$55.91 billion, 4.3% (FY02)
India	3,287,590, 1,269,338	1,049,700,1 18, 1.47%	406	Federal republic	$2.664 trillion, 4.3%, $2,600 (2002 est.)	288 million males, 169 million fit	$11.52 billion, 2.3% (FY02)
Indonesia	1,919,440, 741,096	234,893,453, 1.52%	99	Republic	$714.2 billion, 3.7%, $3,100 (2002 est.)	65 million males, 38 million fit	$1 billion, 1.3% (FY98)
Japan	377,835, 145,882	127,214,499 0.11%	67.7	Constitutional monarchy with a parliamentary government	$3.651 trillion, 0.2%, $28,700 (2002 est.)	29 million males, 25 million fit	$39.52 billion, 1% (FY02)
Laos	236,800, 91,429	5,921,545 2.45%	2.4	Communist state	$10.4 billion, 5.7%, $1,800 (2002 est.)	1.4 million males, 759,499 fit	$55 million (FY98), 4.2% (FY96)

Country				Government	GDP	Military	Military expenditures
Malaysia	329,750, 127,317	23,092,940 1.86%	9.9	Constitutional monarchy	$198.4 billion, 4.1%, $8,800 (2002 est.)	6 million males, 3.6 million fit	$1.69 billion, 2.03% (FY00)
Mongolia	1,565,000, 604,247	2,712,315 1.42%	1.4	Parliamentary	$5.06 billion, 3.9%, $1,900 (2002 est.)	796,449 males, 516,502 fit	$23.1 million, 2.2% (FY02)
Nepal	140,800, 54,363	26,469,569 2.26%	10 [3]	Parliamentary democracy and constitutional monarchy	$37.32 billion, -0.6%, $1,400 (2002 est.)	6.6 million males 3.4 million fit	$57.22 million 1.1% (FY02)
New Zealand	268,680, 103,737	3,951,307 1.09%	1.92	Parliamentary democracy	$78.4 billion, 3.3%, $20,100 (2002 est.)	1 million males, 859,505 fit	$605.7 million, 1% (FY02)
North Korea	120,540, 46,541	22,466,481 1.07%	9.6	Authoritarian socialist; one-man dictatorship	$22.26 billion, 1%, $1,000 (2002 est.)	6.1 million males, 3.6 million fit	$5.2 billion, 33.9% (FY02)
Pakistan	803,940, 310,401	150,694,740 2.01%	40.4 [4]	Federal republic	$295.3 billion (2002 est.), 4.4%, $2,000 (FY01/02 est.)	38.1 million males, 23.3 million fit	$2.9 billion, 4.6% (FY02)
The Philippines	300,000, 115,830	84,619,974 1.92%	33.7	Republic	$379.7 billion, 4.4%, $4,600 (2002 est.)	21.9 million males, 15.4 million fit	$995 million, 1.5% (FY98)
Singapore	692.7, 267.5	4,608,595 3.42%	2.19	Parliamentary republic	$112.4 billion, 2.2%, $25,200 (2002 est.)	1.3 million males, 1.0 million fit	$4.47 billion (FY01 est.), 4.9% (FY01)
South Korea	98,480 38.023	48,289,037 0.66%	22	Republic	$941.5 billion, 6.3%, $19,600 (2002 est.)	14.2 million males, 8.9 million fit	$13 billion, 2.8% (FY02)
Sri Lanka	65, 610 25,332	19,742,439 [5] 0.83%	6.6	Republic	$73.7 billion, 3.2%, $3,700 (2002 est.)	5.3 million males, 4.1 million fit	$719 million, 4.2% (FY98)

(continued)

Appendix 1 *(continued)*

Country	Total geographic area (sq km, sq miles)	Population and population growth rate	Labor force (millions)	Government type	Economy: gross domestic product (GDP), real growth rate, and product per capita (purchasing power parity) (U.S. dollars)	Military manpower availability males ages 15–49, those fit for military service	Military expenditures (U.S. dollar figure, percent of GDP)
Taiwan	35,980, 13,892	22,603,001 0.65%	10	Multiparty democratic regime headed by popularly elected president and unicameral legislature	$406 billion, 3.5%, $18,000 (2002 est.)	6.5 million males, 5 million fit	$7.574 billion, 2.7% (FY02)
Thailand	514,000 198,455	64,265,276, 0.95%	33.4	Constitutional monarchy	$445.8 billion, 5.3%, $7,000 (2002 est.)	17.9 million males, 10.7 million fit	$1.775 billion, 1.4% (FY00)
Vietnam	329,560 127,243	81,624,716, 1.29%	38.2	Communist state	$183.8 billion, 7%, $2,300 (2002 est.)	22.8 million males, 14.3 million fit	$650 million, 2.5% (FY98)

Source: Adapted from U.S. Central Intelligence Agency, *The World Factbook 2003,* available at the Web site www.cia.gov/cia/publications/factbook/index.html. Country information is current as of December 18, 2003.

[1]Extensive export of labor to Saudi Arabia, Kuwait, United Arab Emirates, Oman, Qatar, and Malaysia; workers' remittances estimated at US$1.71 billion in 1998–1999 (1998).

[2]Includes foreign workers and military personnel; temporary residents make up about 40 percent of labor force (1999 est.).

[3]Severe lack of skilled labor (1996 est.).

[4]Extensive export of labor, mostly to the Middle East, and use of child labor.

[5]Since the outbreak of hostilities between the government and armed Tamil separatists in the mid-1980s, several hundred thousand Tamil civilians have fled the island; as of year end 2000, approximately 65,000 were housed in 131 refugee camps in south India, another 40,000 lived outside the Indian camps, and more than 200,000 Tamils have sought refuge in the West (July 2003 est.).

FY = Fiscal Year

Appendix 2

Foreign Terrorist Organizations (FTOs) in Asia

Throughout the text, mention is made of Foreign Terrorist Organizations or FTOs. As of 2004, the United States government (through the secretary of state) had designated thirty-seven terrorist groups worldwide as FTOs, pursuant to section 219 of the Immigration and Nationality Act, as amended by the Antiterrorism and Effective Death Penalty Act of 1996. The designations carry the following specific legal consequences:

- It is unlawful to provide funds or other material support to a designated FTO.
- Representatives and certain members of a designated FTO can be denied visas or excluded from the United States.
- U.S. financial institutions must block funds of designated FTOs and their agents and must report the blockage to the U.S. Department of the Treasury.

Of the thirty-seven designated FTOs, we present an abbreviated list of eleven below (by country) whose prime areas of operations are in Asia. Two of these eleven (al Qaeda and Jemmah Islamiyah) are transnational groups operating across the region.

This list and the group descriptions that follow are derived from the U.S. Department of State, *Patterns of Global Terrorism 2002* and *Patterns of Global Terrorism 2003*, released by the Office of the Coordinator for Counterterrorism, April 30, 2003, and April 29, 2004, at www.state.gov.

Transnational

1. al Qaeda
2. Jemaah Islamiyah (JI)

Japan

3. Aum Supreme Truth (Aum), aka Aum Shinrikyo, Aleph

Pakistan

4. Harakat ul-Mujahidin (HUM) (Movement of Holy Warriors)
5. Jaish-e-Mohammed (JEM) (Army of Mohammed)
6. Lashkar-e-Tayyiba (LT) (Army of the Pure or Army of the Righteous)
7. Lashkar I Jhangvi (LJ) (Army of Jhangvi)

Philippines

8. Abu Sayyaf Group (ASG)
9. Communist Party of Philippines/New People's Army (CPP/NPA)

Sri Lanka

10. Liberation Tigers of Tamil Eelam (LTTE)

Uzbekistan

11. Islamic Movement of Uzbekistan (IMU)

Group Descriptions

1. al Qaeda (Al-Qaida, aka Qa'idat al-Jihad)

Al Qaeda was established by Osama bin Ladin in the late 1980s to bring together Arabs who fought in Afghanistan against the Soviet Union. Helped finance, recruit, transport, and train Sunni Islamic extremists for the Afghan resistance. Current goal is to establish a pan-Islamic caliphate throughout the world by working with allied Islamic extremist groups to overthrow regimes it deems "non-Islamic" and expelling Westerners and non-Muslims from Muslim countries—particularly Saudi Arabia. Issued a statement under the banner of the World Islamic Front for Jihad Against the Jews and Crusaders in February 1998, saying it was the duty of all Muslims to kill U.S. citizens—civilian or military—and their allies everywhere. Merged with Egyptian Islamic Jihad (Al-Jihad) in June 2001. First designated in October 1999.

Activities

In 2003 al Qaeda carried out the assault and bombing on May 12 of three expatriate housing complexes in Riyadh, Saudi Arabia, that killed 20 and injured 139. Assisted in carrying out bombings on May 16 in Casablanca, Morocco, of a Jewish center, restaurant, nightclub, and hotel that killed 41 and injured 101. Probably supported the bombing of the J.W. Marriott Hotel in Jakarta, Indonesia, on August 5. Responsible for the assault and bombing on November 9 of a housing complex in Riyadh, Saudi Arabia, that killed 17 and injured 100. Conducted the bombings of two synagogues in Istanbul, Turkey, on November 15 that killed 23 and injured 200, and the bombings in Istanbul of the British consulate and HSBC Bank on November 20 that resulted in 27 dead and 455 injured. Has been involved in some attacks in Afghanistan and Iraq.

In 2002 al Qaeda carried out bombing on November 28 of a hotel in Mombasa, Kenya, killing 15 and injuring 40. Probably supported a nightclub bombing in Bali, Indonesia, on October 12 that killed about 180. Responsible for an attack on U.S. military personnel in Kuwait, on October 8, that killed 1 U.S. soldier and injured another. Directed a suicide attack on the MV *Limburg* off the coast of Yemen, on October 6 that killed 1 and injured 4. Carried out a firebombing of a synagogue in Tunisia on April 11 that killed 19 and injured 22.

On September 11, 2001, 19 al Qaeda suicide attackers hijacked and crashed 4 U.S. commercial jets—two into the World Trade Center in New York City, one into the Pentagon near Washington, DC, and a fourth into a field in Shanksville, Pennsylvania, leaving about 3,000 individuals dead or missing.

Directed the attack on the USS *Cole* in the port of Aden, Yemen, on October 12, 2000, killing 17 U.S. Navy members and injuring another 39. Al Qaeda conducted bombings in August 1998 of U.S. embassies in Nairobi, Kenya, and Dar es Salaam, Tanzania, that killed at least 301 individuals and injured more than 5,000 others. Claims to have shot down U.S. helicopters and killed U.S. servicemen in Somalia in 1993 and to have conducted 3 bombings that targeted U.S. troops in Aden, Yemen, in December 1992.

Al Qaeda is linked to the following plans that were disrupted or not carried out: to assassinate Pope John Paul II during his visit to Manila in late 1994, to kill President Clinton during a visit to the Philippines in early 1995, to bomb in midair a dozen U.S. transpacific flights in 1995, and to set off a bomb at Los Angeles International Airport in 1999. Also plotted to carry out terrorist operations against U.S. and Israeli tourists visiting Jordan for millennial celebrations in late 1999. (Jordanian authorities thwarted the planned attacks and put 28 suspects on trial.) In December 2001 suspected al Qaeda associate Richard Colvin Reid attempted to ignite a shoe bomb on a transatlantic flight from Paris to Miami. Attempted to shoot down an Israeli chartered plane with a surface-to-air missile as it departed the Mombasa airport in November 2002.

Strength

Al Qaeda probably has several thousand members and associates. The arrests of senior-level al Qaeda operatives have interrupted some terrorist plots. It also serves as a focal point or umbrella organization for a worldwide network that includes many Sunni Islamic extremist groups, some members of al-Gama'a al-Islamiyya, the Islamic Movement of Uzbekistan, and the Harakat ul-Mujahidin.

Location/Area of Operation

Al Qaeda has cells worldwide and is reinforced by its ties to Sunni extremist networks. Was based in Afghanistan until coalition forces removed the Taliban from power in late 2001. Al Qaeda has dispersed in small groups across South Asia, Southeast Asia, and the Middle East and probably will attempt to carry out future attacks against U.S. interests.

External Aid

Al Qaeda maintains moneymaking front businesses, solicits donations from like-minded supporters, and illicitly siphons funds from donations to Muslim charitable organizations. U.S. and international efforts to block al Qaeda funding has hampered the group's ability to obtain money.

2. Jemaah Islamiyah (JI)

Description

Jemaah Islamiyah is a Southeast Asian–based terrorist network with links to al Qaeda. The network recruited and trained extremists in the late 1990s, following the stated goal of creating an Islamic state comprising Brunei, Indonesia, Malaysia, Singapore, the southern Philippines, and southern Thailand. First designated as an FTO in October 2002.

Activities

JI was responsible for the bombing of the J.W. Marriott Hotel in Jakarta on August 5, 2003, the Bali bombings on October 12, 2002, and an attack against the Philippine ambassador to Indonesia in August 2000. The Bali plot, which left more than two hundred dead, was reportedly the final outcome of meetings in early 2002 in Thailand, where attacks against Singapore and soft targets such as tourist spots in the region were also considered. In December 2001 Singapore authorities uncovered a JI plot to attack the U.S. and Israeli embassies and British and Australian diplomatic buildings in Singapore, and in June 2003, Thai authorities disrupted a JI plan to attack several Western embassies and tourist sites there. Investigations also linked the JI to bombings in December 2000 where dozens of bombs were detonated in Indonesia and the Philippines, killing twenty-two in the Philippines and fifteen in Indonesia.

The capture in August of Indonesian Riduan Isamuddin (aka Hambali), JI leader and al Qaeda Southeast Asia operations chief, damaged the JI, but the group maintains its ability to target Western interests in the region and to recruit new members through a network of radical Islamic schools based primarily in Indonesia.

Strength

Exact numbers are currently unknown, and Southeast Asian authorities continue to uncover and arrest additional JI elements. Elements of total JI members vary widely from the hundreds to the thousands.

Location/Area of Operation

JI is believed to have cells spanning Indonesia, Malaysia, the Philippines, southern Thailand, and Pakistan and may have some presence in neighboring countries.

External Aid

Investigations indicate that, in addition to raising its own funds, JI receives money and logistic assistance from Middle Eastern and South Asian contacts, nongovernmental organizations, and other groups—including al Qaeda.

3. Aum Supreme Truth (Aum), aka Aum Shinrikyo, Aleph

Description

A cult established in 1987 by Shoko Asahara, the Aum aimed to take over Japan and then the world. Approved as a religious entity in 1989 under Japanese law, the group ran candidates in a Japanese parliamentary election in 1990. Over time, the cult began to emphasize the imminence of the end of the world and stated that the United States would initiate Armageddon by starting World War III with Japan. The Japanese government revoked its recognition of the Aum as a religious organization in October 1995, but in 1997 a government panel decided not to invoke the Anti-Subversive Law against the group, which would have outlawed the cult. A 1999 law gave the Japanese government authorization to continue police surveillance of the group because of concerns that the Aum might launch future terrorist attacks. Under the leadership of Fumihiro Joyu, the Aum changed its name to Aleph in January 2000 and claimed to have rejected the violent and apocalyptic teachings of its founder. First designated in October 1997.

Activities

On March 20, 1995, Aum members simultaneously released the chemical nerve agent sarin on several Tokyo subway trains, killing twelve persons and injuring perhaps six thousand. The group was responsible for other mysterious chemical accidents in Japan in 1994. Its efforts to conduct attacks using biological agents have been unsuccessful. Japanese police arrested Asahara in May 1995. In February 2004 Asahara received the death sentence for his role in the attacks of 1995. Since 1997, the cult continued to recruit new members, engage in commercial enterprise, and acquire property, although it scaled back these activities significantly in 2001 in response to public outcry. The cult maintains an Internet home page. In July 2001 Russian authorities arrested a group of Russian Aum followers who had planned to set off bombs near the Imperial Palace in Tokyo as part of an operation to free Asahara from jail and then smuggle him to Russia.

Strength

The Aum's current membership is estimated to be less than one thousand persons. At the time of the Tokyo subway attack, the group claimed to have nine thousand members in Japan and as many as forty thousand worldwide.

Location/Area of Operation

The Aum's principal membership is located in Japan, but a residual branch comprising perhaps a few hundred followers has surfaced in Russia.

External Aid

None.

4. Harakat ul-Mujahidin (HUM) (Movement of Holy Warriors)

Description

The HUM is an Islamic militant group based in Pakistan that operates primarily in Kashmir. It is politically aligned with the radical political party Jamiat Ulema-i-Islam Fazlur Rehman faction (JUI-F). The longtime leader of the group, Fazlur Rehman Khalil, stepped down as HUM emir in mid-February 2000, turning the reins over to his second in command, Farooq Kashmiri, the popular Kashmiri commander. Khalil, who has been linked to Osama bin Ladin and in February 1998 signed his *fatwa*, calling for attacks on U.S. and Western interests, assumed the position of HUM secretary general. HUM operated terrorist training camps in eastern Afghanistan until coalition air strikes destroyed them during the fall of 2001. In 2003 HUM began using the name Jamiat ul-Ansar (JUA); Pakistan banned JUA in November 2003. First designated in October 1997.

Activities

The HUM has conducted a number of operations against Indian troops and civilian targets in Kashmir. Linked to the Kashmiri militant group al-Faran that kidnapped five Western tourists in Kashmir in July 1995; one was killed in August 1995, and the other four reportedly were killed in December of the same year. The HUM is responsible for the hijacking of an Indian airliner on December 24, 1999, which resulted in the release of Masood Azhar—an important leader in the former Harakat ul-Ansar imprisoned by the Indians in 1994—and Ahmed Omar Sheik, who was convicted of the abduction-murder in January–February 2002 of U.S. journalist Daniel Pearl.

Strength

Several hundred armed HUM supporters are located in Azad Kashmir, Pakistan, and India's southern Kashmir and Doda regions and in the Kashmir valley. Supporters are mostly Pakistanis and Kashmiris and also include Afghans and Arab veterans of the Afghan war. Uses light and heavy machine guns, assault rifles, mortars, explosives, and rockets. HUM lost a significant share of its membership in to defections in 2000.

Location/Area of Operation

HUM is based in Muzaffarabad, Rawalpindi, and several other towns in Pakistan, but members conduct insurgent and terrorist activities primarily in Kashmir. The HUM trained its militants in Afghanistan and Pakistan.

External Aid

HUM collects donations from Saudi Arabia and other Gulf and Islamic states and from Pakistanis and Kashmiris. The HUM's financial collection methods also include soliciting donations with magazine ads and pamphlets. The sources and amount of HUM's military funding are unknown. In anticipation of asset seizures in 2001 by the Pakistani government, the HUM withdrew funds from bank accounts and invested in such legal businesses as commodity trading, real estate, and production of consumer goods. Its fundraising in Pakistan has been constrained since the government clampdown on extremist groups and freezing of terrorist assets. The United States announced the addition of HUM to the FTO list in 1997.

5. Jaish-e-Mohammed (JEM) (Army of Mohammed)

Description

The Jaish-e-Mohammed is an Islamic extremist group based in Pakistan that was formed by Masood Azhar upon his release from prison in India in early 2000. The group's aim is to unite Kashmir with Pakistan. It is politically aligned with the radical political party Jamiat Ulema-i-Islam Fazlur Rehman faction (JUI-F). The United States announced the addition of JEM to the U.S. Treasury Department's Office of Foreign Asset Control (OFAC) list—which includes organizations that are believed to support terrorist groups and have assets in U.S. jurisdiction that can be frozen or controlled—in October 2001 and the FTO list in December 2001. By 2003 JEM had splintered into Khuddam ul-Islam (KUI) and Jamaat ul-Furqan (JUF). Pakistan banned KUA and JUF in November 2003. First designated in December 2001.

Activities

JEM's leader, Masood Azhar, was released from Indian imprisonment in December 1999 in exchange for 155 hijacked Indian Airlines hostages. The HUA kidnappings in 1994 by Omar Sheik of U.S. and British nationals in New Delhi and the HUA/al-Faran kidnappings in July 1995 of Westerners in Kashmir were two of several previous HUA efforts to free Azhar. The JEM on October 1, 2001, claimed responsibility for a suicide attack on the Jammu and Kashmir legislative assembly building in Srinagar that killed at least thirty-one people but later denied the claim. The Indian government has publicly implicated the JEM—along with Lashkar-e-Tayyiba—for the attack on December 13, 2001, on the Indian Parliament that killed nine and injured eighteen. Pakistani authorities suspect that perpetrators of fatal anti-Christian attacks in Islamabad, Murree, and Taxila during 2002 were affiliated with the JEM.

Strength

JEM has several hundred armed supporters located in Pakistan, in India's southern Kashmir and Doda regions, and in the Kashmir valley, including a large cadre of former HUM members. Supporters are mostly Pakistanis and Kashmiris but also include Afghans and Arab veterans of the Afghan war. Uses light and heavy machine guns, assault rifles, mortars, improvised explosive devices, and rocket grenades.

Location/Area of Operation

Pakistan. The JEM maintained training camps in Afghanistan until the fall of 2001.

External Aid

Most of the JEM's cadre and material resources have been drawn from the militant groups Harakat ul-Jihad-i-Islami (HUJI) and the Harakat ul-Mujahidin (HUM). The JEM had close ties to Afghan Arabs and the Taliban. Osama bin Ladin is suspected of giving funds to the JEM. The JEM also collects funds through donation requests placed in magazines ads and pamphlets. In anticipation of asset seizures by the Pakistani government, the JEM withdrew funds from bank accounts and invested in legal businesses, such as commodity trading, real estate, and production of consumer goods.

6. Lashkar-e-Tayyiba (LT) (Army of the Pure or Army of the Righteous)

Description

The LT is the armed wing of the Pakistan-based religious organization Markaz-ud-Dawa-wal-Irshad (MDI)—a Sunni anti-U.S. missionary organization formed in 1989. The LT is led by Hafiz Muhammad Saeed and is one of the three-largest and best trained groups fighting in Kashmir against India; it is not connected to a political party The United States in October 2001 announced the addition of the LT to the OFAC list. The group was banned, and the Pakistani government froze its assets in January 2002. The LT is also known by the name of its associated organization, Jamaat ud-Dawa (JUD). Musharraf placed JUD on a watch list in November 2003. First designated in December 2001.

Activities

The LT has conducted a number of operations against Indian troops and civilian targets in Jammu and Kashmir since 1993. The LT claimed responsibility for numerous attacks in 2001, including an attack in January on the Srinagar airport that killed five Indians along with six militants; an attack on a police station in Srinagar that killed at least eight officers and wounded several others; and an attack in April against Indian border-security forces that left at least four dead. The Indian government publicly implicated the LT—along with JEM—for the attack on December 13, 2001, on the Indian Parliament building, although concrete evidence is lacking. The LT is also suspected of involvement in the attack on May 14, 2002, on an Indian Army base in Kaluchak that left thirty-six dead. Senior al Qaeda lieutenant Abu Zubaydah was captured at an LT safe house in Faisalabad in March 2002, suggesting some members are facilitating the movement of al Qaeda members in Pakistan.

Strength

LT has several thousand members in Azad Kashmir, Pakistan, in southern Jammu and Kashmir and Doda regions, and in the Kashmir valley. Almost all LT cadres are Pakistanis from madrasas across Pakistan as well as Afghan veterans of the Afghan wars. Uses assault rifles, light and heavy machine guns, mortars, explosives, and rocket-propelled grenades.

Location/Area of Operation

Based in Muridke (near Lahore) and Muzaffarabad.

External Aid

Collects donations from the Pakistani community in the Persian Gulf and from the United Kingdom, Islamic NGOs, and Pakistani and other Kashmiri businesspeople. The LT also maintains a Web site (under the name of its associated organization Jamaat ud-Daawa), through which it solicits funds and provides information on the group's activities. The amount of LT funding is unknown. The LT maintains ties to religious-military groups around the world, ranging from the Philippines to the Middle East and Chechnya through the fraternal network of its parent organization Jamaat ud-Dawa (formerly Markaz Dawa ul-Irshad). In anticipation of asset seizures by the Pakistani government, the LT withdrew funds from bank accounts and invested in such legal businesses as commodity trading, real estate, and production of consumer goods.

7. Lashkar I Jhangvi (LJ) (Army of Jhangvi)

Description

Lashkar I Jhangvi (LJ) is the militant offshoot of the Sunni sectarian group Sipah-i-Sahaba Pakistan (SSP). The group focuses primarily on anti-Shia attacks and was banned by President Musharraf of Pakistan in August 2001 as part of an effort to rein in sectarian violence. Many of its members then sought refuge with the Taliban in Afghanistan, with whom they had existing ties. After the collapse of the Taliban, LJ members became active in aiding other terrorists with safe houses, false identities, and protection in Pakistani cities, including Karachi, Peshawar, and Rawalpindi. In January 2003 the United States added LJ to the FTO list.

Activities

LJ specializes in armed attacks and bombings. The group attempted to assassinate former prime minister Nawaz Sharif and his brother Shabaz Sharif, chief minister of Punjab Province, in January 1999. Pakistani authorities have publicly linked LJ members to the kidnap and murder of U.S. journalist Daniel Pearl in early 2002. Police officials initially suspected LJ members were involved in the two suicide car bombings in Karachi in 2002 against a French shuttle bus in May and the U.S. consulate in June. Their subsequent investigations have not led to any LJ members being charged in the attacks. Similarly, press reports have linked LJ to attacks on Christian targets in Pakistan, including a grenade assault on the Protestant International Church in Islamabad in March 2002 that killed two U.S. citizens, but no formal charges have been filed against the group. Pakistani authorities believe LJ was responsible for the bombing in July 2003 of a Shiite mosque in Quetta, Pakistan.

Strength

Probably fewer than 100.

Location/Area of Operation

LJ is active primarily in Punjab and Karachi. Some members travel between Pakistan and Afghanistan.

External Aid

Unknown.

8. Abu Sayyaf Group (ASG)

Description

The ASG is a small, brutally violent Muslim separatist group operating in the southern Philippines. Some ASG leaders allegedly fought in Afghanistan during the Soviet war and are students and proponents of radical Islamic teachings. The group split from the much larger Moro National Liberation Front in the early 1990s under the leadership of Abdurajak Abubakar Janjalani, who was killed in a clash with Philippine police on December 18, 1998. His younger brother, Khadaffy Janjalani, has replaced him as the nominal leader of the group, which is composed of several semiautonomous factions. First designated in October 1997.

Activities

The ASG engages in kidnappings for ransom, bombings, beheadings, assassinations, and extortion. Although from time to time it claims that its motivation is to promote an independent Islamic state in western Mindanao and the Sulu Archipelago—areas in the southern Philippines heavily populated by Muslims—the ASG has primarily used terror for financial profit. Recent bombings may herald a return to a more radical, politicized agenda, at least among the factions. The group's first large-scale action was a raid on the town of Ipil in Mindanao in April 1995. In April of 2000 an ASG faction kidnapped twenty-one people—including ten Western tourists—from a resort in Malaysia. Separately, in 2000, the group briefly abducted several foreign journalists, three Malaysians, and a U.S. citizen. On May 27, 2001, the ASG kidnapped three U.S. citizens and seventeen Filipinos from a tourist resort in Palawan, Philippines. Several of the hostages, including one U.S. citizen, were murdered. During a Philippine military hostage rescue operation on June 7, 2002, U.S. hostage Gracia Burnham was wounded but rescued, but her husband Martin Burnham and Filipina Deborah Yap were killed during the operation. Philippine authorities say that the ASG had a role in the bombing near a Philippine military base in Zamboanga on October 2 that killed three Filipinos and one U.S. serviceman and wounded twenty others. It is unclear what role ASG has played in subsequent bombing attacks in Mindanao.

Strength

Estimated to have two hundred to five hundred members.

Location/Area of Operation

The ASG was founded in Basilan Province and operates there and in the neighboring provinces of Sulu and Tawi-Tawi in the Sulu Archipelago. It also operates in the Zamboanga peninsula, and members occasionally travel to Manila. In mid-2003 the group started operating in the major city of Cotobato and on the coast of Sultan Kudarat on Mindanao. The group expanded its operational reach to Malaysia in 2000 when it abducted foreigners from a tourist resort.

External Aid

Largely self-financing through ransom and extortion; the ASG may receive support from Islamic extremists in the Middle East and South Asia. Libya publicly paid millions of dollars for the release of the foreign hostages seized from Malaysia in 2000.

9. Communist Party of Philippines/New People's Army (CPP/NPA)

Description

The military wing of the Communist Party of the Philippines (CPP), the NPA is a Maoist group formed in March 1969 with the aim of overthrowing the government through protracted guerrilla warfare. The chairman of the CPP's Central Committee and the NPA's founder, Jose Maria Sison, reportedly directs CPP and NPA activity from the Netherlands, where he lives in self-imposed exile. Fellow Central Committee member and director of the CPP's overt political wing, the National Democratic Front (NDF), Luis Jalandoni also lives in the Netherlands and has become a Dutch citizen. Although primarily a rural-based guerrilla group, the NPA has an active urban infrastructure to conduct terrorism and uses city-based assassination squads. Derives most of its funding from contributions of supporters in the Philippines, Europe, and elsewhere and from so-called revolutionary taxes extorted from local businesses and politicians. First designated in August 2002. Designations by the United States and the European Union may have had an impact on funding.

Activities

The NPA primarily targets Philippine security forces, politicians, judges, government informers, former rebels who wish to leave the NPA, rival splinter groups, and alleged criminals. Opposes any U.S. military presence in the Philippines and attacked U.S. military interests, killing several U.S. service personnel, before the U.S. base closures in 1992. Press reports in 1999 and in late 2001 indicated that the NPA is again targeting U.S. troops participating in joint military exercises as well as U.S. embassy personnel. The NPA claimed responsibility for the assassination of two congressmen from Quezon in May 2001 and Cagayan in June 2001 and many other killings. In January 2002 the NPA publicly expressed its intent to target U.S. personnel if discovered in NPA operating areas.

Strength

Although the NPA is slowly growing—estimated at more than 10,000—this number is significantly lower than its peak strength of around 25,000 in the 1980s.

Location/Area of Operations

The NPA operates in rural Luzon, Visayas, and parts of Mindanao. It has cells in Manila and other metropolitan centers.

External Aid

Unknown.

10. *Liberation Tigers of Tamil Eelam (LTTE)*

Known front organizations: World Tamil Association (WTA), World Tamil Movement (WTM), the Federation of Associations of Canadian Tamils (FACT), the Ellalan Force, the Sangilian Force.

Activities

The Tigers have integrated a battlefield insurgent strategy with a terrorist program that targets not only key personnel in the countryside but also senior Sri Lankan political and military leaders in Colombo and other urban centers. The Tigers are most notorious for their cadre of suicide bombers, the Black Tigers. Political assassinations and bombings are commonplace.

Strength

Exact strength is unknown, but the LTTE is estimated to have eight thousand to ten thousand armed combatants in Sri Lanka, with a core of trained fighters of approximately three thousand to six thousand. The LTTE also has a significant overseas support structure for fund raising, weapons procurement, and propaganda activities.

Location/Area of Operations

The Tigers control most of the northern and eastern coastal areas of Sri Lanka but have conducted operations throughout the island. Headquartered in northern Sri Lanka, LTTE leader Velupillai Prabhakaran has established an extensive network of checkpoints and informants to keep track of any outsiders who enter the group's area of control.

External Aid

The LTTE's overt organizations support Tamil separatism by lobbying foreign governments and the United Nations. The LTTE also uses its international contacts to procure weapons, communications, and any other equipment and supplies it needs. The LTTE exploits large Tamil communities in North America, Europe, and Asia to obtain funds and supplies for its fighters in Sri Lanka.

11. Islamic Movement of Uzbekistan (IMU)

Description

The IMU is a coalition of Islamic militants from Uzbekistan and other Central Asian states. The IMU is closely affiliated with al Qaeda and, under the leadership of Tohir Yoldashev, has embraced Osama bin Ladin's anti-U.S., anti-Western agenda. The IMU also remains committed to its original goals of overthrowing the Uzbekistani president, Islam Karimov, and establishing an Islamic state in Uzbekistan. First designated in September 2000.

Activities

The IMU in recent years has participated in attacks on U.S. and coalition soldiers in Afghanistan and plotted attacks on U.S. diplomatic facilities in Central Asia. In May 2003 Kyrgyzstani security forces disrupted an IMU cell that was seeking to bomb the U.S. embassy and a nearby hotel in Bishkek, Kyrgyzstan. The IMU primarily targeted Uzbekistani interests before October 2001 and is believed to have been responsible for five car bombs in Tashkent in February 1999. Militants also took foreigners hostage in 1999 and 2000, including four U.S. citizens who were mountain climbing in August 2000, four Japanese geologists, and eight Kyrgyzstani soldiers in August 1999.

Strength

Probably fewer than 700 militants.

Location/Area of Operation

Militants are scattered throughout South Asia, Tajikistan, and Iran. Area of operations includes Afghanistan, Iran, Kyrgyzstan, Pakistan, Tajikistan, Kazakhstan, and Uzbekistan.

External Aid

The IMU receives support from other Islamic extremist groups and patrons in the Middle East and Central and South Asia.

About the Editors
and Contributors

The Editors

William M. Carpenter is a consultant on international security affairs. Formerly Assistant Director of the Strategic Studies Center of SRI International, Arlington, Virginia, he is now President and Registered Agent of The American-Pacific Sealanes Security Institute, a research organization that conducts conferences in East Asia focusing on threats to the region's vital sea-lanes. A retired U.S. Navy captain, he served in command and staff assignments at sea and in Japan in three wars, and also in planning and policy offices in Washington, DC, before extending his career into the research field of international security studies with a specialty in East Asian affairs. He is a 1940 graduate of the United States Naval Academy. His publications include *The America That Can Say No* (Tokyo Press, 1994, coauthored with Stephen P. Gibert and translated into Japanese), and *America and Island China: A Documentary History* (University Press of America, 1989) with Stephen P. Gibert.

David G. Wiencek is President of International Security Group, a consulting company based near Washington, DC, that provides threat and risk analysis, global intelligence, and security-related research to international clients. Previously he served as Director of Research with Armor Group, an international security and risk management company in Washington, DC. Mr. Wiencek specializes in East and Southeast Asian political-security affairs, weapons of mass destruction and proliferation studies, terrorism assessment, kidnap-for-ransom issues, and corporate security matters. He holds BA and MA degrees in international affairs from American University, Washington, DC. He is coeditor with John C. Baker of *Cooperative Monitoring in the South China Sea: Satellite Imagery, Confidence-Building Measures, and the Spratly Islands Disputes* (Praeger Publishers, 2002). His articles have appeared in *The Washington Times, Jane's Intelligence Review, Defense News,* the *Journal of Counterterrorism and Homeland Security International,* and other publications. Since 1996, Mr. Wiencek has participated as a panel speaker on a semiannual basis at the John F. Kennedy Special Warfare Center's Regional Studies Symposium at Fort Bragg, North Carolina.

The Contributors

Maureen Aung-Thwin is director of the Burma Project/Southeast Asia Initiative of the New York-based Open Society Institute (OSI), part of the network of foundations created and funded by philanthropist George Soros. A graduate of Northwestern University, Ms. Aung-Thwin did postgraduate work at New York University. She serves on the advisory boards of Human Rights Watch/Asia and the Burma Studies Foundation, which oversees the Center for Burma Studies at Northern Illinois University, De Kalb, Illinois. Before joining OSI she worked at the Asia Society in New York and was a freelance journalist based in Hong Kong. Ms. Aung-Thwin recently contributed an article, "Burma's Modern Tragedy" to *The Virginia Review of Asian Studies* (vol. 6, 2004). She has also contributed articles on Burma to such publications as the *Christian Science Monitor,* the *Far Eastern Economic Review, Foreign Affairs,* and *Ms Magazine.*

Joseph G.D. (Geoff) Babb is a retired U.S. Army lieutenant colonel who served in both Military Intelligence and Special Forces positions. Mr. Babb holds an AB from Bowdoin College, Brunswick, Maine, an MPA from Clark University, Worcester, Massachusetts, and an MA in East Asian Languages from the University of Kansas, Lawrence. Mr. Babb was trained as a China Foreign Area Officer and fulfilled his in-country training in Hong Kong and Beijing. He also served in Washington, DC, at the Defense Intelligence Agency as a China ground forces analyst and on the Joint Chiefs' Staff. He was the Senior China Analyst and Deputy Director of Current Intelligence at U.S. Pacific Command. He also served as an Operations Officer and Northeast Asia Desk Officer at U.S. Army, Pacific. His last active military tour of duty was at Fort Leavenworth as the Chief of the Strategic Studies Division of the Department of Joint and Multinational Operations, where he is now employed as an Assistant Professor. He frequently lectures at the University of Kansas, at the Special Warfare Center at Fort Bragg, North Carolina, and at the Joint Forces Staff College in Norfolk, Virginia. Mr. Babb has authored several articles and book chapters on China and Asia and contributed to *The Savage Wars of Peace: Toward a New Paradigm in Peace Operations* (Westview Press, 1998). He teaches the regional studies course "China: Military Thought,

Wars and Revolutions, and the People's Liberation Army" at the United States Army Command and General Staff College at Fort Leavenworth, Kansas.

Paul C. Grove is Clerk of the Foreign Operations Subcommittee, Senate Appropriations Committee. Previously he served as the Regional Director for the International Republican Institute's (IRI) Asia and Middle East Division in Washington, DC, where he was responsible for the overall management and implementation of IRI's programs in Burma, Cambodia, Indonesia, Mongolia, Morocco, the People's Republic of China, Thailand, Vietnam, and the West Bank. From 1994 to 1996 he served as IRI's Chief of Delegation in Phnom Penh, Cambodia, and from 1989 to 1994 he was a Legislative Assistant and Legislative Aide to U.S. Senator Mitch McConnell (R-KY). Mr. Grove received his BA from Bates College, Lewiston, Maine, and studied two terms at the London School for Economics and Political Science.

John B. Haseman retired from the U.S. Army in 1995 with the rank of colonel. He served three tours of duty in Indonesia, culminating as Defense and Army Attaché from 1990 to 1994. Colonel Haseman had eighteen years of duty in Asia and spent most of his thirty-year military career dealing with Southeast Asian issues. Beside Indonesia, Colonel Haseman served in the Republic of Korea, the Republic of Vietnam, Thailand, and Burma, and had Army Staff duties dealing with political-military policy in Asia. A linguist in the Burmese, Indonesian, and Thai languages, Colonel Haseman is the author of two books, numerous book chapters, and more than one hundred articles on Southeast Asian political-military affairs published in professional journals in the United States, Asia, Australia, and Europe. His most recent works include "The Military and Democracy in Indonesia: Challenges, Politics, and Power" (coauthored with Angel Rabasa, The RAND Corporation, 2002); and "Indonesia: Turbulent Times—From Autocracy to Democracy," in *Fragility & Crisis: Strategic Asia 2003–04* (The National Bureau of Asian Research, 2003). Mr. Haseman lives in Colorado.

Dennis Van Vranken Hickey is Professor of Political Science and University Fellow in Research at Southwest Missouri State University. His publications include articles in *Asian Survey, The Journal of Contemporary China, Orbis,* and *Pacific Review.* Professor Hickey has also published three books: *U.S.-Taiwan Security Ties: From Cold War to Beyond Containment* (Praeger, 1994), *Taiwan's Security in the Changing International System* (Lynne Rienner, 1997), and *The Armies of East Asia: China, Taiwan, Japan and the Koreas* (Lynne Rienner, 2001), and has contributed op-eds to a number of newspapers, including *The Wall Street Journal, Chicago Tribune,* and *The Los Angeles Times.*

K. Alan Kronstadt is an Analyst in Asian Affairs for the Congressional Research Service (CRS) in Washington, DC, where he covers Pakistan and India for Members of the U.S. Congress and their staff. Before joining CRS, Mr. Kronstadt was an instructor in writing and international relations at the University of Southern California (USC), Los Angeles. He currently is completing a PhD-dissertation at USC's School of International Relations, concentrating on international, societal, and human security in South Asia. Mr. Kronstadt has published and done extensive research on South and Southeast Asian issues and has worked for more than a decade as an analyst of U.S. foreign policy and international security. He holds a BA in international relations from San Francisco State University, an MA in international affairs from The American University's School of International Service, Washington, DC, and an MA in international relations from USC.

Cheng-Chwee Kuik is currently a PhD candidate at The Johns Hopkins University's School of Advanced International Studies in Washington, DC, specializing in Southeast Asian relations. He has been a Lecturer in the Strategic Studies Unit at the National University of Malaysia.

Satu P. Limaye is the Director of Research & Publications at the Asia-Pacific Center for Security Studies (APCSS), a direct reporting unit to the United States Pacific Command. Previously, he was an Abe Fellow with the National Endowment for Democracy's International Forum for Democratic Studies. He also served as a Luce Scholar and Head of Program on South Asia at the Japan Institute of International Affairs (JIIA) in Tokyo. Dr. Limaye has taught at Georgetown University, Washington, DC, and at Sophia University in Tokyo. His articles appear in such leading journals as *The Washington Quarterly, Contemporary Southeast Asia,* and *Southeast Asian Affairs* and in such newspapers as the *International Herald Tribune.* He recently edited *Asia's Bilateral Relations* (2004), *Asia-Pacific Responses to U.S. Security Policies* (APCSS, 2003) and *Asia's China Debate* (APCSS, 2003). He is also the author of *U.S.-Indian Relations: The Pursuit of Accommodation* (Westview Press). Dr. Limaye graduated magna cum laude and Phi Beta Kappa from Georgetown University, Washington, DC, with a Bachelor of Science degree in Foreign Service, and he received his PhD in International Relations from Oxford University where he was a Marshall Scholar.

Mark Manyin works as a Specialist in Asian Affairs with the Congressional Research Service (CRS), a nonpartisan agency that provides information and analysis to members of the U.S. Congress and their staff. At CRS, Dr. Manyin's general area of expertise is U.S. foreign economic policy toward East Asia, particularly Japan, Korea, and Vietnam. Prior to joining CRS in 1999, Dr. Manyin completed his PhD in Japanese trade policy at the Fletcher School of Law and Diplomacy at Tufts University, Medford, Massachusetts. He has taught courses in East Asian international relations, worked as a business consultant, and lived in Japan for three years.

Michael J. Mitchell is a partner at Orion Strategies, a Washington, DC-based consulting group that specializes in strategic communications and political advocacy. Previously he was Senior Program Officer at the International Republican Institute, Washington, DC, where he specialized in Central and Southeast Asian affairs. During the George H.W. Bush administration, he was Director of Congressional Relations for the Department of State's Office of International Narcotics and Law Enforcement Affairs. He also served as a special assistant to Senator Mitch McConnell (R-KY) during his tenure on the Senate Foreign Relations Committee's Terrorism and Narcotics Subcommittee. Mr. Mitchell holds an MA in International Trade from George Mason University, Fairfax, Virginia, and a BA in Communications from Clarion University of Pennsylvania, Clarion. He is the author of several articles on building democracy in Mongolia and Burma. He has spoken to a wide variety of civic, political, and corporate groups, including guest lecturing at the U.S. Army's John F. Kennedy Special Warfare Center at Fort Bragg, North Carolina. Mr. Mitchell also has testified before the U.S. Congress on human rights and democracy issues involving Burma. In 1999, he was awarded the Order of Freedom by the Mongolian government for his work in building democratic institutions.

Larry A. Niksch is a Specialist in Asian Affairs with the Congressional Research Service of the Library of Congress. He is also a Senior Adviser on East Asia to The PRS (Political Risk Services) Group and is a consultant to Lloyd, Thomas and Ball international business consulting service. He is a member of the editorial board of *New Asia*, published by the New Asia Research Institute in Seoul, Korea. Dr. Niksch received a Bachelor of Arts degree in History from Butler University, Indianapolis, Indiana, a Master of Science in Foreign Service from Georgetown University, Washington, DC, and a PhD in History from Georgetown University. In his current positions, he specializes in U.S. security policy in East Asia and the Western Pacific, internal political conditions of the countries of the region, and foreign policy developments within the region. In addition to his reports published by the Congressional Research Service, Dr. Niksch has written articles for a number of journals and newspapers in the United States and the Asia-Pacific countries. He has spoken and presented papers at numerous conferences in the United States and abroad. He is interviewed frequently by East Asian, U.S., and British media outlets and by the Voice of America and Radio Free Asia. Dr. Niksch served as a member of the U.S. presidential observer group to the Philippine presidential election in February 1986.

Steven R. Saunders is President of Saunders & Company, an international public policy consulting firm in Alexandria, Virginia, that has advised the governments of eight Pacific Basin nations and scores of North American and Asian multinational companies, trade associations, and Non-Governmental Organizations (NGOs) since 1982. His family has done business in East Asia for more than a century. Formerly Assistant United States Trade Representative in the Executive Office of the President and Staff Director of the Republican Conference of the U.S. Senate, he is former Contributing Editor and columnist of *The Japan Times* and is a member of the Editorial Advisory Board of *The Japan Digest*. Mr. Saunders also serves on the International Council of the American Management Association and as President of the North America-Mongolia Business Council. He received a BA in history from Washington and Lee University, Lexington, Virginia, and has taught at Georgetown University and the University of Pittsburgh. He directed research for former CIA director William J. Casey's book, *Where and How the War Was Fought: An Armchair Traveler's History of the American Revolution* (Morrow: 1976) and was editor *of Japan Hands: Who's Who in Japan-U.S. Relations in the U.S. Government* (Japan Times, 1990).

M.A. Thomas has been the South Asia Analyst for the 4th Psychological Operations Group (Airborne) at Fort Bragg, North Carolina, since September 1993. He received his undergraduate degree from Loyola College, Baltimore, Maryland (1990), and a MA degree in International Relations and South Asia Regional Studies from the University of Pennsylvania, Philadelphia (1993). Mr. Thomas has participated in a number of military training exercises in Thailand and Korea, helped coordinate mine-awareness information campaigns in Cambodia, and has assisted in running terrorism workshops in Singapore. He has managed many U.S. Army Special Operations training programs in Sri Lanka, Nepal, and Bangladesh in conjunction with the Army Special Forces and Navy Seals, and has made a number of official visits to India. Recently he has worked in the Strategic Communications department of the Multi-National force—Iraq based at the U.S. Embassy in Baghdad. Mr. Thomas specializes in nuclear nonproliferation, political-military issues in South Asia, and terrorist organizations in South Asia. He has written analytical studies on these topics for the U.S. Department of Defense. Since 1994, Mr. Thomas has participated as a panel speaker on a semi-annual basis at the John F. Kennedy Special Warfare Center's Regional Studies Symposium at Fort Bragg, North Carolina. Mr. Thomas has served as an adjunct instructor on South Asian Studies for Campbell University, Buies Creek, North Carolina, and has consulted for International Security Group.

Bruce Vaughn is currently an Analyst in Asian Affairs with the Congressional Research Service in Washington, DC. He is concurrently an Adjunct Associate Professor with the School of Foreign Service at Georgetown University, Washington, DC, where he has taught courses on Southeast Asia, Australia, New Zealand and the South Pacific. He edited *The Unraveling of Island Asia? Governmental, Communal, and Regional Instability* (Praeger Publishers, 2002). Vaughn has also coedited *Among Friends: Australian and New Zealand Voices From America* (Otago University Press, Dunedin, New Zealand, 2004). Vaughn spent ten years as the Senior Defence Analyst for the Embassy of Australia in Washington, DC, after completing his PhD in Political Science at the Australian National University, Canberra, where he focused on the comparative politics and security of South Asia. While at the embassy, he focused on Asia-Pacific security issues and America's regional strategic posture. He has published articles on Asia-Pacific security in *Contemporary Southeast Asia, Geopolitics, Intelligence and National Security, Central Asian Survey, Indian Ocean Review, Strategic Analysis,* and the *Strategic and Defence Studies Centre Working Papers Series.* He has also contributed chapters to the previous two editions of *Asian Security Handbook.* Vaughn worked on foreign and defense policy issues for the U.S. Senate Democratic Policy Committee, the U.S. Senate Treaty Review Support Office, and the U.S. Senate Select Committee on Secret Military Assistance to Iran and the Nicaraguan Opposition.

Bridget Welsh is an Assistant Professor in the Southeast Asia Studies Program at the Johns Hopkins University's School of Advanced International Studies (SAIS), Washington, DC, where she teaches courses on Southeast Asian history, violence and political conflict, Malaysian/Singaporean/Brunei politics, development, and regional international relations. She received her MA and PhD degrees from Columbia University, New York, language training (FALCON) from Cornell University, Ithaca, New York, and a BA from Colgate University, Hamilton, New York. She recently edited a volume entitled *Reflections: The Mahathir Years* (SAIS, 2004). She has also written about attitudes toward democracy in Malaysia, the effects of globalization on contemporary political conflicts, human rights, U.S.-Southeast Asia relations, and Malaysian politics. She is currently completing an analysis of Malaysian voting behavior and the electoral system during the last ten years, and a project examining local dynamics in elections. She is also working on ongoing projects examining electoral, vigilante and gangster violence in Indonesia. In the fall of 2004 she was a Henry Luce Fellow at the Australian National University in Canberra. Bridget Welsh is the Chair of the Malaysia, Singapore, Brunei Studies Group, a member of the Southeast Asia policy survey team at Georgetown University, and a consultant to Freedom House.

Index